CONTRIBUTORY NEGLIGENCE IN THE TWENTY-FIRST CENTURY

CONTRIBUTORY NEGLIGENCE IN THE TWENTY-FIRST CENTURY

James Goudkamp

and

Donal Nolan

OXFORD
UNIVERSITY PRESS

OXFORD
UNIVERSITY PRESS

Great Clarendon Street, Oxford, OX2 6DP,
United Kingdom

Oxford University Press is a department of the University of Oxford.
It furthers the University's objective of excellence in research, scholarship,
and education by publishing worldwide. Oxford is a registered trade mark of
Oxford University Press in the UK and in certain other countries

First Edition published in 2019

Impression: 1

Published in the United States of America by Oxford University Press
198 Madison Avenue, New York, NY 10016, United States of America

British Library Cataloguing in Publication Data
Data available

Library of Congress Control Number: 2018961852

ISBN 978–0–19–881424–5

Printed and bound by
CPI Group (UK) Ltd, Croydon, CR0 4YY

Para a Rita e a Maria

PREFACE

This volume came together over the course of around five years. In 2013, we embarked on an empirical study of the law of contributory negligence at first instance. That study focused on decisions delivered by first instance courts in England and Wales between 2000 and 2014. During the course of that project, we felt that there could be value in conducting a similar study in relation to appellate courts, and we duly embarked on that research, which was also limited to England and Wales, and captured judgments handed down in the period 2000–2015. Subsequently, we decided further to extend our investigation of the law of contributory negligence by collecting data from cases decided in Northern Ireland and Scotland, as well as both first instance and appellate decisions for the period until the end of 2016. The additional data gathered at this stage substantially enlarged the size of our samples and so gives the results generated by our study additional weight. In the present volume we present the results of the expanded study and offer a commentary on them.

Research on this scale is inevitably very time-consuming, and in conducting it we have drawn upon the assistance of a number of people who have worked tirelessly on the project and played an indispensable role in relation to it. Charles Austin and Scarlett Ying focused on the data collection process. Lindsay Lee performed the statistical analysis for the initial studies, and Mercy Akoth assumed that role following our decision to enlarge the scope of the research. Javier Pardo Diaz assisted us at the end of the project in connection with, in particular, refinements to many of the figures and Eleni Katsampouka provided indispensable, multifaceted support throughout several major stages of the research. We are enormously grateful to Charles, Scarlett, Lindsay, Mercy, Javier, and Eleni for the many hours that each of them devoted to the project, for the very high quality of their work, and for their patience in tolerating our many adjustments to the methodology and datasets, which often required them to redo significant amounts of work, sometimes more than once.

The results of our original first instance study appeared in the *Modern Law Review* (James Goudkamp and Donal Nolan, 'Contributory Negligence in the Twenty-First Century: An Empirical Study of First Instance Decisions' (2016) 79 MLR 575), and the results of our original appellate study were published in *Legal Studies* (James Goudkamp and Donal Nolan, 'Contributory Negligence in the Court of Appeal: An Empirical Study' (2017) 37 LS 437). A version of chapter 8 appeared in the edited collection *Apportionment in Private Law* (James Goudkamp and Donal Nolan, 'Contributory Negligence and Professional Negligence: An Empirical Perspective' in Kit Barker and Ross Grantham (eds), *Apportionment in Private Law* (Hart Publishing 2018)). We are grateful to the *Modern Law Review, Legal Studies*, and Hart Publishing for allowing us to incorporate material from these earlier contributions into the present book.

We presented some of the results of our study at the *Obligations VIII* conference in 2016, at a lecture in the Reader's Lecture series at the Inner Temple in 2016, at the PEOPIL Annual Conference in 2016, at the Professional Negligence Bar Association's Professional Liability Day 2017, and at the Personal Injuries Bar Association Annual Conference in 2017. Presentations on our research were also given at symposia that were convened by the TC Beirne School of Law at the University of Queensland, the Melbourne Law School, the University of Oxford's Centre for Socio-Legal Studies, and the Faculty of Law at the University of Hong Kong.

We are grateful to all those who gave us valuable comments in connection with these earlier publications and presentations, including Elise Bant, Kit Barker, Susan Bright, Eric Descheemaeker, Matthew Dyson, David Hoffman, Michael Kirby, Mark Lunney, David Marks, Barbara McDonald, John McKenna, James Plunkett, Andrew Robertson, Paul Stanley, and Stephen Tomlinson. We would also like to thank the referees of the two journal articles for their many helpful observations, and the Oxford University Press referees who provided constructive comments on our book proposal.

We were fortunate to receive funding from the John Fell Oxford University Press (OUP) Research Fund in relation to our initial study of first instance decisions. The analysis of the law of contributory negligence in the context of professional negligence was facilitated by an award from the Travers Smith Oxford Law Faculty Fund. Essential financial support was provided throughout the life of this project by the Oxford Law Faculty's Research Support Fund. Had it not been for the financial support from these sources, neither this book, nor its companion volume, James Goudkamp and Donal Nolan, *Contributory Negligence: Principles and Practice* (OUP 2018), would ever have seen the light of day.

James Goudkamp
Donal Nolan
Cala Millor and Santo António do Baldio
3 September 2018

SUMMARY CONTENTS

CONTENTS

LIST OF FIGURES AND TABLES

Figures

Tables

TABLE OF CASES

OTHER JURISDICTIONS

Australia

Canada

Ireland

TABLE OF LEGISLATION

STATUTORY INSTRUMENTS

1

INTRODUCTION

The Contributory Negligence Doctrine: A Cornerstone of Private Law

The doctrine of contributory negligence reduces the compensation that the victim of a wrong receives where the victim was partly to blame for his or her own damage. Paradigmatic examples of conduct that is likely to constitute contributory negligence include failing to wear a seatbelt while a passenger in a motor vehicle, failing to check the depth of a swimming pool before diving into it, and failing to use protective work equipment provided by an employer. In these and countless other situations, the damages recoverable by the victim are diminished on account of the victim's failure to take reasonable care of his or her own safety or interests. Frequently, the reductions that are made are significant both in monetary terms and as a percentage of the amount that the victim would otherwise have received. **1.01**

Because of the very wide range of situations in which it applies, coupled with the powerful effect that it can exert on the quantum of recovery, the contributory negligence doctrine is one of the most important rules in private law.[1] It is regularly relied on by defendants both in litigation and in negotiating settlements.[2] With regard to settlements, it has been said that 'much of the negotiation' may involve trying to agree a discount to reflect the possibility of a finding of contributory negligence were the case to go to court.[3] Two further points attest to the practical significance of the contributory negligence doctrine. One is that the doctrine has **1.02**

---

[1] '[T]he defence [of contributory negligence] is used on a daily basis': Jenny Steele, 'Law Reform (Contributory Negligence) Act 1945: Collisions of a Different Sort' in TT Arvind and Jenny Steele (eds), *Tort Law and the Legislature: Common Law, Statute and the Dynamics of Legal Change* (Hart Publishing 2013) 165.

[2] An American study found that defendants pleaded claimant negligence in 63 per cent of the automobile accident trials surveyed: Michael Shanley, *Comparative Negligence and Jury Behavior* (Rand Graduate Institute 1985) 39.

[3] Peter Cane and James Goudkamp, *Atiyah's Accidents, Compensation and the Law* (9th edn, CUP 2018) 255.

a personal impact on claimants, as it usually leaves them with uninsured losses,[4] especially in the personal injury context. The other is that the operation of the doctrine probably affects the public generally through its impact on liability insurance premiums (it is plausible to think that premiums would be higher without the doctrine and perhaps significantly so[5]).

Investigating a Poorly Understood Rule

1.03 Despite the importance of the contributory negligence doctrine, remarkably little is known about how it works 'on the ground'.[6] When we embarked on this project, we were struck by the fact that no concrete, up-to-date information was available as to, for example, how often the plea of contributory negligence succeeds, the amount by which compensation is reduced when it does, or whether assorted claims made by the courts and commentators regarding the operation and impact of the law of contributory negligence were accurate. Nor was much known about how frequently appellate courts interfered with decisions regarding contributory negligence and, when they did, the manner in which they did so.

1.04 In order to help to fill this major gap in knowledge about a doctrine of central importance to private law, we studied 572 first instance decisions and 129 appellate decisions on contributory negligence in all parts of the United Kingdom between 2000 and 2016. These 701 decisions comprise every judgment that the courts handed down during the study period that we were able to access electronically in which a relevant determination was made regarding contributory negligence. In this book we report the results of our analysis of those decisions and discuss our findings in the light of the case law and literature on contributory negligence. Our study tests a range of received opinions about the judicial application of the contributory negligence doctrine against hard empirical data.

---

[4] Where the claimant has first-party insurance—as will frequently be the case in a property damage claim—his or her contributory fault is unlikely as such to affect any insurance claim, although some types of behaviour that might amount to contributory negligence (such as drink driving) may have this effect: see ibid, 295–96.

[5] It has frequently been argued in the United States that the doctrine of contributory negligence should not be watered down because doing so would result in an increase in insurance premiums. The suggestion that the doctrine has some effect on insurance premiums seems to be tenable. The precise nature of any link is something with which we cannot engage properly here. For discussion, see Cornelius Peck, 'Comparative Negligence and Automobile Liability Insurance' (1960) 58 Mich L Rev 689; John Fleming, 'Comparative Fault at Last—By Judicial Choice' (1976) 64 Calif L Rev 239, 243–44; Victor Schwartz, *Comparative Negligence* (5th edn, LexisNexis 2012) para 2.04.

[6] 'Relatively little is known about the quantitative effect of the law of contributory negligence': Cane and Goudkamp (n 3) 50. See also Lesley-Anne Barnes, 'Contributory Negligence and the Child' [2010] Jur Rev 195, 201n, remarking that there has been 'little in the way of recent studies' of the doctrine's operation.

1.05 In our study of first instance decisions, the two central questions at which we looked were: (i) how often a defendant's plea of contributory negligence was successful; and (ii) the amount by which a claimant's damages were reduced when a finding of contributory negligence was made. We also considered the extent to which the answers to these questions depended on several variables, including: the claimant's age; the claimant's gender; the type of damage suffered by the claimant (personal injury, property damage, or pure economic loss); the contextual setting of the claim (eg, road accident, employers' liability, occupiers' liability, and so on); and the region of the United Kingdom in which the decision was made. We also explored various other matters, such as the distribution of discounts that the courts made for contributory negligence, the year of the decision, and the ages of the youngest and oldest claimants who were found guilty of contributory negligence.

1.06 We should explain why we thought it worthwhile to conduct a study of the operation of the contributory negligence doctrine at first instance as well as on appeal. The doctrine is obviously in issue far more frequently in absolute terms at first instance than on appeal for the simple reason that only a small minority of the cases that are heard at first instance are the subject of an appeal. This meant that by focusing on first instance decisions we were able to draw upon a much larger number of cases. Furthermore, very little is known about how the doctrine of contributory negligence is applied by trial judges. Discussions of contributory negligence in textbooks tend, understandably, to focus on the decisions of appellate courts. This made an investigation of the operation of the doctrine at the trial court level particularly valuable.

1.07 In our study of appellate decisions, in addition to considering the post-appeal success rate of the plea of contributory negligence and the post-appeal discount where the plea succeeded, we asked several further questions, including: how often did appellate courts overturn decisions of trial judges regarding either the existence of contributory negligence or, in cases where a finding of contributory negligence had been made, the amount by which damages were discounted; to what extent did appellate courts vary the discount in cases where they overturned a first instance decision on apportionment; and how often did claimants and defendants respectively succeed in appeals on contributory negligence. Furthermore, we factored into our analysis whether the first instance ruling was a decision of the High Court (or equivalent) or a county court (or equivalent).

1.08 Finally, we considered in depth the application of the doctrine of contributory negligence in three contextual settings, namely road traffic accidents, employers' liability, and professional negligence. In our study of the operation of the doctrine in the road accident context we factored additional variables into our analysis, namely the type of road user (driver, motorcyclist, pedestrian, etc) who had brought the claim, and whether the claimant or defendant had been intoxicated at the time of the accident. In our study of the employers' liability setting, we supplemented our quantitative analysis with a qualitative analysis of the decisions in our appellate dataset, and in the professional negligence context we also engaged in a qualitative analysis, this time of both the first instance and appellate claims, as well as breaking down the professional negligence claims by the profession of the defendant (lawyer, medical practitioner, etc).

Earlier Studies

1.09 Although the apportionment legislation that moulded the law of contributory negligence into its current shape was enacted throughout much of the Commonwealth in the first half of the twentieth century,[7] there have been only four previous empirical investigations of the doctrine in Commonwealth jurisdictions, the most recent of which was conducted well over two decades ago. It is worth briefly reviewing those studies in order to set the scene for our investigation and to demonstrate why it is distinct. The first such study was a 1973 survey of insurance claims in the United Kingdom (excluding Northern Ireland) conducted on behalf of the Royal Commission on Civil Liability and Compensation for Personal Injury. According to that survey, 26 per cent of the settled personal injury claims were disposed of on the basis that the claimant had been guilty of contributory negligence.[8]

1.10 The second study was conducted for the National Committee of Inquiry on Compensation and Rehabilitation in Australia. It surveyed 2,200 personal injury liability insurance files that had been closed in four Australian states in 1972 and 1973. According to that survey, 'a significant number' of all claimants had their compensation reduced by 'substantial sums' because of contributory negligence, with more than one-fifth of all payments in cases of permanent disability being reduced.[9] It was also found that when a deduction was made for contributory negligence the average deduction was 39.5 per cent.[10]

1.11 The third study was a survey of settlements of personal injury claims conducted by the Oxford Centre for Socio-Legal Studies, the results of which were published in 1984.[11] According to that survey, the doctrine of contributory negligence placed 'a

---

[7] The legislation that applies in England, Wales, and Scotland is the Law Reform (Contributory Negligence) Act 1945. In Northern Ireland, the relevant statute is the Law Reform (Miscellaneous Provisions) Act (Northern Ireland) 1948.

[8] *Report of the Royal Commission on Civil Liability and Compensation for Personal Injury*, Cmnd 7054 (1978) vol 2, 163 (Table 117).

[9] *Report of the National Committee of Inquiry on Compensation and Rehabilitation in Australia* (Australian Government Publishing Service 1974) vol 1, paras 129–30. The percentage of all cases in which deductions were made for contributory negligence was however somewhat lower: ibid, vol 3, 97 (Table 13).

[10] Ibid, vol 1, para 131.

[11] Donald Harris et al, *Compensation and Support for Illness and Injury* (Clarendon Press 1984).

powerful negotiating weapon in the hands of the defendant's solicitors or insurance company', which was 'extensively used', and taken into account in 45 per cent of the 51 settlements surveyed.[12] Furthermore, it was found that in about a quarter of the settlements surveyed the contributory negligence doctrine had caused difficulties in the negotiation process.[13]

1.12 The final study was conducted by the English Law Commission in 1994. The Commission surveyed victims of personal injury who had obtained compensation in settlements.[14] In lower-value claims, 8–10 per cent of the 761 victims surveyed said that they had been held partly to blame for their injury, but this figure jumped to 19 per cent in higher-value claims.[15] Respondents who reported that they had been held partly responsible for their injury were generally unable to provide the percentage of the blame attributed to them, but when such a figure was given the quartile into which it most often fell was 25 per cent to 49 per cent.[16] In 92 cases, the survey information was matched with data from solicitors' files,[17] and in 13 per cent of these cases the files indicated that the settlement had been reduced for contributory negligence, with the reductions ranging from 10 per cent to 75 per cent.[18]

The Distinctiveness of the Present Project

1.13 As is apparent from the previous section, our study is the first investigation of the practical operation of the contributory negligence doctrine for over 20 years, and is the only sustained analysis of the handling of the doctrine by the courts in a Commonwealth jurisdiction.[19] Furthermore, our study is very different from these earlier investigations for a number of reasons. First, unlike the earlier studies, we are concerned not with settlements but solely with judicial decisions.[20] Second,

---

[12] Ibid, 91.

[13] Ibid, 111.

[14] Law Commission, *Personal Injury Compensation: How Much is Enough? A Study of the Compensation Experiences of Victims of Personal Injury* (Law Com No 225, 1994). About half the settlements arose out of work-related accidents or disease, and most of the remainder arose out of road accidents (ibid, para 2.1).

[15] Ibid, para 4.10 (Table 407).

[16] Ibid.

[17] Ibid, para 11.7.

[18] Ibid, para 11.9.

[19] There is only a very sketchy and now dated discussion of the question in the classic English study of contributory negligence, Glanville Williams, *Joint Torts and Contributory Negligence: A Study of Concurrent Fault in Great Britain, Ireland and the Common-Law Dominions* (Stevens & Sons 1951) 480–84. For brief accounts of appellate review in contributory negligence cases in the United States, see Henry Woods and Beth Deere, *Comparative Fault* (3rd edn, Clark Boardman Callaghan 1996) ch 21; and Schwartz (n 5) 415–22.

[20] Although the Australian survey dealt with claims that were resolved by court verdict as well as by settlement, in none of the four states surveyed did these account for more than 10 per cent of the claims, and in two states they accounted for only 2.3 per cent of them: *Report of the National Committee of Inquiry on Compensation and Rehabilitation in Australia* (n 9) vol 3, 96 (Table 10).

while we consider the operation of the doctrine of contributory negligence in all the contexts in which it operates, these studies were concerned only with personal injury claims. Third, we address a much greater range of issues relating to the contributory negligence doctrine—none of these previous studies, for example, looked at the relationship between the contributory negligence doctrine and variables such as the claimant's age and gender. A fourth difference is, however, perhaps the most important, and explains some of the others. All the earlier studies, unlike ours, were conducted in the course of a broader inquiry into the operation of tort law as a compensation mechanism for personal injury. This explains the focus on personal injury, of course, but also the emphasis on settlements, as far more compensation is paid pursuant to settlements than court decisions. In addition, it explains why the analysis of contributory negligence was relatively cursory, since the doctrine was not the key item on the agenda of these studies. They concentrated on other issues, such as whether a no-fault compensation system would be preferable to the current system, or whether the levels of compensation received by tort victims were adequate.

1.14 It is important to emphasize that our study is concerned with how judges apply the contributory negligence doctrine. The significance of this focus should not be underestimated. The settlement process is conducted in the 'shadow of the law'.[21] It follows that reliable information about judicial decisions regarding the doctrine of contributory negligence should facilitate the settlement of disputes by giving litigants and their advisers a clearer picture of the likely outcome of possible litigation. In particular, it is hoped that greater clarity may aid claimants, whom it has been suggested may be induced by the uncertainty surrounding the doctrine to accept low settlement offers.[22] Furthermore, the frequency with which the contributory negligence doctrine arises in tort litigation means that our sample of judicial decisions on the topic is large enough for us to be able to draw meaningful conclusions about the doctrine's operation.

1.15 We also hope that this book, along with a companion volume concerned in large part with how the courts discount damages for contributory negligence in a range of frequently recurring situations,[23] will help judges to decide what discount to

---

[21] 'The formal legal rules of the law of negligence provide the structure for all [personal injury claim] negotiation': Hazel Genn, *Hard Bargaining: Out of Court Settlement in Personal Injury Actions* (Clarendon Press 1987) 11; 'The process of bargaining in the shadow of the law is therefore very much what tort in practice is all about' (Richard Lewis, 'Tort Tactics: An Empirical Study of Personal Injury Litigation Strategies' (2017) 37 LS 162, 163). For a seminal account of this relationship, see Robert Mnookin and Lewis Kornhauser, 'Bargaining in the Shadow of the Law: The Case of Divorce' (1979) 88 Yale LJ 950.

[22] Alastair Mullis and Ken Oliphant, *Torts* (4th edn, Palgrave Macmillan 2011) 156.

[23] James Goudkamp and Donal Nolan, *Contributory Negligence: Principles and Practice* (OUP 2018).

impose when a finding of contributory negligence has been made. The majority of cases that raise issues of contributory negligence are heard in county courts (and their institutional equivalents in other parts of the United Kingdom).[24] However, county court judgments are generally not reported or published online. As a result, there is a serious lack of transparency in the discounting process. By revealing information about the discounts that courts have previously imposed for contributory negligence, our study should make the task of apportioning responsibility a little easier.[25]

Structure of the Book

1.16 Chapter 2 canvasses the central features of the law of contributory negligence. The intention in that chapter is simply to give an explanation of the doctrine's content that is sufficient to enable the reader to understand the empirical analysis that follows. In chapter 3, we describe the methodology that we employed in our study. Chapter 4 describes the results of our analysis of first instance decisions and discusses our findings. Chapter 5 embarks on the same exercise in relation to appellate decisions. In chapters 6–8, we drill down into the data and case law to consider in more depth three important contexts in which the contributory negligence operates. Thus, in chapter 6 we examine how the law of contributory negligence is applied in the road accident context, in chapter 7 we focus on employers' liability, and chapter 8 is concerned with the professional negligence setting. A brief conclusion follows in chapter 9.

[24] Most civil disputes are heard in the county courts (and equivalent courts): see 3.03.

[25] For a recent example of a court using analogous cases to help determine the appropriate discount for contributory negligence, see *Sabir v Osei-Kwabena* [2015] EWCA Civ 1213; [2016] RTR 9 [14]–[18] (Tomlinson LJ). For discussion, see Goudkamp and Nolan (n 23) para 3.14.

2

THE LAW OF CONTRIBUTORY NEGLIGENCE

Introduction

2.01 It will be helpful if we start by outlining the central features of the law governing contributory negligence. This discussion is intended to serve simply as a reminder of the key features of the law in this regard. A full exposition of the relevant law should be sought elsewhere.[1] The first point that should be made is that contributory negligence must be pleaded by the defendant. The court cannot raise it on its own motion.[2] Where contributory negligence has been pleaded, and provided that the doctrine applies to the cause of action in respect of which the claimant has sued,[3] the judge will normally address the issue of contributory negligence.[4] A two-stage analysis is used. At the first stage, the judge determines whether the claimant is guilty of contributory negligence. The defendant carries the burden of establishing this,[5] with proof to the civil standard being required to discharge

---

[1] See James Goudkamp and Donal Nolan, *Contributory Negligence: Principles and Practice* (OUP 2018). The classic study of contributory negligence is Glanville Williams, *Joint Torts and Contributory Negligence: A Study of Concurrent Fault in Great Britain, Ireland and the Common-Law Dominions* (Stevens & Sons 1951).

[2] In *UCB Bank Plc v David J Pinder Plc* [1998] CLC 1262 (QBD) [17], HHJ Hicks QC said that the 'authorities establish the necessity of pleading contributory negligence before it can be considered'. See also *Fookes v Slaytor* [1978] 1 WLR 1293 (CA).

[3] Regarding the causes of action to which the contributory negligence doctrine applies, see Goudkamp and Nolan (n 1) paras 2.01–2.06.

[4] When the defendant is found not liable, judges will occasionally abstain from any enquiry regarding contributory negligence. Normally, however, judges consider the question of contributory negligence in this eventuality in order to avoid the need for a retrial on the issue of contributory negligence in the event that the defendant is held liable on appeal. It is convenient to discuss the judicial practice in this regard below: see 3.11.

[5] *Wakelin v London & South Western Railway Co* (1886) 12 App Cas 41 (HL) 47 (Lord Watson) ('I am of opinion that the onus of proving affirmatively that there was contributory negligence on the part of the person injured rests, in the first instance, upon the defendants, and that in the absence of evidence tending to that conclusion, the plaintiff is not bound to prove the negative in order to entitle her to a verdict in her favour').

the onus.[6] At the second stage, the judge apportions responsibility for the damage between the parties in accordance with what is 'just and equitable'. Each of these stages is now considered in turn.

The Existence of Contributory Negligence

A failure to take reasonable care of one's own safety or interests

2.02 In order for contributory negligence to be established, the defendant must show that the claimant failed to take reasonable care of his or her own safety or interests. It has often been said that the standard of care that the claimant is required to meet in this regard is objective,[7] although certain personal characteristics of the claimant are sometimes attributed to the reasonable person, such as his or her age.[8] The claimant 'is not required to attain a standard of perfection'.[9] Rather, the standard that a claimant is expected to achieve balances the cost of taking precautions and the size and magnitude of the risk concerned. It also takes account of 'the realities of ordinary everyday life'.[10] Because contributory negligence comprises a failure to take reasonable care of one's own safety or interests, as opposed to the safety or interests of others, the claimant's conduct must involve self-regarding fault to amount to contributory negligence.[11] The mere fact that a claimant failed to look out for the concerns of others will not constitute contributory negligence.

The claimant's fault must be causally relevant

2.03 Contributory negligence comprises two elements—fault and causation—and both must be present for the doctrine to apply. It follows that the doctrine will not be engaged by causally irrelevant fault. As Lord Atkin said in *Caswell v Powell Duffryn Associated Collieries Ltd*, 'if the plaintiff were negligent, but his negligence was not

---

[6] *Dawes v Aldis* [2007] EWHC 1831 (QB); [2007] All ER (D) 451 (Jul) [33] (Eady J) (holding that establishing a 'strong possibility' that the claimant was guilty of contributory negligence was insufficient) **[1:270]**; **[3:84]**. Cases that fall within our first instance or appellate datasets are listed in the appendices to this book, where essential details are given about them. Throughout this book, we refer to entries in the appendices by numbers in square bold brackets in the format **[__:___]**. The first number refers to the relevant appendix. The second relates to the relevant entry in the appendix concerned.

[7] 'In determining [the issue of contributory negligence], the law eliminates the personal equation': *Froom v Butcher* [1976] QB 286 (CA) 294 (Lord Denning MR). In practice, the standard of care that is used in the contributory negligence context may be more personalized than that used to determine whether a defendant was negligent: see 7.42.

[8] *Gough v Thorne* [1966] 1 WLR 1387 (CA) (holding child claimants to the standard of a reasonable child of the same age).

[9] *Crew v Ash* [2008] EWHC 3068 (QB) [28] (Lloyd Jones J) **[1: 315]**; **[3:109]**.

[10] *Howe v Houlton* [2009] EWHC 3344 (QB); [2009] All ER (D) 184 (Dec) [123] (Swift J) **[1:353]**; **[3:122]**.

[11] *Froom* (n 7) 291 (Lord Denning MR).

a cause operating to produce the damage, there would be no defence'.[12] Thus, if the damage would have happened even if the claimant had taken reasonable care for his or her own safety or interests, a finding of contributory negligence will not be made.

Apportionment of Responsibility

2.04 The second stage of the analysis centres on the statutory apportionment provisions. These provisions are found in section 1 of the Law Reform (Contributory Negligence) Act 1945, which applies in all parts of the United Kingdom except for Northern Ireland, and in the materially identical provision in section 2 of the Law Reform (Miscellaneous Provisions) Act (Northern Ireland) 1948. Section 1 of the 1945 Act stipulates:

> Where any person suffers damage as a result partly of his own fault and partly of the fault of any other person or persons, a claim in respect of that damage shall not be defeated by reason of the fault of the person suffering the damage, but the damages recoverable in respect thereof shall be reduced to such extent as the court thinks just and equitable having regard to the claimant's share in the responsibility for the damage.

By convention, a judge who has made a finding of contributory negligence must assess the parties' respective shares of responsibility for the damage as two percentages that add up to 100.[13] The respective shares of responsibility are determined by reference to the parties' comparative blameworthiness and the relative causative potency of their faulty conduct.[14] There is relatively little jurisprudence on how these twin criteria are to be applied[15] and some doubt exists as to precisely what they entail, the exact nature of the relationship between them, and whether they are exhaustive of the circumstances that can be considered in determining the proper apportionment. According to Lloyd Jones LJ in *Department for Communities and Local Government v Shirley*, these touchstones are 'not precise or mutually exclusive'.[16] Once the court has assigned a percentage of responsibility for the damage to the claimant, the court will reduce the claimant's damages by that figure. Judges

---

[12] [1940] AC 152 (HL) 165.

[13] The combined percentages must not exceed 100 per cent: *Black v McCabe* [1964] NI 1 (CA). Cases involving multiple defendants are subject to special rules: see *Fitzgerald v Lane* [1989] 1 AC 328 (HL).

[14] *Stapley v Gypsum Mines Ltd* [1953] AC 663 (HL) 682 (Lord Reid).

[15] For discussion of the causal potency criterion, see James Goudkamp and Lewis Klar, 'Apportionment of Damages for Contributory Negligence: The Causal Potency Principle' (2016) 53 Alb L Rev 1.

[16] [2017] EWCA Civ 1136; [2017] All ER (D) 2 (Sep) [16].

are not supposed to treat the apportionment exercise as a scientific exercise but to approach it 'in a broad, jury-like and commonsense way'.[17]

Appeals

Permission to appeal

2.05 In the case of England and Wales, permission is needed to appeal to the Court of Appeal from a decision of a county court or of the High Court.[18] Permission will be given only where the court from which permission is sought considers that the appeal would have a 'real prospect of success' or 'there is some other compelling reason for the appeal to be heard'.[19] An appeal will have 'a real prospect of success' when the prospect is realistic as opposed to fanciful.[20] In relation to Scotland, a litigant can appeal against the decision of a sheriff to the Sheriff Appeal Court without permission.[21] However, appeals lie from the Sheriff Appeal Court to the Court of Session only with permission.[22] Permission is granted only where the appeal would 'raise an important point of principle or practice' or 'there is some other compelling reason for the Court of Session to hear the appeal'.[23] Permission is not required to appeal to the Court of Appeal in Northern Ireland save in relation to issues that are presently irrelevant.[24]

Appellate review generally

2.06 The vast majority of appeals involve a 'review' of the lower court's decision.[25] Such appeals will be allowed only where the decision of the lower court is found to be either (i) 'wrong' or (ii) unjust because it was tainted by a serious procedural irregularity.[26] It is only the first of these situations that is relevant for present purposes. The circumstances in which a lower court decision will be found to be 'wrong' depend on the nature of the decision,[27] with more discretionary decisions being more resistant to having that label applied to them, but in all cases it is impermissible

---

17 *Badger v Ministry of Defence* [2005] EWHC 2941 (QB); [2006] 3 All ER 173 [16] (Stanley Burnton J) [**1:210**].

18 Civil Procedure Rules ('CPR') r 52.3(1)(a).

19 CPR 52.6(1).

20 *Tanfern Ltd v Cameron-MacDonald* [2000] 1 WLR 1311 (CA) [21] (Brooke LJ).

21 Courts Reform (Scotland) Act 2014, s 110.

22 Ibid, s 113(1).

23 Ibid, s 113(2).

24 See Judicature (Northern Ireland) Act 1978, s 35.

25 CPR 52.11(1). Exceptionally, appeals may be conducted differently, eg, by way of a rehearing: CPR 52.11(1)(b).

26 CPR 52.11(3).

27 '[T]here is no single standard which is appropriate to every case': *South Cone Inc v Bessant* [2002] EWCA Civ 763; [2002] All ER (D) 426 (May) [26] (Robert Walker LJ).

for the appellate court 'to interfere merely because left to its own devices it would have reached a different conclusion'.[28] Appropriate respect must be afforded to the decision of the lower court.[29]

Appeals regarding contributory negligence

The decision as to whether a claimant is guilty of contributory negligence is one of fact.[30] It has been said that 'normally an appellate court is properly reluctant to disturb' a determination of a trial court judge on the issue,[31] and that intervention is warranted only if the trial judge's decision in this regard 'was manifestly wrong'.[32] Disturbance of apportionment decisions is particularly discouraged. According to Lord Reed in *Jackson v Murray*,[33] apportionment 'is inevitably a somewhat rough and ready exercise', and since 'different judges may legitimately take different views of what would be just and equitable in particular circumstances, it follows that those differing views should be respected, within the limits of reasonable disagreement'.[34] Hence, he said, in the absence of an identifiable error (such as an 'error of law, the taking into account of an irrelevant matter, or the failure to take account of a relevant matter'[35]), an appellate court should intervene with respect to an apportionment decision only where it is 'satisfied that the apportionment made by the court below was not one which was reasonably open to it'.[36] Similarly, Lord Hodge said in the same case that the apportionment exercise was one 'of broad judgment', and that an appellate court could overturn an apportionment decision only if the court below had 'manifestly and to a substantial degree gone wrong'.[37] **2.07**

Perhaps the most eloquent explanation for the appellate reticence to intervene with regard to apportionment decisions was provided by Kirby J in the decision of the High Court of Australia in *Roads and Traffic Authority of NSW v Dederer*. According to Kirby J: **2.08**

[28] Adrian Zuckerman, *Zuckerman on Civil Procedure: Principles of Practice* (3rd edn, Sweet & Maxwell 2013) para 24.197.

[29] *E I Du Pont de Nemours & Co v S T Dupont* [2003] EWCA Civ 1368; [2006] 1 WLR 2793 [94] (May LJ). See also Zuckerman (n 28) para 24.6 ('[l]ower court decisions are accorded a large measure of respect').

[30] *Grant v Sun Shipping Co Ltd* [1948] 2 All ER 238 (HL) 242 (Lord Porter), 246 (Lord du Parcq).

[31] Ibid, 246 (Lord du Parcq).

[32] *Kerley v Downes* [1973] RTR 188 (CA) 193 (Edmund Davies LJ).

[33] [2015] UKSC 5; [2015] 2 All ER 805 [**2:124**].

[34] Ibid, [28].

[35] Ibid, [35].

[36] Ibid.

[37] Ibid, [46]. The sentiments expressed in *Jackson* echoed numerous earlier judicial remarks to similar effect. See, eg, *C (a child) v Imperial Design* [2001] Env LR 33 (CA) [**2:12**], where Hale LJ said (at [36]) that the Court of Appeal was 'normally most reluctant to interfere' with apportionment decisions, and Arden LJ stated (at [45]) that it was well established that review by the Court of Appeal of the apportionment by a trial judge 'was of a very limited nature'.

> This Court has said many times that appellate courts must show restraint in disturbing the apportionment ordered for contributory negligence as between a plaintiff and a defendant, having regard to their respective shares of responsibility for the damage. The point is self-evident. Involved in such an apportionment is a comparative examination of the whole conduct of each negligent party in relation to the circumstances of the accident and an evaluation of the comparative importance of the respective acts and omissions of the parties in causing the damage. Such decisions are evaluative and multi-factorial. Generally speaking, a trial judge, who has full knowledge of all of the evidence, will be in a better position to make such an apportionment correctly. An appellate court, even if it would have reached a different conclusion, will usually be hard pressed to identify an error that warrants disturbance of the primary judge's conclusion on such an issue. Tinkering with apportionments is to be discouraged.[38]

[38] [2007] HCA 42; (2007) 234 CLR 330 [168]. See also *Jackson* (n 33) [27] **[2:124]**, where Lord Reed observed that in making a decision on apportionment, the court is not only required to consider factors that are 'incapable of precise measurement', but is also required to compare incommensurables, since the fault of the defendant (which lies in exposing others to risk) and the fault of the claimant (which lies in want of regard for the claimant's own interests) are very different kinds of things.

3

METHODOLOGY

Introduction

3.01 In this chapter, we outline the methodology that we employed in our analysis so that readers can evaluate the methods that we used and draw their own conclusions regarding the results. We highlight both the strengths and weaknesses of our methodology. The chapter begins by setting out the methodology of our study of first instance decisions (chapter 4) and then turns to additional issues relating to the methodology of our study of appellate decisions (chapter 5). Our more specific enquiries into the operation of the law of contributory negligence in the road accident (chapter 6), employers' liability (chapter 7), and professional liability (chapter 8) contexts raised no additional methodological issues save for some relatively minor exceptions in relation to road accident claims, and we make a few remarks in this regard in the road accident chapter. It should be noted at the outset that the data collection and coding was done by research assistants who had legal backgrounds and a sound understanding of the law of contributory negligence and tort law more generally. We defined the parameters of the process, supervised it closely to ensure that the work was being done properly, and resolved issues that the research assistants brought to our attention.

Contributory Negligence at First Instance

The scope of the study

3.02 Our analysis of the handling of the contributory negligence doctrine at first instance extended to all parts of the United Kingdom. For convenience, unless otherwise indicated references to the 'High Court' and 'county courts' in the discussion of first instance decisions should be taken to include their equivalents in Northern Ireland and Scotland. We located the relevant cases both directly and indirectly. We were able to obtain decisions directly where the full text of the judgment was electronically available. We also gleaned the salient facts of many other cases indirectly either from a reported summary of the decision or, where an appeal had been brought against the judgment, from the judgment of the appellate court.[1]

3.03 The fact that we proceeded in this way introduced two selection biases into our study. The first selection bias arose because the decisions that were directly available were predominantly High Court decisions. This was because the proportion of High Court decisions available online greatly exceeds the proportion of county court decisions available online. The allocation of cases as between the High Court and county courts is complex, and the details are relatively unimportant for present purposes.[2] It suffices to say that most civil cases are heard in the county courts, and only higher value and more complex cases are allocated to the High Court.[3] It follows that, overall, the claims in the cases that were directly accessible to us were likely to be larger and more complex than the general population of claims.

3.04 The second selection bias arose because most of the decisions that were only indirectly accessible to us had either been the subject of an appeal or had been summarized by a law reporter, and it may well be that such cases are unrepresentative. The fact that an appeal was brought, and the fact that permission to appeal was granted, may indicate a higher value or more complex claim, but also the very fact that a trial judge's decision was the subject of an appeal may suggest that the decision is inconsistent with the general tenor of first instance decisions.[4] Similarly, the fact that a law reporter thought it worth summarizing a decision may indicate that the

---

[1] Where insufficient information was supplied about any given first instance decision in the reasons of the appellate court, the case was excluded from the study: see, eg, *Akers v Motor Insurers' Bureau* [2003] EWCA Civ 18; [2003] Lloyd's Rep IR 427. It is of course possible that any given appeal court mistakenly recounted the details of the decision at first instance. However, the risk of errors in relation to whether a finding of contributory negligence was made at first instance, and, if so, the discount that the trial judge applied to the claimant's damages, is surely minimal. These matters are usually stated very clearly by the trial judge. Moreover, draft judgments of appellate courts are generally shown to the parties' legal representatives prior to their being published so that they can alert the court to any factual errors (see Practice Direction ('PD') 40E). This provides an additional reason to be confident regarding the accuracy of the essential details reported in the appellate court judgments.

[2] The central provisions in this regard are Civil Procedure Rules ('CPR') rr 2.1–2.4. See also PD 7A. For discussion, see Adrian Zuckerman, *Zuckerman on Civil Procedure: Principles of Practice* (3rd edn, Sweet & Maxwell 2013) paras 4.7–4.9, although even this leading and comprehensive text glosses over much of the detail.

[3] In relation to England and Wales, it has been said that '[c]ivil cases … are mainly dealt with by county courts … Particularly important, complex or substantial cases are instead dealt with in the High Court' (Ministry of Justice, *Civil Justice Statistics Quarterly, England and Wales* (2015) 3). Also, in the case of England and Wales, a claim cannot be commenced in the High Court unless its value exceeds £100,000, and if proceedings include a claim for damages in respect of personal injury, the value of the personal injury component must exceed £50,000 before the claim can be filed in the High Court. See PD 7A, rr 2.1–2.2. Similar rules exist in relation to Northern Ireland and Scotland.

[4] In England and Wales, litigants require permission to appeal, but this is not necessarily the case in Scotland and Northern Ireland: see 2.05.

claim in the case concerned is rather different from claims in the general population of cases.

How important are these selection biases? We investigated the extent to which the likelihood of a finding of contributory negligence and the size of the discounts imposed for contributory negligence varied both as between High Court cases and county court cases, and as between directly and indirectly accessed cases. We also conducted statistical analysis in order to ascertain the probability that any such differences were attributable to chance. Contributory negligence was found in 56 per cent of High Court claims in our dataset, as opposed to 62 per cent of county court claims, and in 55 per cent of claims in directly accessed cases, as opposed to 65 per cent of claims in indirectly accessed cases. Statistical analysis suggests that the first of these disparities may well be down to chance while the latter is very unlikely to be.[5] If these disparities are not down to chance then the more significant disparity (which is between directly and indirectly accessed cases) may be attributable to the fact that defendants are more likely to bring appeals as to the existence of contributory negligence than claimants.[6] It would then follow that the figures in this book for the success rate of pleas of contributory negligence at first instance may be a little higher than one would find if one looked at the claims in the general population of cases. **3.05**

Differences were also observed in relation to the average discounts imposed in High Court claims (39 per cent) and claims in cases that were directly accessed (37 per cent) on the one hand and in county court claims (42 per cent) and claims in indirectly accessed cases (44 per cent) on the other hand. This time statistical analysis suggested that both of these disparities were unlikely to be attributable to chance.[7] The explanation here may be that an appeal regarding the discount is more likely where a substantial discount has been made at first instance, since this will usually mean that more is at stake. In any case, it seems quite likely that the average discount figures that are reported in this book for first instance decisions may again be a little higher than one would find if one looked at the general population of claims in first instance cases. **3.06**

[5] The statistical tests returned what are known as *p*-values. It is convenient to introduce the concept of *p*-values below: see 4.07. Here, we simply report the values. A Pearson's chi-square test of the difference in the rate at which contributory negligence was found as between High Court cases and county court cases yielded a *p*-value of 0.235. The *p*-value produced by the same test carried out in relation to the mode by which cases were accessed was 0.029.

[6] See 5.09.

[7] A two-sided *t*-test comparing the average discounts in High Court cases and county court cases returned a *p*-value of 0.111. The *p*-value fell to 0.035 when we ran a Wilcoxon rank sum test with continuity correction. The *p*-values for the same tests comparing the average discount for directly accessed cases and indirectly accessed cases were 0.002 (two-sided *t*-test) and < 0.001 (Wilcoxon rank sum test with continuity correction).

3.07 Despite these caveats, we feel confident that the claims in our dataset of first instance decisions are *reasonably* representative of the general population of relevant claims.[8] After all, the selection biases may in fact have no bearing on the incidence with which contributory negligence is found. Furthermore, the two biases may to some extent offset each other. This is because including indirectly accessed cases considerably increased the number of county court decisions in the first instance sample, while the vast majority of the cases that we accessed directly were not the subject of an appeal. Nevertheless, the selection biases that we have identified should be borne in mind in interpreting our results.

3.08 The study was limited to cases that were decided between 1 January 2000 and 31 December 2016.[9] There were three main reasons why we chose to look at decisions made during this period: first, we were interested in the contemporary operation of the contributory negligence doctrine; second, a 17-year period produced a sufficiently large sample of cases to enable us to make meaningful claims about the operation of the doctrine; and, third, since 2000 there has been an explosion in the online availability of decisions. Making use of online decisions made the data collection process vastly less expensive and time-consuming than it would otherwise have been.

Finding the cases

3.09 Cases within the scope of our first instance study were entered into a spreadsheet.[10] In order to locate the cases in which we were interested, 'contributory negligence' was entered as a search term into LexisNexis, and the results were then ordered by date. The full text dialogue box was used (ie, we did not enter these search terms merely into, for example, the catchword dialogue box). Searches were also run using the phrases 'apportionment' and 'Law Reform Contributory Negligence Act 1945' and 'Law Reform Miscellaneous Provisions Act Northern Ireland 1948'

[8] It is worth remembering that '[a]ll empirical studies are imperfect, especially observational (non-experimental) social science studies' and that the goal in selecting cases 'is not a perfect match between sample frame and research conclusions, but only a reasonable connection between the two' (Mark A Hall and Ronald F Wright, 'Systematic Content Analysis of Judicial Opinions' (2008) 96 Calif L Rev 63, 105).

[9] In cases where the salient facts of a first instance decision were gleaned from the judgment of an appellate court, the date of the first instance decision was often given by the appeal court. Where it was not, the decision date was estimated using the following method. We calculated the average number of days between the date of first instance decisions and appellate decisions using the cases for which the dates of both of those decisions were known that were decided between 2000 and 2014 (this came to 328 days). We focused on the period 2000–2014 in this regard simply because that was the temporal scope of the first phase of our empirical investigation into the contributory negligence doctrine. We then subtracted the average number of days from the date of the relevant appellate decisions in order to produce an estimated date for first instance decisions of unknown dates.

[10] Appendix 1 records the key details from the first instance spreadsheet.

to ensure that no relevant cases were omitted. A cross-check was then run with Westlaw and Lawtel, and additional cases added to the dataset as necessary.

All the search results were then filtered so that the only cases left were those in which the court made a formal determination as to whether or not the claimant was guilty of contributory negligence. Cases in which contributory negligence was pleaded in response to a counter-claim[11] or cross-claim[12] were included. Where a deduction for contributory negligence had been agreed by the parties, the case was included only if the agreement had been formally approved by the judge (which approval is required where the claimant is a protected party).[13] Where a case involved multiple claimants or multiple defendants[14] we generally created separate entries for each individual claim in which contributory negligence was an issue.[15] This reflected the fact that in such cases claims that are technically distinct from each other are joined together in the same set of proceedings merely for reasons of convenience. Accordingly, throughout this book we use the language of 'claims' rather than 'cases'. **3.10**

The following categories of claim were excluded from the study: **3.11**

(1) *Claims where the first instance decision on contributory negligence was a contingent finding that did not affect the outcome of the claim at that stage.* When a trial judge determines that there is no liability on the part of the defendant, the judge will nevertheless often proceed to consider issues that would have arisen had the defendant been found liable—such as the doctrine of contributory negligence—in case the decision on liability is reversed on appeal.[16] Where

---

[11] See, eg, *Logical Computer Supplies Ltd v Euro Car Parks Ltd* [2002] IP & T 233 (QBD) **[1:54]**; [4:4]; *Withers LLP v Harrison* [2010] EWHC 2769 (QB); [2010] All ER (D) 41 (Nov) **[1:499]**; [4:45].

[12] See, eg, *Dunlop Haywards Ltd v Barbon Insurance Group Ltd* [2009] EWHC 2900 (Comm); [2010] Lloyd's Rep IR 149 **[1:321]**; **[4:29]**.

[13] There were four such cases: *Al Gouri v Achkar* [2007] CLY 3079 (QBD) **[1:234]**; **[3:75]**; *Sklair v Haycock* [2009] EWHC 3328 (QB); [2009] All ER (D) 159 (Dec) **[1:352]**; **[3:121]**; *Edwards v Martin* [2010] EWHC 570 (QB); [2010] All ER (D) 68 (Jun) **[1:360]**; **[3:123]**; and *Ali v Caton* [2013] EWHC 1730 (QB); [2013] All ER (D) 94 (Jul) **[1:475]**; **[3:167]**. The claimant in *McCracken v Smith* [2013] EWHC 3620 (QB) **[1:491]**; **[2:125]**; **[3:171]** was a protected party and an agreement was reached between the parties as to the discount that a given act of contributory negligence should attract, with the court being left to decide the overall discount.

[14] We did not treat actions brought against an employee and his or her employer as involving multiple defendants since, in reality, the employer is the only defendant in such cases.

[15] The qualification is needed because in one case, *Adams v Atlas International Property Services Ltd* [2016] EWHC 3120 (QB) **[1:569]**; **[4:56]**, there were 16 separate but similarly situated claimants, and in this instance we treated their actions as one claim to avoid distorting the data by giving undue prominence to a single case.

[16] The practice is not universal, however. There are numerous cases in which judges who have absolved the defendant of liability have explicitly refused to address the issue of contributory negligence, sometimes on the basis that their finding on liability made it impossible sensibly to consider the criteria of relative blameworthiness and causal potency: see, eg, *Norman v Theodore Goddard* [1992] BCC 14 (Ch D) 27 (Hoffmann J); *Gorham v British Telecommunications Plc* [2000] 1 WLR

the issue of contributory negligence arose only in this contingent way, we did not include the claim in our study. This was partly because we were concerned that in this kind of case the trial judge might not engage with the contributory negligence question as fully and thoroughly as in cases where the decision on contributory negligence would affect the outcome of the first instance claim. Our sense from reading the relevant cases is that when judges appear confident in their conclusion that the defendant was not liable at all the treatment of contributory negligence is often very perfunctory.[17] Furthermore, judges who address the issue of contributory negligence contingently sometimes give only a rough indication of the size of the discount that they would have imposed but do not descend to specific percentages.[18] We also felt justified in excluding contingent rulings regarding contributory negligence from consideration given that our dataset was large enough for us to be confident that it was representative of the general population of claims.

(2) *Professional negligence claims concerning an underlying claim in which contributory negligence was potentially an issue.* We encountered several claims that had the following structure: (i) a claimant brought proceedings against his or her former lawyers alleging that the lawyers were negligent in handling an action that the claimant had against a third party, with the result that the action failed, or that the damages awarded were less than they should have been; and (ii) the lawyers sought to diminish their liability by arguing that the claimant's action against the third party would have been affected by the claimant's contributory negligence.[19] Professional negligence claims with this structure were excluded from our study.

(3) *Claims where the judge discussed contributory negligence, but did not make a formal determination on the issue.* Examples include a discussion of the possibility of the claimant being guilty of contributory negligence in an application for an interim remedy[20] or summary judgment.

2129 (CA) 2144 (Pill LJ); *Probert v Moore* [2012] EWHC 2324 (QB); [2012] All ER (D) 75 (Aug) [49] (David Pittaway QC); *Seery v Leathes Prior (a firm)* [2017] EWHC 80 (QB) [68] (Sir David Eady); *Webster v Ridgeway Foundation School* [2010] EWHC 157 (QB); [2010] ELR 694 [196] (Nicol J). Consider, also, the remarks in *HIH Casualty and General Insurance Ltd v JLT Risk Solutions Ltd* [2007] EWCA Civ 710; [2008] Bus LR 180 [111] (Auld LJ).

[17] Good illustrations include *Joyce v O'Brien* [2012] EWHC 1324 (QB); [2012] PIQR P18 [48] (Cooke J); *Vaughan v Ministry of Defence* [2015] EWHC 1404 (QB) [2015] All ER (D) 207 (May) [38] (Davis J). In these cases, it was held that the defendant was not liable, and the contingently relevant question of contributory negligence was addressed within the space of just a single paragraph. See also *Sutherland v McConechy's Tyre Service Ltd* [2012] CSOH 28; 2012 Rep LR 46 [54]–[56] (Lord Stewart).

[18] See, eg, *Calvert v William Hill Credit Ltd* [2008] EWHC 454 (Ch); [2008] All ER (D) 170 (Mar) [218] (Briggs J) (stating that had the defendant been liable, a 'very large' discount for contributory negligence would have been imposed).

[19] See, eg, *Hunter v Earnshaw* [2001] PNLR 42 (QBD).

[20] See, eg, *Morris v Buckle (t/a Melplash Court Farm)* 2004 WL 1640368.

(4) *Claims in which the* only *determination pertaining to contributory negligence was whether the doctrine applied to the cause of action for which the claimant was suing.*[21] Judges are periodically required to decide whether the doctrine of contributory negligence applies to a particular cause of action, such as battery or deceit. We did not include such claims in our study unless the judge in question proceeded to make a formal determination as to whether the claimant was guilty of contributory negligence on the facts of the case.[22]

(5) *Claims in which the contributory negligence question was governed by foreign law.* We encountered several claims in which a United Kingdom court was required to consider the doctrine of contributory negligence as a matter of foreign law.[23] We excluded such claims from our study.

The total number of claims in the first instance spreadsheet was 572. Of these, 178 were decided in the county courts (or equivalents) and 394 were decided in the High Court (or equivalents). 383 claims were directly accessed while 189 were accessed indirectly. **3.12**

Coding the claims

The research assistants scrutinized the claims in the dataset in order to ascertain whether the plea of contributory negligence succeeded and, if so, the discount that the judge had applied to the damages award as a result. They also abstracted other relevant information from the judgments and populated the spreadsheet accordingly. The 15 columns in the spreadsheet (A–P) were as follows: **3.13**

A: *The name of the case.*

B: *The citation of the case.* We included the medium neutral citation where one was available along with the citation for the best report where the case had been reported. Where neither was available, we included the Westlaw citation, if there was one. Where the first instance data had been gleaned from an appellate decision, and no neutral citation or report citation of the first instance decision was available, the citation for the appellate decision was entered.

C: *The date of the decision.* Where we had had to estimate the date of the decision,[24] the estimated date was entered.

D: *The jurisdiction of the decision.* The jurisdictions were England and Wales, Northern Ireland, and Scotland.

E: *The court that decided the case.*

---

[21] See, eg, *Hurst v Hone* [2010] EWHC 1159 (QB); [2010] All ER (D) 256 (May) (deceit).

[22] See, eg, *Parmer v Big Security Co Ltd* [2008] EWHC 1414 (QB); [2008] All ER (D) 268 (Apr) (battery) [**1:287**].

[23] See, eg, *Barings Plc (in liq) v Coopers & Lybrand (No 7)* [2003] EWHC 1319 (Ch); [2003] Lloyd's Rep IR 566; *Vann v Ocidental-Companhia De Seguros SA* [2015] EWCA Civ 572; [2015] All ER (D) 36 (Jun).

[24] See n 9.

F: *The institutional status of the court.* We distinguished between the High Court and institutional equivalents, and county courts and institutional equivalents (such as Sheriffs' courts in Scotland).

G: *Whether the case was accessed directly or indirectly.*

H: *The type of claim.* The categories of claim were: (1) road accident; (2) employers' liability;[25] (3) occupiers' liability;[26] (4) public liability;[27] (5) professional negligence; (6) sports injury; and (7) 'other'. If a claim was capable of being classified as falling into more than one category, we made a judgment as to which classification was the most appropriate.[28]

I: *The nature of the damage suffered by the claimant.* The categories of damage were: (1) personal injury (including fatal accident and psychiatric injury claims[29]); (2) property damage; and (3) pure economic loss.[30]

J: *Whether a finding of contributory negligence was made.*

K: *Where a finding of contributory negligence was made, the percentage by which the claimant's damages were discounted as a result.*

L: *The claimant's gender.* Where the claimant was not a natural person, 'N/A' was entered. Where the claim was in respect of a fatal accident, the gender of the deceased was given.

M: *The claimant's age at the time of the act or (where contributory negligence was not found) alleged act of contributory negligence.* Fractions of years were given where they were available. This was done primarily because the courts have often made a point of recording fractions of years, especially in the case of children, the implication being that even small differences in the age of a child can make

---

25 Defined as claims in which the defendant was sued in their capacity as the claimant's employer. This was extended to relationships akin to employment: see, eg, *Commissioner of Police of the Metropolis v Lennon* [2004] EWCA Civ 130; [2004] ICR 1114 **[1:132]** (police officer suing Metropolitan Police Commissioner for failing to give advice about preservation of housing allowance entitlement).

26 Defined as claims in which the defendant was sued in their capacity as the occupier of premises. Applying this definition, several claims where the claimant had suffered injury because of an alleged defect in premises in which she was staying were classified as 'other' (claim type (7)) because the defendant was not sued as the occupier of the premises but in some other capacity, typically that of a tour operator in a contractual relationship with the claimant.

27 Defined as claims in which the defendant was sued in their capacity as a public authority.

28 If an employer, occupier, or public authority was sued in that capacity, the claim was always classified as a type (2), (3), or (4) claim respectively, even if (for example) the claim also involved a road accident or sports injury. This decision was made because our sense from reading the decisions in the (relatively uncommon) claims concerned was that the capacity in which the defendant was sued was the best and most straightforward guide as to how the claim in question should be categorized.

29 At an early stage in the study, psychiatric injury claims were treated as a separate category, but as there were very few claims in this category we decided to merge it with category (1), which had originally been 'physical injury claims'.

30 There was only a single claim (*Renton v Riddell* 2002 Scot (D) 27/4 (OH) **[1:89]**) in which the claimant sued for more than one type of damage (personal injury and property damage). In respect of this claim, 'N/A' was entered with respect to the type of damage.

a difference to findings of contributory negligence and apportionment. These fractions were rounded to the nearest quarter of a year. If the precise age of the claimant was unknown, or if the alleged contributory negligence persisted for over 10 years,[31] then either 'Child' or 'Adult' was entered where it was clear that the claimant had been under or over 18 years of age at the relevant time or throughout the relevant time period.[32] In some claims where the claimant's age was not apparent from the court's judgment, it was possible to obtain it from another source, such as a contemporary news report. The age thus obtained was then entered in the age column, and the source of the information recorded in the notes column (column P). 'N/A' was entered where the claimant was not a natural person, and 'Unknown' was entered where the claimant was a natural person, but it was not possible to tell whether the claimant was a child or adult at the relevant time.

N: *A brief description of the act or (where contributory negligence was not found) alleged act of contributory negligence.* Examples included: 'Failing to wear a seat belt'; 'Failing to keep a proper lookout for pedestrians'; 'Driving at excessive speed'; 'Lying in road when intoxicated'; 'Failing to make a payment on time'; 'Smoking'; 'Rushing down stairs'; and 'Failing to check architect's drawing'. The research assistants were instructed to try to maintain some consistency in the formulae used in this column. Where multiple acts of contributory negligence were found or alleged, this was noted, but only the most significant such acts were entered. Where the plea of contributory negligence succeeded, only those acts that the court found amounted to contributory negligence were entered. Where insufficient detail was available to ascertain the actual or alleged contributory negligence, 'Unknown' was entered.

O: *A brief description of the wrongful conduct of the defendant.*

P: *Notes.* Any interesting or unusual features of the claim were entered in this column, and also such matters as the fact that contributory negligence had been pleaded in response to a counter-claim or cross-claim, the fact that the age of the claimant had been ascertained from a news report, and the fact that either the existence of contributory negligence and/or the discount had been agreed by the parties.

[31] The most common example of an act of contributory negligence that persisted over a long period of time was smoking: see, eg, *Badger v Ministry of Defence* [2005] EWHC 2941 (QB); [2006] 3 All ER 173 [**1:210**]. In one claim (*Rowntree v Commissioner of Police of the Metropolis* [2001] Po LR 404 (QBD) [**1:67**]), the alleged contributory negligence continued for three years, and in this instance we entered the claimant's median age in this period. Where we could tell that the age of the claimant was one of two years we split the difference (so, eg, in the case of a claimant who must have been aged 46 or 47 years we treated the claimant as being aged 46.5 years).

[32] We erred on the side of caution here, and entered 'Child' or 'Adult' only if we were virtually certain that this was the case.

Checking the data

3.14 The data were collected and coded by research assistants. In order to confirm that the assistants were not incorrectly excluding claims from the sample, we instructed them to send us a list of the claims that contained at least one of the relevant search terms but which the assistants thought should be excluded from the sample on the ground that they did not meet the criteria we had prescribed for inclusion. We checked random samples of 15 of these claims in respect of each assistant to determine whether they had been right to exclude them. We were satisfied that the assistants had proceeded correctly in respect of all of the claims.

3.15 Following the initial coding of the first 30 claims, we personally checked the results against the judgments in the cases concerned. This process led to the identification of some errors (which were corrected) and also to clarification of some of the coding instructions. A further 30 claims were then coded, and all of these were again checked by us. Following this, the remainder of the claims were coded. The research assistants were told that if any difficulties were encountered during the coding process, they should be referred to us for resolution (the research assistants consulted us intermittently when they had doubts as to how to proceed and we resolved the relevant queries). The entire first instance spreadsheet was then double-checked by a research assistant who had not been involved in the initial coding. Possible errors identified by that research assistant were brought to our attention and we then decided whether an error had been made, and, if so, modified the spreadsheet accordingly. As the foregoing reveals, all entries in the spreadsheet were double-checked by different people and many were triple-checked, again by different people.

Statistical analysis

3.16 The data were analysed by trained statisticians. The statisticians used a statistical programme known as 'R' to run the tests and to produce the graphs. They ran Pearson's chi-square tests to test independence between categorical variables (such as the frequency with which claimants were found guilty of contributory negligence) and *t*-tests or analysis of variance (ANOVA) as appropriate to measure the significance of observed disparities in the values of continuous variables (such as the size of discounts for contributory negligence) across different categories of data (such as male claimants and female claimants). Wilcoxon rank sum tests with continuity correction were run as a cross-check of the results produced by the *t*-tests. Linear and logistic regression analyses were conducted in order to control for confounding variables.

Reporting the data

3.17 We have endeavoured to report the results of our study in a way that we hope will be readily comprehensible to this book's likely readership, namely, legal academics and practising lawyers who are interested in the law of torts. Accordingly, we have prioritized the use of descriptive concepts that are in general well understood by lawyers, such as the average and the range. The median—the centremost value when the data are arranged in a list—is frequently reported, too, but typically only in graphical representations of the data. We feel that it is preferable to prioritize reporting mean rather than median values as we suspect that many lawyers are more comfortable in thinking in terms of average values rather than median values. More importantly, there are relatively few outliers in our samples. The fact that the samples contain so few outliers means that the average values are unlikely to be distorted and, consequently, provide a reasonable means by which the data can be understood. Furthermore, when it comes to the discounts made for contributory negligence, the mean is more meaningful than the median because (as we show[33]) the courts typically use only a small number of quite coarse discounts (eg, 25 per cent, 50 per cent), and avoid making fine-grained discounts. As a result, the median is likely to be misleading as it is susceptible to being significantly influenced in a way that the mean (given our data) is not. A single case could cause the median to swing by a sizeable amount. We rounded all figures that we report to the nearest whole number except where we considered that greater precision might be useful (eg, to facilitate a comparison with the results found by other investigators).[34]

Contributory Negligence on Appeal

In this section, we outline the methodology of our appellate study. For the most part, the approach was exactly the same, *mutatis mutandis*, as in relation to the first instance study. Thus, the appellate study has the same temporal and jurisdictional scope; cases were identified for inclusion within the appellate spreadsheet in the same way; the same checks were performed; where a case involved multiple claimants or defendants, separate entries for each individual claim in which contributory negligence was in issue were added to the spreadsheet; the same categories of case were excluded; the statistical analysis was carried out in the same way; and the same conventions regarding reporting of the data were followed. Where a claim involved both an appeal and a cross-appeal on contributory negligence, we did not create separate entries in the spreadsheet but simply made a note of that fact.[35] **3.18**

33 See 4.20.

34 To be precise, numbers greater than *X*.444 were rounded up to the nearest whole number and numbers less than *X*.444 were rounded down to the nearest whole number.

35 There were nine such claims, namely *Slack v Glenie* [2000] All ER (D) 592 (CA) **[2:4]**; **[2:5]** (two claims); *Watson v Skuse* [2001] EWCA Civ 1158; [2001] All ER (D) 208 (Jul) **[1:26]**; **[2:26]**; **[3:15]**; *Anderson v Newham College for Further Education* [2002] EWCA Civ 505; [2003] ICR 212 **[1:52]**; **[2:30]**; *Lunt v Khelifa* [2002] EWCA Civ 801; [2002] All ER (D) 352 (May) **[2:36]**; *Noble v de Boer* 2004 SC 548 (IH) **[2:58]**; *Home Office v Lowles* [2004] EWCA Civ 985; [2004] All ER (D) 538 (Jul) **[1:152]**; **[2:64]**; *West Sussex CC v Russell* [2010] EWCA Civ 71; [2010] RTR 19 **[2:93]**; and *Phethean-Hubble v Coles* [2012] EWCA Civ 349; [2012] RTR 31 **[2:109]**. The existence

To minimize duplication, we set out the methodology employed in relation to the appellate study only to the extent that it differed from that adopted in relation to the first instance study.

3.19 We should say something about two recurrent scenarios that we encountered and how we dealt with them. In the first, the trial court absolved the defendant of primary liability, but nonetheless considered whether a finding of contributory negligence would have been made had the defendant been found liable. The appellate court then reversed the first instance court on the primary liability question, and made a real finding on the contributory negligence issue.[36] The research assistants were instructed that when populating the spreadsheet in such a situation they should treat the trial judge's contingent findings regarding contributory negligence (both as to guilt and apportionment) as 'determinations' on the issue. They were also instructed to treat a challenge by one of the parties to either form of 'determination' as an 'appeal' by that party on the issue.

3.20 In the second recurrent scenario, the first instance court again absolved the defendant of primary liability, but this time *did not* go on to consider whether a finding of contributory negligence would have been made if the defendant had been found liable.[37] As in the first scenario, the appellate court then reversed the first instance court on the primary liability question, and made a determination regarding the contributory negligence issue, which had been raised for the first time on appeal. This time, the spreadsheet was populated on the basis that there had been no determination on contributory negligence by the first instance court (and hence no possibility of the appellate court overturning any such determination) and no appeal on contributory negligence by either party. We included claims of this kind in our study because our interest lay in the operation of the contributory negligence doctrine in appellate courts, and not only in the narrower question of appeals in relation to contributory negligence.

3.21 The 26 columns in the appellate spreadsheet (A–Z) were as follows.[38] For the most part, their contents are self-explanatory, and to some extent they simply track the columns that were used in the first instance spreadsheet. We elaborate on their contents only to the extent that doing so is necessary to make plain matters that may otherwise be unclear.

A: *The name of the case.*
B: *The citation of the case.*
C: *The date of the first instance decision.*

of cross-appeals was also made apparent by entries in columns W–Z of the spreadsheet (see 3.13 for descriptions of the columns), where we entered data for each and every appeal in a given claim.

36 See, eg, *Sykes v Harry* [2001] EWCA Civ 167; [2001] QB 1014 [**2:18**].
37 See, eg, *Tasci v Pekalp of London Ltd* [2001] ICR 633 (CA) [**2:13**].
38 Appendix 2 records the key details from the appellate spreadsheet.

D: *The date of the appellate decision.*

E: *The jurisdiction of the decision.* The jurisdictions were the same as in the first instance spreadsheet.

F: *The name of the first instance court.*

G: *The name of the appellate court.*

H: *Whether the judge at first instance was a permanent judge or acting judge.*

I: *The type of claim.* The categories of claim were the same as in the first instance spreadsheet.

J: *The nature of the damage suffered by the claimant.* The categories of damage were the same as in the first instance spreadsheet.[39]

K: *Whether a finding of contributory negligence had been made at first instance.* If no determination had been made, 'N/A' was entered.

L: *Where a finding of contributory negligence had been made at first instance, the percentage by which the claimant's damages were discounted.* If no finding of contributory negligence had been made, 'N/A' was entered. 'Unknown' was entered where it was clear that a finding had been made but, because the text of the first instance decision was unavailable, and because the discount was not reported by the appellate court, the quantum of the discount was unascertainable.[40]

M: *The claimant's gender.*

N: *The claimant's age at the time of the act or (where contributory negligence was not found) alleged act of contributory negligence.*

O: *A brief description of the act or (where contributory negligence was not found) alleged act of contributory negligence.* Examples included 'Failing to keep a proper lookout', 'Stepping into the road without looking', 'Placing hand too close to circular wood-cutter' and 'Carelessly undertaking patient lifting'. Where multiple acts of contributory negligence were found or alleged, only the most significant such acts were entered. Where the appellate court held that the claimant had been guilty of contributory negligence, only those acts which that court found amounted to contributory negligence were entered.

P: *A brief description of the wrongful conduct of the defendant.* Where the first instance court and the appellate court came to different conclusions on this issue, a description of the wrongful conduct as found by the appellate court was entered.

Q: *Whether the appellate court acceded to a request to overturn the determination of the first instance court regarding the existence of contributory negligence.* If the existence of contributory negligence had not been considered at first instance, or if the appellate court had not been asked to disturb the first instance determination on the issue, 'N/A' was entered. 'No' was therefore entered only in cases

[39] There were no claims in the appellate dataset in which the claimant was suing for more than one type of damage.

[40] *Robinson v Midland Bank Plc* [2000] All ER (D) 1560 (CA) [**2:9**] and *Kennedy v Chivas Brothers Ltd* [2013] CSIH 57; 2014 SLT 981 [**2:118**] were the only instances in the appellate dataset in which this occurred.

where the appellate court was specifically asked to disturb the first instance court's determination of the issue, and declined to do so.

R: *Whether the appellate court acceded to a request to overturn the determination of the first instance court regarding apportionment.* If apportionment had not been considered at first instance, or if the appellate court had not been asked to disturb the first instance determination on the issue, 'N/A' was entered. 'No' was therefore entered only in cases where the appellate court was specifically asked to disturb the first instance court's determination of the issue, and declined to do so.

S: *Whether the claimant was found guilty of contributory negligence following the appeal.*

T: *Where the claimant was found guilty of contributory negligence following the appeal, the percentage by which the claimant's damages were discounted.* If the claimant was not found guilty of contributory negligence following the appeal, 'N/A' was entered.

U: *The size of any difference in the discount made for contributory negligence by the first instance court and by the appellate court.* The figure entered in this column represented the direction of the difference from first instance to appellate decision. For example, if the discount at first instance was 20 per cent and the discount imposed by the appellate court was 40 per cent, '20' was entered. Negative values were entered where the appellate court had reduced the discount. Where the appellate court did not overturn the first instance court on apportionment, 'N/A' was entered.

V: *Whether the claimant had succeeded in an appeal on the existence of contributory negligence.* If there had been no such appeal, 'N/A' was entered.

W: *Whether the claimant had succeeded in an appeal on apportionment.* If there had been no such appeal, 'N/A' was entered. 'N/A' was also entered in one case in which the claimant appealed on both the existence of contributory negligence and apportionment, and where the appellate court did not have to deal with apportionment because it allowed the appeal on the former issue.[41]

X: *Whether the defendant had succeeded in an appeal on the existence of contributory negligence.* If there had been no such appeal, 'N/A' was entered.

Y: *Whether the defendant had succeeded in an appeal on apportionment.* If there had been no such appeal, 'N/A' was entered.

Z: *Notes.* Any interesting features of the claim were entered in this column, and also such matters as the fact that the age of the claimant had been gleaned from a news report, and that there had been both an appeal and a cross-appeal on the contributory negligence issue.

[41] *CTO Gesellschaft Fur Containertransport MBH and Co v Dziennik* [2006] EWCA Civ 1456; [2006] All ER (D) 157 (Nov) [1:197]; [2:74].

4

CONTRIBUTORY NEGLIGENCE AT FIRST INSTANCE

Introduction

This chapter concerns the handling of the contributory negligence doctrine at first instance. As explained above,[1] we see value in understanding how the courts apply the law of contributory negligence in everyday situations, and this requires a shift from the usual scholarly diet of decisions of high authority to judgments of trial courts. **4.01**

Results

We begin by setting out some general information about the claims in the sample, and then proceed to the findings. We divide our discussion of the findings into four parts: the success rate of the plea of contributory negligence; the discount applied when contributory negligence is found; the relationship between contributory negligence and claimant age; and the relationship between contributory negligence and claimant gender. Our primary aim in this section of this chapter is simply to present the study's findings, although we also make some observations about their importance. Fuller discussion of key findings in the light of the case law and academic literature is postponed until the next section. **4.02**

General information

Our dataset contained entries for 572 claims in which the defendant had pleaded contributory negligence.[2] 402 (70 per cent) of these claims were from England and Wales, 42 (7 per cent) from Northern Ireland, and 128 (22 per cent) from Scotland. 178 claims (31 per cent) were decided by the High Court (or equivalent) and 394 (68 per cent) by the county courts (or equivalent). We coded for the type **4.03**

---

[1] See 1.06.

[2] A list of the first instance claims is set out in Appendix 1.

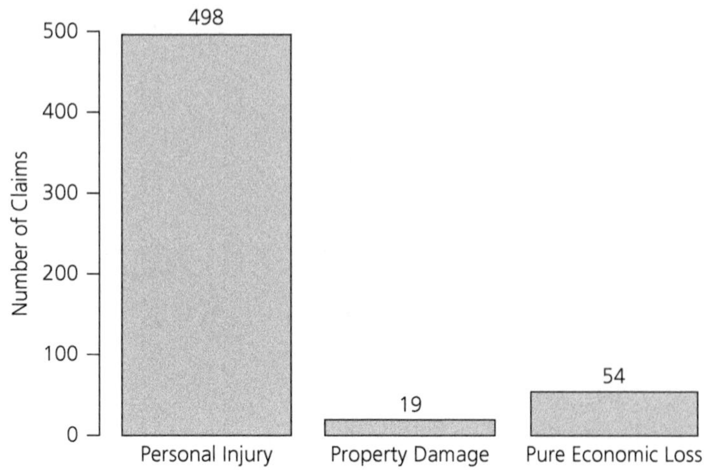

Figure 4.1 Number of claims by damage type at first instance

of damage in 571 claims[3] and, as seen in Figure 4.1, most of those claims (87 per cent) were for personal injury, with the remaining claims being in respect of pure economic loss (10 per cent) or property damage (3 per cent). The small number of property damage claims in our sample should be borne in mind when assessing the results concerning that type of damage. It is impossible to know for certain why there were so few property damage claims. However, one plausible explanation is the fact that many property damage claims are likely to be relatively low value.[4] This is significant because claimants may be less inclined to commence proceedings in respect of lower-value claims, and defendants may be more inclined to settle such claims when proceedings are brought. Furthermore, lower-value claims are determined in the county courts (and institutional equivalents) and, as we observed above,[5] county court decisions, because of their relative inaccessibility, are under-represented in our study.

4.04 There was a slightly more even spread of the claims across our seven categories of claim type (or contextual setting), as seen in Figure 4.2. Nevertheless, road accident

[3] The exception is *Renton v Riddell* 2002 Scot (D) 27/4 (OH) [**1:89**]. As we explained above (see 3.13), we did not code for the type of damage in respect of that case, as it involved both personal injury and property damage.

[4] The Department of Transport publishes estimates annually regarding the cost to society of personal injury and property damage resulting from road accidents. The cost to society per accident involving only property damage pales in comparison to the cost of even trivial personal injuries: Department of Transport, *Reported Road Casualties Great Britain: 2016 Annual Report* (2017) 26 (Table RAS60003): <https://assets.publishing.service.gov.uk/government/uploads/system/uploads/attachment_data/file/668504/reported-road-casualties-great-britain-2016-complete-report.pdf> (accessed 3 November 2018).

[5] See 3.03, 3.12.

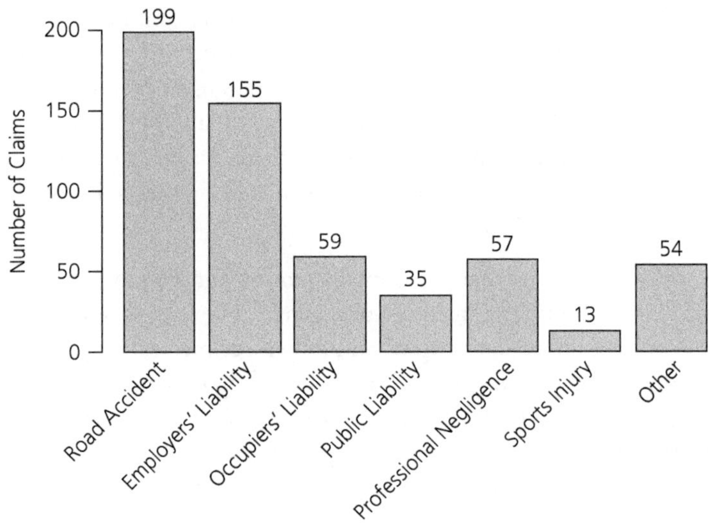

Figure 4.2 Number of claims by claim type at first instance

claims were the most common type of claim (35 per cent of claims), followed by employers' liability claims (27 per cent), and professional negligence claims and occupiers' liability claims (both 10 per cent). The 102 claims in the three remaining categories (public liability, sports injury, and 'other') amount to only 18 per cent of all the claims in the sample. Once again, the small number of claims in these categories must be kept in mind when assessing the relevant results. Claims in the 'other' category included several claims arising out of accidents on boats or ships, on trains, and in the air, as well as attacks by animals, accidents in a prison, and accidents during training courses. This category also included claims where the cause of action was not common law negligence, but another tort, such as battery, false imprisonment, or nuisance, and claims for pre-contractual misrepresentation under section 2(1) of the Misrepresentation Act 1967. The prevalence of road accident and employers' liability claims in the sample is unsurprising, as these are contexts where liability insurance is compulsory, and it is likely that claims in these two categories comprise a high proportion of personal injury actions that go to trial.[6]

The relatively small number of occupiers' liability and public liability claims is, however, noteworthy. Recent data suggest that claims in these two categories account for some 10 per cent of all personal injury claims, a slightly higher proportion than **4.05**

[6] According to the Compensation Recovery Unit (CRU), what it calls 'Motor' claims accounted for 78 per cent of all personal injury claims registered with the CRU in the period 2010–2016: <https://www.gov.uk/government/publications/compensation-recovery-unit-performance-data> (accessed 3 November 2018).

employers' liability claims.[7] Yet in our sample there were considerably more claims in the employers' liability category than in these two categories combined. This disparity might be attributable to (i) a higher proportion of employers' liability claims reaching trial; (ii) a higher proportion of employers' liability claims being tried in the High Court or institutional equivalents (such claims being over-represented in our sample[8]); and/or (iii) contributory negligence being pleaded more frequently in employers' liability claims.

4.06 Finally, we should note that we initially coded for two other categories of claim: product liability and medical negligence. However, there was only one product liability claim in the sample,[9] and only three medical negligence claims.[10] We therefore decided to eliminate both these categories from the dataset, and added the product liability claim to the 'other' category and the medical negligence claims to the professional negligence category (which had originally been a 'professional negligence (non-medical)' category). Our study therefore suggests that these are contexts in which pleas of contributory negligence are rare,[11] although the dearth of product liability claims may also reflect the small number of such claims that have been litigated in recent times.

Success rate of the plea of contributory negligence

4.07 Out of the 572 claims in our sample, the plea of contributory negligence succeeded in 331 claims (58 per cent) and failed in 241 claims (42 per cent). As

[7] The total number of employers' liability claims registered with the CRU in the period 2010–2016 was 555,122, while the total number of 'public liability' claims (a category roughly equivalent to our 'occupiers' liability' and 'public liability' categories combined) was 599,078: see <https://www.gov.uk/government/publications/compensation-recovery-unit-performance-data> (accessed 3 November 2018).

[8] See 3.03, 3.12.

[9] *Abouzaid v Mothercare (UK) Ltd* (Mayor's and City of London CC, 30 May 2000) **[1:19]**. The plea of contributory negligence in this claim failed.

[10] The three medical negligence claims were *Pidgeon v Doncaster HA* [2002] Lloyd's Rep Med 130 (Sheffield CC) **[1:63]**; [4:5]; *P (decd) v Sedar* [2011] EWHC 1266 (QB) **[1:393]**; [4:35] and *Spencer v Hillingdon Hospital NHS Trust* [2015] EWHC 1058 (QB) **[1:531]**; [4:47]. The plea of contributory negligence succeeded in *Pidgeon* and failed in the other two claims.

[11] Although s 6(4) of the Consumer Protection Act 1987 makes it clear that contributory negligence is a defence to an action for damages under the strict product liability regime introduced by that Act, we are not aware of any claims in which a claimant under that legislation has had his or her damages reduced for contributory negligence. There are, however, some claims that pre-date our study where contributory negligence has been found in a product liability action brought in common law negligence: see, eg, *Devilez v Boots Pure Drug Co Ltd* (1962) 106 Sol Jo 552 (QBD). As for medical negligence, the dearth of claims in our sample is unsurprising when one considers that *Pidgeon* (n 10) **[1:63]**; [4:5] (one of the three medical negligence claims in our sample) is apparently the only reported English clinical negligence claim in which there was a finding of contributory negligence: see Jonathan Herring and Charles Foster, 'Blaming the Patient: Contributory Negligence in Medical Malpractice Litigation' (2009) 25 PN 76, 76. For further discussion of contributory negligence in the medical negligence context, see 8.31–8.36.

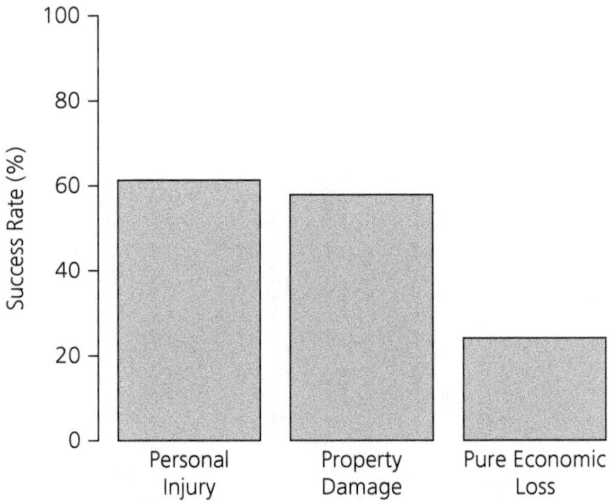

Figure 4.3 Success rate of plea by damage type at first instance

shown in Figure 4.3, the success rate of the plea of contributory negligence was almost identical for personal injury claims and property damage claims (61 and 58 per cent respectively), but markedly lower in pure economic loss claims (24 per cent). Statistical analysis suggests that this disparity is unlikely to be attributable to chance.[12]

4.08 A possible explanation for the difference in the success rate of the plea of contributory negligence between personal injury and property damage claims on the one hand, and pure economic loss claims on the other hand, emerges when we break down the success rate of the plea by type of claim (Figure 4.4). This reveals that

[12] A Pearson's chi-square test on the null hypothesis that the success rate of the plea of contributory negligence is the same across all types of damage gave a p-value of < 0.001. A p-value is the probability of obtaining an effect at least as extreme as the one in the sample data, assuming the truth of the null hypothesis. Hence, the lower the p-value, the more likely it is that the null hypothesis is false. The p-value in this instance is very low, which strongly suggests that the observed disparity is not attributable to chance (in the form of the sample of claims we happened to survey), so that the data provide strong evidence that the success rate of the plea does indeed vary across the different damage types. This evidence is reinforced by logistic regression analysis. This analysis showed that when pure economic loss claims were compared with personal injury claims, the odds of a finding of contributory negligence were notably lower in pure economic loss claims ($p < 0.001$). In many academic disciplines, a p-value of less than 0.05 is regarded as statistically significant, but the appropriateness of the use of this test of statistical significance in legal contexts has been questioned, and properly so in our view: see Neil B Cohen, 'Confidence in Probability: Burdens of Persuasion in a World of Imperfect Knowledge' (1985) 60 NYU L Rev 385, 412; David H Kaye, 'Is Proof of Statistical Significance Relevant?' (1986) 61 Wash L Rev 1333, 1342–45; Douglas W Vick, 'Statistical Significance and the Significance of Statistics' (2000) 116 LQR 575. Accordingly, in this book we eschew the language of 'statistical significance' in this binary sense and instead provide the p-values themselves in the footnotes, and more general observations on the cogency of a given finding in the text.

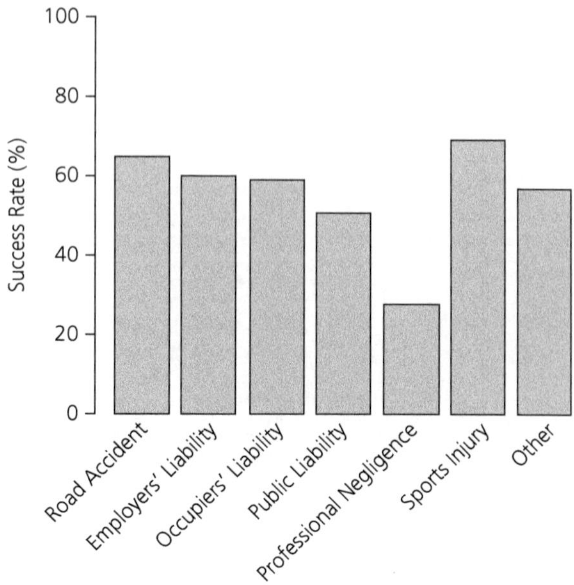

Figure 4.4 Success rate of plea by claim type at first instance

the plea of contributory negligence has a very low success rate in professional negligence claims (28 per cent). This success rate is roughly half that of the success rate of the plea across all types of claim in our study. Again, statistically, this difference is unlikely to be down to chance.[13] The reason for the close association between the success rate in pure economic loss claims and in professional negligence claims is not hard to find. Of the 54 pure economic loss claims, the vast majority (48 claims) fell into the professional negligence category; similarly, of the 57 professional negligence claims, the preponderance (48 claims) were for pure economic loss.

4.09 Two other features of Figure 4.4 should be highlighted. The first is the relatively high success rate of the plea of contributory negligence in sports injury claims (69 per cent). However, this result should be interpreted with great caution since there were very few sports injury claims in the sample (13 claims), and statistical analysis suggests that the higher success rate of the plea in this context is likely to be down to chance.[14] The other feature of the graph that should be noted is the

---

13 Pearson's chi-square test, $p < 0.001$. And logistic regression analysis showed that when professional negligence claims were compared with road accident claims (the largest category of claim), the odds of a finding of contributory negligence were markedly lower in professional negligence claims ($p < 0.001$).

14 Eg, logistic regression analysis showed that when sports injury claims were compared with road accident claims, the odds of a finding of contributory negligence were higher in sports injury claims, but the p-value was too high ($p = 0.747$) for much to be made of this difference.

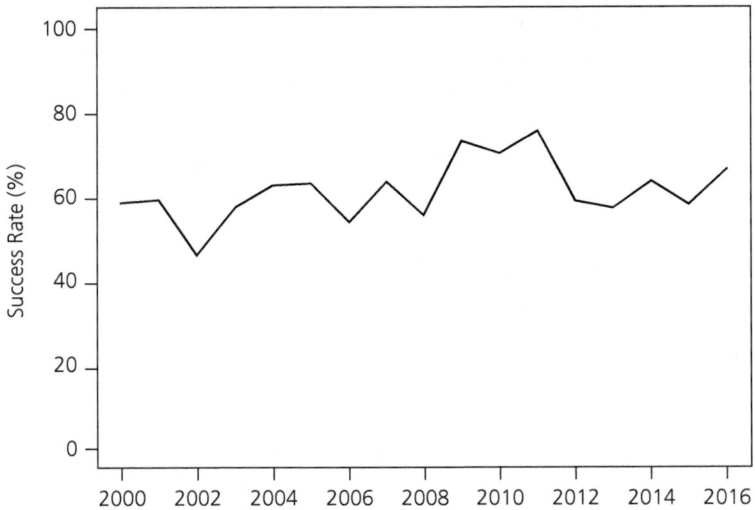

Figure 4.5 Success rate of plea by year at first instance (personal injury claims)

relatively low success rate of the plea in public liability claims (51 per cent).[15] The success rates in the other four categories of claim were fairly similar to each other, as follows: road accident claims, 65 per cent; employers' liability claims, 60 per cent; occupiers' liability claims, 59 per cent; and 'other' claims, 57 per cent.[16]

Figure 4.5 shows the success rate of the plea of contributory negligence by year. We limited this graph to personal injury claims because we thought that in certain years media and political attention on an alleged proliferation of tort claims and a so-called compensation culture might have caused judges to take a harsher view of alleged contributory fault in the personal injury context. However, statistical analysis suggests that there is no association between success rate of the plea and year in personal injury claims.[17] **4.10**

[15] Logistic regression analysis revealed that when public liability claims were compared with road accident claims, the odds of a finding of contributory negligence were lower in public liability claims ($p = 0.134$). And when we controlled for damage type, age, jurisdiction, and gender, the p-value dropped considerably ($p = 0.073$). In this chapter, whenever we controlled for age, age was treated as a categorical variable, with values for 'Adult' whenever the claimant was 18 or older and 'child' whenever the claimant was younger than 18.

[16] The disparities between these categories may well be down to chance. Eg, logistic regression analysis showed that when employers' claims were compared with road accident claims, the odds of a finding of contributory negligence were lower in employers' liability claims, but the p-value was too high ($p = 0.352$) for much to be made of this difference. Furthermore, the p-value increased significantly when we controlled for damage type, age, jurisdiction, and gender ($p = 0.657$), casting further doubt on the significance of the disparity.

[17] Pearson's chi-square test, $p = 0.682$.

4.11 Finally, we also looked at the success rate of the plea of contributory negligence in the different parts of the United Kingdom. The average success rate of the plea was 60 per cent in England and Wales, 60 per cent in Northern Ireland, and 52 per cent in Scotland. Statistical analysis suggests that the difference between the success rate in Scotland and in other parts of the United Kingdom may well be attributable to chance.[18]

Discount where contributory negligence found

4.12 In the 331 claims in which the claimant was found guilty of contributory negligence, the average amount by which the claimant's damages were reduced was 39.8 per cent (which figure we will round hereafter to 40 per cent save where greater precision is meaningful). This is very close to the average deduction of 39.5 per cent found by the Australian study we discussed in chapter 1,[19] which looked both at court decisions and settlements, but was heavily weighted towards the latter.[20]

4.13 Figure 4.6 shows the average discount by damage type. As the graph indicates, the average discounts in property damage claims and pure economic loss claims were 43 per cent and 44 per cent respectively, somewhat higher than the average discount in personal injury claims (40 per cent). In relation to pure economic loss claims, this disparity is likely to be bound up with the higher discounts found in professional negligence claims,[21] as we have seen that most of the pure economic loss claims involved professional negligence (and vice versa). With respect to property damage claims, statistical analysis provided some evidence of an association between damage type and size of discount,[22] but since there were only 11 property damage claims in which findings of contributory negligence were made, further research is required before it justifiably can be concluded that this disparity reflects a broader pattern. Additional detail regarding the discounts made in respect of the three types of damage can be seen in boxplots of discounts by damage type (Figure 4.7). Boxplots show how the data are spread over the range. The thick black line in the boxplot represents the median (ie, midpoint) discount value,[23] the bottom of the box represents the first quartile (ie, the number below which a quarter of the data points lie), the top of the box the

---

[18] A Pearson's chi-square test on the null hypothesis that the success rate of the plea of contributory negligence is the same across all three jurisdictions gave a p-value of 0.261.

[19] See 1.10.

[20] *Report of the National Committee of Inquiry on Compensation and Rehabilitation in Australia* (Australian Government Publishing Service, 1974) vol 3, 97 (Table 14).

[21] See Figure 4.8 and accompanying text.

[22] Linear regression analysis of the change in the average discount from personal injury claims to property damage claims (controlling for type of claim, age, gender, and jurisdiction) returned a p-value of 0.073.

[23] When there are an even number of claims, the median is the average of the centremost values.

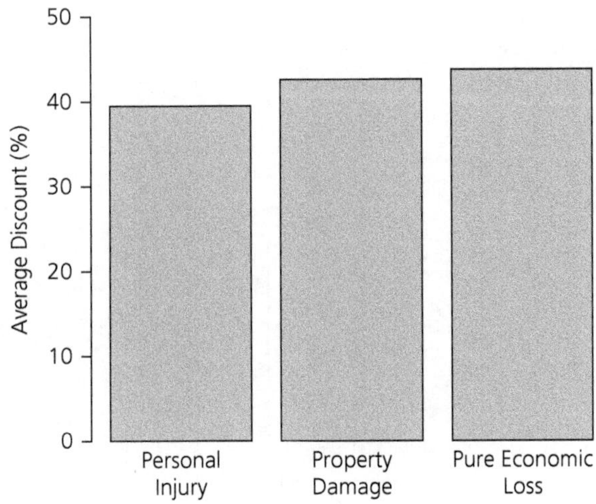

Figure 4.6 Average discount by damage type at first instance

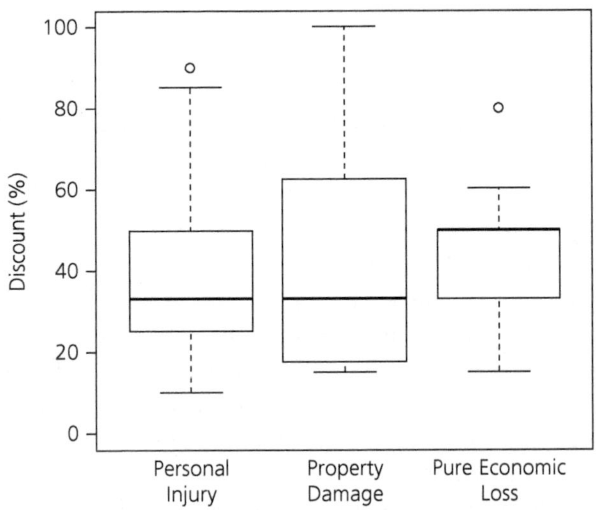

Figure 4.7 Discount by damage type at first instance

third quartile (ie, the number above which a quarter of the data points lie) and the whiskers show the full range of values disregarding outliers, which are shown as dots. An outlier is a value that falls below the first quartile or above the third quartile by more than 1.5 times the interquartile range (ie, the difference between the top and bottom of the box).

Turning from type of damage to type of claim, the average discount by type of claim is shown in Figure 4.8. Several features of this graph are noteworthy. One **4.14**

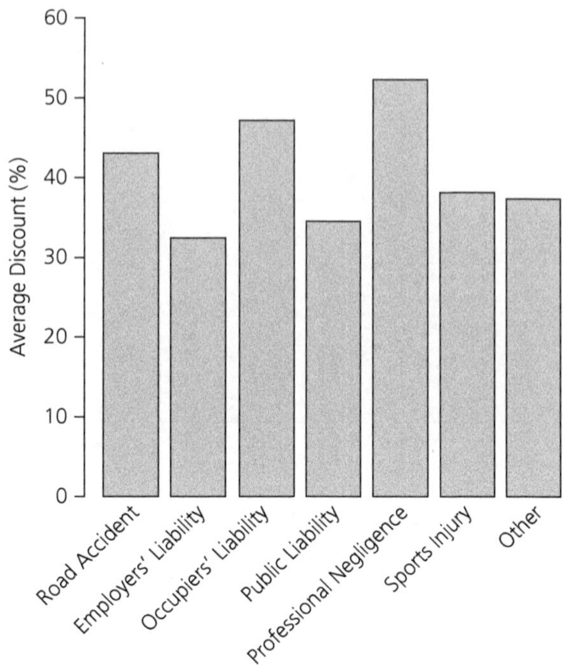

Figure 4.8 Average discount by claim type at first instance

is that the highest average discount (52 per cent) was found in professional negligence claims. However, it should be noted that there were only 16 professional negligence claims in the sample where a discount was made, and while statistical analysis suggests that the disparity between the average discount in professional negligence claims and employers' liability, public liability, and 'other' claims was very unlikely to be down to chance,[24] when it came to other categories of claim, there was a significant likelihood that the disparity was attributable to chance.[25] Nevertheless, the relatively high average discount in professional negligence cases suggests that while the courts are reluctant to find contributory negligence in professional negligence claims,[26] when they do so the discount tends to be higher than in other types of claim.

[24] Two-sided *t*-tests of the differences between the average discounts in the different types of claim gave relatively low *p*-values in the pairings of professional negligence claims with employers' liability claims ($p = 0.005$), public liability claims ($p = 0.014$), and 'other' claims ($p = 0.036$).

[25] Eg, a paired *t*-test of professional negligence claims and road accident claims—the largest category of claim—returned a *p*-value of 0.154. The results of this *t*-test were consistent with the results of a Wilcoxon rank sum test with continuity correction ($p = 0.152$).

[26] See 4.08.

A second noteworthy finding is that the average discount in employers' liability claims was relatively low (32 per cent). The disparity between this figure and the average discounts in road accident claims (43 per cent) and in occupiers' liability claims (47 per cent) was extremely unlikely to be down to chance, meaning that on the whole employees who are found guilty of contributory negligence are almost certainly treated more leniently than road users and those suing occupiers.[27] This is an important finding, as the number of employers' liability claims is very high,[28] and in our sample was second only to the number of road accident claims.[29] **4.15**

We should clarify what we mean by 'leniently'. Whenever damages are discounted for contributory negligence, the court does not consider the claimant's conduct in isolation. The claimant's responsibility for the damage is compared with the defendant's. Accordingly, a given act of contributory negligence by a claimant might attract different discounts depending on the relative significance to be attached to the defendant's negligence. The importance that a court attaches to a defendant's negligence depends, of course, on the entire factual matrix and dynamics of the claim. Our use of the word 'leniently' should be understood in this light. We mean only that, *on average,* claimants in employers' liability claims are treated more sympathetically than claimants in road accident claims or employers' liability claims *simply in terms of the discount imposed* (ie, in a raw mathematical sense). We recognize that a given discount in a specific claim, however low, may well not be 'lenient' in view of the facts in question. We acknowledge, too, that a certain discount in an individual claim may be more lenient (or harsher) than the same discount made in the context of another claim. **4.16**

A third important finding concerns the relatively high average discount in occupiers' liability claims (47 per cent). Statistical analysis suggests that the disparity between the average discount in occupiers' liability claims and in employers' liability and public liability claims was unlikely to be down to chance.[30] Our study therefore indicates that when it comes to discounting damages for contributory negligence, the courts may well in general be harder on claimants in occupiers' liability claims, **4.17**

---

27 Two-sided t-tests of the differences between the average discounts in employers' liability claims and road accident and occupiers' liability claims respectively gave very low p-values ($p < 0.001$ in both instances). These results were consistent with the results of Wilcoxon rank sum tests with continuity correction (again, $p < 0.001$ in both claims). Linear regression analysis of the change in the average discount from road accident claims to employers' liability claims (controlling for damage type, age, gender, and jurisdiction) also returned a p-value of <0.001.

28 See the data reported in n 7.

29 See Figure 4.2.

30 A two-sided t-test of the differences between the average discounts in occupiers' liability claims and employers' and public liability claims gave low p-values ($p < 0.001$ and $p = 0.007$ respectively). This result was broadly consistent with the result of a Wilcoxon rank sum test with continuity correction ($p < 0.001$ and $p = 0.030$ respectively). By contrast, linear regression analysis of the change in the average discount from road accident claims to occupiers' liability claims (controlling for damage type, age, gender, and jurisdiction) returned a higher p-value of 0.259.

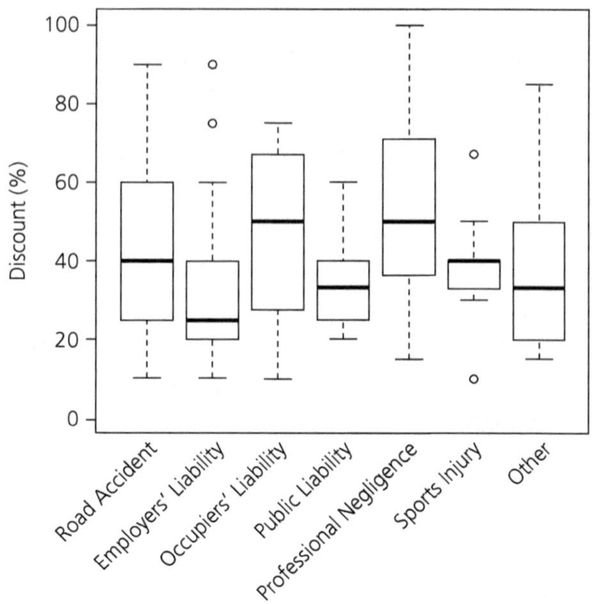

Figure 4.9 Discount by claim type at first instance

not only in comparison with claimants in employers' liability claims but in comparison with claimants in public liability claims as well.

4.18 The average discounts in the other four types of claim were all fairly close to the overall average discount of 40 per cent (road accidents, 43 per cent; public liability, 35 per cent; sports injury, 38 per cent; 'other', 37 per cent) and no significance can be attached to the minor disparities observable between the average discounts across these claim types. More detail on the interaction between discount and claim type is shown in Figure 4.9.

4.19 Once again, no discernible trend emerges when we look at the average discount by year in personal injury claims (Figure 4.10). Statistical analysis strongly suggests that there was no association between average discount and year.[31]

4.20 Our study also reveals important facts about the range and frequency of discounts used by the courts. The lowest discount that we observed was 10 per cent (used in 11 claims, all of them personal injury claims). In one property damage claim a discount of 100 per cent was made.[32] By far the most popular discount was 50 per cent

[31] An analysis of variance ('ANOVA') comparing the average discount for each year produced a high *p*-value ($p = 0.531$).

[32] *Six Continents Retail Ltd v Carford Catering Ltd* [2003] EWCA Civ 1790 [1:139]; [2:52]; [4:13]. We address the appropriateness of 100 per cent discounts later: see 4.41.

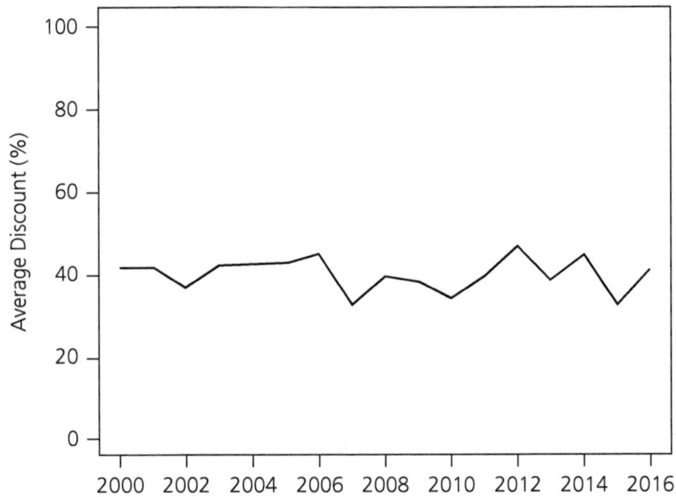

Figure 4.10 Average discount by year at first instance (personal injury claims)

Table 4.1 Most frequently used discounts at first instance

Number of claims	Discount (%)
68	50
46	25
44	20
37	33.3
22	40
17	15
16	66.6
15	75
15	60
15	30
11	10
8	80

(68 claims), followed by 25 per cent and 20 per cent (46 and 44 claims respectively). Table 4.1 sets out the most common discounts. Other discounts used were: 12.5 per cent (one claim); 35 per cent (two claims); 45 per cent (one claim); 55 per cent (two claims); 65 per cent (two claims); 70 per cent (two claims); 85 per cent (two claims); 90 per cent (three claims). The most popular discounts

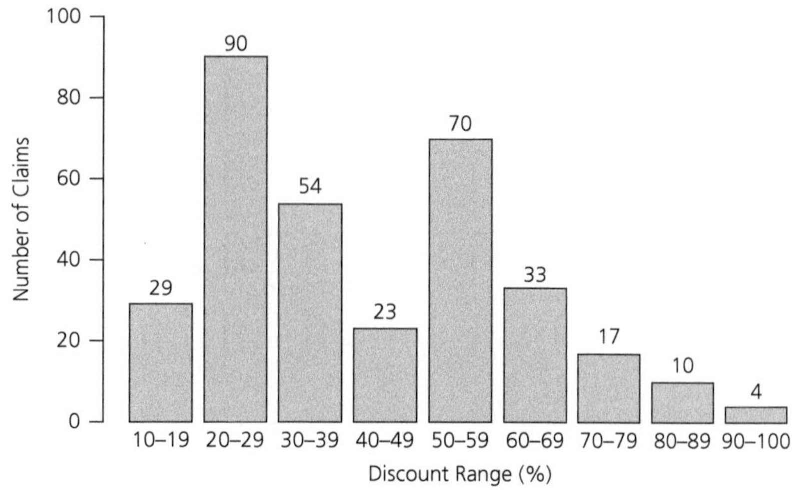

Figure 4.11 Number of claims by discount range at first instance

are of course fractions that are frequently used in everyday life, namely one-half, one-quarter, and one-fifth.[33]

4.21 A graph of the number of claims by discount range (Figure 4.11) gives a clearer indication of the distribution of discounts, with a marked preference for discounts between 10 per cent and 50 per cent, and a pronounced falling off in the number of claims beyond the 50 per cent mark (in only two of the 70 claims in the 50–59 per cent range was the discount greater than 50 per cent—in both instances, 55 per cent). The relatively low number of claims in the 40–49 per cent range (23 claims, in all but one of which the discount was 40 per cent) can probably be explained by the fact that none of the fractions most commonly used in daily life (one-half, one-third, one-quarter, two-thirds, one-fifth, etc) falls within this range.

4.22 Finally, we investigated the size of the average discount imposed in the different parts of the United Kingdom. The average discount was 40 per cent in England and Wales, 39 per cent in Scotland, and 38 per cent in Northern Ireland. Statistical

[33] cf *Jackson v Murray* [2015] UKSC 5; [2015] 2 All ER 805 [28] **[2:124]**, where Lord Reed said that apportionment for contributory negligence is 'inevitably a somewhat rough and ready exercise', and that this is a 'feature reflected in the judicial preference for round figures'. See, similarly, Robert Stevens, 'Contributory Fault: Analogue or Digital?' in Andrew Dyson et al (eds), *Defences in Tort* (Hart Publishing 2015) 259 (noting that when deciding on discounts for contributory negligence, 'judges seldom select finely tuned figures, 73/27 for example'). It has also been observed in connection with the apportionment regime for collisions at sea laid down by the Maritime Conventions Act 1911 that 'the general tendency of courts … has been to deal with apportionment in a fairly broad way', and that 'the most usual divisions have been one-quarter and three-quarters, one-third and two-thirds, and one-half and one-half' (Henry V Brandon, 'Apportionment of Liability in British Courts under the Maritime Conventions Act of 1911' (1977) 51 Tul L Rev 1025, 1041).

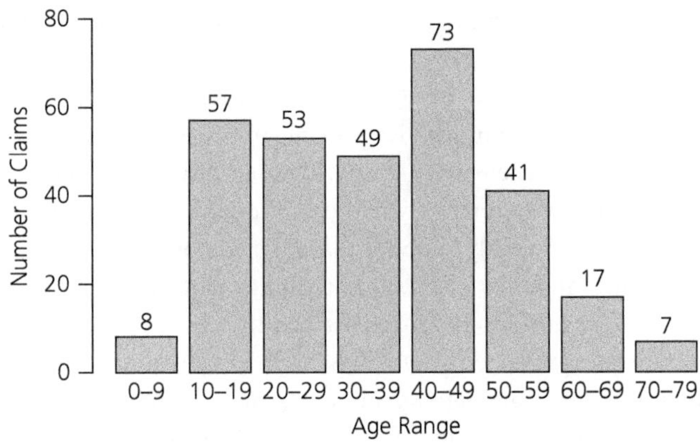

Figure 4.12 Number of claims by claimant age range at first instance

analysis suggests that these minor differences are very likely to be attributable to chance.[34]

Contributory negligence and claimant age

4.23 Of the 572 claims in our sample, 96 were brought by non-human claimants or claimants whose age was left too unclear by the court for it to be determined whether they were children or adults. Of the remaining 476 claims, 52 (11 per cent) were brought by children and 424 (89 per cent) were brought by adults. We were able to discern the age of the claimant with precision in 305 claims. The youngest claimant was aged six,[35] while the oldest was 79.[36] The distribution of these 305 claims by claimant age range is shown in Figure 4.12.

4.24 As can be seen from this graph, the claimant age range with the largest number of claims is 40–49 years (24 per cent of all claims), followed by 10–19 years (19 per cent), and then 20–29 years (17 per cent). There are relatively few claims in which the claimant was aged 60 or over (8 per cent). When looking at these figures, it should be borne in mind that it seems likely that the incidence of personal injury claims generally is relatively low in respect of young children and the elderly.[37] It should also be borne in mind that there were a large number of claims in the sample (171) where it was clear that the claimant was an adult but where we could

34 ANOVA, $p = 0.913$.

35 *Boardman v Ministry of Defence* (High Court, 12 November 2010) [**1:379**]; [**3:130**].

36 *Palfrey v WM Morrisons Supermarkets Plc* [2012] EWCA Civ 1917 [**1:422**]; [**2:111**].

37 In the Australian survey of personal injury claims discussed in chapter 1 (see 1.10), the proportions of claims by children under 14 and by elderly persons aged over 65 were much lower than the proportions of the general population in these age groups: *Report of the National Committee of Inquiry on Compensation and Rehabilitation in Australia* (n 20) vol 3, 91–92 (Tables 1 and 2).

not discern the age of the claimant more precisely. These claims are not included in Figure 4.12, which therefore over-represents the proportion of claimants in the sample who were under 18 (as in all the claims where it was possible to discern that the claimant was a child it was also possible to discern the claimant's age more precisely). Furthermore, there were a considerable number of additional claims in the sample where it was unclear whether a human claimant was a child or an adult, and we might reasonably suppose that most if not all of these claims in fact involved adults, since it seems unlikely that a judge would fail to mention the age of a claimant who was under 18 (not least because this might affect the analysis of the contributory negligence issue).[38] It is highly likely, therefore, that if we had age data for all of the human claimants in our sample, the number of claims in all the age ranges from and including 20–29 years and above would be higher, and in some instances substantially so.

4.25 Turning to the relationship between age and the success rate of the plea of contributory negligence, the plea succeeded in 69 per cent of claims where the claimant was a child, and 59 per cent of claims where the claimant was an adult. This striking result suggests that, if anything, courts are *more* likely to find contributory negligence against a child claimant, although statistical analysis showed that this disparity might well be down to chance.[39] The youngest claimant found guilty of contributory negligence was aged 7;[40] the oldest was 79.[41]

4.26 A breakdown of the success rate of the plea of contributory negligence by age range can be seen in Figure 4.13. As this graph shows, the age range where the plea of contributory negligence was most likely to succeed in our sample was 10–19 (success rate of 72 per cent). This figure is considerably higher than the success rate across all claims of 58 per cent, and allows us to finesse our earlier proposition about success rate and children to the claim that the plea of contributory negligence was substantially more likely to succeed where the claimant was aged 10–19 years. Statistical analysis was inconclusive as to whether this was attributable to chance.[42] Success rates in the remaining age ranges were more tightly clustered, as

---

[38] Judges have often emphasized that the fact that the claimant is a child is a particularly relevant consideration in the contributory negligence context: see, eg, *Gough v Thorne* [1966] 1 WLR 1387 (CA). The fact that judges sometimes leave it unclear whether a human claimant is an adult or child is attributable to the fact that 'judges' factual presentations are meant only to explain as much of the case as is necessary to justify the outcome': Mark A Hall and Ronald F Wright, 'Systematic Content Analysis of Judicial Opinions' (2008) 96 Calif L Rev 63, 95–96.

[39] Pearson's chi-square test with Yates's continuity correction, $p = 0.202$. Logistic regression (controlling for claim type, damage type, gender, and jurisdiction) returned a p-value of 0.403.

[40] *N (a child) v Newham LBC* [2007] CLY 2931 (Central London CC) [1:248] (the claimant punched a pane of glass while at school).

[41] *Palfrey* (n 36) [1:422]; [2:111].

[42] A Pearson's chi-square test on the null hypothesis that the success rate of the plea of contributory negligence is the same across all age ranges gave a high p-value of 0.402). However, logistic regression analysis comparing the odds of a finding of contributory negligence where the claimant

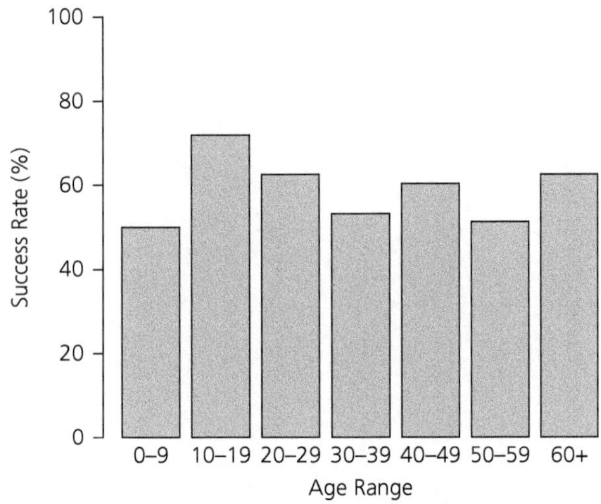

Figure 4.13 Success rate of plea by claimant age range at first instance

follows: 0–9 years, 50 per cent; 20–29 years, 62 per cent; 30–39 years, 53 per cent; 40–49 years, 60 per cent; 50–59 years, 51 per cent; and 60+ years, 63 per cent.

4.27 Turning to the relationship between discount and age, the average discount for children was 41 per cent, and the average discount for adults was 39 per cent. In other words, not only is a finding of contributory negligence more likely where the claimant is a child, but in such claims the average discount is also higher. However, statistical analysis suggests that this modest disparity is either down to chance, or is attributable to other factors, such as the prevalence of child claimants in claim types where higher discounts tend to be made.[43]

4.28 Figure 4.14 shows the average discount by claimant age range. No strong trend is discernible, although the highest average discount is found in the 0–19-year age range (42 per cent). The average discounts in four of the other age ranges are very similar (20–29 years, 35 per cent; 30–39 years, 34 per cent; 40–49 years, 36 per cent; 50–59 years, 35 per cent), although the average discount in the 60+ years age range is somewhat higher, at 40 per cent. It should be noted that although the average discounts for claimants in the 0–19 and 60+ age ranges look high, they are

was in the 10–19 age range with the odds of such a finding in the four other age ranges in which there were substantial numbers of claimants returned a range of p-values, two of which were low enough effectively to discount chance as an explanation for the relevant disparity (20–29: $p = 0.282$; 30–39: $p = 0.046$; 40–49: $p = 0.167$; 50–59, $p = 0.038$).

[43] A two-sided t-test of the difference between the average discounts in child claimant and adult claimant claims gave a p-value of 0.566. This result was broadly consistent with the result of a Wilcoxon rank sum test with continuity correction ($p = 0.616$). Furthermore, linear regression analysis (controlling for case type, damage type, jurisdiction, and gender) returned a p-value of 0.611.

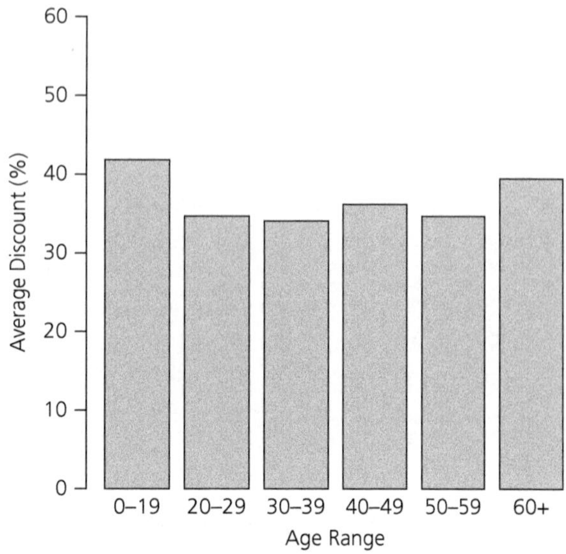

Figure 4.14 Average discount by claimant age range at first instance

not far from the average discount across all claims in the sample (39.8 per cent). It follows that when compared with the average discount across all claims, it is the average discounts in the other four of the five adult age ranges that are marginally out of line. A possible explanation for this situation is that the age of an adult claimant is more likely to be discernible in types of claim where a lower discount tends to be made, in particular employers' liability claims (where the average discount is a mere 32 per cent).[44] All in all, it seems that the size of the discount is probably more strongly associated with type of claim than with age.

Contributory negligence and claimant gender

4.29 Of the 572 claims in our sample there were 57 where the claim was brought by a non-human claimant or where it was not possible to discern the claimant's gender. Of the 515 claims remaining, 370 (72 per cent) were brought by men, and 145 (28 per cent) were brought by women. Since all but five of these claims were brought for personal injury, this disparity may reflect the fact that men bring more personal injury claims than women, but although men are undoubtedly more likely to be injured in circumstances where compensation may be payable, such as on the roads,[45]

[44] See Figure 4.8 and the accompanying text.

[45] Eg, 70 per cent of those reported as killed or seriously injured in road accidents in the United Kingdom (excluding Northern Ireland) in the period 2005–2009 were men: <https://www.gov.uk/government/statistics/reported-road-casualties-great-britain-annual-report-2013> (accessed 3 November 2018). Similarly, in the *Report of the Royal Commission on Civil Liability and Compensation*

it is unclear whether they bring more personal injury claims as a result.[46] In any case, there is a distinct possibility that this disparity is attributable (at least in part) to the fact that women are generally more risk-averse than men,[47] and so less likely to act in such a way as to expose them to a plausible plea of contributory fault.

With respect to the relationship between success rate of the plea of contributory negligence and gender, this was higher for male claimants than for female claimants (62 per cent and 57 per cent respectively), though statistical analysis suggests that this disparity may well be down to chance.[48] If the disparity is not down to chance, then it might again be attributable to women being more risk-averse, and so more likely to be able successfully to rebut a plea of contributory fault. As for the relationship between size of discount and claimant gender, the average discount in claims involving male claimants was 39 per cent, and the average discount in claims involving female claimants was 41 per cent. Further detail on the relationship between discount and gender can be gleaned from Figure 4.15. **4.30**

Statistical analysis of these figures shows that there is a decent probability that the disparity between the average discount for male and female claimants is due to chance.[49] Furthermore, a possible explanation for the lower average discount for male claimants is the fact that men are over-represented in employers' liability **4.31**

for Personal Injury, Cmnd 7054 (1978) vol 2, 9 (Table 2) it was estimated that at the time men suffered work injuries over six times more often than women, even though only 50 per cent more men were working at that time than women (ibid, para 334), although under modern employment conditions, the gender gap is likely to be much narrower.

[46] There appear to be no concrete contemporary data on the relationship between gender and personal injury claims in the United Kingdom. In the early 1990s, men accounted for 80 per cent of respondents in the three lower settlement bands in the Law Commission's survey of compensated victims of personal injury, and 65 per cent of respondents in the highest settlement band: Law Commission, *Personal Injury Compensation: How Much is Enough? A Study of the Compensation Experiences of Victims of Personal Injury* (Law Com No 225, 1994) para 2.4. However, more recent figures from Ireland indicate that any gender gap in terms of claiming may now be much reduced, or even non-existent. According to the Irish Personal Injuries Assessment Board, in 2012, 51 per cent of motor liability awards and 30 per cent of workplace liability awards for personal injury were made to women (*Annual Report of the Personal Injuries Assessment Board 2013* (2014) 18–19), while in 2010, 72 per cent of public liability awards for personal injury were made to women (*Annual Report of the Personal Injuries Assessment Board 2010* (2011) section 4).

[47] The literature in this regard is extensive. A widely cited study of over 150 published articles regarding gender differences in the propensity to run risks concluded that 'our results clearly support the idea that male participants are more likely to take risks than female participants': James P Byrnes, David C Miller and William D Schafer, 'Gender Differences in Risk Taking: A Meta-analysis' (1999) 125 Psychol Bull 367, 377. For more recent analyses to similar effect, see Jonathan J Rolison et al, 'Risk-Taking Differences Across the Adult Life Span: A Question of Age and Domain' [2013] Journals of Gerontology, Series B, 5; Christine R Harris and Michael Jenkins, 'Gender Differences in Risk Assessment: Why Do Women Take Fewer Risks than Men?' (2006) 1 Judgm Decis Mak 48.

[48] Pearson's chi-square test, $p = 0.311$. Logistic regression analysis (controlling for claim type, damage type, age, and jurisdiction) returned a p-value of 0.426.

[49] Two-sided t-test, $p = 0.523$. This result was broadly consistent with the result of a Wilcoxon rank sum test with continuity correction ($p = 0.501$).

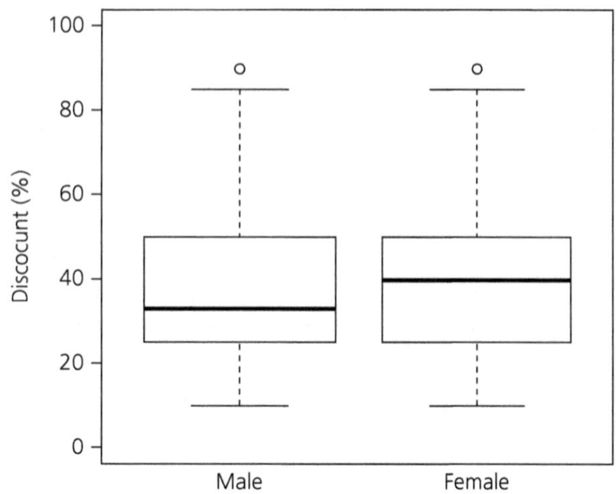

Figure 4.15 Discount by claimant gender at first instance

claims,[50] since we have seen that this is the type of claim in which the average discount is the lowest.[51]

Discussion

4.32 In this section of this chapter, we highlight what we consider to be some of the most important findings of our first instance study and discuss those findings in the light of the relevant academic literature. We do not discuss in detail here the findings of our first instance study in respect of road accidents, employers' liability, and professional negligence, since each of those claim types is the subject of a separate chapter of this book, and the relevant first instance findings are discussed in the chapter in question.[52]

Overall success rate and average discount

4.33 The plea of contributory negligence succeeded in 58 per cent of the claims in our first instance study. In claims where a finding of contributory negligence was made, the

[50] 20 per cent of the claims in which female claimants were found guilty of contributory negligence were employers' liability claims; the equivalent figure for male claimants was 34 per cent. This hypothesis is supported by the fact that linear regression analysis of the change in average discount from male claimant claims to female claimant claims (controlling for claim type, damage type, age, and jurisdiction) returned a higher *p*-value of 0.959.

[51] See Figure 4.8 and accompanying text.

[52] See chapter 6 (road accidents); chapter 7 (employers' liability); and chapter 8 (professional negligence).

average discount was 40 per cent. Given that it appears that contributory negligence is pleaded very frequently,[53] these findings underscore the practical importance of the contributory negligence doctrine.

Claimant age

Our study contains several interesting findings about the relationship between contributory negligence and claimant age. One is that of the 16 claims where contributory negligence was pleaded against children under 12, the plea was successful in 10, with the youngest claimant accused of contributory negligence aged six,[54] and the youngest claimant found guilty of contributory negligence aged seven.[55] Although the relevant sample size is admittedly small, our study therefore suggests that while contributory negligence is not often pleaded against children under 12, when it is, the courts are not averse to making a finding against a young claimant on this issue. However, while our findings are not inconsistent with Lord Denning MR's declaration that '[a] very young child cannot be guilty of contributory negligence',[56] our study suggests that in practice 'very young' means younger than seven years old.[57] **4.34**

It is also noteworthy that of the ten claimants younger than 12 found guilty of contributory negligence in our sample, six were injured in road accidents. In 1978, the Pearson Commission stated that the courts were 'increasingly reluctant to reduce **4.35**

---

53 See 1.02.

54 *Boardman v Ministry of Defence* (QBD, 12 October 2010) [**1:379**]; [**3:130**].

55 *N (a child)* (n 40) [**1:248**]. For a finding of contributory negligence against an eight-year old who fell while climbing on a farm gate, see *Anderson v Imrie* [2016] CSOH 171; 2017 Rep LR 21 [**1:570**]. See generally on children and contributory negligence, Lesley-Anne Barnes, 'Contributory Negligence and the Child' [2010] Jur Rev 195; and Lesley-Anne Barnes Macfarlane, 'Rethinking Childhood Contributory Negligence' [2018] Jur Rev 75.

56 *Gough* (n 38) 1390. See also *Gardner v Grace* (1858) 1 F & F 359, 359; 175 ER 763, 763 (Channell B) ('The doctrine of contributory negligence does not apply to an infant of tender age').

57 According to Glanville Williams (writing in 1951), some courts in Canada and the United States had held that as a matter of law no child under seven could be guilty of contributory fault: Glanville Williams, *Joint Torts and Contributory Negligence: A Study of Concurrent Fault in Great Britain, Ireland and the Common-Law Dominions* (Stevens & Sons 1951) 355. The age of seven also marked the boundary in Roman law between *infantia* and *infantia maior*, and is treated by many continental jurisdictions as a basic 'age of discernment' for the purposes of tort law: see Marta Pantaléon Díaz, 'Children's Liability in Negligence' (2018) 9 JETL 25, 27. Contrast the claim that in this context children of 'tender years' means those under four (Barnes [2010] (n 55) 205). Admittedly, this claim is consistent with a handful of Scottish decisions pre-dating our study in which children aged between four and six were found guilty of contributory negligence (see *Cass v Edinburgh & District Tramways Co Ltd* 1909 SC 1068 (IH) (four); *McKinnell v White* 1971 SLT (notes) 61 (OH) (five); *Banner's Tutor v Kennedy's Trustees* 1978 SLT (notes) 83 (OH) (five); *Harvey v Cairns* 1989 SLT 107 (OH) (six)). According to Christopher Walton et al, *Charlesworth & Percy on Negligence* (14th edn, Sweet & Maxwell 2018) para 4.47, '[t]here is a perception that Scottish courts have been readier to find contributory negligence against children than their English counterparts', but we suspect that these days even in Scotland a finding of contributory negligence is very unlikely to be made against a child aged under seven (see also Michael Jones et al, *Clerk & Lindsell on Torts*

damages awarded to young children for motor vehicle injury on the grounds of the child's contributory negligence', and argued that this development should be given statutory force by a provision barring reliance on contributory negligence in motor vehicle injury claims where the claimant was under 12 years of age at the time of the accident.[58] Only recently, a distinguished scholar claimed that such an enactment 'would make very little difference to the practical position at present'.[59] Our study suggests otherwise.

4.36 Another significant finding of our study on the age front was that the success rate of the plea of contributory negligence was higher for claimants in the 10–19 years age range than for claimants in any other age range. To reiterate, 72 per cent of claimants aged between 10 and 19 were found guilty of contributory negligence, a figure 14 per cent higher than the average success rate across the whole sample. Furthermore, the average discount in the 0–19 age range was also the highest, at 42 per cent. 77 per cent of the claimants in the 10–19 age range were children, and we have also seen that the plea of contributory negligence was successful in 69 per cent of claims where the claimant was a child, and 59 per cent of claims where the claimant was an adult, and that the average discount was marginally higher where the claimant was a child (41 per cent, as against 39 per cent for adults).

4.37 The foregoing findings cast doubt on the accuracy of the commonly expressed perception that courts treat children more leniently than adults when it comes to the application of the contributory negligence doctrine. According to one leading textbook, for example, '[t]he courts have been singularly lenient to children both in terms of finding them guilty of contributory negligence and in apportioning damages'.[60] Similar remarks have been made elsewhere.[61] Our study suggests that in fact pleas of contributory negligence are more likely to succeed against children

(22nd edn, Sweet & Maxwell 2017) para 3.82). For a brief but illuminating discussion of whether a fixed minimum age should apply for both liability and contributory fault in tort (the suggested age again being seven), see the Scottish Law Commission, *Report on the Legal Capacity and Responsibility of Minors and Pupils* (Scot Law Com No 110, 1987), Pt V.

[58] Pearson Commission (n 45) vol 1, para 1077.

[59] Peter Cane, *Atiyah's Accidents, Compensation and the Law* (8th edn, CUP 2013) 53.

[60] Carolyn Sappideen and Prue Vines (eds), *Fleming's The Law of Torts* (10th edn, Thomson Reuters Professional (Australia) Ltd 2011) 330.

[61] The author of *Street on Torts* claims that 'it is ordinarily more difficult for the defendant to establish contributory negligence if the claimant is an infant than where he is an adult' and that when it comes to apportionment 'infant claimants are treated very leniently because of their vulnerability', with decisions on apportionment 'often made very much in their favour': Christian Witting, *Street on Torts* (15th edn, OUP 2018) 195. (Note, however, that it is not entirely clear what the author means by the word 'infant' here, and, in particular, whether the word is being used in a legal sense, to refer to persons under the age of 18 years, or in a colloquial sense, to refer to young children.)

aged 10 or over than against adults, despite the fact that an age-relative standard of care is applied to child claimants.[62]

4.38 This seems to us to be both an important and (to a certain extent) a surprising finding. One possible explanation for it might be that defendants are reluctant to plead contributory negligence against children, and thus only do so in the most obvious instances of claimant fault. There are several reasons why defendants might be reluctant to plead contributory negligence against children, including the possibility of adverse publicity, sympathy on the part of claims handlers and lawyers, and the risk of alienating a judge sympathetic to an injured child. However, we think such an explanation unlikely. After all, a defendant has little reason not to plead contributory negligence if there is a chance that the plea will be successful given the significant effect that the doctrine can have on the extent of the claimant's recovery, and in our sample there were a substantial number of claims involving claimants aged between 10 and 19 years old. Two other possible explanations present themselves. One is that in practice, judges are not, contrary to authority, applying an age-relative standard of care to child claimants, but are holding them to an adult standard. The other is that children (or perhaps more specifically teenagers) are less risk-averse than people in other age groups, and so tend to take less care of their own safety. There is considerable evidence to support this final possibility: according to one commentator, neuroscience research demonstrates that 'adolescents as a class of person possess an unavoidable predisposition to engage in physical risk-taking that increases both their exposure to harm and the likelihood of its occurrence'.[63]

Claimant gender

4.39 Turning to gender, it is interesting to note that in our sample pleas of contributory negligence were more frequently successful against male claimants (62 per cent) than against female claimants (57 per cent), though statistical analysis shows that this disparity may well be down to chance. Conversely, the average discount was higher in claims involving female claimants than in claims involving male claimants, although the difference was small and, statistically speaking, justifiably attributable to chance. It is also important to recall that in our sample male claimants

[62] See 2.02.

[63] David Thorpe, 'Adolescent Negligence, "Obvious Risk" and Recent Developments in Neuroscience' (2014) 21 Torts LJ 195, 219. See also Rolison et al (n 47) 6 (reporting that risk-taking attitudes in the recreational domain reduce sharply from age 18 upwards); Laurence Steinberg, 'Risk Taking in Adolescence: New Perspectives from Brain and Behavioral Science' (2007) 16 Curr Dir Psychol Sci 55 (noting that 'statistics on automobile crashes, binge drinking, contraceptive use, and crime' reveal that '[a]dolescents and college-age individuals take more risks than children or adults do'. In *Morton v Glasgow CC* 2007 SLT (Sh Ct) 81 (Glasgow and Strathkelvin Sheriff Court) [21] [1:254], the sheriff accepted the evidence of a psychologist that children aged 14 lacked the capability of adults when it came to assessing risks.

(72 per cent) far outnumbered female claimants (28 per cent), although since it appears that there are no data on the overall number of personal injury claims brought by men and women respectively in the study period, it is impossible to know to what extent this evidences a greater propensity for defendants to plead contributory negligence against male claimants.

4.40 Mayo Moran's gender-centred analysis of the operation of the contributory negligence doctrine in claims involving children led her to conclude that:

> assumptions about what kind of behaviour is natural for girls as opposed to boys effectively results in different standards for contributory negligence. The normal boy, it seems, seeks risks and is therefore not chastised for so doing; in contrast, the normal girl seeks safety and avoids risks and is held to that standard. The consequence is that the range of situations in which the playing girl will be able to recover damages from a tortfeasor will be far more limited than the situations in which the boy will be permitted to recover.[64]

We found little evidence to support this claim in our study, although the success rate of the plea of contributory negligence was slightly higher for female claimants aged under 18 (73 per cent[65]) than for male claimants aged under 18 (68 per cent[66]), and the average discount for female children found guilty of contributory negligence was also slightly higher than the average discount applied in the case of male children (45 per cent and 40 per cent respectively). Nor does our study provide any evidence that different standards for contributory negligence are applied to female and male claimants more generally.

The range of discounts imposed

4.41 Another interesting point that emerges from our study concerns the range of discounts.[67] The lowest discount in our sample was 10 per cent. This is consistent with the observation made in the academic literature that holdings that the claimant's share of responsibility is less than 10 per cent are 'unusual'.[68] At the other end of

---

[64] Mayo Moran, *Rethinking the Reasonable Person: An Egalitarian Reconstruction of the Objective Standard* (OUP 2003) 128–29. See also ibid, 153–54 ('Conceptions of what is normal and natural mean that the girl must inhabit the public world with more caution').

[65] 11 out of 15 claims.

[66] 25 out of 37 claims.

[67] See 4.20–4.21.

[68] See, eg, James Goudkamp, 'Rethinking Contributory Negligence' in Erika Chamberlain et al (eds), *Challenging Orthodoxy in Tort Law* (Hart Publishing 2013) 350. See also Jones et al (n 57) para 3.98 ('where one of the parties is less than 10 per cent responsible no apportionment should normally be made'); and Barnes [2010] (n 55) 200 n 35 (remarking that it is standard practice not to make a deduction of less than 10 per cent). For rare examples of a discount of less than 10 per cent from the English case law, see *Laszczyk v National Coal Board* [1954] 3 All ER 205 (Manchester Assizes) (5 per cent); *Pasternack v Poulton* [1973] 1 WLR 476 (QBD) (5 per cent). 5 per cent deductions have also been made by courts in other jurisdictions where a similar

the scale, the highest discount that was made for contributory negligence in our sample of claims was 100 per cent, and the next highest was 90 per cent (three claims[69]). It has been argued that findings of 100 per cent contributory negligence are incoherent,[70] since the contributory negligence doctrine applies only when the damage suffered by the claimant is partly the fault of the defendant and partly the fault of the claimant, an analysis inconsistent with a finding that the claimant is entirely responsible for his or her injury. If this is correct, then the claim in our sample where a judge purported to make a discount of 100 per cent for contributory negligence is best understood as a decision that on the facts the defendant's wrongful conduct was not causative of the injury in respect of which the claimant was bringing the claim.[71] The discounts of 90 per cent are not open to the same objection, but there were only three claims in our sample in which this discount was made, and only two where the next highest discount (85 per cent) was made,[72] which bears out the claim that reductions in damages approaching 100 per cent are rare.[73] That the courts avoid extremes of the spectrum, such as discounts below 10 per cent or (save for the aberration that we have mentioned) above 90 per cent, is unsurprising. Such discounts suggest that something has gone wrong with other findings. Very low discounts raise the issue of whether the claimant was in fact properly found guilty of contributory negligence,[74] while very high discounts suggest that perhaps the defendant should have been absolved of responsibility altogether.[75]

---

legislative regime governs contributory negligence: see, eg, *Snushall v Fulsang* (2006) 258 DLR (4th) 425 (Ont CA); *Nominal Defendant v Rooskov* [2012] NSWCA 43; (2012) 60 MVR 350. That deductions of less than 10 per cent are *permissible* (if unusual) has been accepted by the Court of Appeal: see *Capps v Miller* [1989] 1 WLR 839 (CA) 848–49 (Croom-Johnson LJ) (cf Walton et al (n 57) para 4.34).

69 *Anderson v Newham College for Further Education* [2002] EWCA Civ 505; [2003] ICR 212 **[1:52]**; **[1:30]**; *Stephen v Peters* 2005 SCLR 513 (OH) **[1:186]**; and *Jackson v Murray* [2012] CSOH 100; 2012 SCLR 605 **[1:432]**; **[3:155]**.

70 See *Pitts v Hunt* [1991] 1 QB 24 (CA) 48 (Beldam LJ), 51 (Balcombe LJ); *Brumder v Motornet Service and Repairs Ltd* [2013] EWCA Civ 195; [2013] ICR 1069 [4] (Beatson LJ); Goudkamp (n 68) 344–46.

71 Consider *HIH Casualty and General Insurance Ltd v JLT Risk Solutions Ltd* [2007] EWCA Civ 710; [2008] Bus LR 180 [111], in which Auld LJ seemed to equate a finding of 100 per cent contributory negligence with a denial of causation.

72 *Smith v Bluebird Buses Ltd* [2014] CSOH 75; 2014 Rep LR 91 **[1:505]**; **[3:179]**; *Ferguson v Ferguson* [2015] CSIH 63; 2015 SLT 561 **[1:518]**; **[2:126]**.

73 Goudkamp (n 68) 348. For examples of discounts of 90 per cent or above in claims falling outside the scope of this study, see *Hodkinson v Henry Wallwork & Co Ltd* [1955] 1 WLR 1195 (CA) (90 per cent); and *Cummings v Murphy* [1967] VR 865 (Full Ct) (95 per cent deduction at trial not challenged on appeal).

74 See *Butcher v Cornwall CC* [2002] EWCA Civ 1640 [13] (Sedley LJ) **[1:79]**; **[2:41]**; *Cooper v Carillion Plc* [2003] EWCA Civ 1811 [11] (Keene LJ) **[1:110]**; **[2:54]**.

75 See *Toole v Bolton MBC* [2002] EWCA Civ 588 [13] (Buxton LJ) **[1:51]**; **[2:31]**.

Two negative findings

4.42 Sometimes the importance of empirical work lies in a finding that there is no significant association between variables, and there are a number of examples of such negative findings in our study. We wish to highlight two. The first is that it seems that it is very unlikely that the success rate of the plea of contributory negligence varies significantly across the categories of claim that account for the vast majority of personal injury claims in which contributory negligence is commonly pleaded, namely road accident claims, employers' liability claims, occupiers' liability claims, and public liability claims. Second, we uncovered no evidence that in personal injury claims either the success rate of the plea of contributory negligence or the average discount varied significantly across the 17-year period of our study. We had thought that we might find some indications that judges had been harsher towards claimants who were alleged to be guilty of contributory negligence in time periods in which there was a heightened media and political focus on the so-called compensation culture, in particular 2003–2005 and 2009–2013.[76] However, statistical analysis revealed no association in personal injury claims between success rate or average discount and year. It appears that—as regards contributory negligence, at least—the judiciary are largely impervious to being influenced in the way that we thought possible.[77]

Occupiers' liability

4.43 Since we do not devote space elsewhere in this book to occupiers' liability claims in particular, we conclude our discussion of the first instance study with some observations about the operation of contributory negligence in this category of claim. We have seen that in total there were 59 occupiers' liability claims, which

---

[76] A crude but plausible measure of such focus is the number of stories in UK national newspapers in a given year that feature the phrase 'compensation culture'. A LexisNexis search produces the following figures for the years in our study period: 2000 (190); 2001 (279); 2002 (267); 2003 (297); 2004 (479); 2005 (297); 2006 (149); 2007 (146); 2008 (128); 2009 (129); 2010 (264); 2011 (292); 2012 (298); 2013 (381); 2014 (211); 2015 (162); and 2016 (180). A trawl through the footnotes of some of the leading early academic literature on the compensation culture amply bears out the claim that there was a particular focus on this issue in the period 2003–2005: see, eg, Kevin Williams, 'State of Fear: Britain's "Compensation Culture" Reviewed' (2005) 25 LS 500; and Annette Morris, 'Spiralling or Stabilising? The Compensation Culture and Our Propensity to Claim Damages for Personal Injury' (2007) 70 MLR 349. And a similar review of footnotes of a more recent book chapter evidences a renewed focus on the issue in media and political circles in 2009–2010 (which culminated at that end of that period in the publication of Lord Young of Graffham's report *Common Sense, Common Safety* for Prime Minister David Cameron): see Annette Morris, 'The "Compensation Culture" and the Politics of Tort' in TT Arvind and Jenny Steele (eds), *Tort Law and the Legislature: Common Law, Statute and the Dynamics of Legal Change* (Hart Publishing 2013).

[77] For evidence that the attitudes of American jurors towards tort litigation are susceptible to media influence, see William Haltom and Michael McCann, *Distorting the Law: Politics, Media and the Litigation Crisis* (University of Chicago Press 2004) 297–99.

accounted for 10 per cent of the claims in our first instance study. Of these, only six were brought by non-visitors, under the Occupiers' Liability Act 1984. The success rate of the plea of contributory negligence in occupiers' liability claims was 59 per cent, which breaks down to 57 per cent in the case of claims by visitors and 83 per cent in the case of claims by non-visitors. In the light of the small number of non-visitor claims in our sample, little weight should be placed on this disparity, which statistical analysis suggests may well be attributable to chance.[78] Conversely, it seems plausible to suppose that there is a particularly high likelihood that a finding of contributory negligence will be made against a trespasser who ought not to be on the land in question in the first place, and the disparity in success rates of the plea as between visitors and non-visitors is consistent with this supposition.

It is also noteworthy that the average discount in occupiers' liability claims generally was relatively high, at 47 per cent, and that the higher average discount in such claims compared with employers' liability and public liability claims was unlikely to be down to chance. This may be attributable to the fact that many of the claimants in such claims behave in a particularly foolhardy manner. It is interesting to note, for example, that although in total there were only 15 instances in which a discount of 75 per cent was made in the claims in our sample, of these no fewer than six were in occupiers' liability cases. Examples of conduct by claimants in occupiers' liability cases that attracted a 75 per cent discount included diving into a harbour late at night while the worse for drink,[79] attempting to jump from one section of a climbing wall to another,[80] and running over rough ground in the dark while intoxicated after failing to pay a taxi fare.[81] **4.44**

Again, when we disaggregate visitor and non-visitor claims, we see that the courts come down harder on non-visitors at the apportionment stage, with the average discount in non-visitor claims being considerably higher (58 per cent) than the average discount in visitor claims (45 per cent). Once again, the fact that there were only five non-visitor claims in the sample in which a discount was made means that we should not attach great significance to this disparity,[82] but nor is it altogether surprising that the higher likelihood of a finding of contributory negligence in the case of non-visitors is matched by a tougher approach at the apportionment stage of the enquiry. **4.45**

[78] Pearson's chi-square test, $p = 0.410$.

[79] *Donoghue v Folkestone Properties Ltd* [2003] EWCA Civ 231; [2003] QB 1008 [**1:100**].

[80] *Poppleton v Trustees of the Portsmouth Youth Activities Committee* [2008] EWCA Civ 646; [2009] PIQR P1 [**1:267**].

[81] *Harvey v Plymouth City Council* [2010] EWCA Civ 860; [2010] PIQR P18 [**1:347**].

[82] A two-sided t-test of the difference between the average discounts in visitor and non-visitor claims returned a p-value of 0.249. A Wilcoxon rank sum test with continuity correction yielded a p-value of 0.189.

Conclusion

4.46 In this chapter we reported the key findings of our study of 572 first instance decisions on contributory negligence in the United Kingdom in the first 17 years of this century. Perhaps the most important of the findings we have highlighted in this chapter are as follows:

1. The plea of contributory negligence succeeded in 58 per cent of the claims.
2. Where a finding of contributory negligence was made, the average discount was 40 per cent.
3. The most popular discounts were fractions that are commonly used in everyday life, namely, one-half, one-third, one-quarter, and one-fifth. Although judges use essentially the full spectrum of discounts, discounts at the higher end of the spectrum are relatively infrequent. This latter finding is consistent with frequently expressed views to the same effect.
4. Judges do not appear to be especially reluctant to find claimants guilty of contributory negligence in employers' liability claims. We found no evidence of such reticence. However, when contributory negligence was found in this category of claim, the discount tended to be relatively small.
5. Larger discounts from damages tend to be made in occupiers' liability claims than in employers' liability and public liability claims.
6. Judges are very slow to find contributory negligence in professional negligence claims. However, when contributory negligence is found in such claims, the discount tends to be relatively high.
7. Judges treat children aged over 10 more harshly than adult claimants, both when deciding whether to make a finding of contributory negligence and when determining the discount where contributory negligence has been found.
8. We found little evidence of a gender difference in relation to either the frequency with which contributory negligence is found or in terms of the size of the discount.
9. In personal injury claims, both the success rate of the plea of contributory negligence and the size of the discounts imposed remained fairly constant during the study period.

5

CONTRIBUTORY NEGLIGENCE ON APPEAL

Introduction

In this chapter, we present the results of our study of appellate court decisions on contributory negligence. Our main aim in the first section of the chapter is simply to describe our findings, though we make some observations about them as well. Further discussion of certain key findings is offered in the next section. We are unaware of any previous sustained studies of the operation of the contributory negligence doctrine at the appellate level in this or any other common law jurisdiction.[1] Furthermore, of the decisions in our study from England and Wales[2] all but one was a decision of the Court of Appeal,[3] and it has been pointed out that that court has been the subject of relatively little academic investigation more generally.[4] This part of our study thus addresses largely unexplored issues. **5.01**

---

[1] See n 19 in chapter 1.

[2] Almost all of the claims in our appellate study are from England and Wales. Only three claims (2 per cent) came from Northern Ireland (*Ward v Chief Constable of the Royal Ulster Constabulary* [2000] NI 543 (CA) **[2:7]**; *Smyth v Smyth* [2004] NICA 16 **[2:62]** and *Neeson v Acheson* [2008] NIQB 12 **[2:81]**), and 15 (12 per cent) from Scotland (*Noble v de Boer* 2004 SC 548 (IH) **[2:58]**; *McFarlane v Scottish Borders Council* 2005 SLT 359 (IH) **[2:66]**; *Duncan v Walshe* [2005] CSIH 49; 2005 Scot (D) 19/6 **[2:69]**; *Robb v Salamis (M&I) Ltd* [2006] UKHL 56; [2007] 2 All ER 97 **[2:75]**; *McGowan v W&JR Watson Ltd* [2006] CSIH 62; 2007 SC 272 **[1:211]**; **[2:76]**; *Johnstone v AMEC Constructions Ltd* [2010] CSIH 57; 2011 SCLR 178 **[2:96]**; *Swilas v Clyde Pumps Ltd* 2012 SLT (Sh Ct) 146 (Glasgow and Strathkelvin Sheriff Court) **[2:99]**; *Wardle v Scottish Borders Council* 2011 SLT (Sh Ct) 199 (Lothian and Borders Sheriff Court) **[2:100]**; *Wallace v Glasgow CC* [2011] CSIH 57; 2011 Rep LR 96 **[2:104]**; *Phee v Gordon* [2013] CSIH 18; 2013 SC 379 **[2:113]**; *Hill v Norside Ltd* [2013] CSIH 44; 2013 GWD 19-387 **[2:115]**; *Kennedy v Chivas Brothers Ltd* [2013] CSIH 57; 2013 SLT 981 **[2:118]**; *Jackson v Murray* [2015] UKSC 5; [2015] 2 All ER 805 **[2:124]**; *Ferguson v Ferguson* [2015] CSIH 63; 2015 SLT 561 **[1:518]**; **[2:126]**; *Wagner v Grant* [2016] CSIH 34; 2016 SLT 699 **[2:129]**).

[3] The exception is *Nixon v Thames Water Utilities Ltd* [2006] CLY 2913 (Romford CC) **[1:131]**; **[2:61]**, a decision of a county court in the exercise of its appellate jurisdiction (as to this jurisdiction, see the Access to Justice Act 1999 (Destination of Appeals) Order 2000, r 3(2)).

[4] See Gavin Drewry et al, *The Court of Appeal* (Hart Publishing 2007) 2. That book is itself the most notable exception to the more general academic neglect that its authors highlight, though see also Burton M Atkins, 'Interventions and Power in Judicial Hierarchies: Appellate Courts in England and the United States' (1990) 24 Law & Soc'y Rev 71; Burton M Atkins, 'Party Capability

5.02 More concretely, we hope that the appellate part of our study will be of value in the following respects. First, we believe that by providing reliable information about appellate decisions on contributory negligence our study will facilitate the settlement of disputes by giving litigants and their advisers a clearer picture of the likely outcome of a possible appeal on the issue. Second, by revealing when and how appellate courts have intervened on the apportionment issue, this chapter should help trial judges to decide what discount to impose following a finding of contributory negligence. Third, this chapter, read together with the results of our first instance study as reported in chapter 4, will enable comparisons to be drawn between the operation of the contributory negligence doctrine at first instance and on appeal (and indeed we make some such comparisons in this chapter).

5.03 It is important to note that we distinguish in this chapter between *claims* and *appeals*. By a 'claim', we mean an action by a particular claimant against a particular defendant.[5] By an 'appeal', we mean each and every challenge mounted in the appellate proceedings to a determination of the first instance court on either the existence of contributory negligence or the appropriate discount. Suppose, for example, that the trial judge had found the claimant guilty of contributory negligence and imposed a discount of 50 per cent. And suppose that in the appellate proceedings the claimant challenged both the finding of contributory negligence and the size of the discount, and that the defendant had cross-appealed on the basis that the discount should have been higher than 50 per cent. This would be treated as three appeals in total: two by the claimant, and one by the defendant. The number of claims and appeals differ in this study.[6] This is because in some of the claims (as in our example) there was more than one appeal, while in others contributory negligence was considered for the first time on appeal, so that there was no appeal by either party on the issue.

Results

General information

5.04 Our dataset contained entries for 129 claims in which an appellate court dealt with contributory negligence.[7] 55 of the entries (43 per cent) concerned appeals from

Theory as an Explanation for Intervention Behavior in the English Court of Appeal' (1991) 35 Am J Polit Sci 881. For a recently published study of personal injury cases in the Court of Appeal, see Per Laleng, 'Winners and Losers in the Court of Appeal: An Empirical Study of Personal Injury Cases (2002–2016)' [2018] JPIL 36.

[5] See 3.10.

[6] As can be seen, for example, by comparing the numbers of *claims* in the various contextual categories (Figure 5.1) with the overall number of *appeals* in those categories (Figure 5.3).

[7] A list of the claims is set out in Appendix 2.

the High Court and 74 (57 per cent) related to appeals from a county court.[8] There were only two second appeals in our study, one to the House of Lords[9] and one to the Supreme Court.[10] Both were Scottish appeals, and the fact that these cases reached the ultimate appellate level is doubtless attributable to the fact that, at the time, permission to appeal to the House of Lords/Supreme Court was not required in civil cases in Scotland.[11]

5.05 121 claims (94 per cent) were for personal injury, with seven of the remaining claims (5 per cent) being for property damage, and only one (1 per cent) being for pure economic loss. Because there were so few cases in our appellate dataset that were not personal injury cases, the results of the appellate study relating to type of damage will not be reported. There were also few property damage claims in our study of first instance decisions on contributory negligence, which we have suggested might be because many property damage claims are likely to be relatively low value.[12] The same explanation may account for the dearth of contributory negligence cases concerning property damage that reach an appellate court.

5.06 There was a more even spread of the claims across our six categories of claim type (or contextual setting), as seen in Figure 5.1. Road accident claims were the most common type of claim (42 per cent of claims), followed by employers' liability claims (29 per cent), and occupiers' liability claims (12 per cent). The 21 claims in the three remaining categories (public liability, professional negligence, and 'other') amount to only 16 per cent of the claims in the dataset. The small number of claims in these categories should be kept in mind when assessing the relevant results. The claims in the 'other' category included claims arising out of accidents at sea,[13] on a train,[14] and in a prison,[15] as well as attacks by animals,[16] and a case concerning vandals letting off fire extinguishers in a church.[17] The prevalence of road accident and employers' liability claims (which together account for over 70 per cent of the

[8] Because the overwhelming majority of the claims in our appellate dataset are from England and Wales (see (n 2)), in this chapter we use the terminology that is applicable in those parts of the United Kingdom. We similarly focus, for the most part, on the procedural apparatus in England and Wales, and on the Court of Appeal of England and Wales.

[9] *Robb* (n 2) [2:75].

[10] *Jackson* (n 2) [2:124].

[11] This has now changed: see the Courts Reform (Scotland) Act 2014, s 117, amending the Court of Session Act 1988, s 40.

[12] See 4.03.

[13] *Owners of the Selat Arjuna v Owners of the Contship Success* [2000] 1 All ER (Comm) 905 [2:3]; *Noble* (n 2) [2:58].

[14] *Collins-Williamson v Silverlink Train Services Ltd* [2009] EWCA Civ 850 [2:90].

[15] *St George v Home Office* [2008] EWCA Civ 1068; [2009] 1 WLR 1670 [2:82].

[16] *Neeson v Acheson* [2008] NIQB 12 [2:81]; *Ferguson* (n 2) [1:518]; [2:126].

[17] *Chubb Fire Ltd v Vicar of Spalding* [2010] EWCA Civ 981; [2010] 2 CLC 277 [1:330]; [2:98].

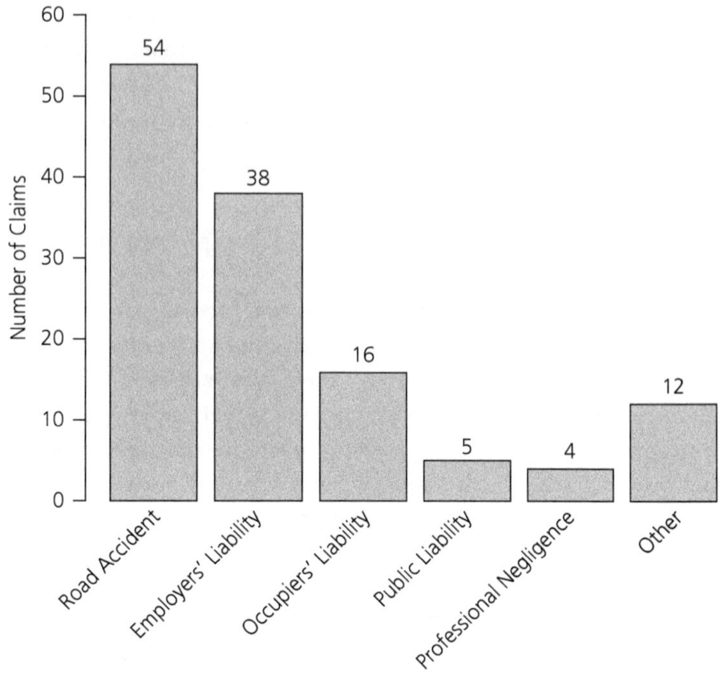

Figure 5.1 Number of claims by claim type on appeal

claims in the dataset) was predictable, as these are contexts where liability insurance is compulsory.

5.07 Figure 5.2 shows the number of claims in the dataset by year. The falling off in claims after 2003 is very marked. For the period 2000–2003, the average number of claims in the dataset per year rounds up to 14. For the remainder of the study period, the average number of claims per year rounds up to five. We consider possible explanations for this decline below.[18]

5.08 Switching from the number of claims to the number of appeals,[19] there was a total of 130 appeals in the dataset, of which 57 (44 per cent) were against determinations as to the existence of contributory negligence, and 73 (56 per cent) were against determinations as to the appropriate discount. The fact that more appeals concerned apportionment than guilt is noteworthy. This is because, as discussed in chapter 2, the judicial guidance on appeals in this context emphasises that apportionment is a highly discretionary exercise and that appellate courts should

[18] See 5.39–5.41.

[19] Regarding this distinction between claims and appeals, see 5.03.

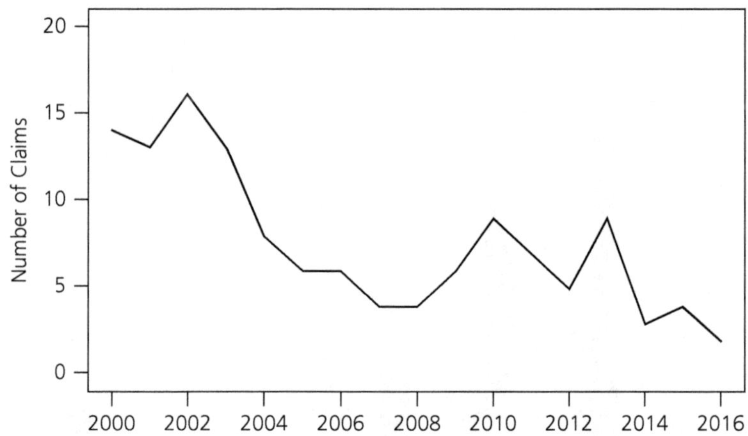

Figure 5.2 Number of claims by year on appeal

therefore be particularly slow to intervene on this issue.[20] In the light of this, one might expect to see fewer appeals on apportionment than on guilt, but in our study the reverse was true.

Claimants brought 57 (44 per cent) of the appeals, and defendants 73 (56 per cent). Breaking this down by appeal type, of the appeals on guilt, 23 (40 per cent) were brought by claimants, and 34 (60 per cent) by defendants. In relation to appeals on apportionment, 34 (47 per cent) were brought by claimants, and 39 (53 per cent) were brought by defendants. **5.09**

Figure 5.3 shows the number of appeals by type of claim. One point of interest that emerges from this graph is that the two contexts in which appeals on apportionment substantially outnumber appeals on guilt are road accident and occupiers' liability cases. **5.10**

Appellate intervention

The appellate court overturned the determination of the first instance court regarding guilt in 39 per cent of cases, and the determination of the first instance court in respect of apportionment in 33 per cent of cases.[21] The overall level of appellate **5.11**

---

[20] See 2.07–2.08.

[21] We should be clear about what we mean by these statements. When we say, for example, that the appellate court overturned the determination of the first instance court regarding guilt in *x* per cent of cases, we mean that the appellate court acceded to a request to overturn the determination of the first instance court regarding guilt in *x* per cent of the cases *in which it was asked to do so*. See further the descriptions of columns Q and R of the spreadsheet (see 3.21), from which results on intervention rates were generated.

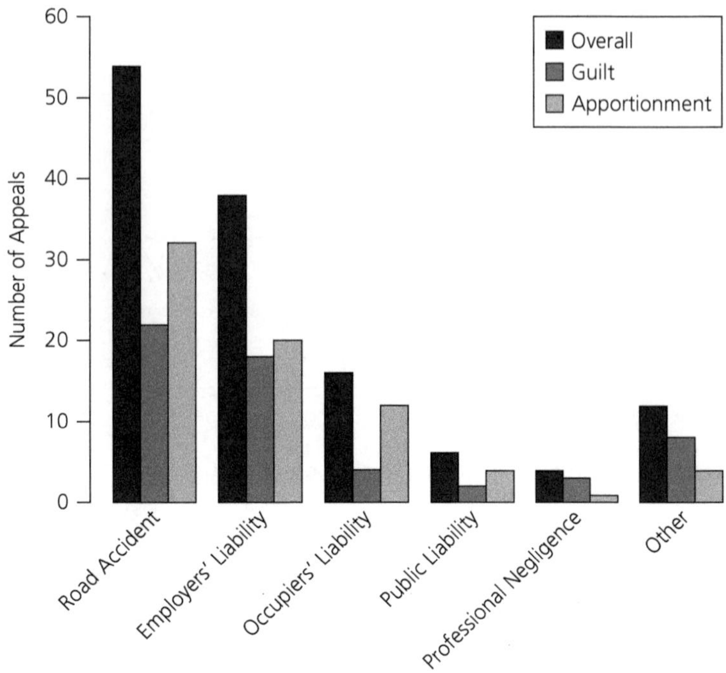

Figure 5.3 Number of appeals by claim type

intervention[22] was 35 per cent. When looking at these figures, readers should bear in mind that by the time a case reaches the Court of Appeal it has passed through a preliminary filter in the form of the permission to appeal process, and that this process has not been captured by our study (because the relevant data are not publicly available).[23] The proportion of first instance decisions on both the existence of contributory negligence and apportionment that are challenged successfully is therefore bound to be considerably lower than these figures would indicate.

5.12 Figure 5.4 shows appellate intervention rates by claim type for the three claim types with the most claims (and where, therefore, the results carry more weight). As the graph shows, the overall appellate intervention rate was lower in employers' liability claims (41 per cent) than in road accident claims (47 per cent). However, statistical analysis suggests that this disparity may well be down to chance.[24] As for occupiers'

---

[22] For a definition of appellate 'intervention' in this sense, see Atkins (1990) (n 4) 73.

[23] For a publicly available judgment of the Court of Appeal on permission to appeal against a first instance decision on apportionment for contributory negligence, see *Parkinson v Chief Constable of Dyfed Powys Police* [2004] EWCA Civ 802.

[24] Logistic regression analysis showed that when employers' liability claims were compared with road accident claims, the odds of appellate intervention were lower in the former, but not significantly so ($p = 0.545$). More generally, a Pearson's chi-square test on the null hypothesis that the

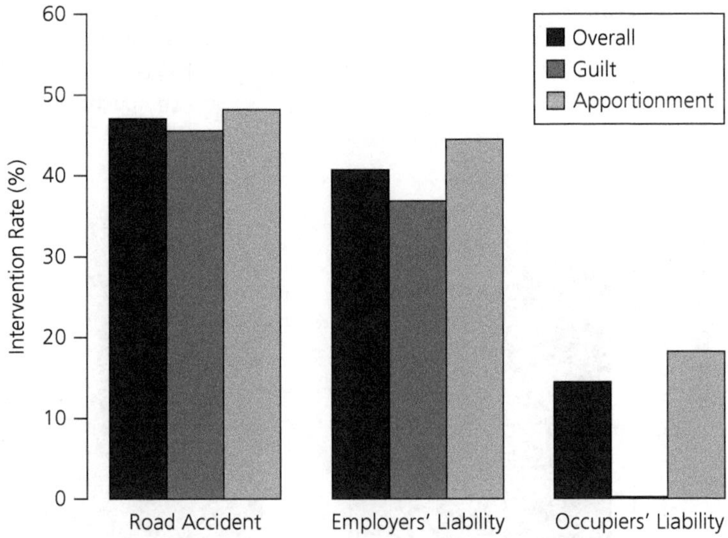

Figure 5.4 Appellate intervention rate by claim type

The intervention rate on guilt in occupiers' liability cases was zero, which explains the presence of a line rather than a bar in the relevant section of the figure.

liability claims, although the figures are relatively low, the results are nonetheless striking in that in claims of this type, an appellate court intervened with respect to a first instance decision on guilt or apportionment on only two of the 14 occasions on which it was asked to do so, giving a very low overall intervention rate in that category of 14 per cent. Furthermore, statistical analysis suggests that the low rate of intervention in occupiers' liability cases as compared with road accident cases is unlikely to be attributable to chance.[25]

Another noteworthy aspect of Figure 5.4 is that in all three of these common claim types, the level of appellate intervention regarding apportionment was higher than the level of appellate intervention in connection with guilt, though in the two most common claim types the disparity was more marked in the case of employers' liability claims (44 per cent and 37 per cent respectively) than in the case of road accident claims (48 per cent and 45 per cent respectively). **5.13**

In Figure 5.5, the data on appellate intervention are broken down by the court of first instance. The overall intervention rate in claims on appeal from a county **5.14**

appellate intervention rate is the same across all types of claim returned a p-value of 0.169 (suggesting no strong association between intervention rate and claim type at a general level).

[25] Logistic regression analysis showed that when occupiers' liability claims were compared with road accident claims, the odds of appellate intervention were substantially lower in the former ($p = 0.040$).

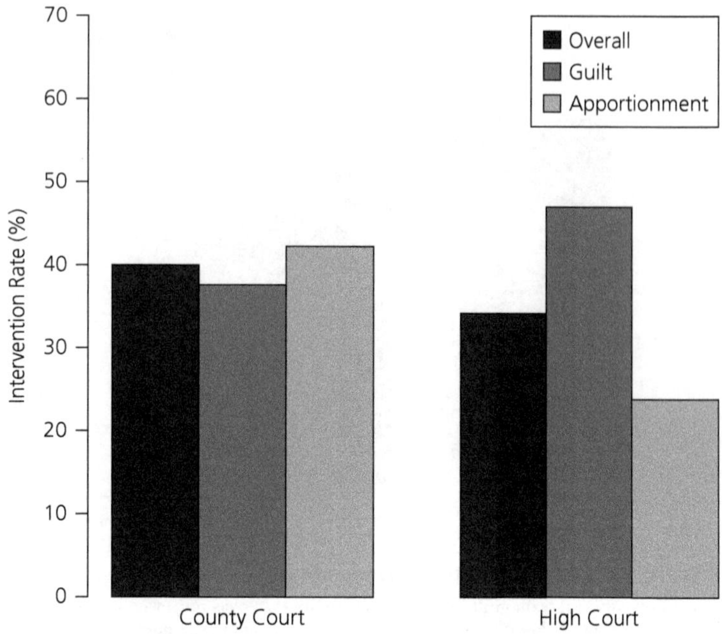

Figure 5.5 Appellate intervention rate by trial court

court (or equivalents) was 40 per cent, and, as the graph shows, in such cases the intervention rate regarding apportionment (42 per cent) was slightly higher than the intervention rate with respect to guilt (38 per cent). The overall intervention rate in claims on appeals from the High Court (or equivalents) was 34 per cent, but this time the intervention rate regarding guilt (47 per cent) was considerably higher than the intervention rate with respect to apportionment (24 per cent). Hence, in our dataset, county court decisions on contributory negligence were overturned on appeal more frequently than High Court decisions, and while appellate intervention in relation to guilt was more likely where the first instance court was the High Court, appellate intervention with respect to apportionment was more likely where the first instance court was a county court. However, statistical analysis suggests that these disparities may well be down to chance.[26]

5.15 We also looked at whether appellate intervention rates differed according to whether the judge at first instance had been a permanent judge or an acting judge.

[26] A Pearson's chi-squared test with Yates's continuity correction on the null hypothesis that the overall appellate intervention rate is the same for both types of first instance court returned a very high p-value of 0.682. A Pearson's chi-square test on the null hypothesis that the appellate intervention rate with regard to guilt is the same for both types of first instance court returned a p-value of 0.501. Running the same test with regard to appellate intervention with respect to apportionment also yielded a relatively high p-value (p = 0.148).

Our hypothesis here was that appellate courts might be more inclined to intervene where the judge at first instance was an acting judge, on the assumption that appellate judges may be more deferential to the decisions of permanent judges simply because they are career judges.[27] Of the 129 claims in our dataset, the judge at first instance was identifiable as permanent in 91 claims, and as acting in 30 claims. In the remaining eight claims, it was not possible to tell whether the first instance judge had been permanent or acting. Contrary to our hypothesis, the overall appellate interference rate in claims where the first instance judge had been permanent (41 per cent) was in fact higher than where the first instance judge had been acting (30 per cent). Breaking this down as between guilt and apportionment, we found that the intervention rate on guilt was 46 per cent where the judge below had been permanent, and only 20 per cent where the judge had been acting. However, when it came to intervention on apportionment, the intervention rate for permanent judges (36 per cent) was marginally lower than for acting judges (40 per cent). Statistical analysis suggests that while the small disparity on apportionment intervention was quite possibly down to chance,[28] this was unlikely in the case of the much more substantial disparity in the other direction on guilt intervention.[29] All in all, then, our study provides no support for the hypothesis that appellate courts are more likely to intervene where the first instance judge is temporary, and to some extent it even suggests that the opposite may be true. Exactly why this is the case is unclear.

Who wins appeals?

Turning to the question of who wins appeals on contributory negligence, Figure 5.6 shows that claimants are more likely to win than defendants, and that appeals by claimants regarding the existence of contributory negligence have a particularly high success rate. To put some flesh on these bones, in the claims in our dataset, claimants succeeded in 44 per cent of appeals overall, with a success rate of 57 per cent in appeals on guilt and 35 per cent in appeals on apportionment. By contrast, defendants won only 29 per cent of their appeals overall, and were *less* likely to win an appeal on guilt (26 per cent success rate) than an appeal on apportionment (31 per cent success rate). Thus, in our dataset, while the chances of a successful appeal on apportionment were only marginally higher for claimants **5.16**

[27] It has also been suggested, perhaps rather implausibly, that 'temporary judges may be both less familiar with current law and precedent and less attuned to the [appellate] court's norms and roles': Atkins (1991) (n 4) 890.

[28] A Pearson's chi-squared test on the null hypothesis that the appellate intervention rate with regard to apportionment is the same for both permanent and temporary first instance judges returned a very high p-value of 0.789.

[29] A Pearson's chi-squared test on the null hypothesis that the appellate intervention rate with regard to guilt is the same for both permanent and temporary first instance judges returned a p-value of 0.077.

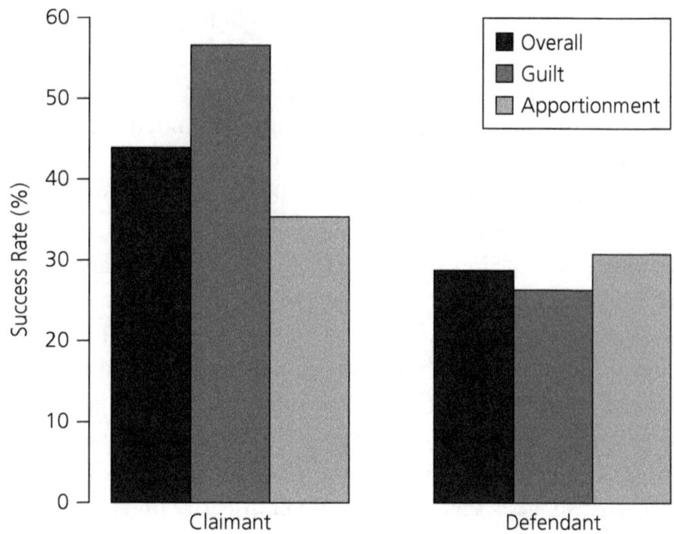

Figure 5.6 Success rate of appeal by party

than for defendants, claimants were more than twice as likely to succeed in appeals on guilt as defendants.

5.17 Statistical analysis suggests that the disparities in the success rates of claimants and defendants in appeals overall, and particularly in the success rates in appeals on guilt, were unlikely to be down to chance.[30] It should be borne in mind here that defendants brought considerably more appeals in our dataset than claimants.[31] It may therefore be that claimants are more selective in deciding whether to appeal. If so, that may explain why claimants are more likely to win appeals, though it would not explain the disparity in this regard between appeals on guilt and appeals on apportionment. It is also interesting to note in this connection that a recent empirical study found that in personal injury claims generally defendants were more likely to succeed in an appeal to the Court of Appeal than claimants (the success rates being 49.1 per cent and 37.4 per cent respectively).[32] It is unclear why the Court of Appeal looks more favourably upon claimants when applying the doctrine of contributory negligence than in the personal injury context more generally.

[30] A Welch two-sample *t*-test comparing the success rates of claimants and defendants in appeals overall returned a *p*-value of 0.079. When we used the same test to compare the success rates of claimants and defendants in appeals on guilt, the *p*-value dropped to 0.026.

[31] See 5.09.

[32] Laleng (n 4) 44–45 (Table 2). The figures in the text exclude cross-appeals. Note also Laleng's later reference (at 52) to earlier studies 'demonstrating a general pro-defendant bias at appellate level'.

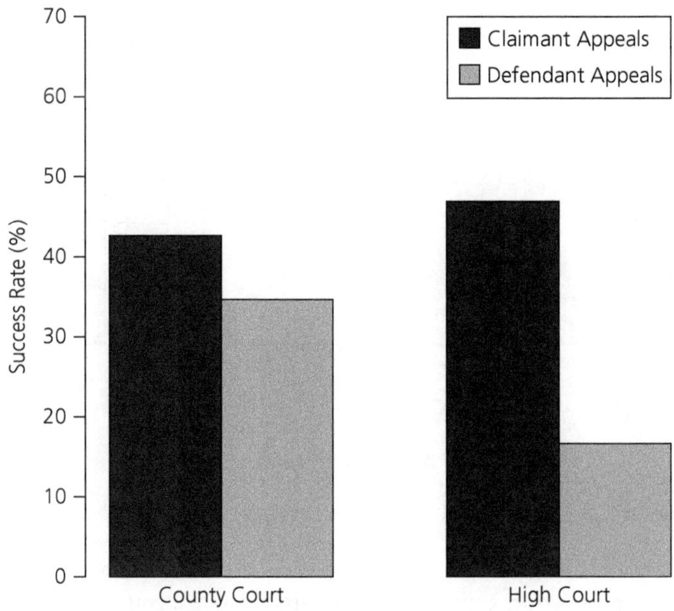

Figure 5.7 Success rate of appeal by trial court and party

Turning to the success rate of appeal by trial court and party (as shown in Figure 5.7), whereas the chances of a claimant appeal from the High Court (or equivalents) succeeding (47 per cent) were only a little higher than the chances of a claimant appeal from a county court (or equivalents) succeeding (43 per cent), defendant appeals from a county court were more than twice as likely to succeed as defendant appeals from the High Court (the relevant figures being 35 per cent and 17 per cent respectively). Statistical analysis suggests that the disparity in the success rates of claimants and defendants in appeals from county courts may well be down to chance[33] but that the reverse is true with respect to appeals from the High Court.[34] **5.18**

Extent of appellate intervention with respect to the discount

There were 24 claims in our dataset where the appellate court intervened in relation to a first instance decision on apportionment. In 12 of these cases, the discount was reduced, and in the other 12 it was increased. Figure 5.8 shows the extent to **5.19**

[33] A Welch two-sample *t*-test comparing the success rates of claimants and defendants in appeals from county courts returned a *p*-value of 0.459.

[34] A Welch two-sample *t*-test comparing the success rates of claimants and defendants in appeals from the High Court yielded a *p*-value of 0.048.

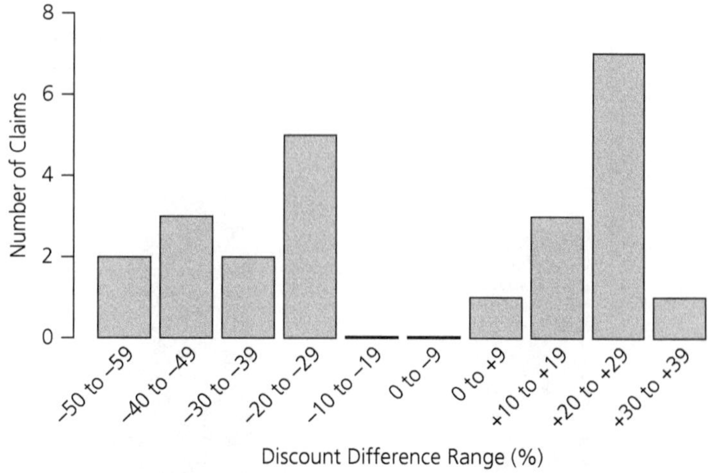

Figure 5.8 Post-appeal difference in discount

which the appellate court differed from the first instance court in these cases. The average reduction in the discount (32 per cent) was considerably larger than the average increase in the discount (20 per cent), and similarly both the smallest reduction (20 per cent)[35] and the largest reduction (50 per cent)[36] were greater than the equivalent figures for increases in the discount (8 per cent[37] and 30 per cent[38] respectively). Furthermore, statistical analysis suggests that the disparity between the average increase and the average reduction is unlikely to be down to chance.[39] Hence it appears that when appellate courts *reduce* the discount, they tend to do so by larger amounts than when they *increase* the discount.[40] Set alongside Figure 5.6, these results suggest that appellate courts tend to look favourably upon claimants in contributory negligence cases.

5.20 Finally, we can see from the way that the heights of the bars dip in the middle of Figure 5.8 (a roughly bimodal distribution) that appellate courts rarely change the

---

[35] *C (a child) v Imperial Design Ltd* [2001] Env LR 33 (CA) **[2:12]**; *Eagle v Chambers (No 1)* [2003] EWCA Civ 1107; [2004] RTR 9 **[1:102]**; **[2:49]**; **[3:36]**; *Johnstone* (n 2) **[2:96]**; *Starks v Chief Constable of Hertfordshire* [2013] EWCA Civ 782; [2014] RTR 4 **[2:119]**.

[36] *King v Rco Support Services Ltd* [2001] ICR 608 **[2:14]**; *Robb* (n 2) 97 **[2:75]**.

[37] *Eyres v Atkinsons Kitchens & Bedrooms Ltd* [2007] EWCA Civ 365; (2007) 151 SJLB 576 **[2:77]**.

[38] *Watson v Skuse* [2001] EWCA Civ 1158 **[1:26]**; **[2:26]**; **[3:15]**.

[39] A Welch two-sample *t*-test comparing the average increase in discount with the average reduction returned a *p*-value of 0.006. This result was broadly consistent with the result of a Wilcoxon rank sum test with continuity correction ($p = 0.014$).

[40] In one employers' liability case, *Toole v Bolton MBC* [2002] EWCA Civ 588 **[1:51]**; **[2:31]**, the Court of Appeal found that there had been no contributory negligence at all, when at first instance a 75 per cent discount had been imposed for contributory fault.

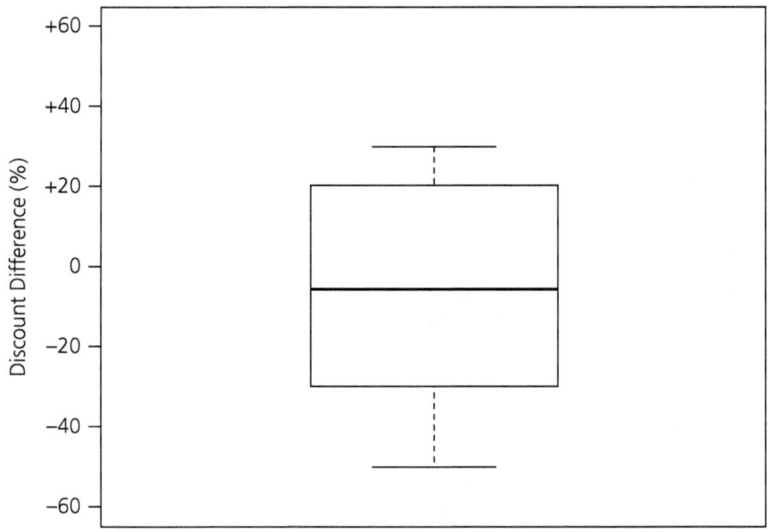

Figure 5.9 Post-appeal difference in discount

discount in either direction by a small amount. Indeed, there is only one claim in which the discount difference was less than 10 per cent,[41] and only four claims in which it was less than 20 per cent. Figure 5.9 presents the same data in a boxplot, which may assist understanding of the variability observed.

Success of the plea and discount imposed following appeal

Our study also produced interesting data on the post-appeal success rate of the plea of contributory negligence and the post-appeal discounts imposed, which tended to reinforce some of the conclusions of our study of first instance decisions. Out of the 129 claims in our appellate dataset, the plea of contributory negligence succeeded following the appeal in 92 claims (71 per cent), and failed in 37 claims (29 per cent). **5.21**

Figure 5.10 shows the post-appeal success rate of the plea of contributory negligence by type of claim. Statistical analysis suggests that these variables might well be associated.[42] As can be seen from the graph, the post-appeal success rate of the plea was fairly similar across the road accident (80 per cent), occupiers' liability (81 per cent), and public liability (80 per cent) categories. However, the post-appeal **5.22**

[41] *Eyres* (n 37) [2:77].

[42] A Pearson's chi-square test on the null hypothesis that the post-appeal success rate of the plea of contributory negligence is the same across all types of claim returned a low *p*-value of 0.094.

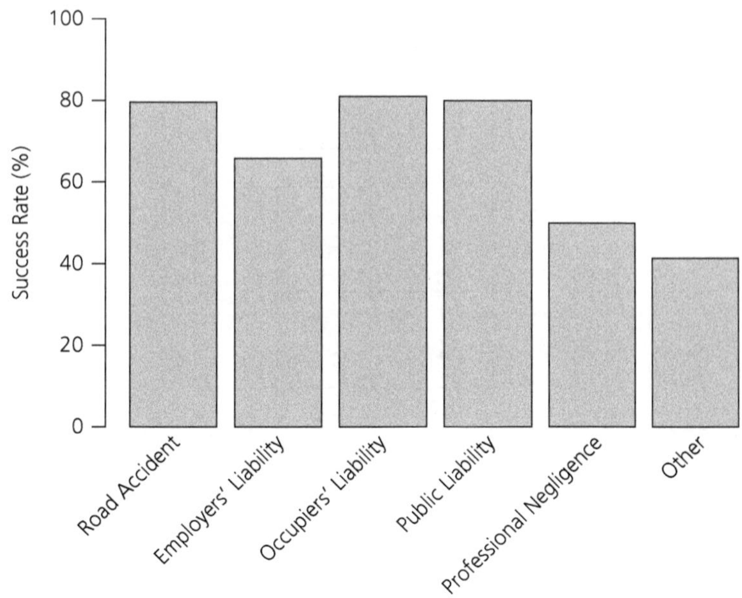

Figure 5.10 Post-appeal success rate of plea by claim type

success rate was substantially lower than this in the three other categories: employers' liability (66 per cent); professional negligence (50 per cent); and 'other' (42 per cent). The small number of relevant claims means that the low success rate in the final two categories should be treated with caution. Nevertheless, statistical analysis suggests that the very low post-appeal success rate of the plea in claims in the 'other' category was unlikely to be attributable to chance.[43]

5.23 As for the low post-appeal success rate of the plea in the professional negligence category, while statistical analysis suggests that this might well be attributable to chance,[44] it does tally with a key finding of our first instance study, namely that at first instance the plea of contributory negligence was significantly less likely to succeed in claims of this type than in other types of claim.[45] Turning to the relatively low post-appeal success rate of the plea in employers' liability claims, the substantial number of claims in this category allows us to attach greater significance to this result, and statistical analysis provides some evidence

[43] Logistic regression analysis showed that when claims in the 'other' category were compared with road accident claims (the largest category of claim), the odds of the plea of contributory negligence succeeding post-appeal were significantly lower in 'other' claims ($p = 0.010$).

[44] Logistic regression analysis revealed that when professional negligence claims were compared with road accident claims, the odds of the plea of contributory negligence succeeding post-appeal were lower in professional negligence claims, but not significantly so ($p = 0.197$).

[45] See 4.08.

of an association between this type of case and the post-appeal success rate of the plea.[46]

Any explanations offered for the relatively low post-appeal success rate of the plea in the 'other' and employers' liability categories are inevitably speculative. However, it is perhaps noteworthy that in *all* the seven claims in the employers' liability category in which the appellate court intervened with respect to a finding as to guilt at first instance it did so in favour of the claimant, whereas across the entire dataset the appellate court intervened in favour of the claimant on guilt only 57 per cent of the time. Hence, while our first instance study uncovered no evidence that trial judges were particularly lenient[47] towards employees when it came to the existence of contributory negligence,[48] our appellate study suggests that appellate courts may well be. **5.24**

Turning to the discount imposed for contributory negligence following an appeal, the average post-appeal discount across the dataset was 50 per cent, so substantially higher than the average discount in our first instance study, which was 40 per cent.[49] This disparity—which statistical analysis suggests is extremely unlikely to be down to chance[50]—is doubtless connected to the fact that it seems that decisions regarding contributory negligence are more likely to be the subject of an appeal if a relatively large discount has been imposed at first instance.[51] This may be because in these cases there is a perception that more is at stake when it comes to contributory negligence, and hence that an appeal on the issue is more worthwhile. **5.25**

Figure 5.11 shows the average post-appeal discount by claim type. It reveals that the average post-appeal discounts for four of the categories of claim were fairly tightly clustered on or just above the overall average figure of 50 per cent, namely road accidents (52 per cent); occupiers' liability (52 per cent); public liability (52 per cent); and 'other' (50 per cent). By contrast, the average post-appeal discount in employers' liability cases was quite a bit lower than the average (45 per cent), while in professional negligence cases it was quite a bit higher (58 per cent). Statistical analysis suggests that the lower average discount in employers' liability cases is unlikely to be **5.26**

---

[46] Logistic regression analysis revealed that when employers' liability claims were compared with road accident claims, the odds of the plea of contributory negligence succeeding post-appeal were lower in employers' liability claims ($p = 0.140$).

[47] On what we mean by 'lenient', see 4.16.

[48] See 4.09. Leniency towards employees was, however, manifested at the apportionment stage: 4.15. See also 7.20–7.37

[49] See 4.12.

[50] A Welch two-sample t-test of the difference between the average discount in the first instance study and the average post-appeal discount in the current study gave a very low p-value ($p < 0.001$). This result was consistent with the result of a Wilcoxon rank sum test with continuity correction ($p < 0.001$).

[51] In the claims in the appellate study dataset, the average discount at first instance was 53 per cent, which is (again) considerably higher than the average discount in our first instance study of 40 per cent.

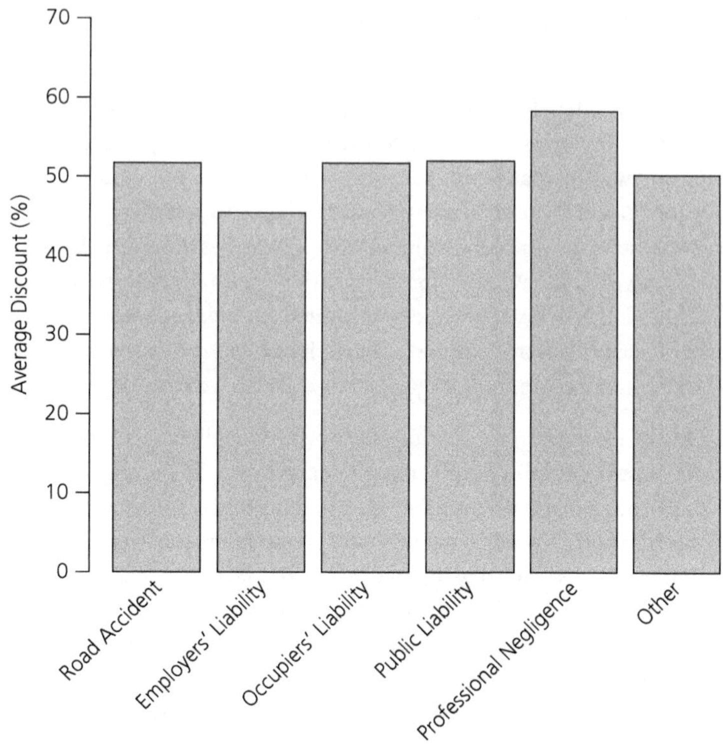

Figure 5.11 Average post-appeal discount by claim type

down to chance, but that the higher average discount in professional negligence cases could well be.[52] These results can usefully be compared with the corresponding findings of our first instance study.[53] That study provided evidence that at the trial court level, discounts for contributory negligence tended to be low in employers' liability claims and high in professional negligence claims, tendencies which this study suggests may well carry through into appellate decisions. Conversely, there is no echo in the appellate study of a third finding of our first instance study, which was that the discounts imposed in occupiers' liability claims tended to be on the high side.[54]

---

52 A Welch two-sample *t*-test comparing the average post-appeal discounts in road accident and employers' liability claims returned a *p*-value of 0.101, although the *p*-value rose to 0.160 when we ran a Wilcoxon rank sum test with continuity correction. The *p*-values for the same tests comparing the average post-appeal discounts in employers' liability and professional negligence claims were 0.506 and 0.526 respectively. However, when the average post-appeal discounts in road accident and professional negligence claims were compared using the same tests, the *p*-values were considerably higher (0.963 and 1 respectively).

53 See 4.14–4.15.

54 The average discount in occupiers' liability claims at first instance (47 per cent) was considerably higher than the overall average discount of 40 per cent (see 4.17). By contrast, in the appellate study the equivalent disparity in the post-appeal discount was much smaller (52 per cent as against

Figure 5.12 gives more detail on the interaction between post-appeal discount and claim type. **5.27**

As Figure 5.12 shows, the lowest post-appeal discount imposed in the appellate dataset was 20 per cent (four claims),[55] while the highest was 85 per cent (one claim).[56] As in our first instance study,[57] by far the most popular discount was 50 per cent (33 claims), which was more than three times more common than the next most popular discount, 33.3 per cent (10 claims). Table 5.1 sets out all the discounts imposed following appeal in the dataset. **5.28**

Contributory negligence on appeal and claimant age

Of the 129 claims in our appellate dataset, 23 were brought by corporate entities or human claimants whose age was left too unclear by the court for it to be determined whether they were children or adults. Of the remaining 106 claims, 14 (13 per cent) were brought by children and 92 (87 per cent) were brought by adults. We were able to discern the age of the claimant with precision in 53 claims. The youngest claimant was aged nine,[58] while the oldest was 79.[59] The distribution of these 53 claims by claimant age range is shown in Figure 5.13. **5.29**

When looking at this graph, it should be borne in mind that in 53 claims in the dataset it was clear that the claimant was an adult but we could not discern the age of the claimant more precisely. These claims are not included in Figure 5.13, which therefore significantly over-represents the proportion of claimants in the dataset who were under 18 (as in all the claims where we knew that the claimant was a child it was possible to discern the claimant's age more precisely). Furthermore, there were 15 additional claims in the dataset where it was unclear whether a human claimant was a child or an adult, and we might reasonably suppose that these claims in fact involved adults, since it seems most unlikely that a judge would fail to mention the age of a claimant who was under 18 (not least because this might affect the analysis of the contributory negligence issue[60]). It is inevitable, therefore, that had we been able to obtain age data for all of the human claimants **5.30**

50 per cent). This disparity is particularly interesting in the light of Laleng's finding that personal injury claimants are less likely to win appeals in occupiers' liability cases than in other types of case: Laleng (n 4) 45 (Table 3).

55 *Purdue v Devon Fire and Rescue Service* [2002] EWCA Civ 1538 [**1:68**]; [**2:40**]; [**3:30**]; *Dorning v Personal Representative of Paul Rigby* [2007] EWCA Civ 1315 [**2:80**]; *Palfrey v WM Morrisons Supermarkets Plc* [2012] EWCA Civ 1917 [**1:422**]; [**2:111**]; *Hill v Norside Ltd* [2013] CSIH 44; 2013 GWD 19-387 [**2:115**].

56 *Ferguson* (n 2) [**1:518**]; [**2:126**].

57 See 4.20.

58 *Wardle* (n 2) [**2:100**].

59 *Palfrey* (n 55) [**1:422**]; [**2:111**].

60 See n 38 in chapter 4.

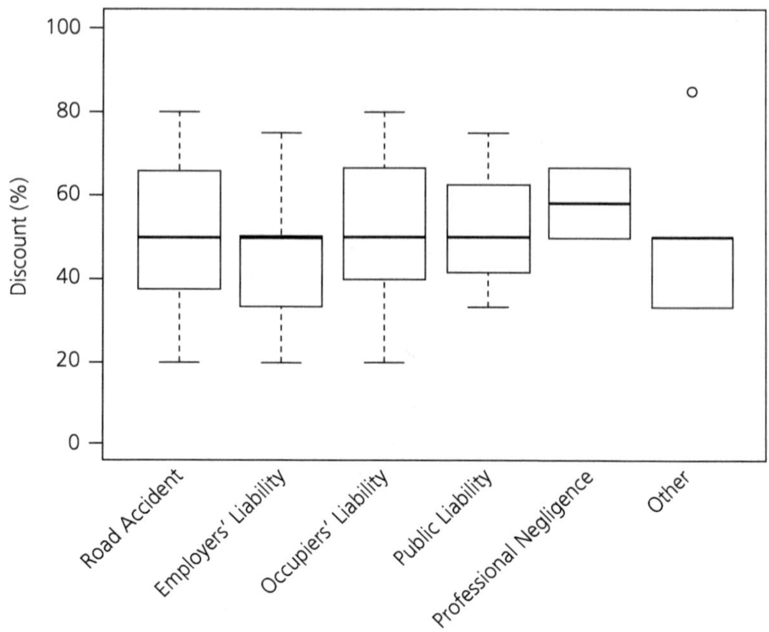

Figure 5.12 Post-appeal discount by claim type

Table 5.1 Post-appeal discounts

Number of claims	Discount (%)
33	50
10	33.3
8	60
8	40
7	75
6	80
5	25
4	66.6
4	20
3	30
1	85
1	70
1	65
1	35

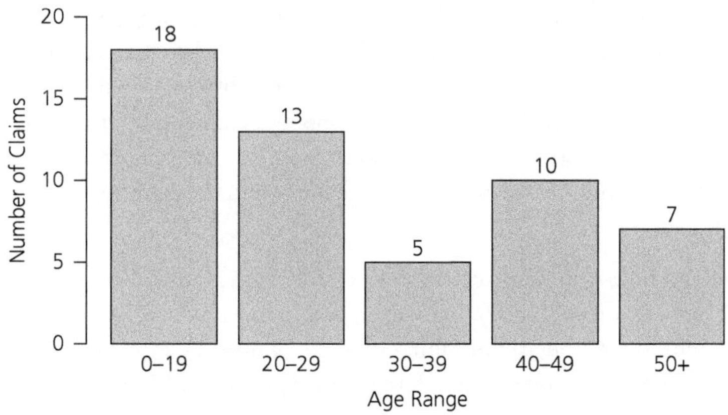

Figure 5.13 Number of claims by claimant age range on appeal

in our dataset, the number of claims in all the age ranges from 20–29 years upwards would be higher, and probably substantially so.

5.31 Moving on to the results of our study regarding contributory negligence in appellate courts and claimant age, by far the most noteworthy is the fact that in the claims in our dataset appellate courts were much more likely to intervene with respect to a first instance decision regarding apportionment where the claimant was a child. The relevant figures are striking. In cases involving child claimants, the appellate court intervened in relation to apportionment in 80 per cent of cases, whereas in cases involving adult claimants, it did so in only 28 per cent of cases. Furthermore, statistical analysis showed that this disparity was very unlikely to be attributable to chance.[61] Where the appellate court did intervene in relation to apportionment, it increased the discount in 50 per cent of cases involving children and in 54 per cent of cases involving adults. It would appear, then, that while appellate courts are much more likely to differ from first instance courts on the appropriate discount where the claimant is a child, this does not translate into any clear tendency on their part to lean either in favour of or against child claimants on the apportionment question. Furthermore, we discerned no similar disparity when it came to the existence of contributory negligence, albeit that there were only four claims in the dataset involving child claimants in which an appellate court was asked to overturn a first instance decision on this question.[62]

---

61 Pearson's chi-square test with Yates's continuity correction, $p = 0.008$.

62 In those four claims, the appellate court intervened with respect to guilt in one claim (*Osei-Antwi v South East London & Kent Bus Co* [2010] EWCA Civ 132 [**1:332**]; [**2:92**]; [**3:116**]), and refused to do so in the other three (*Stanton v Collinson* [2010] EWCA Civ 81; [2010] RTR 26 [**2:94**]; *Phethean-Hubble v Coles* [2012] EWCA Civ 349; [2012] RTR 31 [**2:109**]; and *Jackson* (n 2) [**2:124**]).

5.32 The post-appeal success rate of the plea of contributory negligence was 86 per cent where the claimant was a child, and 72 per cent where the claimant was an adult. However, statistical analysis showed that this disparity could well be down to chance.[63] When we broke down the post-appeal success rate of the plea by age range, no discernible trend was observable[64] and statistical analysis suggests that there is no association between claimant age range and the post-appeal success rate of the plea.[65]

5.33 The average post-appeal discounts for children and adults were 52 per cent and 49 per cent respectively. However, statistical analysis suggests that this disparity could well be attributable either to chance, or to other factors, such as the prevalence of child claimants in claim types where higher discounts tend to be made.[66] Figure 5.14 shows the average post-appeal discount by claimant age range. No strong trend is discernible, although the highest average post-appeal discounts are found in the 0–19 years age range (55 per cent), and the average post-appeal discounts in the other four age ranges are somewhat lower (20–29 years, 50 per cent; 30–39 years, 44 per cent; 40–49 years, 51 per cent; 50+ years, 48 per cent). A similar trend was observable in our first instance study where we noted that a possible explanation for it was that the age of an adult claimant was more likely to be identifiable in types of claim where a lower discount tends to be made, in particular employers' liability claims.[67] There is any case nothing in the results of the appellate study that is inconsistent with our tentative conclusion in the first instance study that the size of the discount is probably more strongly associated with type of claim than with age.[68]

5.34 Further detail regarding the relationship between post-appeal discount and claimant age range is shown in Figure 5.15. The first two boxplots reveal that there was no claim in the dataset brought by a claimant who was under 30 years of age in which the post-appeal discount was less than 33.3 per cent.

---

63 Pearson's chi-square test with Yates's continuity correction, $p = 0.436$. Logistic regression (controlling for claim type and gender) returned a p-value of 0.528.

64 The results were as follows: 0–19 years, 83 per cent post-appeal success rate; 20–29 years, 77 per cent; 30–39 years, 80 per cent; 40–49 years, 60 per cent; 50+ years, 86 per cent.

65 Logistic regression analysis comparing the odds of a finding of contributory negligence post-appeal where the claimant was in the 0–19 age range with the odds of such a finding in the two other age ranges in which there were substantial numbers of claimants returned relatively high p-values (20–29 years: $p = 0.713$; 40–49 years: $p = 0.211$).

66 A Welch two-sample t-test of the difference between the average post-appeal discounts in child claimant and adult claimant claims returned a p-value of 0.477. This result was broadly consistent with the result of a Wilcoxon rank sum test with continuity correction ($p = 0.55$). Linear regression analysis (controlling for case type and gender) returned a p-value of 0.739.

67 See 4.28.

68 See 4.27–4.28.

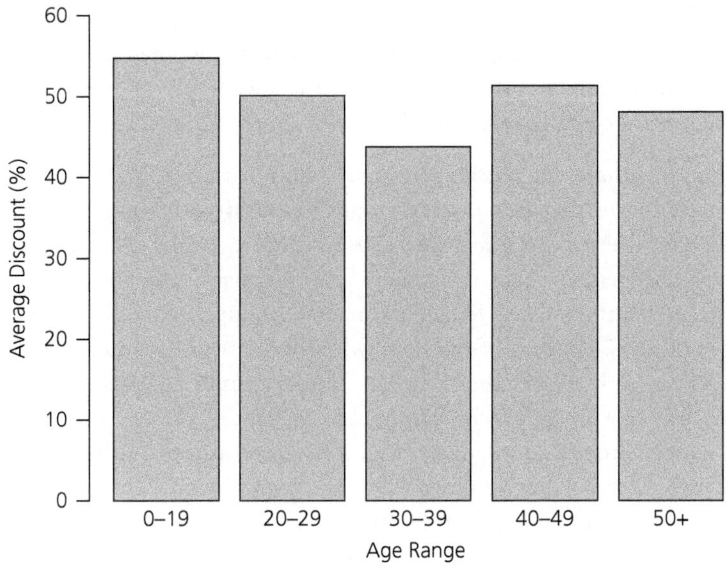

Figure 5.14 Average post-appeal discount by claimant age range

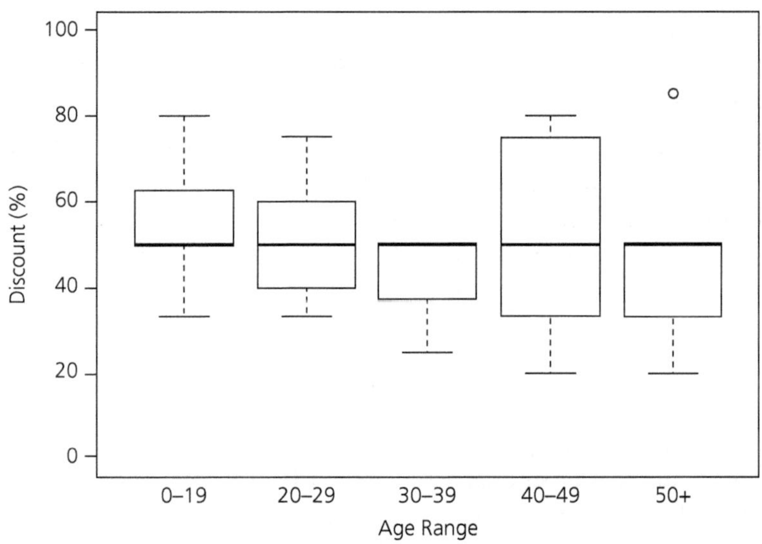

Figure 5.15 Post-appeal discount by claimant age range

Contributory negligence on appeal and claimant gender

Of the 129 claims in our appellate dataset, eight were brought by a corporate entity. **5.35**
Of the remainder, 82 (68 per cent) were brought by men, and 39 (32 per cent) were brought by women. A similar gender balance was observed in our first instance

study.[69] We speculated that it might be attributable to the fact that men bring more personal injury claims than women and/or that women are generally more risk-averse than men, and so less likely to act in such a way as to expose them to a plausible plea of contributory fault.[70]

5.36 In any case, perhaps the most noteworthy result of the appellate study regarding claimant gender is that in our dataset appellate courts were much more likely to intervene with respect to a first instance decision regarding the existence of contributory negligence where the claimant was female. The relevant figures are striking. In claims involving female claimants, the appellate court intervened with regard to guilt 67 per cent of the time, whereas the corresponding figure for male claimants was only 31 per cent. Furthermore, statistical analysis showed that this disparity was very unlikely to be attributable to chance.[71] Where the appellate court did intervene with regard to guilt, it found for the claimant on the point in 60 per cent of the claims involving female claimants, and in 55 per cent of the claims involving male claimants. It would appear, then, that although appellate courts are considerably more likely to differ from first instance courts on the guilt issue where the claimant is female, this does not translate into any strong tendency on their part to lean either in favour of or against female claimants on this question. Furthermore, when it came to apportionment, the trend was reversed: in claims involving female claimants, the appellate court intervened with regard to apportionment only 24 per cent of the time, whereas in claims involving male claimants, the interference rate was 44 per cent.[72]

5.37 Finally, the post-appeal success rate of the plea of contributory negligence was 71 per cent where the claimant was male, and 79 per cent where the claimant was female, and average post-appeal discounts for male and female claimants were 50 per cent and 49 per cent respectively. In both cases, statistical analysis suggests that the disparities are probably attributable to chance.[73]

Discussion

5.38 In this section, we highlight what we consider to be some of the most interesting findings of our appellate study and discuss those findings in the light of the relevant case law and academic literature.

---

69 See 4.29.

70 See ibid.

71 Pearson's chi-square test with Yates's continuity correction, $p = 0.038$.

72 However, statistical analysis suggests that this disparity could well be attributable to chance: Pearson's chi-square test with Yates's continuity correction, $p = 0.192$.

73 Success rate of the plea post-appeal and claimant gender: Pearson's chi-square test with Yates's continuity correction, $p = 0.424$. Average discount post-appeal and claimant gender: Welch two-sample t-test, $p = 0.718$.

The decline in the number of appellate decisions on contributory negligence

We have seen (in Figure 5.2) that there was a marked falling off in the number of appellate decisions concerning contributory negligence after 2003.[74] A similar downward trend is observable in personal injury appeals more generally over roughly the same time period.[75] Two explanations for this decline initially struck us as plausible, but neither is entirely convincing.[76] The first potential explanation relates to permission to appeal. Since 2 May 2000, as we noted above,[77] it has generally been necessary for prospective appellants to obtain permission to appeal. Before that date, when permission to appeal was required, a less demanding test for permission prevailed.[78] However, while—if we bear in mind the time lag between first instance and appellate decisions—this may explain why there was a relatively high number of appellate decisions regarding contributory negligence in 2000, and possibly even in 2001, it is difficult to see how this can explain a decline in such decisions more than three years after the changes to the permission to appeal requirement came into force. **5.39**

Another potential explanation lies in civil litigation funding arrangements. Legislation significantly extending the conditional fee agreement ('CFA') regime was passed in 1999.[79] The extended scheme took effect on 1 April 2000. It is certainly possible that lawyers acting for claimants funded by a CFA may be more reluctant to advise their client to appeal, since they would go unpaid in the event that the appeal fails (although set against this is the fact that, all other things being equal, the more difficult the appeal, the greater the lawyer's success fee). One problem with this explanation, however, is that defendant appeals dropped off even more markedly than claimant appeals after 2003.[80] And **5.40**

---

[74] It would have been interesting to know whether the decline in the number of appeals was specific to contributory negligence appeals or was true of appeals generally. However, while data are available on the number of appeals determined by the Court of Appeal (Ministry of Justice, *The Royal Courts of Justice Annual Tables: Supplementary Data for Additional Courts* (Ministry of Justice 2016) Table 3.9 (<http://www.gov.uk/government/uploads/system/uploads/attachment_data/file/643446/rcj-tables-2016.xlsx>, accessed 3 November 2018), unfortunately these only date back to 2003.

[75] See Laleng (n 4) 41 (Figure 2).

[76] We are grateful to Andrew Higgins and Adrian Zuckerman for sharing their thoughts with us on these points.

[77] See 2.05.

[78] See *Smith v Cosworth Casting Processes Ltd* [1997] 1 WLR 1538 (CA) 1538 (Lord Woolf MR), explaining that, at the time, the Court of Appeal could grant permission to appeal even if it was not satisfied that the applicant had a realistic prospect of success. Cf the current test for permission to appeal: see 2.05.

[79] Access to Justice Act 1999, s 27.

[80] In 2000–2003 there was an average of 5.5 claimant appeals per year in our dataset, and an average of 8.75 defendant appeals. From 2004–2016 there was an average of 2.15 claimant appeals per year, and an average of 2.92 defendant appeals.

it is hard to see why the number of defendant appeals should be affected by the extension of the CFA regime, when defendants do not generally use CFAs to fund litigation.[81]

5.41 Accordingly, we are unable to identify a clear cause of the precipitous decline in the number of appellate decisions regarding contributory negligence after 2003.[82] We suspect that the decline and/or the fact that the number of appellate decisions subsequently remained fairly low are attributable to a combination of factors. Possible influences in this regard additional to those that we have already mentioned include the clamping down on second appeals,[83] a 'recent substantial increase in immigration appeals'[84] (which leaves less time for contributory negligence appeals to be decided), and increased emphasis on the need to divert cases from the judicial system to mediation and other forms of alternative dispute resolution.[85] However, further exploration of these matters would take us deep into a jungle of procedural rules and well beyond the scope of this book.

The number of claims in the dataset

5.42 Notwithstanding the drop-off in appellate decisions concerning contributory negligence after 2003, the fact that there are 129 claims in our dataset suggests that litigants are not particularly slow to appeal on the issue of contributory negligence. In particular, the claim in a leading textbook that litigants appeal against apportionment decisions 'only rarely'[86] is not borne out by the cases in our dataset, where appeals on apportionment outnumbered appeals on guilt. As Figure 5.3 shows, this tendency to launch appeals on apportionment was particularly marked in road accident and occupiers' liability cases.

---

[81] It is conceivable that a threatened appeal by a defendant (or the actual filing of an appeal notice/obtaining of permission to appeal) could induce a claimant to settle because he or she is funded by a CFA. However, we have no way of knowing whether or not this is the case.

[82] It is, of course, possible that what looks like a decline in appellate decisions concerning contributory negligence after 2003 may in fact be a spike in such decisions from (at the latest) 2000 until 2003. However, as Court of Appeal judgments were only routinely uploaded onto the internet from 2000 onwards, we have no ready means of checking the number of such decisions before the beginning of the study period.

[83] See the onerous test in Civil Procedure Rules ('CPR') r 52.13. This change was described as 'major' in *Tanfern Ltd v Cameron-Macdonald* [2000] 1 WLR 1311 (CA) [42] (Brooke LJ).

[84] Michael Burton (ed), *Civil Appeals* (2nd edn, Sweet & Maxwell 2013) para 1.300.

[85] Consider, for example, the court's duty actively to manage cases, including by 'encouraging the parties to use an alternative dispute resolution procedure' and 'helping the parties to settle the whole or part of the case' (CPR 1.4(2)(e)–(f)) and the Court of Appeal's Mediation Scheme (as to which, see HM Courts & Tribunal Service, 'Court of Appeal Mediation Scheme (CAMS)' (<http://www.cedr.com/docslib/56D_CA_Mediation_Scheme_rules_for_1_April_13_final.pdf>, accessed 3 November 2018).

[86] Simon Deakin, Angus Johnston and Basil Markesinis, *Markesinis and Deakin's Tort Law* (7th edn, OUP 2013) 756.

The incidence of appellate intervention

Tony Weir once remarked that '[a]lthough the Court of Appeal keeps saying that it is reluctant to interfere with the trial judge's apportionment, in fact it keeps doing so'.[87] Was this a fair criticism? According to our study, the overall level of appellate intervention with respect to first instance decisions on contributory negligence was 35 per cent. This is quite a bit lower than the percentage of appeals allowed by the Court of Appeal across all cases that came before it in the period 2003–2016 (48 per cent),[88] and also substantially lower than the reversal rate in personal injury claims more generally (44 per cent to the nearest percentage point).[89] The Court of Appeal is therefore at least more reluctant to reverse a trial court on contributory negligence than it is to reverse trial courts on certain other issues, even in the personal injury context. We also found that the intervention rate when it came to the existence of contributory negligence (39 per cent) was higher than the intervention rate in relation to apportionment (33 per cent), a disparity that is consistent with the principle that appellate courts should be particularly slow to intervene in relation to apportionment decisions.[90] Nor should it be forgotten that all appeals heard by the Court of Appeal will have passed through the permission to appeal filter. Overall, therefore, while it is certainly true that appellate intervention with respect to apportionment is not uncommon, it would appear that appellate courts are reasonably restrained in this regard. **5.43**

We had suspected that the Court of Appeal might intervene more readily in connection with decisions of county courts than decisions of the High Court. This was because the Court of Appeal overturns county courts decisions more frequently than decisions of the High Court across appeals of all types.[91] Indeed, this suspicion was borne out by our data, which showed that the overall intervention rate was 6 per cent higher in appeals on contributory negligence from county courts than in appeals on contributory negligence from the High Court[92] (although this disparity was a little lower than the 10 per cent disparity observable across appeals of all types in the period 2008–2016[93]). **5.44**

---

[87] Tony Weir, *A Casebook on Tort* (10th edn, Sweet & Maxwell 2004) 247.

[88] Ministry of Justice (n 74) Table 3.9 (this figure disregards appeals that were dismissed by consent, struck out, or disposed of by other means). In an earlier study, Atkins found that the Court of Appeal intervened on average in 35 per cent of appeals in all types of case decided between 1952 and 1983, with 'a remarkable degree of consistency' through this period: Atkins (1990) (n 4) 83.

[89] Laleng (n 4) 44.

[90] See 2.07–2.08.

[91] According to statistics published by the Ministry of Justice, in the period 2008–2016 the rate of appellate intervention with respect to decisions of the Queen's Bench Division of the High Court was 36 per cent. The corresponding intervention rate for decisions from county courts (excluding appeals in family and admiralty matters) was 46 per cent. See Ministry of Justice (n 74) Table 3.9.

[92] See Figure 5.5.

[93] See n 91.

5.45 Writing in 1991, Burton Atkins argued that the greater readiness of the Court of Appeal to intervene in appeals from county courts could be explained by two factors: first, the fact that 'county courts hear the more routine cases in which appeals are likely to rest upon narrow questions of procedure and law'; and, second, the fact that both solicitors and barristers had rights of audience in county courts and were eligible for appointment as county court judges, whereas only barristers had rights of audience before the High Court and were eligible for appointment as justices of the High Court, with the 'broader participation of the legal profession' in the county courts necessitating 'a more intensive degree of oversight'.[94] However, to the extent that our study lends supports to the hypothesis that the Court of Appeal is more likely to interfere with a county court decision than a High Court decision, we are unpersuaded that these two factors explain the disparity we observed. As to the first factor, there is no reason to suppose that decisions as to the existence of contributory negligence or the appropriate apportionment following a finding of contributory negligence are likely to pose 'narrow[er] questions of procedure and law' if those decisions are reached in a county court rather than by the High Court. And Atkins's second factor rests on the speculative proposition that wider involvement in the practices of judging and lawyering results in inferior decision-making. In our view, therefore, the explanation for the disparity that we observed in intervention rates by court type probably lies elsewhere, perhaps in a more general sense at the appellate level that decisions in the High Court or equivalent are more likely to be reliable than decisions of courts lower down in the judicial hierarchy.

The extent of appellate intervention with respect to apportionment

5.46 Our study shows that when appellate courts intervene in relation to first instance decisions on apportionment, they rarely change the discount by a small amount, and that a change of 20 per cent or more in either direction is the norm.[95] These findings are consistent with the principle that an appellate court should intervene with respect to a decision on apportionment only where it concludes that the first instance court got it badly wrong.[96] After all, it is implicit in the stringency of the tests that must be satisfied before appellate intervention in relation to apportionment is permissible that when an appellate court does intervene, it should not do so only to a small extent, since a minor adjustment would be inconsistent with the conclusion that the lower court's decision on the point was manifestly flawed. As Lord Reed said in *Jackson v Murray*, '[t]he need for the appellate court to be

[94] Atkins (1991) (n 4) 889–90.
[95] See 5.20.
[96] See 2.07–2.08.

satisfied, in the absence of an identifiable error, that the apportionment made by the court below was outside the range of reasonable determinations is reflected in the fact that apportionments are not altered by appellate courts merely on the basis of a disagreement as to the precise figure'.[97]

Furthermore, the results of our study are also consistent with the suggestion that appellate intervention with respect to apportionment is more justifiable where the appellate court favours an apportionment of responsibility that is 'qualitatively different' from that favoured by the first instance court, so that (for example) replacing a 60 per cent discount with a 40 per cent discount is more justifiable than replacing a 40 per cent discount with a 20 per cent one.[98] This is because in all but four of the 24 claims in our study in which the appellate court intervened in relation to apportionment, it either changed the apportionment from an unequal division of responsibility to an equal one or vice versa, or it shifted the bulk of the responsibility from one party to the other. **5.47**

Post-appeal discounts

Several interesting points emerge in relation to the spread of post-appeal discounts. **5.48** In the dataset, appellate courts tended to use fractions that are routinely encountered in everyday life, such as one-half and one-quarter, to express the division of responsibility between the parties.[99] This result is unsurprising. The same tendency was visible in the dataset for our first instance study,[100] and the preference for round figures coheres with the fact that apportionment is not an exact science. Attempts to fine-tune the apportionment would be inconsistent with this reality, and would falsely suggest that degrees of responsibility are amenable to exact specification. The range of post-appeal discounts in our dataset (20 per cent being the lowest and 85 per cent being the highest) was also similar to that reported in the first instance study.[101]

---

[97] *Jackson* (n 2) [**2:124**]. See also *Sabir v Osei-Kwabena* [2015] EWCA Civ 1213; [2016] RTR 9 [3] [**1:496**]; [**2:127**]; [**3:174**], where Tomlinson LJ said that even a conclusion that the claimant's share of responsibility was 40 per cent rather than the 25 per cent as found by the trial judge 'might not be enough to warrant [appellate] interference'.

[98] For this suggestion, see *Jackson* (n 2) [38] (Lord Reed) [**2:124**], drawing on *Eagle* (n 35) [16] (Hale LJ) [**1:102**]; [**2:49**]; [**3:36**]. See also at [44], where Lord Reed said that '[t]he view that parties are equally responsible for the damage suffered by the pursuer is substantially different from the view that one party is much more responsible than the other'. In a Court of Appeal hearing on permission to appeal an apportionment decision, counsel for the party seeking the permission was said to have accepted 'that if he was simply asking [the Court of Appeal] to adjust the contributory negligence of the claimant from 35 per cent upwards or downwards but still remaining a minority of responsibility, that would not be something which [the Court of Appeal] would properly entertain as a proper ground of appeal': *Parkinson* (n 23) [3] (Latham LJ).

[99] See Table 5.1.

[100] See 4.20–4.21.

[101] See 4.20, 4.41.

Conclusion

5.49 In this chapter we reported the key findings of our empirical study of the handling of the doctrine of contributory negligence by appellate courts in the United Kingdom. It is the first study of its kind in any common law jurisdiction. Perhaps the most important of our findings are as follows:

1. 44 per cent of the appeals were against determinations as to the existence of contributory negligence, and 56 per cent were appeals against determinations regarding apportionment. Claimants brought 44 per cent of the appeals, and defendants 56 per cent.
2. Appellate courts overturned determinations as to the existence of contributory negligence in 39 per cent of cases, and determinations in respect of apportionment in 33 per cent of cases. The overall level of appellate intervention was 35 per cent.
3. The chances of having a county court decision (or decision of equivalent courts) on contributory negligence overturned on appeal were somewhat higher than the chances of having a High Court decision (or decision of equivalent courts) overturned.
4. Claimants succeeded in 44 per cent of their appeals, while defendants won only 29 per cent of their appeals. And while the chances of a successful appeal on apportionment were only marginally higher for claimants than for defendants, claimants were more than twice as likely to succeed in appeals on guilt as defendants.
5. When appellate courts reduce discounts in contributory negligence cases, they tend to do so by larger amounts than when they increase discounts. And appellate courts rarely change the discount in either direction by a small amount.
6. The post-appeal success rate of the plea of contributory negligence is lower in employers' liability cases and cases in the 'other' category than in relation to the rest of the claim types. Furthermore, in all the cases in the employers' liability category in which the appellate court intervened in relation to a finding as to guilt it did so in favour of the claimant.
7. The average post-appeal discount across all cases was 50 per cent. The average post-appeal discount in employers' liability cases was quite a bit lower (at 45 per cent), while in professional negligence cases it was quite a bit higher (at 58 per cent). The lowest post-appeal discount imposed was 20 per cent, while the highest was 85 per cent. By far the most popular post-appeal discount was 50 per cent.
8. Appeal courts are much more likely to differ from first instance courts on apportionment where the claimant is a child, but this does not translate into any clear tendency on their part to lean either in favour of or against child claimants on the apportionment question.

9. Appeal courts are much more likely to intervene with respect to a first instance decision regarding the existence of contributory negligence where the claimant is female, but, again, are not markedly inclined in favour of or against female claimants on this issue.

As well as illuminating the way in which the contributory negligence doctrine is applied at the appellate court level, the results presented in this chapter also have more general implications for the study of the intermediate appellate courts of the United Kingdom. Three of our findings in particular can be highlighted in this respect. **5.50**

First, the overall level of appellate intervention in contributory negligence cases demonstrates that in the contributory negligence context the UK's intermediate appellate courts are reasonably interventionist, and are perhaps more inclined to interfere with first instance decisions than judicial pronouncements on the subject of appellate intervention in this context may suggest. This finding is consistent with Atkins's observation that 'the English [Court of Appeal] is relatively active in supervising actions of lower courts',[102] even if at the same time our study suggests that the UK's intermediate appellate courts are perhaps more restrained in the contributory negligence context than in appeals generally. In any case, there is nothing in our study that is inconsistent with the claim that the intermediate appellate courts in the United Kingdom 'routinely participate in the judicial process and are active in determining the burdens and benefits being distributed in the system' and hence 'can wield significant power'.[103] **5.51**

Second, the findings of our study lend tentative support to the hypothesis that intermediate appellate courts are more likely to interfere with decisions of county courts and their equivalents than with decisions of the High Court and its equivalents. **5.52**

Finally, our study also suggests that in personal injury cases, intermediate appellate courts may be more sympathetic to claimants than to defendants, although we are acutely conscious that there may be other explanations for the fact that claimants win more appeals on contributory negligence than defendants. On these and other questions that arise out of our study, we hope that we have demonstrated that there is considerable scope for further research into the operations of intermediate appellate courts, both generally and in particular legal contexts. **5.53**

[102] Atkins (1990) (n 4) 87 (see also at 92: 'a relatively active role').
[103] Ibid, 78.

6

CONTRIBUTORY NEGLIGENCE ON THE ROADS

Introduction

6.01 This chapter explores how first instance courts apply the contributory negligence doctrine in the context of road accidents. This setting merits extended treatment for two main reasons. First, in terms of the number of claims, it is by far the most important context in which the law of contributory negligence is relevant.[1] Second, grounds exist for thinking that the contributory negligence doctrine may be applied in a distinctive way in this area. Defendants in road accident claims, who are almost always drivers, will often have exposed claimants to asymmetrical risks of serious injury,[2] and it is possible that this influences how the courts apply the law of contributory negligence.

Results

Number of claims

6.02 Our first instance dataset contains 199 claims that we coded as road accident claims,[3] all of which were for personal injury.[4] Figure 6.1 shows the number of

---

[1] See 4.04, 5.06.

[2] 'A car can do so much more damage to a person than a person can usually do to a car' (*Eagle v Chambers (No 1)* [2003] EWCA Civ 1107; [2004] RTR 9 [15] (Hale LJ) [**1:102**]; [**2:49**]; [**3:36**]); 'the driver of a car has a far greater power than a pedestrian to cause injury' (*Green v Bannister* [2003] EWCA Civ 1819; [2003] All ER (D) 279 (Dec) [6] (Sedley LJ) [**1:122**]; [**2:55**]; [**3:40**]).

[3] Each of these claims features in Appendix 1. However, because some additional coding of these 199 claims was done for the purposes of the present analysis of the contributory negligence doctrine in the road accident context (see 6.12, 6.14), and in the interests of permitting all of these claims to be seen easily alongside each other, they also feature in Appendix 3, which is specifically concerned with road accident claims. Because we do not discuss jurisdiction and gender in detail in this chapter, we briefly set out the relevant details here. Most of the 199 road accident claims related to England and Wales (151 claims (76 per cent)) while 11 (6 per cent) pertained to Northern Ireland, and 36 (18 per cent) to Scotland. Of the 199 road accident claims, 139 claims (70 per cent) were brought by men and 58 (29 per cent) by women (in two claims the claimant's gender could not be ascertained). The plea succeeded in 67 per cent of the claims brought by men and in 62 per cent of claims brought by women. The average discount was almost identical: 43 per cent in claims by men and 42 per cent in claims by women.

[4] The results that are presented in this section of this chapter are based solely on the 199 claims in our first instance dataset that were coded as being road accident claims. Claims that were

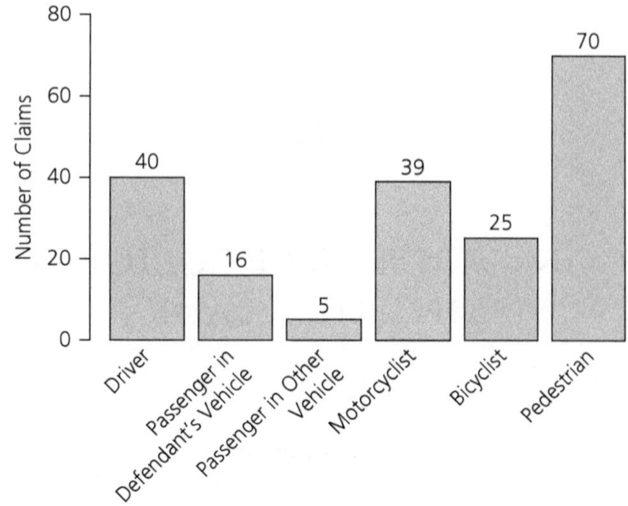

Figure 6.1 Number of road accident claims by claimant type

claims by claimant type. It captures all the road accident claims in the dataset except for two claims that could not be classified because of a lack of information regarding the claimant,[5] and two claims that did not fit into any of the categories.[6] By far the largest number of claims were brought by pedestrians (36 per cent), followed by claims by drivers of cars or other large motor vehicles[7] (21 per cent), and then claims by motorcyclists[8] (20 per cent). It is noteworthy that there were roughly the same number of claims by car drivers and motorcyclists despite there being far more cars in the United Kingdom than motorcycles. This may reflect the fact that motorcyclists are far more likely to suffer injury than other types of road user, and also the fact that motorcyclists may be less risk-averse and hence more likely to have contributory negligence alleged against them. The number of claims in the remaining categories is much lower. The fact that only five of the claims were brought by passengers in

coded as pertaining to a different contextual setting are disregarded even if they involved a road accident.

[5] *Al Gouri v Achkar* [2007] CLY 3079 (QBD) **[1:234]**; **[3:75]** (claimant a passenger but unclear whether or not he was travelling in the defendant's vehicle); *Edwards v Martin* [2010] EWHC 570 (QB); [2010] All ER (D) 68 (Jun) **[1:360]**; **[3:123]** (circumstances of the injury unclear save that the claimant was injured in a road accident).

[6] *Stoddart v Perucca* [2011] EWCA Civ 290; [2011] All ER (D) 16 (Mar) **[1:362]**; **[2:101]**; **[3:124]** (horse rider); *Devereux v Hayward* [2011] EWHC 2780 (QB); [2011] All ER (D) 49 (Nov) **[1:417]**; **[3:147]** (same).

[7] Henceforward, in this chapter references to 'cars' should also be understood as references to other large vehicles.

[8] The category of motorcyclists includes pillion passengers. In the end, there was only one claim involving a pillion passenger: *McCracken v Smith* [2013] EWHC 3620 (QB) **[1:491]**; **[3:171]**.

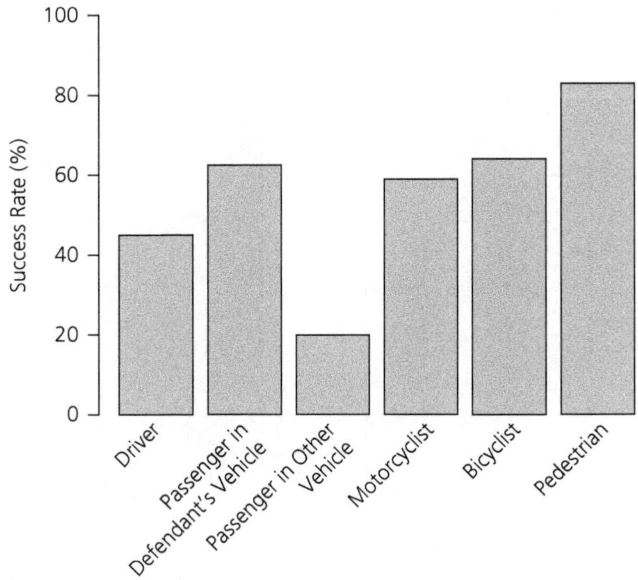

Figure 6.2 Success rate of plea in road accident claims by claimant type

vehicles not driven by the defendant[9] perhaps reflects the fact that it would be relatively unusual for such a claimant to be partly responsible for their injuries, since they have not chosen to (for example) travel in a vehicle with an intoxicated driver. Of the 21 claims by both types of passengers, in 10 of them (48 per cent) the alleged contributory negligence was failing to wear a seat belt.[10]

Success rate of the plea

The plea of contributory negligence succeeded in 129 of the road accident claims (65 per cent), which is a little higher than the success rate of 58 per cent across all types of claim in the first instance dataset. Figure 6.2 shows the success rate of the plea by type of claimant. It reveals striking differences in the success rate. Statistical analysis suggests **6.03**

[9] *Taylor v Rashid* [2008] CLY 2661 (Bow CC) **[1:251]**; **[3:79]**; *Garth v Grant* [2007] All ER (D) 459 (May) (QBD) **[1:259]**; **[3:82]**; *McCrory v Hutchinson's Coaches (Overtown) Ltd* 2007 SLT (Sh Ct) 187 (South Strathclyde, Dumfries and Galloway Sheriff Court) **[1:272]**; **[3:86]**; *Minh Lac v Clayton* [2009] EWCA Civ 106; [2009] All ER (D) 159 (Apr) **[1:293]**; **[1:294]**; **[2:86]**; **[2:87]**; **[3:98]** **[3:99]** (two claims).

[10] *W v Hardman* [2001] CLY 4452 (Leeds CC) **[1:40]**; **[3:22]**; *Mattar v Shenouda* [2001] All ER (D) 362 (Feb) (QBD) **[1:45]**; **[3:24]**; *Welsh v Messenger* [2006] CLY 2875 (Newcastle upon Tyne CC) **[1:208]**; **[3:68]**; *Gawler v Raettig* [2007] EWHC 373 (QB); [2007] All ER (D) 10 (Mar) **[1:247]**; **[3:78]**; *Taylor* (n 9) **[1:251]**; **[3:79]**; *Garth* (n 9) **[1:259]**; **[3:82]**; *Palmer v Kitley* [2008] EWHC 2819 (QB); [2008] All ER (D) 305 (Nov) **[1:313]**; **[3:107]**; *Stanton v Collinson* [2009] EWHC 342 (QB); [2009] All ER (D) 172 (Mar) **[1:322]**; **[3:112]**; *Hazlett v Robinson* [2014] NIQB 17 **[1:497]**; **[3:175]**; *Pearson v Anwar* [2015] EWCA Civ 1011 **[1:512]**; **[3:182]**.

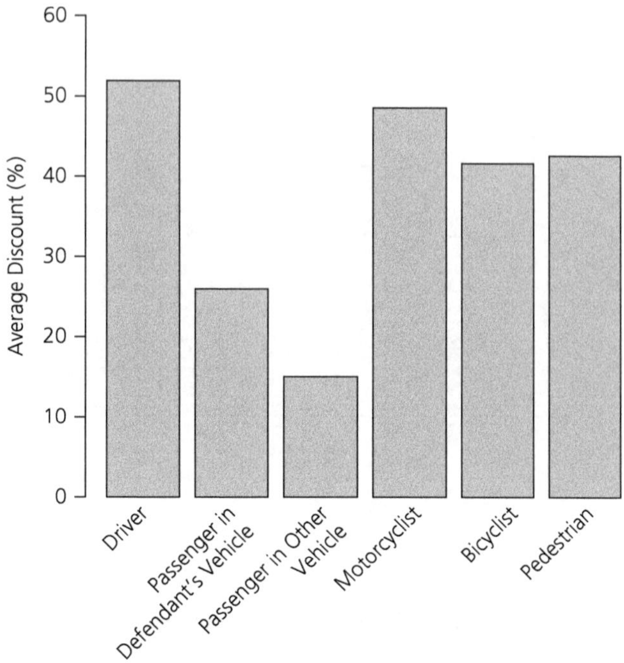

Figure 6.3 Average discount in road accident claims by claimant type

that these differences are very unlikely to be down to chance.[11] By category, the success rates were as follows: driver (45 per cent); passenger in defendant's vehicle (63 per cent); passenger in other vehicle (20 per cent); motorcyclist (59 per cent); bicyclist (64 per cent); and pedestrian (83 per cent). Note that relatively little weight should be placed on the low success rate in claims by passengers injured while travelling in a vehicle not driven by the defendant, since only five claims fell within this category.

Discount

6.04 The average discount across all road accident claims was 43 per cent, which is a little higher than the average discount of 40 per cent across all types of claim in the first instance dataset. Figure 6.3 shows the average discount by type of claimant in road accident claims. The average discount was broadly the same across all categories save for the two passenger groups. The average discounts were as follows: driver (52 per cent); passenger in defendant's vehicle (26 per cent); passenger in other vehicle (15 per cent); motorcyclist (49 per cent); bicyclist (42 per cent); and pedestrian (43 per cent). Statistical analysis suggests that these differences are

[11] Pearson's chi-square test, $p < 0.001$.

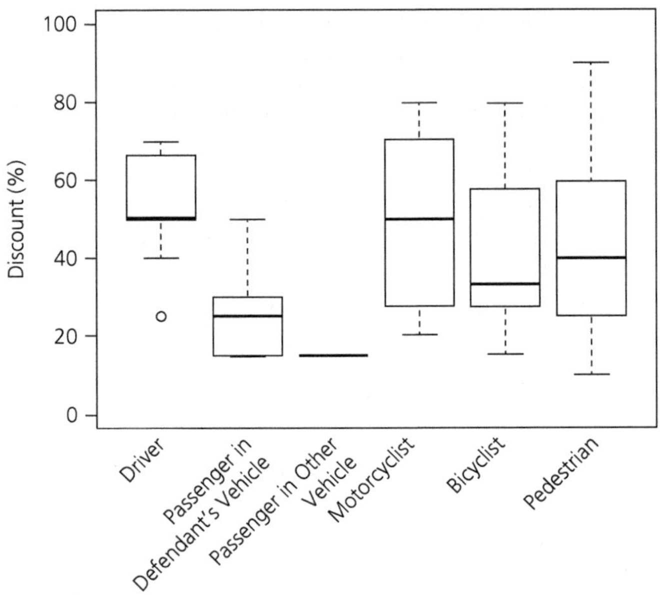

Figure 6.4 Discount in road accident claims by claimant type

very unlikely to be down to chance,[12] although when claims by passengers who were in the defendant's vehicle are excluded from the analysis, the probability that the remaining differences are attributable to chance is much higher.[13] That claims by passengers who were in the defendant's vehicle have an important effect on the analysis is unsurprising given that the average discount in that category of claim is so low relative to the other categories in which a meaningful number of findings of contributory negligence were made.

6.05 Figure 6.4 provides further detail as to the discount by claimant type. One interesting feature of the data revealed by Figure 6.4 is that there was much more variability in the discount where the claimant was a pedestrian than where the claimant was (in particular) a driver or passenger. This perhaps lends some weight to the complaint by a practitioner that it is 'often difficult to predict the likely apportionment' in claims by pedestrians.[14] Substantial variability in the discount is also apparent in relation to the motorcyclist and bicyclist categories. The discounts in the category of passengers in a vehicle not driven by the defendant exhibit no variability because the plea of contributory negligence succeeded in only one claim within that category.[15] It follows that little weight should be put on the average discount for this category.

[12] ANOVA, $p = 0.014$.
[13] ANOVA, $p = 0.198$.
[14] Daniel Dyal, 'Contributory Negligence in Pedestrian Road Traffic Accidents' [2018] JPIL 23, 23.
[15] *Garth* (n 9) **[1:259]**; **[3:82]**.

Table 6.1 Discounts in road accident claims

Number of claims	Discount (%)
24	50
14	25
13	33.3
12	20
10	66.6
9	40
8	15
7	80
7	60
7	30
5	75
3	10
2	70
2	55
1	90
1	85
1	65
1	45
1	35
1	12.5

6.06 Table 6.1 sets out all the discounts used in the road accident claims, Figure 6.5 shows the distribution of these discounts by discount range, and Figure 6.6 provides further detail as regards the distribution. The most popular discount by far was 50 per cent (which is consistent with the results of the first instance study generally[16]), and there was a marked preference for discounts falling between 20–29 per cent and 50–59 per cent. The lowest discount was 10 per cent (three claims),[17] and the highest was 90 per cent (one claim).[18] High discounts were less common than low discounts.

[16] See 4.20.

[17] *Sklair v Haycock* [2009] EWHC 3328 (QB); [2009] All ER (D) 159 (Dec) [**1:352**]; [**3:121**]; *McDermott v Pettit* [2011] EWHC 3074 (QB); [2011] All ER (D) 33 (Dec) [**1:420**]; [**3:148**]; *Low v Duncan* [2015] CSOH 133; 2015 Scot (D) 4/10 [**1:547**]; [**3:192**].

[18] *Jackson v Murray* [2012] CSOH 100; 2012 SCLR 605 [**1:432**]; [**3:155**]. On appeal to the Inner House, the discount was reduced to 70 per cent ([2012] CSIH 100; 2013 SLT 153), and the Supreme Court further reduced the discount to 50 per cent: [2015] UKSC 5; [2015] 2 All ER 805 [**2:124**].

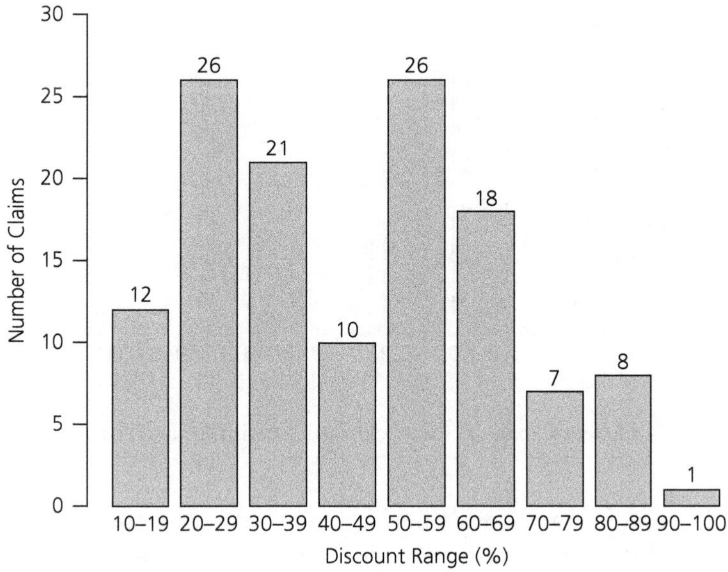

Figure 6.5 Number of road accident claims by discount range

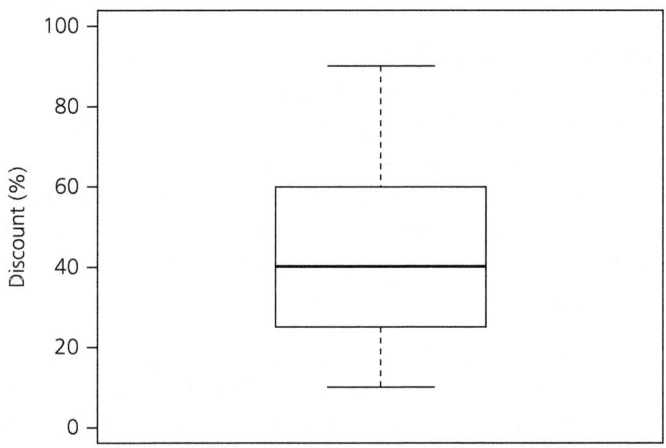

Figure 6.6 Discount in road accident claims

Claimant age

There were considerably more road accident claims in the first instance dataset by claimants aged between 10 and 19 years at the time of the accident than there were claims by claimants falling within all other age groups (Figure 6.7). 38 claims (33 per cent) of the 117 claims in which the age of the claimant could be ascertained involved claimants who fell within that band. This constitutes a noteworthy **6.07**

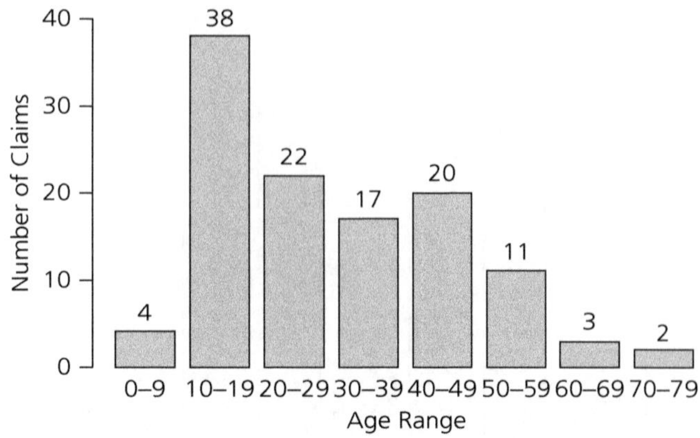

Figure 6.7 Number of road accident claims by claimant age range

respect in which road accident claims differ from claims in our first instance dataset generally. In the first instance dataset, the 10–19 age bracket contained 19 per cent of claims, and the most populous age bracket, 40–49 years, captured 24 per cent of claims.[19] This difference is probably largely due to the substantial number of employers' liability claims in the first instance dataset, in which the claimants were of course overwhelmingly adults.[20]

6.08 In interpreting the results regarding age, it is important to remember that in 82 of the road accident claims (41 per cent) the precise age of the claimant could not be ascertained. We might reasonably suppose that most if not all of these claims in fact involved adults, since it seems unlikely that a judge would fail to mention the age of a claimant who was under 18 at the time of the accident, not least because this might affect the contributory negligence analysis. There are therefore good grounds for thinking that the results significantly understate the number of claims that fell into the adult age brackets.

6.09 Where the claimant was a child, the success rate of the plea of contributory negligence was 77 per cent, whereas for adult claimants it was 63 per cent. Statistical analysis suggests that this difference may well be down to chance.[21] These results can be compared with the corresponding figures across all first instance claims, where the plea succeeded 69 per cent of the time where the claimant was a child and 59 per cent of the time where the claimant was an adult.[22] It would appear,

---

[19] See 4.24.

[20] Of the total employers' liability claims, just two involved claimants who were known to be children: see *M v Parsons* 2000 WL 33122496 (QBD) [1:5]; *Mosson v Spousal (London) Ltd* [2016] EWHC 53 (QB); [2016] 4 WLR 28 [1:553].

[21] Pearson's chi-square test, $p = 0.195$.

[22] See 4.25.

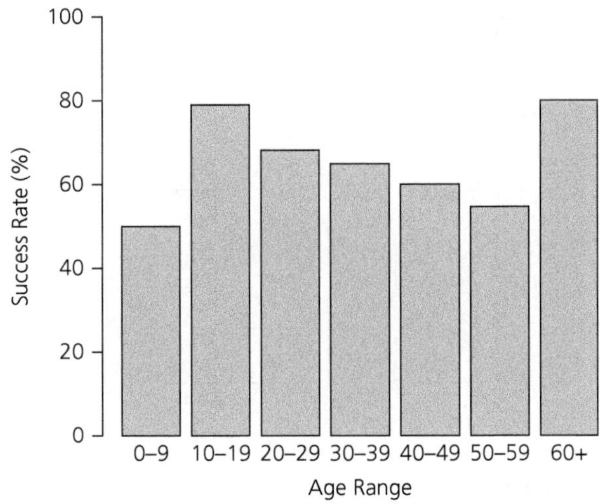

Figure 6.8 Success rate of plea in road accident claims by claimant age range

therefore, that the greater likelihood of a finding of contributory negligence against a child that is observable in first instance claims generally is even more marked in the road traffic context. The youngest claimant found guilty of contributory negligence in the road accident context was aged 9[23] and the oldest was aged 78.[24]

6.10 Figure 6.8 shows the success rate of the plea by claimant age range. The low success rate of the plea in the 0–9 age bracket (50 per cent) is unsurprising, although not much can be read into that result given that only four claims fell within that band.[25] The age ranges where the plea of contributory negligence was most likely to succeed in our sample were 60+ (80 per cent) and 10–19 (79 per cent), although, again, not much weight should be placed on the success rate for the former band since it was computed on the basis of just five claims.[26] These figures are considerably higher than the success rate across all road traffic claims (65 per cent) and all claims at first instance generally (58 per cent). Success rates in the remaining four age ranges were closer to the average discount across all road accident claims, as follows: 20–29 years, 68 per cent; 30–39 years, 65 per cent; 40–49 years, 60 per cent; and 50–59 years, 55 per cent.

[23] *AB v Main* [2015] EWHC 3183 (QB) [1:548]; [3:193].

[24] *Moreh v O'Neill* [2008] NIQB 28 [1:283]; [3:93].

[25] *Boardman v Ministry of Defence* (QBD, 12 November 2010) [1:379]; [3:130]; *Re Kelly v Nugent* [2011] NIQB 79 [1:396]; [3:138]; *Rehman v Brady* [2012] EWHC 78 (QB); [2012] All ER (D) 157 (Jan) [1:424]; [3:151]; *AB* (n 23) [1:548]; [3:193].

[26] *Gilfillan v Barbour* 2003 SLT 1127 (OH) [1:144]; [3:48]; *Maughan v Boylan* [2006] NIQB 38 [1:225]; [3:71]; *Welsh* (n 10) [1:208]; [3:68]; *Moreh* (n 24) [1:283]; [3:93]; *McCreery v Letson* [2015] CSOH 153; 2015 Scot (D) 6/11 [1:551]; [3:195].

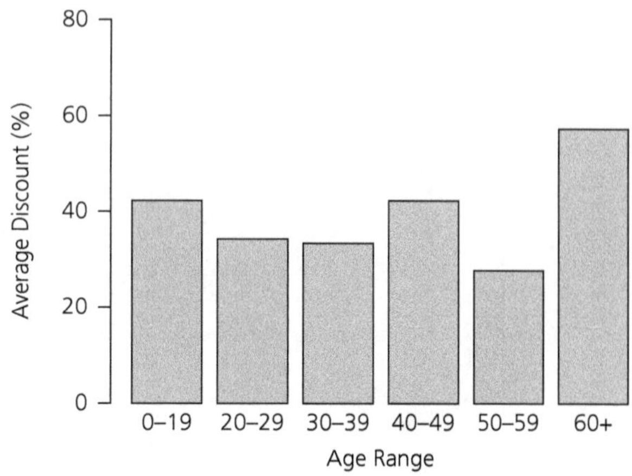

Figure 6.9 Average discount in road accident claims by claimant age range

6.11 As for the relationship between discount and age, the average discount was 42 per cent for children and 44 per cent for adults, which difference may well be attributable to chance[27] (the corresponding figures for all first instance claims were 41 per cent and 39 per cent, respectively). Figure 6.9 shows the average discount by claimant age range. The figures are as follows: 0–19 years, 42 per cent; 20–29 years, 34 per cent; 30–39 years, 33 per cent; 40–49 years, 42 per cent; 50–59 years, 28 per cent; and 60+ years, 58 per cent). In broad terms, therefore, the average discount was much the same across all age categories save for the 60+ category, where it was considerably higher than the average (although, as observed earlier, this result should be treated with caution, since there were very few claims in that category where a discount was imposed).

Frequently recurring types of contributory negligence

6.12 In road accident claims in our first instance dataset where the claimant was found guilty of contributory negligence, three acts of contributory negligence frequently recurred. These three frequently recurring acts accounted for 85 claims, some 66 per cent of the 129 road accident claims in which contributory negligence was established. The frequently recurring acts were: entering or remaining in the carriageway when it was unsafe to do so; speeding; and failing to wear a seat belt or helmet. A research assistant coded for claims falling within each of these categories. We included in the speeding category claims in which the court indicated that the claimant was driving too quickly in the circumstances

[27] Welch two-sample t-test, $p = 0.689$; Wilcoxon rank sum test with continuity correction, $p = 0.622$.

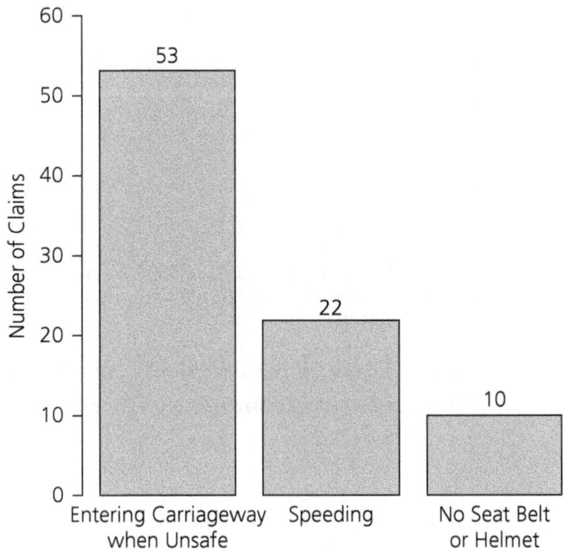

Figure 6.10 Number of road accident claims by frequently recurring act of contributory negligence

although the claimant was not driving in excess of the speed limit.[28] 'N/A' was entered where none of these codes was applicable (including because no contributory negligence was established). Figure 6.10 shows the number of claims falling within each of the three categories. The number of claims falling within the first category (53 claims) is not far short of the total number of claims in which pedestrians were found guilty of contributory negligence (58 claims), which suggests that the first frequently recurring act accounts for the vast majority of cases of pedestrian contributory negligence. The pedestrian claims where a finding of contributory negligence was made that did not involve entering or remaining in the carriageway when it was unsafe to do so included claims by pedestrians who were injured after climbing onto the bumper bar of a lorry,[29] walking between the rear of a trailer and the wall of a loading bay,[30] and standing too close to the edge of the carriageway.[31]

Figures 6.11 and 6.12 show the average discount by frequently recurring act of contributory negligence. The average discount where the claimant was a pedestrian **6.13**

---

28 See, eg, *Edwards v Jerman* [2004] CLY 2743 (Liverpool CC) [**1:149**]; [**3:52**].

29 *North v TNT Express (UK) Ltd* [2001] EWCA Civ 853; [2001] All ER (D) 358 (May) [**1:17**]; [**3:10**].

30 *Donaldson v Hays Distribution Services Ltd* [2007] CSOH 31 [**1:243**]; [**3:76**].

31 *Osei-Antwi v South East London & Kent Bus Co* [2010] EWCA Civ 132; [2010] All ER (D) 207 (Jan) [**1:332**]; [**2:92**]; [**3:116**].

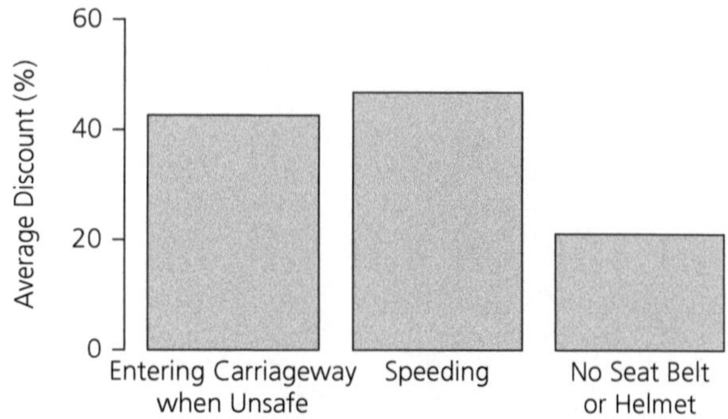

Figure 6.11 Average discount in road accident claims by frequently recurring act of contributory negligence

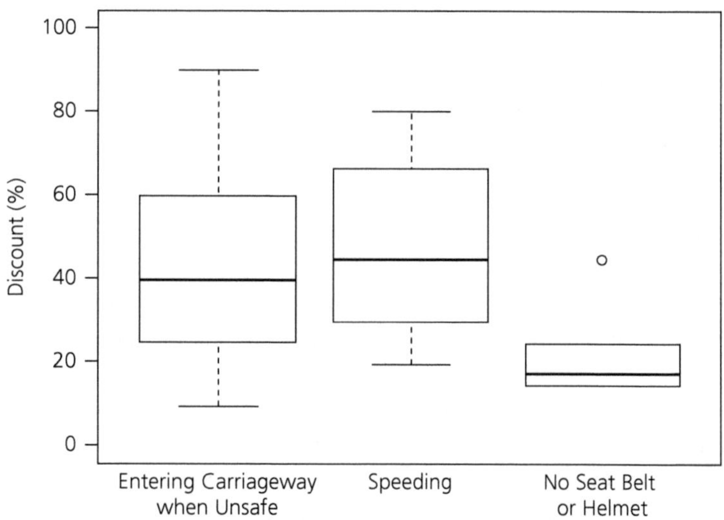

Figure 6.12 Discount in road accident claims by frequently recurring act of contributory negligence

who was injured after entering or remaining in the carriageway when it was unsafe to do so was 43 per cent. Contributory negligence in the form of speeding attracted an average discount of 48 per cent, and failing to wear a seat belt or helmet resulted in an average discount of 22 per cent. Claims involving a failure to use a seat belt or helmet are out of line with the other two categories both in relation to the average discount (which is markedly lower) and also because, as Figure 6.12 reveals, they exhibit much less variability in terms of the discount. Statistical analysis suggests that it is very unlikely that the differences in the average discount are attributable to chance.[32] These phenomena are of course due, at least in large part, to the guideline discounts that were propounded for seat belt cases in *Froom v Butcher*,[33] which have been extended by analogy to helmet cases.[34] We consider these guidelines and their impact in some detail below.[35]

Intoxication

6.14 Intoxication (on the part of either party) is often a matter on which the courts place emphasis when considering contributory negligence in a road accident case.[36] Accordingly, intoxication on the part of either party was one of the variables that we analysed. We instructed a research assistant to code for both the claimant and the defendant in road accident claims with the relevant categories being 'intoxicated' and 'not intoxicated'. A party was treated as being intoxicated whenever a finding was made by the court, explicitly or implicitly, that his or her ability to take reasonable care was impaired by alcohol consumption.[37] In 17 of the road accident claims in our first instance dataset, the claimant was intoxicated[38] (9 per cent) and in eight the defendant was intoxicated[39] (4 per cent). In only two claims (1 per cent)

---

32 ANOVA, $p = 0.004$.

33 [1978] QB 286 (CA).

34 'I see no reason to distinguish between seat belt cases and crash helmet cases and I would apply the dictum of Lord Denning [in *Froom v Butcher*] to crash helmets just as he spoke of it in seat belts': *Capps v Miller* [1989] 1 WLR 839 (CA) 847 (Croom-Johnson LJ); 'In my judgment the observations of Lord Denning MR [in *Froom v Butcher*] ... should apply to the wearing of helmets by cyclists': *Smith v Finch* [2009] EWHC 53; [2009] All ER (D) 158 (Jan) [44] (Griffith Williams J) **[1:318]**; **[3:111]**. For discussion, see Julian Fulbrook, 'Cycle Helmets and Contributory Negligence' [2004] JPIL 171.

35 See 6.17.

36 See, eg, *McDermott* (n 17) [15]–[16], [40] (Parker J) **[1:420]**; **[3:148]**; *McCaughey v Mullan* [2014] NIQB 132 [16] (O'Hara J) **[1:524]**; **[3:185]**.

37 For example, the defendant motorist in *Eagle* (n 2) **[1:102]**; **[2:49]**; **[3:36]** was classified as intoxicated despite his having a concentration of alcohol in his system that was less than the legal limit because he was found to have drunk a sufficient amount that his ability to drive was impaired (at [18]).

38 *Cook v Thorne* [2001] EWCA Civ 81; [2001] All ER (D) 142 (Jan) (two claims) **[1:11]**; **[1:12]**; **[2:16]**; **[2:17]**; **[3:7]**; **[3:8]**; *North* (n 29) **[1:17]**; **[3:10]**; *Currie v Clamp* 2002 SLT 196 (OH) **[1:44]**; **[3:23]**; *Lunt v Khelifa* [2001] All ER (D) 428 (Oct) (QBD) **[1:69]**; **[3:31]**; *Green* (n 2) **[1:122]**; **[2:55]**; **[3:40]**; *Booth v White* [2003] EWCA Civ 1708; (2003) 147 SJLB 1367 **[1:125]**; **[2:53]**; **[3:41]**; *Edwards v Jerman* (n 28) **[1:149]**; **[3:52]**; *Parkinson v Chief Constable of Dyfed Powys* [2004] EWCA Civ 802 **[1:157]**; **[3:54]**; *Dawes v Aldis* [2007] EWHC 1831 (QB); [2007] All ER (D) 451 (Jul) **[1:270]**; **[3:84]**; *Crew v Ash* [2008] EWHC 3068 (QB) **[1:315]**; **[3:109]**; *Sedge v Prime* [2011] EWHC 820 (QB) **[1:385]**; **[3:134]**; *Lightfoot v Go-Ahead Group Plc* [2011] EWHC 89 (QB); [2011] RTR 27 **[1:386]**; **[3:135]**; *Ayres v Odedra* [2013] EWHC 40 (QB); [2013] All ER (D) 114 (Jan) **[1:458]**; **[3:162]**; *MacLeod v Commissioner of the Police of the Metropolis* [2014] EWHC 977 (QB); [2014] All ER (D) 60 (Apr) **[1:501]**; **[3:177]**; *Smith v Bluebird Buses Ltd* [2014] CSOH 75; 2014 Rep LR 91 **[1:505]**; **[3:179]**; *McCaughey* (n 36) **[1:524]**; **[3:185]**.

39 *W* (n 10) **[1:40]**; **[3:22]**; *Currie* (n 38) **[1:44]**; **[3:23]**; *Eagle* (n 2) **[1:102]**; **[2:49]**; **[3:36]**; *Booth* (n 38) **[1:125]**; **[2:53]**; **[3:41]**; *Wakeling v McDonagh* [2007] EWHC 1201 (QB); [2007] All

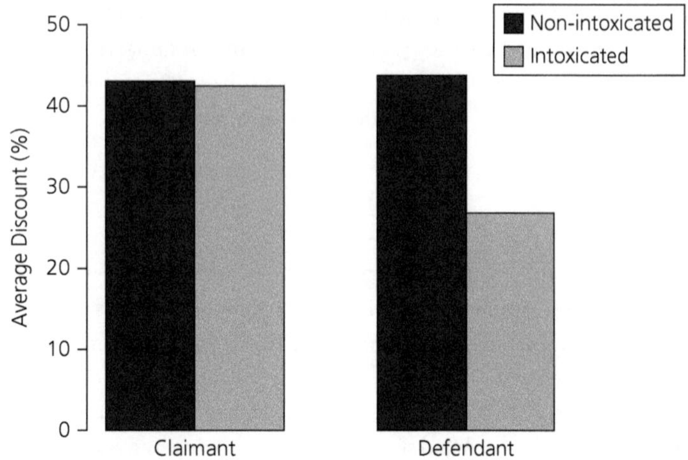

Figure 6.13 Average discount in road accident claims by party and intoxication

were both parties intoxicated.[40] The number of relevant claims is thus small, which diminishes the significance of the results. However, the results are nonetheless of some interest given the prominence that the courts professedly attach to the fact of intoxication.

6.15 The plea of contributory negligence was successful in 77 per cent of claims involving an intoxicated claimant and in 64 per cent of claims where the claimant was not intoxicated. However, this difference may well be attributable to chance.[41] Perhaps surprisingly, claimant intoxication had little effect on the average discount. Where the claimant was intoxicated, the average discount was 42 per cent, and where the claimant was not intoxicated, the average discount was very similar, at 43 per cent. Intoxication on the part of the defendant (which can be relevant to contributory negligence only for the purposes of determining the discount, rather than the success of the plea) presents a different picture. Where the defendant was intoxicated, the average discount was 27 per cent, but in claims where the defendant was not intoxicated it was 44 per cent. This difference is unlikely to be due to chance.[42] Figure 6.13 shows the average discounts by party depending on whether or not they were intoxicated.

ER (D) 455 (May) [**1:258**]; [**3:81**]; *Gleeson v Court* [2007] EWHC 2397 (QB); [2008] RTR 10 [**1:276**]; [**3:88**]; *Douglas v O'Neill* [2011] EWHC 601 (QB) [**1:389**]; [**3:136**]; *McDermott* (n 17) [**1:420**]; [**3:148**].

[40] *Currie* (n 38) [**1:44**]; [**3:23**]; *Booth* (n 38) [**1:125**]; [**2:53**]; [**3:41**].

[41] Pearson's chi-square test, $p = 0.432$.

[42] Welch two-sample *t*-test, $p = 0.079$; Wilcoxon rank sum test with continuity correction, $p = 0.041$.

Defendant's status

6.16 In 189 of the road accident claims (95 per cent), the defendant was driving a car. In the other ten claims (5 per cent), the defendant was either riding a motor cycle,[43] riding a bicycle,[44] or walking a dog.[45] It would be a mistake to place too much weight on the results that follow given the small number of claims in which the defendant was not driving a car. However, two points are nonetheless of interest. First, the success rate of the plea was higher where the defendant was driving a car (66 per cent) than where the defendant was not (38 per cent), although this difference may well be down to chance.[46] Second, the average discount was somewhat higher where the defendant was driving a car (43 per cent) than where the defendant was not (37 per cent). However, this difference may well also be attributable to chance.[47]

Discussion

Seat belts and helmets

6.17 In the landmark decision in *Froom*,[48] Lord Denning MR introduced guideline discounts for seat belt cases. The rule is that a 25 per cent discount should usually be imposed if a seat belt would have prevented the damage altogether, and a 15 per cent discount if using a seat belt would merely have reduced the damage. The same discounts have been adopted in helmet cases.[49] It is clear from Lord Denning's reasons that he propounded these guidelines with a view to reducing the amount of litigation regarding the appropriate discount in seat belt cases.[50] Our results suggest that Lord Denning's efforts have enjoyed a certain amount of success. Of the 199 road accident claims, there were only 12 concerning seat belts[51] and three

---

[43] *Beckley v Crowther* 2000 WL 1544758 (QBD) [1:23]; [3:13]; *Askey v Wood* [2005] EWCA Civ 574; (2005) 149 SJLB 514 [1:166]; [2:68]; [3:56]; *Pesenti v London General Transport Services Ltd* [2006] CLY 2903 (Clerkenwell CC) [1:176]; [3:61]; *Greenwood v Cummings* (QBD, 9 April 2008) [1:286]; [3:95]; *Heaton v Herzog* [2008] EWCA Civ 1636; [2009] RTR 30 [1:288]; [2:83]; [3:96]; *Smith v Finch* (n 34) [1:318]; [3:111]; *Devereux* (n 6) [1:417]; [3:147].

[44] *Brown v Brent* (Croydon CC, 21 June 2011) (cyclist) [1:407]; [3:145].

[45] *Swinton v Annabel's (Berkeley Square) Ltd* [2005] CLY 2842 (Lambeth CC) [1:170]; [3:59]; *Sandison v Coope* 2016 Rep LR 70 (Tayside, Central and Fife Sheriff Court) [1:554]; [3:196].

[46] Pearson's chi-square test, $p = 0.178$.

[47] Welch two-sample *t*-test, $p = 0.230$; Wilcoxon rank sum test with continuity correction, $p = 0.662$.

[48] (n 33).

[49] See the authorities cited in n 34.

[50] 'This question should not be prolonged by an expensive inquiry into the degree of blameworthiness on either side, which would be hotly disputed': *Froom* (n 33) 296 (Lord Denning MR).

[51] *Mattar* (n 10) [1:45]; [3:24]; *W* (n 10) [1:40]; [3:22]; *Welsh* (n 10) [1:208]; [3:68]; *Al Gouri* (n 5) [1:234]; [3:75]; *Garth* (n 9) [1:259]; [3:82]; *Gawler* (n 10) [1:247]; [3:78]; *Taylor* (n 9)

concerning helmets,[52] although the low numbers of such claims is, of course, likely to be due at least in part to increased seat belt[53] and (presumably) helmet[54] use since *Froom* was decided.

6.18 The *Froom* guidelines were followed in all the seat belt claims in our first instance dataset except *Hazlett v Robinson*, which is a decision from Northern Ireland. In that case, a 20 per cent discount was imposed, with the trial judge remarking that the injuries would have been 'very [much] less severe' had a seat belt been used.[55] Contributory negligence was established in only one helmet claim, *McCracken v Smith,* and the discount imposed was 45 per cent.[56] That discount was chosen because the claimant had not only failed to wear a helmet but had travelled as a pillion passenger on a stolen trail bike that was not designed to carry pillion passengers and in circumstances where he knew that the driver was likely to speed.[57] On appeal, the discount was increased to 65 per cent.[58]

6.19 *Froom* strongly encourages the courts to find contributory negligence where the claimant failed to wear a seat belt, provided that that failure was causally linked to the damage.[59] Our results suggest that judges follow this steer. There were only two claims in our first instance dataset in which a failure to wear a seat belt did not constitute contributory negligence, despite there being no apparent issue as to causal relevance. In the first of these, *Welsh v Messenger*,[60] the claimant had been travelling on a coach at the time of the accident. The court emphasized that the accident had happened in 2002, at which time there was no legal requirement to use a seat belt on coaches, although it was mandatory for coaches to be fitted with seat belts. In the second claim, *Taylor v Rashid*,[61] the claimant had not worn a seat

---

[1:251]; [3:79]; *Palmer* (n 10) [1:313]; [3:107]; *Stanton* (n 10) [1:322]; [3:112]; *Edwards v Martin* (n 5) [1:360]; [3:123]; *Hazlett* (n 10) [1:497]; [3:175]; *Pearson* (n 10) [1:497]; [3:175].

52 *Swinton* (n 45) [1:170]; [3:59]; *Smith v Finch* (n 34) [1:318]; [3:111]; *McCracken* (n 8) [1:491]; [3:171].

53 Statistics on seat belt use in the United Kingdom prior to 1999 are difficult to find. However, a Department of Transport survey records increasing seat belt during the period 1999–2014 in England and Scotland, especially among passengers: Department of Transport, *Seat Belt and Mobile Phone Use Surveys: England and Scotland, 2014* (2015) <https://assets.publishing.service.gov.uk/government/uploads/system/uploads/attachment_data/file/406723/seatbelt-and-mobile-use-surveys-2014.pdf> (accessed 3 November 2018).

54 According to a report commissioned by the Department of Transport, '[b]icycle helmet wearing rates in Great Britain have increased steadily in the last decade': Elizabeth Towner et al, *Bicycle Helmets: Review of Effectiveness (No 30)* (Department of Transport 2002) 6.

55 (n 10) [53] (Gillen J) [1:497]; [3:175].

56 (n 8) [1:491]; [3:171].

57 Ibid, [83] (Keith J).

58 *McCracken v Smith* [2015] EWCA Civ 380; [2016] Lloyd's Rep IR 171 [2:125].

59 '[I]n the ordinary way a person who fails to wear a seat belt should accept some share of responsibility for the damage—if it could have been prevented or lessened by wearing it': *Froom* (n 33) 295 (Lord Denning MR).

60 (n 10) [1:208]; [3:68].

61 (n 9) [1:251]; [3:79].

belt while a passenger in a taxi. The plea of contributory negligence failed because the defendant did not adduce any evidence that a working seat belt was available save for an admission by the claimant in cross-examination that there may have been one. One suspects that the court may have decided the point differently but for the fact that the defendant amended his pleading just five weeks before the trial to allege contributory negligence. It is also worth noting that there was only one claim in the dataset in which the court rejected the plea of contributory negligence because the defendant had failed to prove that the claimant's injuries would have been any less had a seat belt been worn.[62]

6.20 It is unclear whether the courts regard failure to use seat belts and helmets differently when it comes to making findings of contributory negligence, although it would not be surprising if they did in circumstances where at least bicyclists are not required to use helmets. Of the three helmet claims in our first instance dataset, the claimant was acquitted of contributory negligence in two of them. In one of these claims, *Swinton v Annabel's (Berkeley Square) Ltd*,[63] the court said that a bicyclist who had been injured while cycling in a London park would have been acting over-cautiously if he had used a helmet. In the other, *Smith v Finch*, it was held that the failure of a bicyclist to wear a helmet was not causally relevant.[64] The third helmet claim, *McCracken*, has already been discussed.[65] In that case, the parties agreed that the claimant's failure to wear a helmet constituted contributory negligence.[66]

Intoxication

6.21 In *Best v Smyth*,[67] Tugendhat J wrote that, since *Owens v Brimmell*,[68] 'the figure of 20% is commonly regarded as the appropriate reduction for a claimant who has got into a vehicle when he must have known that the driver had had too much to drink'.[69] Our study suggests otherwise. There were only three claims in our dataset in which the claimant was found to be guilty of contributory negligence in accepting a ride from an intoxicated driver. In the first of those claims,[70] a discount of 15 per cent was imposed, although it is unclear why the judge arrived at that figure, as the full text of the judge's reasons is not available. In the second, the discount was 33.3 per cent.[71] It was held that the pursuer either knew or ought to have known

---

62 *Stanton* (n 10) [1:322]; [3:112].
63 (n 45) [1:170]; [3:59].
64 (n 34) [1:318]; [3:111].
65 See 6.18.
66 (n 8) [2] [1:491]; [3:171].
67 [2010] EWHC 1541 (QB); [2010] All ER (D) 210 (Jun) [12].
68 [1977] QB 859 (QBD).
69 See also, Christopher Kennedy and Matthew Snarr, 'Intoxication and Inebriation: Another Late Night' [2015] JPIL 84, 90 ('[a] discount of 20 per cent is likely to be seen as a benchmark').
70 *W* (n 10) [1:40]; [3:22].
71 *Currie* (n 38) [1:44]; [3:23].

that the driver was 'heavily intoxicated' and 'clearly unfit to drive'.[72] The judge specifically considered *Owens* but insisted that '[e]ach case … must be decided on its own facts'.[73] In the third claim, damages were reduced by 30 per cent.[74] In that case, the claimant knew that the defendant driver was sufficiently affected by drink that he should not be driving and had also agreed to be carried in the boot of the car. Judge Foster QC said that he could not see 'any convincing reason why the figure of 20 per cent in *Owens v Brimmell* … should not be adopted'[75] had the contributory negligence lain only in accepting a ride from the intoxicated defendant. He also said that had the only act of contributory fault been travelling in the boot, there would have been 'no reason to depart from the conventional figure of 25 per cent' propounded in *Froom*.[76] Judge Foster QC considered that simply combining the figures of 20 per cent and 25 per cent would have amounted to double-counting, since both acts of contributory negligence 'flow[ed] from [the claimant's] impaired decision making',[77] and it was in these circumstances that he settled on the overall figure of 30 per cent.

Pedestrians

6.22 The plea of contributory negligence succeeds more often against pedestrians than against any other type of claimant in the road accident context. Moreover, at 83 per cent, the success rate of the plea in pedestrian claims is very high compared with the success rate of 65 per cent in road accident claims generally, and 58 per cent across all types of claim. One possible explanation for this result lies in the fact that pedestrians will frequently have had some ability to avoid the accident altogether by, for example, looking out for oncoming vehicles.[78] By contrast, this will not so often be the case in relation to other types of claimants, such as car drivers and motorcyclists, who may more easily be able to persuade the court that they were in no way responsible for what happened.

6.23 Turning to the discount, judges routinely remark that, as between motorists and pedestrians, the law tends to assign a greater share of the responsibility for the damage to the former. For example, in *Jackson v Murray*, Lord Reed said that '[t]he trend of the case law is to attribute more responsibility to the driver than to a pedestrian'. He added that this 'principle' exists in 'recognition of the moral

---

72 Ibid, [22] (Lord Clarke).
73 Ibid.
74 *Gleeson* (n 39) [1:276]; [3:88].
75 Ibid, [22].
76 Ibid, [25].
77 Ibid, [26].
78 One practitioner puts the point in the following way: 'in the overwhelming majority of cases it is arguable that there is something the pedestrian could reasonably have done to avoid the accident': Dyal (n 14) 23.

blameworthiness or, alternatively, the causative potency of driving a motor vehicle without exercising reasonable care, because a vehicle can be a dangerous weapon'.[79] Similar claims have also been made by commentators.[80] As the average discount in claims by pedestrians is 43 per cent, our results suggest that typically the courts do indeed regard drivers as more responsible than pedestrians, although not fundamentally more so. However, pedestrians as a category of claimant are not treated leniently in relation to the discount, since the average discount across all claimant categories is also 43 per cent.

There are several cases in the dataset where the 'dangerous weapon' principle was applied in apportioning responsibility between drivers and road users other than pedestrians. In *Russell v Smith*,[81] for example, the judge found that the claimant cyclist, a child of 10, was three-quarters to blame for the accident in which he was injured, but imposed a discount of only 50 per cent in part because he was a vulnerable road user. Similarly, in *Jones v Lawton*[82] the fact that the claimant was a motorcyclist who had collided with a car was taken into account when apportioning responsibility one-third to two-thirds in his favour, and in *Stoddart v Perucca*[83] a car driver's fault was considered to be more causatively potent than that of a horse rider on the basis of the 'dangerous weapon' principle. **6.24**

Judges also often claim that '[i]t is rare indeed for a pedestrian to be found more responsible than a driver unless the pedestrian has suddenly moved into the path of an oncoming vehicle'.[84] The thinking underpinning this proposition is that although a driver will normally be more responsible than a pedestrian because he or she created an asymmetrical risk of serious injury, where a pedestrian moved suddenly in front of a vehicle, 'the more direct and immediate cause of the damage can be said to be the conduct of the pedestrian, which interrupted a situation in which an accident would not otherwise have occurred'.[85] Is this claim borne out **6.25**

---

[79] [2015] (n 18) [50] **[2:124]**. For similar remarks, see *Lunt v Khelifa* [2002] EWCA Civ 801 [20] (Latham LJ), [25] (Brooke LJ) **[2:36]**; *Eagle* (n 2) [15] (Hale LJ) **[1:102]**; **[2:49]**; **[3:36]**; *Pankhurst v White* [2006] EWHC 2093 (Admin); [2006] All ER (D) 308 (Jun) [21]–[22] (Wilkie J) **[1:228]**; **[3:73]**; *Sahakian v McDonnell* [2007] EWHC 3242 (QB); [2008] RTR 19 [18] (Judge Foster QC) **[1:274]**; **[3:87]**; *Stewart v Glaze* [2009] EWHC 704 (QB); [2009] All ER (D) 112 (Apr) [92] (Coulson J); *Toropdar v D* [2009] EWHC 2997 (TCC); [2009] All ER (D) 129 (Dec) [42] (Christopher Clarke J) **[1:344]**; **[3:119]**; *Smith v Chief Constable of Nottinghamshire* [2012] EWCA Civ 161; [2012] RTR 23 [54] (Ward LJ) **[1:383]**; **[2:108]**; **[3:133]**; *Hickman v London Central Bus Co Ltd* [2013] EWHC 1703 (QB); [2013] All ER (D) 272 (Jun) [70] (Sir Robert Nelson) **[1:472]**; **[3:166]**; *Wormald v Ahmed* [2014] EWHC 4498 (QB) [23] (HHJ Forster QC) **[1:519]**; **[3:184]**.

[80] See, eg, Christian Witting, *Street on Torts* (15th edn, OUP 2018) 194.

[81] [2003] EWHC 2060 (QB) **[1:140]**; **[3:46]**.

[82] [2013] EWHC 4108 (QB); [2013] All ER (D) 233 (Dec) **[1:494]**; **[3:172]**.

[83] (n 6) **[1:362]**; **[2:101]**; **[3:124]**.

[84] *Eagle* (n 2) [16] (Hale LJ) **[1:102]**; **[2:49]**; **[3:36]**. In *Callier v Deacon* [2009] EWHC 245 (QB); [2009] All ER (D) 71 (Jan) [25] **[1:317]**; **[3:110]**, HHJ McKenna doubted that Hale LJ was seeking to lay down a definite rule in this regard.

[85] *Jackson* [2015] (n 18) [40] (Lord Reed) **[2:124]**.

by the results of our study? In 58 of the 70 claims by pedestrians in our first instance dataset, the claimant was found guilty of contributory negligence. In 15 of those 58 claims, a discount of greater than 50 per cent was imposed, and in 33 the discount was less than 50 per cent. Of the 15 claims which involved a discount greater than 50 per cent, in two of them the defendant was acquitted of negligence on appeal,[86] and in two of them the discount was reduced by a higher court to 50 per cent or less.[87] Of the remaining 11 claims, seven of them involved a claimant who had moved into the carriageway in a hurry or who the defendant had little opportunity to see before the accident.[88] The other four claims did not. In three of them the claimants had lain drunk in the carriageway,[89] walked down the middle of the carriageway while intoxicated,[90] and allowed a rear door of a vehicle to swing into the carriageway, respectively.[91] The final claim concerned a claimant who had walked into the carriageway and was 'at least 11 feet out from the side of the pavement'[92] when he was struck by the defendant's vehicle. Speaking broadly, these results at least support the proposition that discounts greater than 50 per cent are unusual in pedestrian claims, although they also suggest that it is not entirely right to say that they are 'rare' except where the claimant moved suddenly into the carriageway.[93]

Drivers

6.26 Figure 6.4 reveals that the discounts in claims by drivers of cars were relatively homogenous compared with the discounts imposed in claims by most of the other categories of claimant. If three outlier discounts of 25 per cent are disregarded,[94]

---

[86] *North* (n 29) [1:17]; [3:10]; *B (a child) v Wynn* [2001] EWCA Civ 710; [2001] All ER (D) 148 (May) [1:36]; [3:19].

[87] *Eagle* (n 2) (60 per cent to 40 per cent) [1:102]; [2:49]; [3:36]; *Jackson* [2015] (n 18) (90 per cent to 50 per cent) [2:124].

[88] *Pritchard v Ralph* [2001] All ER (D) 1721 (QBD) [1:3]; [3:3]; *Futter v Bryceland* 2000 GWD 9-339 (OH) [1:9]; [3:5]; *Ehrari (a child) v Curry* [2006] EWHC 1319 (QB); [2006] All ER (D) 61 (Jun) [1:227]; [3:72]; *Belka v Prosperini* [2011] EWCA Civ 623; [2011] All ER (D) 263 (May) [1:373]; [2:129]; [3:129]; *Smith v Chief Constable of Nottinghamshire* (n 79) [1:383]; [2:108]; [3:133]; *Smith v Bluebird Buses* (n 38) [1:505]; [3:179]; *Glass v Donnelly* [2016] NIQB 36 [1:556]; [3:197].

[89] *Green* (n 2) [1:122]; [2:55]; [3:40].

[90] *McCaughey* (n 36) [1:524]; [3:185].

[91] *Brown v First Glasgow Ltd* [2012] CSOH 192; 2013 GWD 2-8 [1:452]; [3:161].

[92] *Maughan* (n 26) [13] (Morgan J) [1:225]; [3:71].

[93] See also *Callier* (n 84) [1:317]; [3:110], where a discount of 55 per cent was made for the contributory negligence of a teenage cyclist hit by a car while stationary at the side of the road at night. Considerations taken into account in this case in apportioning the bulk of responsibility to the claimant included the fact that he was wearing dark clothing, that both the bicycle and the road were unlit, and that he had failed to pay any proper attention to oncoming traffic.

[94] *Edwards v Jerman* (n 28) [1:149]; [3:52]; *Don v Eastern Holdings Ltd* (Edinburgh Sheriff Court, 18 June 2018) [1:297]; [3:101]; *Meaney v Link Rider Coaches Ltd* (Bournemouth CC, 21 June 2012) [1:433]; [3:156].

the lowest discount was 40 per cent[95] and the highest 70 per cent,[96] yielding a range of just 30 per cent. Furthermore, almost three-quarters of the discounts fell within the range of 50 per cent to 66.6 per cent. In addition to the fact that the discounts imposed on drivers are tightly clustered, the discounts converge, approximately, at the level of 50 per cent. These twin features of the data may well be closely related to each other. One possible explanation for both phenomena lies in the fact that car drivers, unlike all other categories of claimant in the road traffic context, will often pose at least roughly symmetrical risks of injury to defendants, almost all of whom in our first instance dataset were also car drivers. In these circumstances, it is unsurprising that where the claimant is a driver the courts often see the responsibility of both parties as being essentially equal. Indeed, it may be a matter of luck whether a driver who is involved in accident is the claimant or defendant. Counterclaims in proceedings between drivers are likely and it is often simply a matter of which party sues first that determines who is the claimant and who the defendant.

Conclusion

The most interesting findings that emerge from our study with regard to road accident claims are as follows: **6.27**

1. The success rate of the plea of contributory negligence was 65 per cent in road accident cases, and the average discount was 43 per cent.
2. The average discount was broadly the same across all categories of road user claimant save for the two passenger groups, where it was markedly lower. There was considerably more variability in the discount where the claimant was a pedestrian than where the claimant was a driver or passenger.
3. By far the most popular discount was 50 per cent, and there was a marked preference for discounts falling between 20–29 per cent and 50–59 per cent.
4. Where the claimant was a child, the success rate of the plea of contributory negligence was 77 per cent, whereas for adult claimants it was 63 per cent. This disparity is slightly greater than the equivalent disparity observable in first instance claims generally. By contrast, the average discount in road accident claims was 42 per cent for children and 47 per cent for adults.
5. The *Froom v Butcher* guidelines for seat belt claims were regularly followed. Although they have been extended by analogy to helmet claims, there were insufficient claims for it to be ascertained whether the guidelines are also adhered to in that context.
6. The courts seem not to stick to the guideline discount traceable to *Owens v Brimmell* that is said to apply where the claimant accepted a lift from an

[95] *Gray v Gibson* [2014] EWCA Civ 355; [2014] All ER (D) 35 (Mar) [1:467]; [2:122]; [3:165].
[96] *Ievers v Prebble* [2010] EWCA Civ 1615; [2010] All ER (D) 265 (Oct) [1:346]; [3:120].

intoxicated driver. More generally, the defendant's intoxication is associated with low discounts whereas it seems that the courts assign relatively little weight to intoxication of the claimant both in terms of the success of the plea of contributory negligence and the discount.

7. Three frequently recurring acts accounted for 66 per cent of the findings of contributory negligence in road accident claims: entering or remaining in the carriageway when it was unsafe to do so; speeding; and failing to wear a seat belt or helmet.
8. In claims by pedestrians against drivers of cars, the courts tend to regard the driver as more responsible than the pedestrian for the damage, although only marginally so. Relatedly, while our study bears out the proposition that it is unusual in such a case for a driver to be held more responsible than a pedestrian, it is not entirely correct to say that pedestrians are rarely held more responsible than drivers unless they moved suddenly into the carriageway.

7

CONTRIBUTORY NEGLIGENCE AT WORK

Introduction

7.01 This chapter explores how the courts apply the contributory negligence doctrine in the context of accidents at work. Extended treatment of this setting is justified by two main considerations. The first is that employers' liability claims were the second most numerous in our first instance dataset, after road accident claims.[1] The second is that, as with the road accident context, there are reasons to believe that this is a setting in which the contributory negligence doctrine may operate in a distinctive way. In particular, both judges and commentators have argued that there are features of many employers' liability cases that may justify the courts in treating claimants relatively leniently in this context.[2]

7.02 In the first section of the chapter, we report the results of our first instance and appellate studies in so far as they pertain to decisions on contributory negligence in employers' liability claims. Thereafter, we discuss these results in the light of qualitative analysis of the employers' liability case law in our appellate dataset, along with the existing literature on the operation of contributory negligence in this context. It should be noted that the claims that are considered in this chapter are those where the defendant was sued in their capacity as the claimant's employer, and that we extended this concept of 'employers' liability' to relationships akin to employment, such as that between a police officer and his or her Chief Constable.[3]

Results

7.03 We begin by setting out some general information about employers' liability claims in the first instance and appellate datasets, and then proceed to the

---

[1] See 4.04.

[2] See 7.20–7.36.

[3] See, eg, *Lennon v Commissioner of Police of the Metropolis* [2004] EWCA Civ 130; [2004] ICR 1114 [**1:132**] (police officer suing Metropolitan Police Commissioner for failing to give advice about preservation of housing allowance entitlement).

findings. We divide our discussion of the findings into four parts: general information about the first instance claims; the success rate of the plea and discount at first instance; frequently recurring types of contributory negligence at first instance; and the appellate claims. As in other chapters, our primary aim in the results section is simply to present the findings of the study, although we do also make some observations about their importance. Fuller discussion of key findings in the light of the case law and literature is postponed until the following section.

General information about first instance claims

7.04 We saw above[4] that the 155 employers' liability claims make up over a quarter (27 per cent) of the total number of 572 claims in our first instance dataset. This is a much higher percentage than the percentage of all personal injury claims in the period 2010–2016 that were classified by the Compensation Recovery Unit as employers' liability claims (9 per cent),[5] and we put forward some possible explanations for this disparity above.[6] Whatever the explanation for the relatively high proportion of employers' liability claims in the dataset may be, it is clear that this is a context in which contributory negligence is pleaded very frequently, and of considerable practical significance.

7.05 All but one of the employers' liability claims at first instance were for personal injury. The exception, *Lennon v Commissioner of Police of the Metropolis*,[7] was a pure economic loss claim in which the defendant had negligently failed to advise the claimant about the preservation of his housing allowance entitlement. The plea of contributory negligence failed. Of the personal injury claims, all but two were for physical injury, with the two exceptions being claims for psychiatric harm caused by stress at work.[8] Again, in neither of these claims was a finding of contributory negligence made.

7.06 86 of the employers' liability claims in the first instance dataset were from England and Wales (56 per cent), 12 from Northern Ireland (8 per cent), and 57 from Scotland (37 per cent). Compared with the first instance dataset as a whole, where Scottish claims accounted for 22 per cent of all claims, the proportion of employers' liability claims heard by a Scottish court was relatively high. Of

---

[4] See 4.04.

[5] The total number of personal injury claims registered with the Compensation Recovery Unit ('CRU') in the period 2010–2016 was 6,073,324, of which 555,122 were classified as employers' liability claims: see <https://www.gov.uk/government/publications/compensation-recovery-unit-performance-data> (accessed 4 November 2018).

[6] See 4.05.

[7] (n 3) [1:132].

[8] *Rowntree v Commissioner of the Police of the Metropolis* (QBD, 26 October 2001) [1:67]; *Young v Post Office* [2002] EWCA Civ 661; [2002] IRLR 660 [1:56]; [2:33].

the claims from England and Wales, 47 of the claims were from county courts (55 per cent) and 39 were from the High Court (45 per cent). All 12 claims from Northern Ireland were decided by the High Court of Justice, and 51 of the Scottish claims (89 per cent) were decided by the Outer House of the Court of Session, with the remaining six claims being decided by Sheriffs' courts. In total, therefore, 102 of the first instance claims (66 per cent) were decided by the High Court or an equivalent court, and 53 claims (34 per cent) by a county court or an equivalent court.

119 of the claims in the employers' liability category were brought by men (77 per cent), and 36 by women (23 per cent). As we saw above,[9] in the first instance dataset as a whole, men accounted for 72 per cent of the claims brought by a human claimant where it was possible to discern the claimant's gender, and women for the remaining 28 per cent of such claims. Hence, while male claimants were over-represented in the claims in the employers' liability category, the disparity was not particularly marked when compared with the gender balance in the first instance dataset as a whole. As for age, unsurprisingly there were only two claims in this category which were brought by claimants who were aged under 18 at the relevant time, in one of which a 14-year-old girl had been injured on a paper round,[10] and in the other of which the claimant had been exposed to asbestos by an employer between the ages of 15 and 16, some 40 years before the action was heard.[11] The oldest claimant in the first instance dataset was a school caretaker who was injured when he fell off a stepladder at the age of 68.[12] **7.07**

Success rate of the plea and discount at first instance

We saw above[13] that in the 572 claims in our first instance dataset, the plea of contributory negligence succeeded in 58 per cent of claims and failed in 42 per cent. When we broke down the success rate of the plea by claim type, the success rate of the plea of contributory negligence in employers' liability claims was 60 per cent,[14] which is very close to the success rate of the plea across all claim types at first instance in our study. **7.08**

We also observed that, in the claims in the first instance dataset, the average amount by which the claimant's damages were reduced was 40 per cent.[15] The average discount in employers' liability claims (32 per cent) was some way **7.09**

---

[9] See 4.29.
[10] *M v Parsons* (QBD, 10 February 2000) [1:6].
[11] *Mosson v Spousal (London) Ltd* [2016] EWHC 53 (QB); [2016] 4 WLR 2 [1:553].
[12] *Gower-Smith v Hampshire CC* (Southampton CC, 27 June 2008) [1:299].
[13] See 4.07, 4.33.
[14] See 4.09.
[15] See 4.12.

Table 7.1 Discounts in employers' liability claims

Number of claims	Discount (%)
21	20
18	25
16	50
13	33.3
6	10
4	40
4	15
3	60
3	30
2	90
2	75
1	35

below this, and indeed the lowest average discount in any contextual category.[16] Furthermore, we saw that the disparities between the average discount in employers' liability claims and the average discounts in road accident claims (43 per cent) and in occupiers' liability claims (47 per cent) were extremely unlikely to be down to chance.[17] Our study therefore suggests that, while the courts are just as likely to make a finding of contributory negligence in an employers' liability claim as in other types of claim, when they do so they tend to impose a relatively low discount.

7.10 Our study also reveals important information about the range and frequency of discounts used by the courts in employers' liability claims. Table 7.1 sets out the discounts in the 93 employers' liability claims in the first instance dataset in which a discount was imposed, Figure 7.1 shows the distribution of these discounts by discount range, and Figure 7.2 provides further detail as regards the distribution. Table 7.1 reveals that the lowest discount was 10 per cent (six claims), while the highest was 90 per cent (two claims). The most frequently observed discount was 20 per cent (21 claims). There were only seven employers' liability claims in which a discount greater than 50 per cent was imposed, a mere 8 per cent of the claims where a finding of contributory negligence was made. Furthermore, while 50 per cent was by far the most popular in the first instance dataset as a whole,[18] in this

[16] See 4.15.
[17] See ibid.
[18] See 4.20.

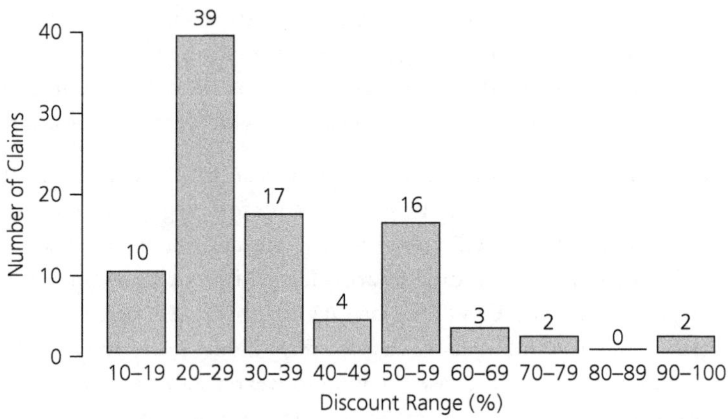

Figure 7.1 Number of employers' liability claims by discount range

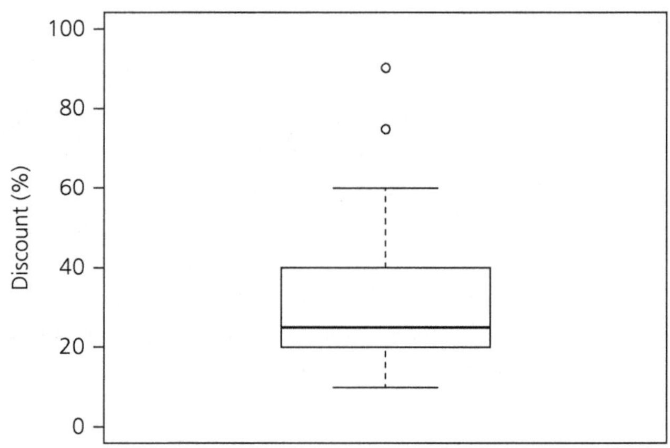

Figure 7.2 Discount in employers' liability claims

setting it was only the third most frequently imposed discount, after 20 per cent and 25 per cent.

Frequently recurring types of contributory negligence

Several forms of contributory negligence frequently recurred in the employers' liability claims in our first instance dataset where the claimant was found guilty of contributory negligence. These frequently recurring forms of contributory fault included: slip-and-fall accidents in the workplace; carelessness in connection with work equipment; carelessness in or while working at height; dangerous lifting; and smoking (where the claim was based on occupational asbestos exposure). In the companion volume to this work we consider the first three of these categories of **7.11** recurrent contributory negligence in some detail, as these were the most commonly occurring types of contributory negligence observed in the employers' liability context.[19] We also list in that work several claims in which the other two recurrent acts featured, although the claims in these two categories were less numerous.[20]

7.12 Examples of contributory negligence in the employers' liability context that fell outside these five frequently occurring types of contributory negligence included: carelessness while driving a vehicle;[21] failing to take precautions against being hit by a vehicle in the workplace;[22] standing at arms-length from a heavy raised load and trying to dislodge the load by pulling or tugging at it;[23] self-exposure to asbestos during a period of self-employment as a plasterer;[24] diving into a river from a bridge while on a military training exercise;[25] failing to wear a stab-proof vest;[26] failing to have regard to the obvious risk of malaria while working abroad;[27] and failing to wear an oven glove and properly to take note of the instructions on a ready-meal container.[28]

The appellate claims

7.13 Of the 129 claims in the appellate dataset, 38 were employers' liability claims, so that, as with the first instance dataset, such claims made up a relatively high proportion (30 per cent) of the total. All of the appellate claims in this contextual category were for personal injury. 30 of the claims were from England and Wales (79 per cent), none was from Northern Ireland, and eight (21 per cent) were from Scotland. 12 of the claims (32 per cent) were from the High Court or equivalent, and 26 (68 per cent) were from a county court or equivalent. 28 of the employers' liability claims in the appellate dataset were brought by men (74 per cent of the total), and 10 by women (26 per cent), a similar gender balance to that in

---

19 James Goudkamp and Donal Nolan, *Contributory Negligence: Principles and Practice* (OUP 2018) chs 13, 16, 17.

20 Ibid, ch 19.

21 *Stephen v Peters* 2005 SCLR 513 (OH) (lorry driver) [**1:186**]; *Steele v WH Malcolm Ltd* 2013 GWD 25-511 (North Strathclyde Sheriff Court) (forklift driver) [**1:455**]. See also *M v Parsons* (n 10) (paper girl on bicycle) [**1:6**]. The plea of contributory negligence failed in *O'Gara v Paul John Construction (Leicester) Ltd* [2005] EWHC 2829 (QB); [2005] All ER (D) 11 (Aug) (dumper driver) [**1:204**]; and *Birch v Ministry of Defence* [2013] EWCA Civ 676; [2014] PIQR P1 (army Land Rover) [**2:117**].

22 *Ceva Logistics Ltd v Lynch (t/a SW Lynch Electrical Contractors)* [2011] EWCA Civ 188; [2011] ICR 746 [**1:363**]; [**1:364**].

23 *Delaney v Beechwood Nurseries Ltd* [2004] CSOH 38; 2004 Rep LR 75 [**1:118**].

24 *Barker v Corus (UK) Ltd* [2006] UKHL 20; [2006] 2 AC 572 [**1:128**].

25 *Ministry of Defence v Radclyffe* [2009] EWCA Civ 635; [2009] Al ER (D) 299 (Jun) [**1:302**]; [**2:89**].

26 *Ormsby v Chief Constable of Strathclyde* [2008] CSOH 143; 2008 SCLR 783 [**1:306**].

27 *Palfrey v Ark Offshore Ltd* [2001] All ER (D) 304 (Feb) (QBD) [**1:42**].

28 *Coldridge v Bury MBC* (Manchester CC, 24 June 2011) [**1:408**].

such claims at first instance. The youngest claimant in the appellate dataset of such claims was 18 at the relevant time,[29] and the oldest was 60.[30]

7.14 As we saw above,[31] the overall appellate intervention rate in employers' liability claims was 41 per cent, compared with an intervention rate across all claim types of 35 per cent. We also saw[32] that in employers' liability claims the level of appellate intervention regarding apportionment (44 per cent) was higher than in connection with guilt (37 per cent), whereas across all claim types the reverse was the case, with the level of appellate intervention on apportionment being 33 per cent, and on guilt 39 per cent. It thus seems that appeals on the existence of contributory negligence are no more likely to succeed in employer's liability claims than in contributory negligence appeals generally, whereas the chances of an appeal on apportionment succeeding are relatively high in this type of claim.

7.15 We also saw above[33] that the post-appeal success rate of the plea of contributory negligence in employers' liability claims was 66 per cent, which is a little lower than the overall post-appeal success rate of 71 per cent. We additionally observed that in all of the seven employers' liability claims where the appellate court intervened with respect to a finding as to guilt it did so in favour of the claimant, whereas across the entire appellate dataset the appellate court intervened in favour of the claimant on this issue only 57 per cent of the time. This seems to suggest that appellate courts tend to look favourably upon employees in contributory negligence cases, at least when it comes to the question of guilt.

7.16 Finally, turning to the question of post-appeal discount in employers' liability claims, we saw above[34] that, at 45 per cent, the average post-appeal discount in employers' liability cases was quite a bit lower than the average post-appeal discount across all claim types of 50 per cent, which is consistent with the finding that discounts tend to be lower in this type of case at first instance. Of the eight employers' liability claims where the appellate court intervened to change the discount, in five it lowered the discount[35] and in three it increased it.[36] Furthermore, when the discount was lowered this tended to be by a greater

---

[29] *Birch v Ministry of Defence* [2013] EWCA Civ 676; [2014] PIQR P1 [**2:117**].

[30] *Wallace v Glasgow CC* [2011] CSIH 57; 2011 Rep LR 96 [**2:104**].

[31] See 5.12.

[32] See 5.13.

[33] See 5.22.

[34] See 5.26.

[35] *King v Rco Support Services Ltd* [2001] ICR 608 (CA) [**2:14**]; *Anderson v Newham College for Further Education* [2002] EWCA Civ 505; [2003] ICR 212 [**2:30**]; *McFarlane v Scottish Borders Council* 2005 SLT 359 (IH) [**2:66**]; *Robb v Salamis (M&I) Ltd* [2006] UKHL 56; [2007] 2 All ER 97 [**2:75**]; *Johnstone v AMEC Construction Ltd* [2010] CSIH 57; 2011 SCLR 178 [**2:96**].

[36] *Butcher v Cornwall CC* [2002] EWCA Civ 1640; [2002] All ER (D) 274 (Oct) [**2:41**]; *Eyres v Atkinsons Kitchens and Bedrooms Ltd* [2007] EWCA Civ 365; (2007) 151 SJLB 576 [**2:77**]; *Ellis v William Cook Leeds Ltd* [2007] EWCA Civ 1232; [2007] All ER (D) 24 (Nov) [**2:79**].

amount than when it was increased. The highest reduction in the discount in an employers' liability claim was 50 per cent (two claims[37]), and the lowest reduction was 20 per cent,[38] with the average reduction being 37 per cent. By contrast, the highest *increase* in the discount was 25 per cent,[39] the lowest increase 8 per cent,[40] and the average increase 19 per cent. These figures are further evidence that appellate courts tend to be claimant-friendly in the employers' liability context.

Discussion

Introduction

7.17 Our study has generated important data concerning the operation of the contributory negligence doctrine in employers' liability cases. Three general conclusions can be drawn: (i) employers' liability claims feature very often in both the first instance and appellate case law on contributory negligence (over a quarter of such cases at both levels); (ii) at first instance, pleas of contributory negligence are as likely to succeed in employers' liability claims as in other types of claim; and (iii) when claimants are found guilty of contributory negligence in employers' liability claims, the discount tends to be lower than in other types of claim.

7.18 The second of those findings is difficult to square with the judicial statements that have frequently been made that courts should be reluctant to find employees guilty of contributory negligence, particularly where an employee sues an employer for a breach of a statutory duty imposed to protect employees.[41] On the contrary, the data generated by our study suggest that at first instance leniency towards employees was manifested only at the apportionment stage, although in the case of appellate courts such leniency did apparently extend to findings of contributory negligence as well.

---

37 *King* (n 35) [2:14]; *Robb* (n 35) [2:75].

38 *Johnstone* (n 35) [2:96].

39 *Ellis* (n 36) [2:79].

40 *Eyres* (n 36) [2:77].

41 See, eg, *Caswell v Powell Duffryn Associated Collieries Ltd* [1940] AC 152 (HL) 179–80 (Lord Wright); *Hutchinson v London and North Eastern Rly Co* [1942] 1 KB 481 (CA) 488 (Goddard LJ); *Hopwood v Rolls-Royce Ltd* (1947) 176 LT 514 (CA) 520 (Lord Greene MR); *Staveley Iron & Chemical Co Ltd v Jones* [1956] AC 627 (HL) 648 (Lord Tucker); *Quintas v National Smelting Co Ltd* [1961] 1 WLR 401 (CA) 408 (Sellers LJ); *Proctor v City Facilities Management Ltd* [2012] NIQB 99 [22] (Horner J) [1:444]. The foregoing are all cases in which explicit statements were made to the effect that judges should be reticent to find employees guilty of contributory negligence. There are countless cases in which this understanding is implicitly endorsed. Such cases include *Toole v Bolton MBC* [2002] EWCA Civ 588; [2002] All ER (D) 133 (Apr), especially at [13] (Buxton LJ) [1:51]; [2:31]; and *Nixon v Chanceoption Developments Ltd* [2002] EWCA 558, especially at [13]–[15] (Sedley LJ). For discussion, see Daniel Bennett (ed), *Munkman on Employer's Liability* (16th edn, LexisNexis 2013) paras 6.47–6.59; Ken Oliphant (ed), *The Law of Tort* (3rd edn, LexisNexis Butterworths 2015) para 15.52.

In the remainder of this section we consider several questions pertaining to contributory negligence in the employers' liability context in the light of a qualitative analysis of the case law. This analysis is focused mainly on the case law in our appellate dataset as this made the task more manageable than it would otherwise have been and because the approach taken at the appellate level may be thought to carry more weight. The principal question that we explore is the extent to which our study bears out propositions that have regularly made in the case law and the literature to the effect that a lenient approach is taken towards employees accused of contributory negligence, particularly where the employee's injury was caused by a breach of statutory duty on the part of the defendant. We also briefly investigate two additional questions, namely: the approach taken by the courts where the contributory negligence of the employee is unrelated to their employment with the defendant; and the extent to which the courts take account of the employee's level of experience or skill when applying the contributory negligence doctrine. **7.19**

The leniency issue in general

One of the difficulties that is encountered when exploring the question of leniency in the application of the contributory negligence to employees is that while several different claims are discernible in the case law and literature on this issue, they tend to blend into each other, so that considering each claim independently of the others is nigh on impossible. Accordingly, we adopt a fairly broad-brush approach to this question, while also seeking to identify and evaluate one or two more specific propositions where possible. **7.20**

The general theme of leniency in the application of the contributory negligence doctrine in the employment context is well known, particularly where the defendant employer breached a specific legal obligation to take precautions either to prevent conduct of the kind that is said to constitute contributory negligence, or to reduce the risks posed by such conduct. A classic judicial proposition to this effect is that of Goddard LJ in *Hutchinson v London & North Eastern Railway Co*: **7.21**

> It is only too common to find in cases where the plaintiff alleges that a defendant employer has been guilty of a breach of a statutory duty, that a plea of contributory negligence has been set up. In such a case I always direct myself to be exceedingly chary of finding contributory negligence where the contributory negligence alleged was the very thing which the statutory duty of the employer was designed to prevent.[42]

Similarly, in *Flower v Ebbw Vale Steel Iron & Coal Ltd*, Lord Wright quoted with approval the trial judge's remark that '[i]t is not for every risky thing which a workman **7.22**

[42] (n 41) 488.

in a factory may do in his familiarity with the machinery that a plaintiff ought to be held guilty of contributory negligence'.[43]

7.23 It is important to remember that these statements predate the introduction of the apportionment legislation, and so were made at a time when a finding of contributory negligence would defeat the employee's claim altogether—indeed it has even been suggested that 'the relaxed standard of care applied to injured workmen originated as a device for mitigating the harshness' of the common law rule that contributory negligence was a complete defence.[44] Nevertheless, the courts continued to endorse this approach after the apportionment regime was introduced, as is shown by two House of Lords decisions from the 1950s. In the first of the cases, *John Summers & Sons Ltd v Frost*, Lord Keith said that:

> The type of accident that happened here is just the type of accident against which section 14 is directed. There is no question here of disobedience to orders, or of reckless disregard by a workman of his own safety. At most there was a mere error of judgment by the plaintiff . . . and possibly only a mere momentary inadvertence.[45]

The following year Lord Tucker observed in *Staveley Iron & Chemical Co Ltd v Jones* that:

> [I]n Factory Act cases the purpose of imposing the absolute obligation is to protect the workmen against those very acts of inattention which are sometimes relied upon as constituting contributory negligence so that too strict a standard would defeat the object of the statute.[46]

7.24 Two points about these comments are particularly noteworthy. First, they relate to the question of whether a finding of contributory negligence should be made at all, and not to the apportionment exercise. And second, they indicate that even after contributory negligence ceased to be a complete defence to an action, it was still felt in breach of statutory duty cases that the purpose of the protective legislation could be undermined by too ready a tendency to find employees guilty of contributory fault.

7.25 At the same time, in a third House of Lords case from the same era, *Smith v Austin Lifts Ltd*, Viscount Simonds expressly deprecated what he called 'any tendency to treat the relation of employer and skilled workman as equivalent to that of a nurse and imbecile child',[47] and it has always been understood that a finding of contributory negligence can rightly be made in a more extreme case of employee fault.

---

[43] [1936] AC 206 (HL) 214.
[44] Ian Fagelson, 'The Last Bastion of Fault: Contributory Negligence in Actions for Employers' Liability' (1979) 42 MLR 646, 650.
[45] [1955] AC 740 (HL) 777.
[46] (n 41) 648.
[47] [1959] 1 WLR 100 (HL) 105.

A recent first instance decision that bears this out is *Ashbridge v Christian Salvesen.*[48] In this case, Lord Glennie acknowledged the protective purpose of the regulations that the employer had breached, and said that it was 'the exceptional case rather than the norm' where a finding of contributory negligence would be made, but took the view that the pursuer's 'cavalier in the extreme' attitude to his own safety warranted a discount for contributory negligence of 50 per cent.

7.26 It would seem to follow from the reasoning in these breach of statutory duty cases that the courts ought also to be wary of finding contributory negligence where a common law duty of care obliged an employer to prevent the very conduct that is said to amount to contributory negligence, or to reduce the risks posed by that conduct, but authority that is directly on point is harder to find.[49] Nevertheless, the general idea that this is a context where leniency is appropriate appears to extend to common law negligence actions, and there are observations by commentators to this effect. According to *Charlesworth & Percy on Negligence*, for example, '[i]t has been generally assumed that the same principles will apply where the allegation against the employer is one of common law negligence', although '[i]t will no doubt depend upon the facts whether they do'.[50] All in all, then, there is a considerable body of authority in favour of the claim that when applying the contributory negligence doctrine to employees a 'more lenient' standard of care should be used 'than that expected of the reasonable employer or the reasonable road user', at least with regard to 'momentary inadvertence or carelessness'.[51]

7.27 Then again, it can be argued that in the apportionment era the appropriate response to considerations of this kind is not to apply a more lenient standard of care, but rather to take these issues into account when deciding how to apportion responsibility as between employee and employer. In the words of one commentator, for example, '[i]t is entirely unnecessary to vary the standard of care expected of a workman when the flexible instrument of apportionment is available'.[52] Furthermore, there is implicit support for this approach in some of the recent case law. In *Shortell v BICAL Construction Ltd*, Mackay J said that the duties of an employer at common law and under asbestos regulations should not be 'emasculated by a *high finding* of contributory negligence',[53] and imposed a low discount of 15 per cent for contributory negligence in the form of smoking, rather than no

---

48 [2006] CSOH 79; 2006 SLT 697 [**1:223**].

49 In *Staveley* (n 41), Lord Tucker made a somewhat ambivalent observation in this regard (at 647).

50 Christopher Walton et al, *Charlesworth & Percy on Negligence* (14th edn, Sweet & Maxwell 2018) para 4.074.

51 *Munkman on Employers' Liability* (n 41) para 6.55.

52 Fagelson (n 44) 453.

53 (QBD, 16 May 2008) [62] (emphasis added) [**1:291**].

discount at all. Similarly, in a recent Court of Appeal decision, also on asbestos and smoking, Lloyd Jones LJ said that:

> There is a particular policy underlying Parliament's strict prohibition of the exposure of workers to asbestos and other harmful substances *which needs to be reflected in the apportionment of responsibility*. Here the judge was right to give very considerable weight to the blameworthiness of the employer in exposing its employee to asbestos in breach of a strict statutory duty in circumstances where the dangers of asbestos to health were well known.[54]

7.28 Nevertheless, these two cases are distinctive, in that the contributory negligence (smoking) was unrelated to the employee's work for the defendant employer[55] and qualitative analysis of the appellate case law more generally suggests that a lenient standard of care continues to be applied, at least at the appellate level. In *McGowan v W & JR Watson Ltd*,[56] for example, where the pursuer was a joiner whose finger was injured when it came into contact with the blade of a circular saw, the Inner House of the Court of Session dismissed an appeal against the finding that there had been no contributory negligence. According to Lord Nimmo Smith, the authorities supported the proposition that a momentary lapse of concentration by a worker did not constitute contributory negligence on the part of an employee injured by an employer's breach of an absolute statutory obligation.

7.29 Another significant appellate decision in this regard is *Toole v Bolton MBC*,[57] where the claimant had been employed by the defendant council as a porter at its town hall. While attempting to retrieve a syringe that had been discarded in a toilet-brush holder, the claimant had pricked his finger on another syringe that he had failed to notice, even though one of his colleagues had warned him that the holder had several syringes in it. The trial judge had found that the defendant's failure to provide the claimant with protective gloves amounted to a breach of its common law duty of care and of various statutory duties, but had discounted the damages by 75 per cent for contributory negligence. However, the Court of Appeal, having cited some of the authorities highlighted earlier, considered that there was insufficient evidence to warrant a finding of contributory negligence at all.[58] Similarly, in *Nixon v Chanceoption Developments Ltd*,[59] where a labourer had been injured after falling from scaffolding that was missing guardrails in violation of various of his employer's statutory duties, the Court of Appeal again rejected the employer's plea

[54] *Blackmore v Department for Communities and Local Government* [2017] EWCA Civ 1136; [2018] QB 471 [39] (emphasis added).

[55] For a discussion of claims with this characteristic, see 7.37–7.41.

[56] [2006] CSIH 62; 2007 SLT 169 [1:211]; [2:76].

[57] (n 41) [1:51]; [2:31].

[58] Ibid, [13].

[59] (n 41).

of contributory negligence. This was despite the fact that on a very windy day the claimant had climbed to an exposed and unfenced point high on the scaffolding while carrying two buckets of mortar. Finally, in *Cooper v Carillion Plc*, Keene LJ remarked that to 'impose too strict a standard of care on the workman would defeat the object of the statutory requirement' that had been breached by the employer in that case.[60]

Pulling the various strings together, it seems that there is a tension in the case law between manifesting leniency towards employees by, on the one hand, finding against the existence of contributory negligence at all, and on the other hand, finding that there was contributory negligence but imposing a low discount. Our study suggests that the latter approach is now the dominant one at the first instance level, in that there we found evidence of leniency in this context only at the apportionment stage, but our analysis of the appellate case law suggests that at that level leniency towards employees is also manifested in a tendency to reject pleas of contributory negligence altogether. **7.30**

Three more specific propositions regarding leniency

In addition to the general idea that leniency is appropriate in the employers' liability context, particularly in breach of statutory duty cases, three more specific propositions have been made in this regard, and we now consider the extent to which these are borne out by our study. **7.31**

The first of these propositions is that 'other than in very exceptional circumstances, there is no basis for a discount above . . . 50 per cent' for contributory negligence of an employee in a breach of statutory duty case.[61] Although there is some support for this proposition in the recent case law,[62] there were several claims in the appellate dataset that contradicted it, in that discounts above 50 per cent were imposed in what would not appear to have been 'very exceptional' circumstances. In *Sherlock v Chester CC*,[63] for example, the damages awarded to a joiner who had lost his thumb and index finger as a result of his employer's negligence and breaches of statutory duty were reduced by 60 per cent for contributory negligence. According to Latham LJ: **7.32**

---

[60] [2003] EWCA Civ 1811; [2003] All ER (D) 31 (Dec) [13] [**1:110**]; [**2:54**].

[61] Nigel Tomkins, 'Getting Contributory Negligence Right (Part 2)' [2008] JPIL 249, 252.

[62] See, eg, *Toole* (n 41) [**1:51**]; [**2:31**], where Buxton LJ said (at [13]) that it was not 'usual for there to be marked findings of contributory negligence in a breach of statutory duty case'. See also *Ashbridge* (n 48) [**1:223**], where, despite Lord Glennie's description of the pursuer's conduct as 'cavalier in the extreme', and demonstrating 'wanton disregard' for his own safety, a discount of only 50 per cent was imposed.

[63] [2004] EWCA Civ 201 [**2:57**].

> [There] may well be some justification for [the] view [that high discounts should not be imposed where there has been a breach of statutory duty by the employer] in cases of momentary inattention by an employee. But where a risk has been consciously accepted by an employee, it seems to me that different considerations may arise. That is particularly so where the employee is skilled and the precaution in question is neither esoteric nor one which he could not take himself.[64]

7.33 The second more specific proposition that has been made is that where an employee was engaged in a repetitive activity and, in the course of that activity, made an error that caused him or her to suffer damage, account will be taken of the repetitive nature of the work that the claimant was required to do and the fatigue and tedium that it was likely to induce. In a case of this kind, provided that the claimant generally acted carefully, it is said that the court will be unlikely to make a finding of contributory negligence.[65] Since this principle applies, classically, to highly repetitive work on production lines and the like, it is arguably of less relevance now that a smaller proportion of the workforce is employed in factories than formerly. However, it was nevertheless possible to find one or two applications of this proposition in the appellate case law in our study, such as *Kennedy v Chivas Brothers Ltd*, where the Inner House of the Court of Session absolved a line operator in a bottling plant of contributory negligence, and Lord Drummond Young commented that:

> Momentary acts of inattention are to be expected, especially when employees are under pressure or are performing repetitive tasks. For that reason a finding of contributory negligence should only be made in a clear case; generally speaking this will be one where the employee has made a conscious decision to embark upon a risky course of action.[66]

7.34 Furthermore, there were also instances[67] where the courts relied upon the related proposition that where an employer is guilty of a breach of statutory duty—and quite apart from the nature of the employee's work—momentary inadvertence or inattention on an employee's part will not amount to contributory fault,[68] though admittedly this more general principle is difficult to separate from the broader question of leniency in this context, as discussed above.[69]

---

64 Ibid, [32]. For other examples of discounts of greater than 50 per cent in breach of statutory duty cases, see *Tasci v Pekalp of London Ltd* [2001] ICR 633 (CA) (60 per cent) **[2:13]**; *Betts v Tokley* [2002] EWCA Civ 52; [2002] All ER (D) 99 (Jan) (60 per cent) **[1:43]**; **[2:28]**; and *Swilas v Clyde Pumps Ltd* 2012 SLT (Sh Ct) 146 (Glasgow and Strathkelvin Sheriff Court) (75 per cent) **[2:99]**.

65 *Caswell* (n 41) 187 (Lord Porter).

66 [2013] CSIH 57; 2013 SLT 981 **[2:118]**.

67 See, eg, *McGowan* (n 56) [14] (Lord Nimmo Smith) **[1:211]**; **[2:76]**; *Jones v BBC* (QBD, 22 June 2007) **[1:262]**; **[1:263]**.

68 See the quotation from Lord Keith in *John Summers* (7.23); *Westwood v Post Office* [1974] AC 1 (HL) 16 (Lord Kilbrandon). See also Tomkins (n 61) 254; Christian Witting, *Street on Torts* (15th edn, OUP 2018) 191.

69 See 7.20–7.30.

7.35 Then again, the courts were not altogether consistent in this regard. In one case, for example, the Court of Appeal held that the trial judge had been entitled to impose a discount of 50 per cent for an inadvertent mistake committed by a worker engaged in an 'extremely monotonous' task on a car production line.[70] And in another case a first instance judge acknowledged the principle that one of the purposes of the regulations in question was to protect workers against acts of inattention or carelessness, and described the claimant's conduct as 'akin to momentary inattention or carelessness', but nevertheless found her guilty of contributory negligence, albeit ascribing to her a mere 10 per cent of the responsibility for her injury.[71]

7.36 Finally, it is also sometimes claimed that particular leniency is appropriate where the motivation of the employee in engaging in the conduct that is alleged to constitute contributory negligence was not the employee's own convenience but to further the interests of the employer's business.[72] Again, express reliance on this principle in the recent case law was rare, but it was possible to identify a few claims where this consideration was taken into account either in deciding whether to make a finding of contributory negligence at all,[73] or in deciding what discount to impose.[74] In *Birch v Ministry of Defence*,[75] for example, an 18-year-old Royal Marine Lance Corporal stationed at a dangerous mountain post in Afghanistan had responded to his commanding officer's request for a volunteer to drive down the mountain to collect personnel and supplies, despite having neither a full UK driving licence nor an army driving permit, both of which were required to drive an army Land Rover. On the way down the mountain, the claimant lost control of the vehicle, which plunged down the mountain side, causing him catastrophic injuries. The Court of Appeal held that, since the claimant's commanding officer had known that he was not qualified to drive, the defendant had breached both its common law duty of care and the Defence Road Transport Regulations, but that in all the circumstances no deduction should be made from the claimant's damages for contributory negligence. Longmore LJ said that he found it 'impossible to attach any blame to Marine Birch for what was a selfless act'.[76]

---

70 *Griffiths v Vauxhall Motors Ltd* [2003] EWCA Civ 412; [2003] All ER (D) 167 (Mar) [**1:101**]; [**2:46**].

71 *Goodchild v Organon Laboratories Ltd* [2004] EWHC 2341 (QB); [2004] All ER (D) 262 (Oct) [**1:174**].

72 See, eg, *Stewart v Killeen Paper Mills Ltd* [1959] IR 436 (SC) 449 (Kingsmill Moore J); *Moffat v Atlas Hydraulic Loaders Ltd* 1992 SLT 1123 (OH) 1124 (Lord Mainoch) (both cited in *Munkman on Employer's Liability* (n 41) para 6.67). See also *Machray v Stewarts and Lloyds Ltd* [1964] 3 All ER 716 (Monmouthshire Assizes) 721 (McNair J).

73 See, eg, *Johnson v Castle Combe Circuit Ltd* (QBD, 7 October 2011) [**1:416**].

74 See, eg, *Parker v PFC Flooring Supplies Ltd* [2001] EWCA Civ 1533; [2001] All ER (D) 168 (Oct) [31] (Potter LJ) [**2:27**].

75 [2013] EWCA Civ 676; [2014] PIQR P1 [**2:117**].

76 Ibid, [24].

Acts of contributory negligence unrelated to the claimant's work

7.37 There is a distinct category of employers' liability claim where the conduct that is said to amount to contributory negligence is not related to the claimant's work, and is therefore, in a sense, far removed from the conduct that grounds the defendant's primary liability. Most claims of this kind that we came across involved employees who had contracted lung cancer after being exposed to asbestos by the defendant, where the contributory negligence consisted of smoking.

7.38 In *Blackmore v Department for Communities and Local Government*,[77] an asbestos/smoking case that post-dates our study period, Lloyd Jones LJ upheld a discount of 30 per cent imposed by the trial judge, observing that this had been consistent with the deductions made for contributory fault in three earlier High Court decisions in similar cases. This was despite the fact that the discounts in those cases had been somewhat lower, at 15 per cent[78] and 20 per cent.[79] Although counsel for the defendant in *Blackmore* observed that the claimant's contributory negligence had been entirely unrelated to his work or to the duty owed by the defendant, Lloyd Jones LJ could see 'no reason for drawing a general distinction' between cases where the conduct that amounted to contributory negligence related to the claimant's work and those where it did not:

> While it may well be appropriate in a given case to accord less weight to contributory negligence arising in the context of the tortfeasor's duty [such as] a failure to wear a protective mask, I do not consider that it is possible to construct a general principle that in all cases greater weight should be attributed to negligent conduct outside the scope of the employer/employee relationship.[80]

7.39 There were only two claims in our study where the contributory negligence was unrelated to the work of the claimant and which did not involve asbestos exposure. In these two claims the contributory negligence related to a second accident which had not occurred in a work context but which was causally connected to an earlier work accident for which the defendant was responsible. The first of these cases was *Spencer v Wincanton Holdings Ltd*,[81] where the claimant had fallen while filling his car with petrol, thereby aggravating a pre-existing leg injury he had suffered at work several years earlier. A one-third deduction was imposed for his failure to notice the trip hazard and to use crutches or a prosthesis for support.

---

77 (n 54).

78 *Shortell* (n 53) [**1:291**].

79 *Badger v Ministry of Defence* [2005] EWHC 2941 (QB); [2006] 3 All ER 173 [**1:210**]; *Horsley v Cascade Insulation Services Ltd* [2009] EWHC 2945 (QB); [2009] All ER (D) 206 (Nov) [**1:348**]. A 20 per cent discount was also imposed at first instance in *Barker* (n 24) [**1:128**], an asbestos case where the contributory negligence took the form of self-exposure to asbestos during a period of self-employment.

80 *Blackmore* (n 54) [25].

81 [2009] EWCA Civ 1404; [2010] PIQR P8 [**1:319**].

The other case was *Dalling v R J Heale & Co Ltd*,[82] where the claimant had suffered a head injury in a fall at work for which the defendant employer had accepted liability. More than three years after that accident, the claimant had sustained further injuries through falling over in a pub while intoxicated. The trial judge found that the initial head injury had reduced the claimant's ability to control his drinking habit, and had thereby played a causative role in relation to the second accident. However, the judge also held that the damages awarded in respect of the second accident fell to be reduced by one-third to reflect the claimant's contributory negligence in relation to that incident. The Court of Appeal upheld the judge's decision that the employer was liable for the second accident, and refused to intervene on the apportionment question. **7.40**

Consistently with Lloyd Jones LJ's observations in *Blackmore*, it is indeed difficult to detect in the rather limited case law on this category of employers' liability any general principle that greater weight should be attributed to contributory negligence that is unrelated to the claimant's employment. Indeed, it is difficult to discern any general differences in the way that the courts treat claimant negligence that is unrelated to the claimant's work and claimant negligence that is so related. **7.41**

The relevance of the employee's experience and skill

Finally, it is worth highlighting that in the cases in the appellate dataset, the courts frequently took an employee's level of experience or skill into account in deciding whether he or she was guilty of contributory negligence, or in deciding what discount to impose after a finding of contributory negligence had been made. A good example of such a case is *Egan v Central Manchester and Manchester Children's University Hospitals NHS Trust*,[83] where the claimant, an 'experienced and highly trained nurse', was using a mobile hoist to move a disabled patient into a bath when the hoist came to a sudden stop, causing her to suffer a back injury. The Court of Appeal held that the claimant's employer had breached its statutory obligation to take all appropriate steps to reduce the risk of injury arising from a handling operation to the lowest level that was reasonably practicable, but that the claimant had also been careless, and shared equal responsibility for her injury with her employer.[84] Conversely, in *Mullaney v Chief Constable of the West Midlands*,[85] where it was held that the defendant Chief Constable had breached his duty of care to the claimant, a probationary police constable who sustained a serious head **7.42**

[82] [2011] EWCA Civ 365; [2011] All ER (D) 54 (Apr) **[1:361]**; **[2:102]**.

[83] [2008] EWCA Civ 1424; [2009] ICR 585 **[2:84]**.

[84] For other examples, see *Coe v The Executors of Mrs D M De Rothschild (The Waddesdon Estate)* (CA, 30 October 2000) **[2:10]**; *King* (n 35) [39] (Kay LJ) **[2:14]**; and *Sherlock* (n 63) [32] (Latham LJ) **[2:57]**.

[85] [2001] EWCA Civ 700; [2001] Po LR 150 **[1:7]**; **[2:23]**.

injury whilst attempting to arrest a suspect without assistance, Clarke LJ said that in the light of the fact that the claimant was 'a very inexperienced officer' it would be unjust to hold that he had been guilty of contributory negligence in entering a public lavatory to carry out reconnaissance on his own.[86] Decisions such as *Egan* and *Mullaney* are consistent with earlier cases in which an employee's experience was taken into account when applying the contributory negligence doctrine,[87] and provide powerful evidence for the proposition that a more subjective standard of care is applied in the contributory negligence context than when determining questions of primary liability.

Conclusion

7.43 The most interesting findings that emerge from our study with regard to employers' liability claims are as follows:

1. Employers' liability is a context in which the doctrine of contributory negligence features very frequently, both at the first instance and appellate levels.
2. The success rate of the plea of contributory negligence was 60 per cent in employers' liability claims at first instance, which is consistent with the success rate of the plea across all types of claim.
3. The average discount in employers' liability claims was 32 per cent at first instance, which is considerably lower than the average discount across all claim types, and the lowest average discount in any contextual category.
4. The most popular discounts in this type of claim were 20 per cent and 25 per cent. Discounts of over 50 per cent were imposed in only 8 per cent of the claims where a finding of contributory negligence was made at first instance.
5. While it would seem that appeals in relation to the existence of contributory negligence are no more likely to succeed in employers' liability claims than in contributory negligence appeals generally, the chances of an appeal on apportionment succeeding are relatively high in this type of claim.
6. Our study suggests that while at the first instance level, leniency towards employees in the contributory negligence context tends now to be manifested only at the apportionment stage, at the appellate level, it is also manifested in a tendency to reject the plea of contributory negligence altogether.
7. There is a particular category of employers' liability claim where the conduct that is said to amount to contributory fault is not related to the claimant's work, but we found no evidence that the courts take a distinctive approach when applying the contributory negligence doctrine in this type of case.

---

86 Ibid, [90].

87 See, eg, *Byers v Head Wrightson & Co Ltd* [1961] 2 All ER 538 (QBD) 543 (Elwes J); *Ball v Richard Thomas & Baldwin Ltd* [1968] 1 All ER 389 (CA) 395 (Davies LJ), 398 (Willmer LJ). See also the cases cited in *Munkman on Employer's Liability* (n 41) para 6.62.

8. The courts frequently take a claimant employee's level of experience or skill into account when applying the contributory negligence doctrine. This provides support for the proposition that a more subjective standard of care is applied in the contributory negligence context than when determining questions of primary liability.

8

CONTRIBUTORY NEGLIGENCE AND PROFESSIONALS

Introduction

Although contributory negligence is usually associated with accident cases, it is frequently pleaded by defendants who have been sued for negligence in the performance of their professional duties, and yet very little is known about the impact of the doctrine in professional negligence litigation.[1] In this chapter, we seek to fill this gap, by means of both empirical and qualitative analysis of recent contributory negligence case law in the United Kingdom. This analysis suggests that there are certain distinctive features of the operation of the contributory negligence doctrine in the professional negligence context. **8.01**

In the first section of the chapter, we report the results of our study in so far as they pertain to decisions in professional negligence cases. In the second section, we discuss these results in the light of qualitative analysis of the professional negligence case law in our study and the existing literature on the operation of contributory negligence in this context. It should be noted that we took a fairly broad view of what amounted to a professional negligence claim, and included within this **8.02**

---

[1] For helpful general treatment of the topic, see David W Marks, 'Professional Negligence: Contribution and Contributory Negligence' (1988–1989) 15 Univ Qld Law J 209; Anthony M Dugdale and Keith M Stanton, *Professional Negligence* (3rd edn, Butterworths 1998) 523–32; and John Murdoch, 'Client Negligence: A Lost Cause?' (2004) 20 PN 97. There is a more extensive body of literature on contributory negligence in the medical negligence context: see especially Robert B Harper, 'The Application of Contributory Negligence Principles to the Doctor/Patient Relationship' (2001) 9 TLJ 1; Yola SH Ventresca, Peter W Kryworuk, and Scott D Chambers, 'With Patient Rights Come Patient Responsibilities: Contributory Negligence in Medical Negligence Actions' (2007) 33 Advoc Q 207; Jonathan Herring and Charles Foster, 'Blaming the Patient: Contributory Negligence in Medical Malpractice Litigation' (2009) 25 PN 76; Ellen I Picard and Gerald B Robertson, *Legal Liability of Doctors and Hospitals in Canada* (4th edn, Carswell 2007) 368–74; William Binchy and RA Komolafe, 'Patients, Contributory Negligence and Medical Negligence Litigation' (2010) 4 QRTL 21; Jennifer M Yule, 'Defences in Medical Negligence: To What Extent Has Tort Law Reform in Australia Limited the Liability of Health Professionals?' (2011) 4 JALTA 53, 54–56.

category claims against (among others) lawyers, medical practitioners, valuers/surveyors, bankers, architects, engineers, accountants, and insurance brokers.

8.03 Before we consider the results of our study in this context, it is important to highlight the fact that most professional negligence claims are pleaded in both tort and contract, with the professional's conduct being alleged to be in breach of concurrent duties of reasonable care.[2] There are, however, cases where only an action in tort is available to the claimant, as where the claimant was not in a direct contractual relationship with the defendant, but was linked to the defendant by a chain of contracts,[3] or where the defendant provided their professional services gratuitously.[4]

8.04 For a time, it was unclear how the contributory negligence doctrine functioned in cases of concurrent liability. However, at least since the decision of the Court of Appeal in *Forsikringsaktieselskapet Vesta v Butcher*,[5] it has been clear that the doctrine may apply where a defendant who owed concurrent duties in tort and contract is alleged to have caused damage by failing to exercise reasonable care, although the position will be otherwise where the complaint is that the professional breached, whether or not through negligence, a strict contractual duty.[6] Furthermore, in such cases the doctrine is potentially applicable irrespective of the precise way in which the claim is framed, so that a claimant cannot avoid the contributory negligence rule by suing only for breach of contract.[7]

Results

8.05 In this section of the chapter, we present the results of our empirical study pertaining to professional negligence. We begin by setting out some general information about the claims in the first instance and appellate datasets, and then proceed to the findings. We divide our discussion of the findings into three parts: the success rate of the plea of contributory negligence; the discount applied when contributory

[2] This has become the norm since the decision of the House of Lords in *Henderson v Merrett Syndicates Ltd* [1995] 2 AC 145 (HL). Since *Henderson*, 'the orthodox analysis [has been] that a professional person in a contractual relationship with a client will ordinarily owe that client a concurrent duty of care': John Powell et al, *Jackson & Powell on Professional Liability* (8th edn, Sweet & Maxwell 2017) para 2.117 (footnote omitted).

[3] See, eg, *Smith v Eric S Bush (a firm)* [1990] 1 AC 831 (HL) and the actions by the 'indirect Names' in *Henderson* (n 2).

[4] As a practical matter, this is most relevant where medical treatment is provided under the National Health Service: see *Jackson & Powell on Professional Liability* (n 2) para 13.002.

[5] [1989] AC 852 (CA).

[6] For a clear statement of the rules in this regard, see *Secretary of State for the Environment, Transport and Regions v Unicorn Consultancy Services Ltd* [2000] NPC 108 (Ch D) [123] (Rimer J) [1:31]; [4:3].

[7] Clearly stated at first instance in *Vesta v Butcher* [1986] 2 Lloyd's Rep 179 (QBD) 197 (Hobhouse J).

negligence is found; and some additional observations about the professional negligence claims in the two datasets. Our primary aim in this section is simply to present the findings of the study, although we also make some observations about their importance. Fuller discussion of key findings in the light of the case law and academic literature is postponed until the following section.

General information

We saw in chapter 4 that our first instance dataset contained entries for 572 claims in which the defendant had pleaded contributory negligence, and that the vast majority of these claims (87 per cent) were for personal injury, with the remaining claims being in respect of pure economic loss (10 per cent) or property damage (3 per cent). **8.06**

We also saw that there was a more even spread of the claims across our seven categories of claim type (or contextual setting), and that the 57 professional negligence claims made up just under 10 per cent of the total number of first instance claims. The essential details of the 57 professional negligence claims in the first instance dataset can be found in Appendix 4. The preponderance of these claims (48 claims) were claims for pure economic loss. Of the other nine professional negligence claims, three were for personal injury (all of which were medical negligence cases), and six were for property damage. **8.07**

In chapter 5, we saw that of the 129 claims in the appellate dataset, only four were professional negligence claims. Of these, three were property damage claims and the fourth was a pure economic loss claim. The number of professional negligence claims in the appellate dataset is so low that no meaningful empirical conclusions can be drawn therefrom. Nevertheless, we will occasionally draw upon the judgments in the four appellate decisions on contributory negligence in the professional negligence context in our qualitative analysis in the next section of the chapter. **8.08**

Success rate of the plea of contributory negligence

We saw in chapter 4 that out of the 572 claims in our first instance dataset, the plea of contributory negligence succeeded in 331 claims (58 per cent) and failed in 241 claims (42 per cent). We also saw that when we broke down the success rate of the plea by type of claim, the plea of contributory negligence had a very low success rate in professional negligence claims (28 per cent)—roughly half that of the success rate of the plea across all types of claim in our study—and that statistically, this difference was very unlikely to be down to chance.[8] **8.09**

[8] See 4.08.

Discount where contributory negligence found

8.10 In the 331 claims in the first instance dataset in which the claimant was found guilty of contributory negligence, the average amount by which the claimant's damages were reduced rounded up to 40 per cent.[9] The highest average discount (52 per cent) was found in professional negligence claims. As we have seen, even though there were only 16 professional negligence claims in the sample where a discount was made, statistical analysis suggests that the disparity between the average discount in professional negligence claims and in claims in three of the other categories of claim type (employers' liability, public liability, and 'other') was very unlikely to be down to chance.[10] These results therefore suggest that, while the courts are reluctant to find contributory negligence in professional negligence claims, when they do so the discount tends to be higher than in other types of claim.

8.11 Our study also reveals important facts about the range and frequency of discounts used by the courts in professional negligence cases. The lowest discount that we observed in such a case was 15 per cent,[11] while the highest was 100 per cent.[12] In *Speshal Investments Ltd v Corby Kane Howard Partnership Ltd,* Hart J referred to a discount below 20 per cent in the context of a claim against a valuer as being a 'token' one.[13] That perhaps suggests that he thought that discounts below that amount should not normally be made at all, and that the proper course to take in such circumstances is to find that there was no contributory negligence in the first place. The most popular discount was 50 per cent (five claims). Table 8.1 sets out all the discounts used in such cases, Figure 8.1 shows the distribution of these discounts by discount range, and Figure 8.2 provides further detail as regards the distribution. As can be seen from Table 8.1, there were more professional negligence claims (six) in which a discount of over 50 per cent was imposed than there were such claims (five) where a discount of less than 50 per cent was imposed.

---

[9] See 4.12.

[10] See 4.14.

[11] *Playboy Club London Ltd v Banca Nazionale del Lavoro SpA* [2014] EWHC 2613 (QB); [2014] All ER (D) 288 (Jul) **[1:509]**; **[4:46]**. On appeal to the Supreme Court, the defendant was held not liable: [2018] UKSC 43; [2018] 1 WLR 4041.

[12] *Six Continents Retail Ltd v Carford Catering Ltd* [2003] EWCA Civ 1790 **[1:139]**; **[2:52]**; **[4:13]**. In this case, a discount of 100 per cent was imposed as an alternative to a finding that the conduct of the claimants had broken the chain of causation between the defendant's negligence and the damage suffered by the claimant. On appeal, the finding on causation was overturned, and it was said that the finding of 100 per cent contributory negligence must fall with it. This would suggest that the finding of 100 per cent contributory negligence was really just another way of repackaging the finding on causation, a suggestion consistent with the view (shared by us) that findings of 100 per cent contributory negligence are both incoherent and impermissible under the apportionment legislation. See 4.41.

[13] [2003] EWHC 390 (Ch); [2003] All ER (D) 31 (Mar) [69] **[1:115]**; **[4:10]**.

Table 8.1 Discounts in professional negligence claims

Number of claims	Discount (%)
5	50
2	75
2	20
1	100
1	80
1	66.6
1	60
1	40
1	33.3
1	15

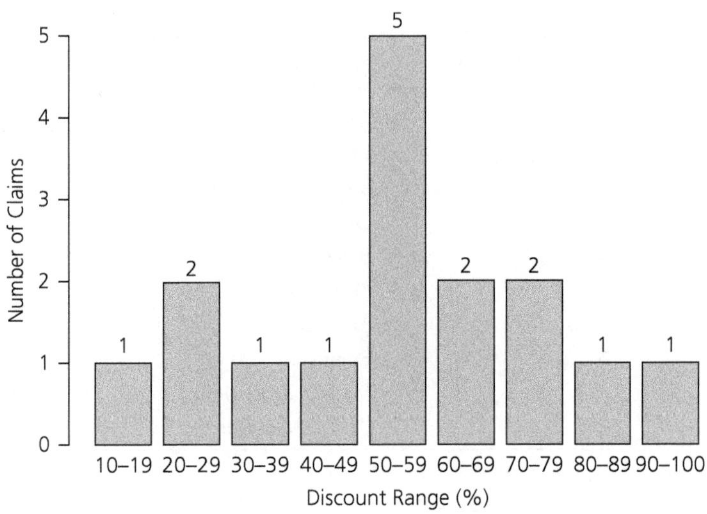

Figure 8.1 Number of professional negligence claims by discount range

Further details of professional negligence claims

Of the 57 professional negligence claims, 51 were from England and Wales, four from Northern Ireland, and two from Scotland. Of the claims from England and Wales, all but one were decisions of the High Court. The exception was a medical negligence claim decided by the Sheffield County Court.[14] The four Northern Irish **8.12**

[14] *Pidgeon v Doncaster HA* [2002] Lloyd's Rep Med 130 (Sheffield CC) [1:63]; [4:5].

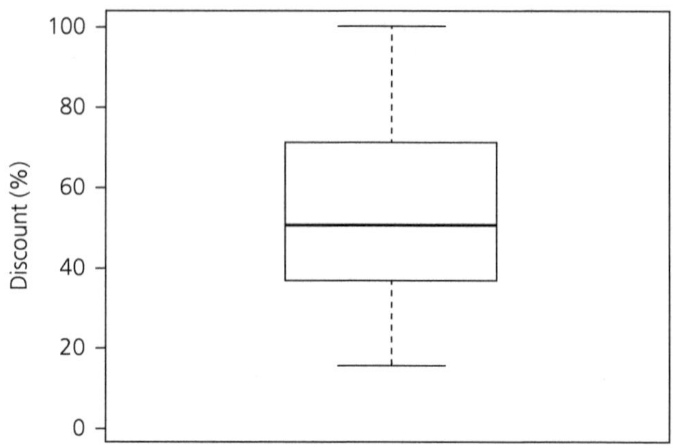

Figure 8.2 Discount in professional negligence claims

Table 8.2 Defendants by profession in professional negligence claims

Number of claims	Profession of defendant
16	Legal Practitioner
9	Valuer/Surveyor
7	Insurance Broker
7	Other
4	Banker
3	Accountant
3	Architect
3	Engineer
3	Medical Practitioner
2	Project Manager

claims were decided by the High Court of Justice, and both the Scottish claims were decided by the Outer House of the Court of Session.

8.13 The types of professional who featured as defendants in the 57 first instance professional negligence claims are shown, in decreasing order of frequency, in Table 8.2. The defendants in the seven claims where the defendant is classified as 'other' in this table were as follows: a financial adviser;[15] a supplier of fire suppression systems

[15] *Chrysalis Scotland Ltd v Clydesdale Bank Insurance Brokers Ltd* [2008] CSOH 144; 2008 GWD 38-578 [1:307]; [4:25].

(two claims);[16] a company that provided a range of services—including assistance, testing and advice—in relation to leather products;[17] a company in the business of the overhaul and/or reconditioning of parts used by the railway industry;[18] a company that (among other things) carried out searches in relation to property for potential purchasers;[19] and an IT firm hired to supply a company with an email system.[20]

As can be seen from Table 8.2, the profession that features by far the most frequently in the contributory negligence case law is the legal profession, which accounts for 28 per cent of the professional negligence claims in the dataset. The only two other professions that account for more than 10 per cent of the dataset are valuers/surveyors (16 per cent) and insurance brokers (12 per cent). By contrast, there are only three claims in the dataset where the defendant was a medical practitioner.[21] Our study therefore suggests that pleas of contributory negligence are rare in the medical negligence context, as might have been expected in the light of the fact that one of these three cases[22] is apparently the only reported English clinical negligence claim in which there was a finding of contributory negligence.[23] **8.14**

Because the numbers of claims in each professional category are relatively low, a comparison of the success rate of the plea across these categories is of limited value, but nevertheless, it is perhaps noteworthy that in our sample pleas of contributory negligence succeeded more often where the defendant was a valuer/surveyor than where the defendant was a lawyer or insurance broker. To be precise, the plea of contributory negligence succeeded in only two of the 16 claims against lawyers[24] (13 per cent), in only one of the seven claims against insurance brokers[25] (14 per **8.15**

---

[16] *Trebor Bassett Holdings Ltd v ADT Fire & Security Plc* [2011] EWHC 1936 (TCC); [2011] BLR 661 [1:411]; [4:35].

[17] *Argos Ltd v Leather Trade House Ltd* [2012] EWHC 1348 (QB); [2012] ECC 34 [1:430]; [4:37].

[18] *Great North Eastern Railway Ltd v Railcare Ltd* [2003] EWHC 1608 (Comm); [2003] All ER (D) 305 (Jul) [1:136]; [4:12].

[19] *Manorgate Ltd v First Scottish Property Services Ltd* [2013] CSOH 108; [2014] PNLR 1 [1:474]; [4:41].

[20] *Logical Computer Supplies Ltd v Euro Car Parks Ltd* [2002] IP & T 233 (QBD) [1:54]; [4:4].

[21] The claims were *Pidgeon* (n 14) [1:63]; [4:5]; *P (decd) v Sedar* [2011] EWHC 1266 (QB) [1:393]; [4:34]; and *Spencer v Hillingdon Hospital NHS Trust* [2015] EWHC 1058 (QB); [2015] All ER (D) 172 (Apr) [1:531]; [4:47]. The plea of contributory negligence succeeded in *Pidgeon*, and failed in the other two cases.

[22] *Pidgeon* (n 14) [1:63]; [4:5].

[23] Herring and Foster (n 1) 76. In *Sims v MacLennan* [2015] EWHC 2739 (QB); [2015] All ER (D) 117 (Oct), a medical negligence claim, the trial judge recorded that he would have reduced the damages by 25 per cent for contributory negligence had he held the defendant liable.

[24] *Unicorn* (n 6) [1:31]; [4:3]; *Alpha Credit Bank v Stephenson Harwood* [2002] EWHC 922 (Ch) [1:87]; [4:6].

[25] *Dunlop Haywards Ltd v Barbon Insurance Group* [2009] EWHC 2900 (Comm); [2010] Lloyd's Rep IR 149 [1:351]; [4:30].

cent), but in four out of the nine claims against valuers/surveyors[26] (44 per cent). The high success rate of the plea in claims against valuers/surveyors is consistent with earlier research where it was found that in 22 out of 39 cases in which contributory negligence was pleaded by a valuer/surveyor between 1991 and 2004, a finding of contributory negligence was made.[27] Discussion of possible explanations for these disparities will be found below.

Discussion

8.16 Intriguing data emerge from our study concerning the operation of the contributory negligence doctrine in the professional negligence context. Three principal conclusions can be drawn: (i) contributory negligence is frequently pleaded in professional negligence litigation (10 per cent of the claims in our first instance dataset were professional negligence claims); (ii) pleas of contributory negligence are considerably less likely to succeed in professional negligence claims than in other types of claim; and (iii) when claimants are found guilty of contributory negligence in professional negligence claims, the average discount is higher than in other types of claim. In the light of (ii), (i) is perhaps surprising although it is important to observe that defendants rarely have anything to lose by pleading contributory negligence, even if the prospects of success on the point are very slim,[28] and that a plea of contributory negligence may be a useful bargaining chip in settlement negotiations, even if it would be unlikely to succeed at trial. It is noteworthy in this connection that, in many of the professional negligence claims in our study where the court found against the defendant on this issue, it seems clear that the plea of contributory negligence was not put forward with any real force or enthusiasm.[29] In one case, for example, Tomlinson J began his discussion of the contributory negligence issue by saying:

> This defence [contributory negligence] was memorably described by Mr Railton [counsel for one defendant] at an early stage of the trial as 'limp'. Mr Railton was

---

[26] *Speshal* (n 13) [**1:115**]; [**4:10**]; *Webb Resolutions Ltd v E.Surv Ltd* [2012] EWHC 3653 (TCC); [2013] PNLR 15 [**1:450**]; [**4:38**]; *Aurora Leasing Ltd v Colliers International Belfast Ltd* [2013] NIQB 116 [**1:480**]; [**4:42**]; *Barclays Bank Plc v Christie Owen & Davies Ltd* [2016] EWHC 2351 (Ch); [2017] PNLR 8 [**1:566**]; [**4:55**].

[27] Murdoch (n 1) 97.

[28] Although defendants who unsuccessfully plead contributory negligence (or who succeed in the plea of contributory negligence, but abandon or lose on particular allegations of contributory negligence) may be required to pay the costs associated with that issue. For an indication that the courts might be relatively reluctant to require defendants to bear costs in these circumstances, see *The Governors and Company of the Bank of Ireland v Watts Group Plc* [2017] EWHC 2472 (TCC); [2017] BLR 625 [12] (Coulson J).

[29] It has been pointed out to us that defendants may not push a plea of contributory negligence very hard because it always needs to be argued on the footing that the defendant himself or herself was guilty of negligence, which is not a scenario that defendants will wish to emphasize.

> not of course involved in this particular argument between Aon and SLAC, but his evaluation was in my view not uncharitable. To be fair to Mr Weitzman [counsel for Aon, a defendant which had pleaded contributory negligence] it was not an argument which he pursued with any more enthusiasm than his professional duty required.[30]

Establishing contributory negligence in a professional negligence case

8.17 Our second general conclusion is consistent with the commonly expressed view that it is difficult for a defendant in a professional negligence claim to make an allegation of contributory negligence stick.[31] There are obvious reasons why a professional will often face 'grave difficulty'[32] and will 'only rarely ... be able to set up allegations of contributory negligence against their clients'.[33] These reasons include the fact that the professional will usually have greater expertise than the client in the relevant field, that the relationship between professional and client is often markedly asymmetrical in terms of power, and that it will often be reasonable for the client to follow professional advice and to rely on the professional to do properly the job that he or she has been engaged to do.

8.18 These explanations are consistent with the differential treatment of human and corporate claimants in this context (since it might plausibly be supposed that corporate claimants are generally more capable of protecting their own interests in the context of professional advice than human claimants, so that the corporate/human claimant distinction can serve as a proxy for a sophisticated/unsophisticated claimant distinction). In our dataset, only two out of 16 human claimants (13 per cent) were found guilty of contributory negligence in professional negligence claims,[34] while the equivalent figures for corporate claimants were 13 out of 40 claimants (33 per cent).[35] Clearly these figures are suggestive, although admittedly

---

[30] *Standard Life Assurance Ltd v Oak Dedicated Ltd* [2008] EWHC 222 (Comm); [2008] 2 All ER (Comm) 916 [109] [**1:281**]; [**4:24**].

[31] See, eg, *Jackson & Powell on Professional Liability* (n 2) para 5.172 ('[i]n the context of professional negligence a successful plea of contributory negligence by the defendant is less common than in other areas of negligence'); Stephen Walmsley et al, *Professional Liability in Australia* (3rd edn, Lawbook Co 2016) para 1.2170 ('In claims against professionals by clients, it is often difficult for the professional to successfully plead contributory negligence').

[32] Marks (n 1) 226–27.

[33] *Unicorn* (n 6) [128] (Rimer J) [**1:31**]; [**4:3**].

[34] The two cases in which findings of contributory negligence were made against human claimants were *Pidgeon* (n 14) [**1:63**]; [**4:5**], a medical negligence claim, and *Slattery v Moore Stephens* [2003] EWHC 1869 (Ch); [2004] PNLR 14 [**1:141**]; [**4:14**], a claim by an investment banker against his tax advisers.

[35] We have excluded from this comparison one case in which the claimants were trustees of a rugby club (*Montlake v Lambert Smith Hampton Group Ltd* [2004] EWHC 938 (Comm); [2004] 3 EGLR 149 [**1:165**]; [**4:15**]), a scenario that does not neatly fit into the human/corporate claimant dichotomy.

the relevant sample size is small and there might be alternative explanations for the differential treatment of human and corporate claimants. For example, it may be that judges are more willing to make discounts from the damages of corporations on the footing that it is usually easier for them to absorb and/or pass on losses than it is for individuals.[36]

8.19 However, it is worth emphasizing that, even in professional negligence claims involving corporate clients, the likelihood of a successful plea of contributory negligence is still considerably lower than in other types of claim, which suggests that the relative sophistication of the parties is only a partial explanation for the low success rate of pleas of contributory negligence in this context. Qualitative analysis of the claims in our dataset suggests that a more powerful explanation for the low success rate of the plea in professional negligence claims is that judges are unimpressed by arguments to the effect that clients should have done more to check the work done, or advice given, by a professional. Put simply, in most cases the courts take the view that a client is entitled to rely on the expertise of a defendant who has (almost always) been paid to provide a professional service.[37]

The high average discount in professional negligence cases

8.20 In the light of these considerations, it is interesting to observe that while pleas of contributory negligence are less likely to succeed in professional negligence claims, when they do succeed the average discount is higher than in all other types of claim. Quite why this inverse relationship exists is unclear. One possible explanation is that claimants need to do something particularly unreasonable in order to be found guilty of contributory negligence in a professional negligence claim. If this is correct, then judges might conclude that claimants who have been found guilty of contributory negligence in professional negligence claims deserve to have

---

[36] Statistical analysis of this disparity by means of a Pearson's chi-square test returned a p-value of 0.175, meaning that it could well be down to chance. It might be thought that the explanation for the disparity lies in the defendant's profession. As we have seen, pleas of contributory negligence were, on average, less likely to succeed when made by lawyers or insurance brokers than when made by valuers/surveyors. It follows that if human claimants brought more claims against lawyers and insurance brokers than they did against valuers/surveyors that could explain (at least in part) why pleas of contributory negligence rarely succeeded against human claimants. However, this explanation is unconvincing in view of the fact that *corporate* claimants accounted for a higher proportion of the claims in our sample against lawyers and insurance brokers (69 per cent and 100 per cent respectively) than they did of the claims against valuers/surveyors (63 per cent).

[37] We return to this theme throughout this section of the chapter. See also Marks (n 1) 219 ('in many factual circumstances, the client will reasonably rely so completely upon the professional's skills that the defence will not succeed'); *Jackson & Powell on Professional Liability* (n 2) para 10.234 (footnote omitted) ('it is often harder to establish contributory negligence against a claimant in a professional negligence context than it might be in other areas of negligence, because in many cases the client will be entitled simply to rely upon the advice he receives from the professional he has retained').

their damages discounted by a sizeable amount. This explanation would suggest that in, say, a borderline road accident case (ie, a case involving relatively minor claimant fault), the typical response is a finding of contributory negligence but the imposition of a small discount, while in a borderline professional negligence case the typical response is a finding that there was no contributory negligence at all.

8.21 Another possible explanation for the relatively high discounts in professional negligence cases is that in other types of case, such as road accident claims, considerations of causative potency play a greater role in the apportionment decision, whereas in professional negligence claims the focus is often exclusively on the relative fault of the parties. Hence, where the relative fault of the parties is thought to be roughly equivalent in a professional negligence claim, an equal division of responsibility is likely to be considered appropriate, so that a relatively high discount of 50 per cent (or thereabouts) is likely to be made. By contrast, in a road accident claim where the relative fault of a pedestrian claimant and a motorist defendant is judged to be roughly equivalent, the fact that the defendant was driving a motor vehicle will tend to mean that greater causative potency is judged to attach to the defendant's negligence,[38] so that a lower discount of, say, one-third, is more likely to be made.

Differing success rates of the plea for different professions

8.22 Our study also suggests that a plea of contributory negligence is more likely to succeed when made by a valuer/surveyor than by a lawyer. There are several possible explanations for this disparity.[39] If we look first at the cases in our dataset involving lawyers, the allegation of contributory negligence usually boils down to a failure on the part of the client to detect an error in draft work produced by the defendant, or to remember to do something which it is the responsibility of the defendant to remind the client to do.[40] The general attitude of the courts in such cases is that (in the words of a leading text on professional negligence) '[i]n most situations it would not be reasonable to expect a client to check on the advice given or service provided by a solicitor'.[41]

---

[38] See 6.23.

[39] Another possible explanation (ie, additional to those set out in the following paragraphs) that has been suggested to us for this disparity is that judges tend to be relatively tough on lawyers in professional negligence cases because they have a good understanding of the nature of the work that lawyers do, and hence feel more comfortable making findings of negligence against lawyers than against other professionals. However, although this seems plausible, such a tendency would not necessarily carry through into a concomitant *reluctance* to find lawyers' clients guilty of *contributory* negligence.

[40] For general discussion of contributory negligence in claims against lawyers, see *Jackson & Powell on Professional Liability* (n 2) paras 11.341ff, 12.043.

[41] Dugdale and Stanton (n 1) para 21.38.

8.23 In *Credit Lyonnais SA v Russell Jones & Walker (a firm)*,[42] for example, the defendant had been negligent in not drawing to the client's attention the fact that time was of the essence in relation to a particular payment that needed to be made in order to exercise a break clause in a lease. The defendant's argument that the claimant (a major bank) had also been guilty of contributory negligence in not making the payment on time was rejected. Similarly, in *Akasuc Enterprise Ltd v Farmar & Shirreff*,[43] where the defendant's negligence consisted of failing to insert a mechanism into a conditional purchase agreement to protect an overage fee, the judge rejected the argument that the corporate client in question had been negligent in not noticing the omission. And in *Feakins v Burstow*,[44] it was said that it would be rare for a client alleging the negligence of a lawyer in the conduct of litigation to be found guilty of contributory fault. Finally, in a case where insurance underwriters had settled a claim in reliance on defective advice provided by their solicitors, Simon J gave short shrift to the defendant's allegation that the claimants had been guilty of contributory negligence in not realising that the advice it had given was flawed:

> The defendant was specifically instructed to consider the issue of coverage and it is difficult to see why the client, who has paid the solicitor to do the work, should check that the solicitor has done the task for which he has been employed . . . To put the matter more proverbially: if you hire a dog you do not expect to have to bark.[45]

8.24 By contrast, analysis of the case law involving valuers and surveyors suggests that claims against such defendants typically arise out of decisions made by institutional lenders which were based on several different considerations, only one of which was the valuation provided by the defendant. Such scenarios lend themselves to allegations of contributory negligence on the grounds that the claimant's decision to lend was imprudent in the light of the other factors in play. In this context, failure by the claimant to act in accordance with prudent lending practices is readily interpreted by judges as a form of negligence on the claimant's part which played as much (if not more) of a causal role in the decision to make a loan to a third party against the security of a property than the negligent over-valuation of that property by the defendant valuer or surveyor.[46] As the leading practitioner text on professional negligence puts it:

---

[42] [2002] EWHC 1310 (Ch); [2003] PNLR 2 [**1:98**]; [**4:7**].

[43] [2003] EWHC 1275 (Ch); [2003] All ER (D) 49 (Jun) [**1129**]; [**4:11**].

[44] [2005] EWHC 1931 (QB); [2006] PNLR 6 [**1:207**]; [**4:18**].

[45] *Newline Corporate Name Ltd v Morgan Cole (a firm)* [2007] EWHC 1628 (Comm); [2008] PNLR 2 [69] [**1:266**]; [**4:23**]. For the same argument in respect of other types of professional adviser, see *Chrysalis Scotland* (n 15) [58] (Lord Glennie) [**1:307**]; [**4:25**] (financial adviser); *Manorgate* (n 19) [58] (Lord Woolman) [**1:474**]; [**4:41**] (property search company). See also the observation of Picard and Robertson (n 1) 373 in the medical negligence context that 'as a general rule it is reasonable for a patient to rely on the professional opinion of their physician'.

[46] For general discussion of contributory negligence in claims against surveyors and valuers, see Hugh Evans, 'Contributory Negligence by Lenders' (1998) 14 PN 43; Murdoch (n 1) 102ff; and *Jackson & Powell on Professional Liability* (n 2) para 10.234ff.

> There are ... areas where the client is a sophisticated entity retaining functions not delegated to the professional for which the client retains responsibility. One such area is that of a lending institution, and it is in this context that most of the contributory negligence cases relating to surveyors have been decided.[47]

It follows that contributory negligence arguments continue to play an important role in claims by mortgage lenders against property valuers.[48] Examples of such claims in our study include *Speshal*,[49] *Webb Resolutions Ltd v E.Surv Ltd*,[50] *Barclays Bank Plc v Christie Owen & Davies Ltd*,[51] and *Aurora Leasing Ltd v Colliers International Belfast Ltd*.[52] **8.25**

Considerable emphasis is placed in cases of this kind on the question of whether the claimant lending institution complied with common practice in the industry. According to Coulson J in *Webb*, for example: **8.26**

> In general terms, the approach is to see what was happening elsewhere in the lending market because, if the claimant was doing what its competitors were doing, negligence was unlikely, unless it could be shown that it was irrational or illogical.[53]

Failures to comply with the prudent lender standard have included not taking account of discrepancies between a borrower's statements as to his debts and those revealed by credit checks;[54] failing to make enquiries regarding a borrower's income and ability to service the loan;[55] and failing to take account of a borrower's misuse of an earlier loan.[56] Furthermore, in cases of this kind, a sophisticated lender may be held to have been at fault simply for not second-guessing the valuation provided by the defendant, though in such a scenario a lower discount can be expected.[57] **8.27**

---

[47] *Jackson & Powell on Professional Liability* (n 2) para 10.234.

[48] See also Murdoch (n 1) 97 arguing that allegations of contributory negligence 'have assumed an extremely high profile' in this context.

[49] (n 13) [**1:115**]; [**4:10**].

[50] (n 26) [**1:450**]; [**4:38**].

[51] (n 26) [**1:566**]; [**4:55**].

[52] (n 26) [**1:480**]; [**4:42**]. See also *Paratus AMC Ltd v Countrywide Surveyors Ltd* [2011] EWHC 3307 (Ch); [2012] PNLR 12, a case excluded from our study because the discussion of contributory negligence was hypothetical, where the judge held that if the defendant surveyors had been found liable, he would have reduced the damages by 60 per cent for the contributory negligence of the claimant lender.

[53] *Webb* (n 26) [71] [**1:450**]; [**4:38**]. See also *Paratus* (n 52) [79]–[80] (HHJ Keyser); *Barclays Bank* (n 26) [232] (Richard Spearman QC) [**1:566**]; [**4:55**] ('if a practice was accepted by a significant section of the banking market at the relevant time, it should not be held to fail to meet the standard of a reasonably competent bank unless plainly illogical').

[54] See, eg, *Paratus* (n 52); *Webb* (n 26) [**1:450**]; [**4:38**].

[55] See, eg, *Paratus* (n 52).

[56] See, eg, *Barclays Bank* (n 26) [**1:566**]; [**4:55**] (40 per cent discount).

[57] See, eg, *Speshal* (n 13) [**1:115**]; [**4:10**] (20 per cent discount for not subjecting to critical analysis the disparity between the purchase price of the properties against which the loan was secured and the valuations provided by the defendants).

8.28 High discounts for contributory negligence can also be found in other types of professional negligence case, where the fault of the claimant is independent of the fault of the defendant (in that it does not lie in not checking or verifying the professional's work),[58] or where the thing that the claimant ought to have done did not require technical competence. A good example of a case in which the claimant's fault was independent of that of the defendant is *Sahib Foods Ltd v Paskin KyriaKides Sands (a firm)*,[59] a case concerning fire damage to the claimant's factory, where liability was imposed on the defendant architects for the inadequate fireproofing of a food preparation room, but the damages were reduced by two-thirds because the claimant's employees had both caused the fire and contributed to its spreading by misinforming the defendants about the nature of the cooking process involved. Similarly, in *Logical Computer Supplies Ltd v Euro Car Parks Ltd*[60] the compensation awarded to a company for damage to its computer files that had been caused by employees of an IT firm hired to supply an email system was reduced by 50 per cent on account of the company's failure to apply 'business common sense and risk management'[61] by properly backing up its data.

8.29 Nevertheless, despite these broader trends, much still depends on the facts of the particular case, and the sophistication of the claimant is clearly a material consideration, since 'the idea of a duty to second-guess an expert adviser is at its weakest in cases where the recipient of the advice is a lay person'.[62] In one claim against a law firm, for example, the judge took account, in finding that there was no contributory negligence, of the fact that the person who ran the claimant company had 'little or no experience' of property development and limited understanding of the 'intricacies of such agreements'.[63] By contrast, in one of the two instances in which a law firm successfully pleaded contributory negligence,[64] the claimant was a government department. The judge held that, as such, it should have had its own system in place for ensuring that it made a vital payment that would have enabled it to exercise a break clause in a lease on time, and ought not to have relied completely on its legal advisers to remind it.[65] It was, however, also a consideration in the latter

---

58 As Murdoch points out (n 1) 98, findings of contributory negligence are more appropriate in professional negligence cases where 'losses suffered by the client are clearly the result, not only of negligence by a professional adviser, but also of some totally independent act or omission by the client which contains no element of second-guessing the expert'.

59 [2003] EWCA Civ 1832; [2004] PNLR 22 [1:114]; [2:56]; [4:9].

60 (n 20) [1:54]; [4:4].

61 Ibid, [14] (Richard Fernyhough QC).

62 Murdoch (n 1) 102.

63 *Credit Lyonnais* (n 42) [21], [80] (Peter Smith J) [1:98]; [4:7].

64 *Unicorn* (n 6) [1:31]; [4:3].

65 For similar reasoning in a Canadian case, see *Doiron v Caisse Populaire* (1985) 17 DLR (4th) 660 (NBCA), where it was held that a financial institution was guilty of contributory negligence for failing to check that the loan documents provided by the defendant solicitor complied with its instructions.

case that the claimant knew that it was vital that the payment was made punctually, and that doing so required no special expertise.[66]

The sophistication of the client is also clearly relevant in claims against insurance brokers, where it is unlikely that a lay client will be found to have been at fault in not checking or failing to understand insurance documentation. To take one example, in *Arbory Group Ltd v West Craven Insurance Services*[67] it was held that a lay businessperson could not be expected to be familiar with the principles of computation of lost profits in the context of business interruption insurance, and that it was the duty of the defendant broker to explain its meaning to such a client.[68] However, such conduct is more likely to be considered negligent where the client is itself an insurance company, and, hence, 'as knowledgeable about insurance matters' as an insurance broker.[69] Overall, however, our finding that pleas of contributory negligence by insurance brokers succeeded in only 14 per cent of the claims in which they were made is consistent with the statement that in this context '[w]hile a reduction for contributory negligence is possible, in practice the courts show a good deal of indulgence towards assureds who assume that their brokers have acted properly and do not take steps to double check'.[70] **8.30**

Contributory negligence in the medical negligence context

Turning to the medical negligence context, the dearth of case law in our study provides further evidence that pleas (let alone successful pleas) of contributory negligence are most unusual in this area of law. It is also instructive to compare the facts of the only such case where a finding of contributory negligence was made, *Pidgeon v Doncaster HA*,[71] with the facts of one of the medical negligence cases in which the plea was unsuccessful, *P (decd) v Sedar*.[72] In *Pidgeon*, the claimant sought damages in respect of a cervical smear which was wrongly evaluated by the defendants as being negative. However, although the judge held that the defendants had indeed been negligent, he also held that two-thirds of the responsibility for the failure to identify the claimant's cancerous condition lay with the claimant herself, who failed **8.31**

---

66 *Unicorn* (n 6) [128] (Rimer J) [1:31]; [4:3].

67 [2007] Lloyd's Rep IR 491 (QBD) [1:249]; [4:21].

68 For a similar analysis in the insurance context, see *Dunlop* (n 25) [224]–[225] (Hamblen J) [1:350]; [1:351]; [4:29]; [4:30].

69 *Jackson & Powell on Professional Liability* (n 2) para 16.182. See also Murdoch (n 1) 99. For examples of the relative sophistication of the client affecting the contributory negligence analysis in claims against insurance brokers in claims not included in our study, see Dugdale and Stanton (n 1) para 21.37.

70 Michael Jones (ed), *Clerk & Lindsell on Torts* (22nd edn, Sweet & Maxwell 2017) para 10.259 (footnote omitted).

71 (n 14) [1:63]; [4:5].

72 (n 21) [1:393]; [4:34].

to have further smear tests, despite being repeatedly urged to do so in strong terms by several doctors. By contrast, in *P (decd) v Sedar*, where the judge described the facts of *Pidgeon* as 'extreme',[73] it was held that the deceased had not been negligent in failing to chase up hospital appointment letters that the defendant GP had sent to the wrong address, with the result that the deceased's breast cancer was incurable by the time it was diagnosed.

8.32 On one level, the lack of case law on contributory negligence in the medical malpractice context is unsurprising. As an Australian commentator has pointed out:

> The paternalistic model [of the doctor/patient relationship] places responsibility for the patient's health and medical treatment squarely on the shoulders of the doctor without reference to any responsibility the patient may have for his or her own health. It follows that contributory negligence principles have little application in a legal system that embodies the paternalistic model . . . .[74]

8.33 On the other hand, whatever model of the doctor–patient relationship is adopted, it is hard to see why clearly negligent conduct on the part of a patient who fails to, for example, disclose highly relevant information, attend a follow-up appointment, or comply with medical advice, should not be met with a modest reduction in damages. Furthermore, as common law legal systems move away from the paternalistic model of the doctor–patient relationship, courts may be more inclined to make findings of contributory negligence in medical malpractice litigation. In Canada, it has been said by commentators that 'the number of cases in which patients have been found contributorily negligent has increased significantly in recent years', a phenomenon linked to patients striving for (and achieving) 'a more equal role in ... the doctor–patient relationship'.[75] Similarly, it has been argued that the shift away from a medical paternalism model towards a patient autonomy model in Australia following the decision of the High Court in *Rogers v Whitaker*[76] has led to increased reliance on the contributory negligence doctrine in medical malpractice litigation before the Australian courts.[77] As Harper says:

> The recognition of greater patient autonomy at law mandates that courts re-evaluate the foundational assumptions upon which the majority of medical law

[73] Ibid, [61] (HHJ Mitchell).

[74] Harper (n 1) 3. See also Herring and Foster (n 1) 83 (under the traditional paternalistic model, '[t]he patients' role is essentially a passive one', with the result that 'there is little the patient can do that would be regarded as negligent').

[75] Picard and Robertson (n 1) 369. Nevertheless, even in Canada, the same authors say that the contributory negligence defence 'has been applied in relatively few medical negligence cases': ibid.

[76] (1992) 175 CLR 479 (HCA).

[77] Harper (n 1) 17. It has also been said that the defence is frequently employed in medical malpractice litigation in the United States, where the courts have also embraced the patient autonomy model: see Herring and Foster (n 1) 76.

> is premised. In the context of the defence of contributory negligence, this means that courts must move away from the implicit assumption of patient dependence, an assumption that, for decades, justified the preclusion of the defence of contributory negligence for defendant-physicians ... There is an argument to be made that the movement for patients' rights demands reciprocity. For example, if patients have the 'right' to full disclosure by their physicians, then it can be argued that they also have the 'obligation' to reciprocate by fully and accurately disclosing to the physician all information that may be relevant to the patient's medical care.[78]

If increased patient autonomy also entails increased patient responsibility, then one by-product of the strong recent emphasis by the UK courts on patient autonomy in the medical non-disclosure context could be an increased focus on patient conduct in medical negligence litigation. After all, in *Montgomery v Lanarkshire Health Board*—where the Supreme Court replaced the *Bolam* test[79] with a patient-sided test of 'material risk' in medical non-disclosure cases—Lord Kerr and Lord Reed said, in the leading judgment, that: **8.34**

> It would ... be a mistake to view patients as uninformed, incapable of understanding medical matters, or wholly dependent on a flow of information from doctors. The idea that patients were medically uninformed and incapable of understanding medical matters was always a questionable generalisation ....[80]

Furthermore, their Lordships argued that the social and legal developments that they highlighted in their judgment pointed away from a model of the relationship between doctor and patient based on medical paternalism. These developments, they said, instead favoured an approach that treats patients, not as placing themselves in the hands of their doctors (and then being prone to sue in the event of a disappointing outcome), but so far as possible as adults who are capable of understanding that medical treatment is uncertain of success and may involve risks, accepting responsibility for the taking of risks affecting their own lives, and living with the consequences of their choices.[81] **8.35**

Nevertheless, judgment in *Montgomery* was handed down near the end of our study period, and so it remains to be seen whether this new-found emphasis on patient responsibility will mean that in future the contributory negligence doctrine will play a greater role in medical negligence litigation in the United Kingdom. **8.36**

---

78 Ventresca, Kryworuk, and Chambers (n 1) 228. To similar effect, see Harper (n 1); Sharon Murphy, 'Contributory Negligence in Medical Malpractice: Are the Standards Changing to Reflect Society's Growing Health Care Consumerism?' (1991) 17 U Dayton L Rev 151; Herring and Foster (n 1) 76.

79 *Bolam v Friern Hospital Management Committee* [1957] 1 WLR 582 (QBD) 587 (McNair J).

80 [2015] UKSC 11; [2015] AC 1430 [76].

81 Ibid, [81].

Conclusion

8.37 Professional negligence cases are often thought of as rather different in certain important respects from other types of negligence proceedings.[82] It therefore stands to reason that the contributory negligence doctrine might also operate in a distinctive way in this context. The burden of this chapter was, accordingly, to explore, employing both quantitative and qualitative analysis, how the doctrine functions in the professional negligence setting. Our findings suggest that the law of contributory negligence indeed adapts to the professional negligence environment. Thus, in our dataset, the plea of contributory negligence succeeded much less frequently in the professional negligence context than in other types of case. However, when the plea did succeed, the average discount was higher than in any other category of case. Interesting differences were also observed in the way in which the contributory negligence doctrine applies to different types of professional. In our sample, the plea of contributory negligence was particularly unlikely to succeed where the defendant was a lawyer or insurance broker. By contrast, valuers and surveyors who alleged contributory negligence had more success in the plea. We identified sophistication of the claimant as an important factor in explaining the handling of the contributory negligence doctrine in this context, although we also observed that this was only one of several considerations to which significance was attached. One thing that is clear, however, is that contributory negligence is regularly relied upon by defendants in professional negligence claims. That is unsurprising, given that it costs little or nothing to plead and yet significantly affects the quantum of recovery when the plea succeeds.

[82] 'The nature and functions of the traditional professions have ... resulted in certain significant distinctions in the application of basic tort rules to professionals. These distinctions have both restricted liability in some contexts and extended it in others': *Clerk & Lindsell on Torts* (n 70) para 10.02.

9

CONCLUSION

Traditionally, the shorthand writers who work in the courts had the copyright in the republication of the judgments that they produced. However, under a new contract that came into effect in 1999, the Court Service became entitled to publish judgments free of copyright. This change, coupled with developments in information technology, precipitated an explosion in the online availability of court decisions, which for the first time made the vast majority of reserved judgments of the higher courts accessible at the click of a mouse.[1] **9.01**

The revolution in the accessibility of court decisions at around the turn of the century creates important new opportunities for those engaged in legal scholarship in the United Kingdom. Previously, UK legal scholars were in practical terms largely reliant on the small minority of cases that were chosen for inclusion in the law reports as significant precedents. Now, however, scholars are realistically capable of engaging in empirical analysis of a large body of case law and drawing reliable conclusions about the practical operation of legal doctrines in the courts. **9.02**

It was in the light of this revolution that we embarked on an empirical study of the operation of the contributory negligence doctrine in the UK courts in the first 17 years of the twenty-first century. Our study of over 700 first instance and appellate decisions on contributory negligence is the first empirical investigation of the contributory negligence doctrine carried out in a Commonwealth jurisdiction for over two decades, and is the only such study ever to have looked exclusively at judicial decisions. In this book we have presented the results of that study and commented on them in the light of qualitative analysis of the case law and the existing scholarship regarding contributory negligence. **9.03**

Readers will have seen that our study uncovered several important truths about the contributory negligence doctrine hidden in this mass of case law. Some of these findings cast significant doubt on the accuracy of widely held views about the doctrine's operation, while others suggest that some commonly expressed **9.04**

[1] See Michael Zander, *The Law-Making Process* (7th edn, Hart Publishing 2015) 302.

perceptions are accurate. Given the centrality of the contributory negligence doctrine in private law litigation, our findings are of considerable significance to both the study and the practice of private law. We hope that they will inform future writing and reform proposals in the field of contributory negligence and will be taken on board by all those who engage with this doctrine as judges, legal practitioners, teachers, and researchers.

9.05 Studies like ours represent a sea-change in the treatment of court decisions as the subject of scholarly analysis. In traditional legal scholarship, court decisions are treated as precedents to be analysed in doctrinal terms. In the new empirical legal scholarship, by contrast, court decisions are treated as data to be subjected to empirical analysis. The focus therefore shifts from the exceptional decision to the run-of-the-mill one, and from where the *most important* decisions are found (in ultimate appellate courts) to where the *most* decisions are found (in trial courts and intermediate appellate courts). As two American commentators have observed, whereas when traditional legal scholars read cases, they are 'auditioning a crowd of singers to find the best soloists', empirical legal scholars 'assemble a chorus, listening to the sound that the cases make together'.[2]

9.06 Certain areas of private law are particularly amenable to empirical analysis of this kind. The doctrine of contributory negligence is a good example. The frequency with which the doctrine arises in litigation means that judicial decisions on contributory negligence are numerous enough for an empirical study to generate meaningful results. Furthermore, the phrase 'contributory negligence' is sufficiently distinctive to make it relatively easy to isolate the cases in which the doctrine is at issue. Also, the key decisions that a court typically makes when faced with a plea of contributory negligence—whether to discount the claimant's damages for contributory fault, and (if so) by how much—are easy to capture and translate into data susceptible to statistical analysis. But there are many areas of law in which such an approach could be of value, as is shown by the fact that several papers have been published in recent years that are the fruit of empirical analysis of UK court decisions dealing with other aspects of the law of tort.[3]

9.07 Empirical legal scholarship has a long and distinguished history in the United States, where it has recently been described as 'a dominant trend',[4] and UK legal scholarship

---

[2] Mark A Hall and Ronald F Wright, 'Systematic Content Analysis of Judicial Opinions' (2008) 96 Calif L Rev 63, 76.

[3] See, eg, David Acheson, 'Empirical Insights into Corporate Defamation: An Analysis of Cases Decided 2004–2013' (2016) 8 JML 32; James Goudkamp and Eleni Katsampouka, 'An Empirical Study of Punitive Damages' (2018) 38 OJLS 90; Per Laleng, 'Winners and Losers in the Court of Appeal: An Empirical Study of Personal Injury Cases (2002–2016)' [2018] JPIL 36.

[4] Jeffrey J Rachlinski, 'Does Empirical Legal Studies Shed more Heat than Light? The Case of Civil Damages Awards' (2016) 29 Ratio Juris 556, 556.

often follows where US legal scholarship has led. This is unsurprising given that there are clear advantages in engaging in the kind of empirical scholarship that underlies this book, one of which is that such scholarship is potentially of value to a variety of audiences, not least legal practitioners, to whom it provides concrete, robust information about the practice of the courts in a particular field of law.[5] But empirical research of this kind poses significant challenges as well. Because content analysis of large numbers of judicial decisions is inevitably very time-consuming, and because a trained statistician is needed to perform the statistical analysis, significant funding is often required to pay research assistants and statisticians. (In future, this difficulty will doubtless be alleviated, at least to some degree, by the use of artificial intelligence technology, which is likely to open up new vistas for empirical analysis of court decisions. For now, however, human beings are still required to do the bulk of the work.) Furthermore, it can be difficult to determine in advance not only what the questions are to which you want answers but also how to structure the coding of the data in such a way as to generate those answers. This was particularly challenging for our study of appellate decisions, where, contrary to our expectations, the dataset and statistical analysis ended up being far more complex than had been necessary for the first instance component of the work.

Perhaps the biggest challenge of all, however, is to gather sufficient data to render one's findings meaningful. In our study, two decisions that we made were particularly helpful in this regard. The first was to include within our first instance dataset salient details of first instance decisions that could be obtained only indirectly, either through summaries of the cases concerned or from appeals therefrom, because the full text of the first instance decision in issue was unavailable. The 189 claims that we indirectly accessed in this way significantly increased the size of our first instance sample, from 383 claims to 572. The other key decision was to extend the geographical scope of our study beyond England and Wales to include Northern Ireland and Scotland, which also substantially increased our first instance sample, this time by 170 claims. By seeking to maximize the size of our samples, we sought to minimize the likelihood that particular findings would be attributable to chance, as opposed to reflecting trends present in the entire body of decided cases. And while of course the possibility that some of the results were simply 'flukes' remained, the use of statistical analysis enabled us to evaluate how likely it was that a particular finding was attributable to chance, and to convey that information to the reader. **9.08**

Finally, in a book on contributory negligence, it seems appropriate to conclude with a word or two about the doctrine itself. Our study certainly suggests that the contributory negligence doctrine is in rude health, and that it continues to play **9.09**

[5] The companion volume to this work is a good example of the operation of this dynamic: see James Goudkamp and Donal Nolan, *Contributory Negligence: Principles and Practice* (OUP 2018).

a central role in the modern-day reality of private law litigation. Our analysis of contributory negligence in three of its most significant contextual settings—road accidents, employers' liability, and professional negligence—also suggests that the operation of the doctrine has a distinctive dynamic in different types of claim. While admittedly there are some types of case where contributory negligence seems rarely to be in issue—most obviously psychiatric injury claims and medical negligence claims—even here there are signs that reliance on the doctrine may be on the rise. In a world of driverless cars and declining manual labour—not to mention the effective abolition of breach of statutory duty actions against employers[6]—it might be thought that the future of the contributory negligence doctrine is uncertain. But we would venture to suggest that it will continue to be a significant feature of the private law landscape, and a fruitful subject of scholarly enquiry, for some time to come.

6 See the Enterprise and Regulatory Reform Act 2013, s 69.

EXPLANATORY MEMORANDUM TO APPENDICES

The following four appendices set out essential information regarding the claims in our first instance and appellate datasets. Appendix 1 comprises all the first instance claims while Appendix 2 captures the appellate claims. Appendix 3 contains all of the road accident claims in Appendix 1 and offers some additional information regarding those claims. Appendix 4 comprises all the claims in our first instance sample that were coded as professional negligence claims, and again offers some additional detail regarding those claims.

There are several important points regarding the appendices that may be worth our emphasizing so that the appendices can be properly understood. First, the listing of certain claims more than once in a given appendix is entirely deliberate. As we explained in our methodology chapter,[1] we carried out our analysis at the level of claims rather than cases, and so where there was more than one claim in a given case we created multiple entries to capture each of the claims.

Second, although it may appear odd that we have included references to appellate decisions in Appendices 1, 3, and 4, given that they are concerned solely with claims at first instance, the citation of appellate decisions is, again, wholly deliberate. As we explained above,[2] we often accessed first instance decisions indirectly, including via judgments given in appellate proceedings. When we cite appellate decisions in Appendices 1, 3, and 4, we have abstracted from those decisions details regarding the claim (or claims) at first instance.

Third, although the appendices (especially Appendices 1 and 2) track the first instance and appellate spreadsheets that we compiled in gathering our data, they do not replicate them in full. As is apparent from our description of our methodology above,[3] our spreadsheets contained considerably more detail than the appendices. In order to fit them onto the page, the appendices contain only the key information that the spreadsheets captured.

The following abbreviations are used in the appendices (Appendix 4 generally eschews the abbreviations as space is not at such a premium in relation to it):

CC: county court
CN: contributory negligence
EL: employers' liability
F: female
FI: first instance
M: male
N: no
NI: Northern Ireland
N/A: not applicable
O: other
OH: Outer House
OL: occupiers' liability
PD: property damage
PEL: pure economic loss

1 See 3.10.
2 See 3.02.
3 See 3.13, 3.21.

PI: personal injury

PL: public liability

PN: professional negligence

RA: road accident

SI: sports injury

U: unknown

Y: yes

APPENDIX 1

FIRST INSTANCE CLAIMS

	Claim	Citation	Court	Claim type	Damage type	Guilty of CN	Discount	Gender	Age	Actual or alleged CN	Defendant's wrongful conduct
1	**McDonald v Chambers**	2000 SLT 454	Court of Session (OH)	RA	PI	Y	33.3	F	25	Stepping into road before confirming that the traffic had stopped.	Failing to brake, swerve, or sound horn upon seeing pursuer.
2	**Ameen v Hunter**	2000 SLT 954	Court of Session (OH)	RA	PI	Y	50	F	27	Failing to stop car to check what was wrong with it; failing to move car off the carriageway; failing to activate hazard lights once car had come to rest.	Failing to move to inside lane to avoid collision.
3	**Pritchard v Ralph**	2000 WL 1791426	High Ct	RA	PI	Y	75	M	Adult	Stepping into road without looking for oncoming traffic.	Failing to keep a proper lookout for pedestrians.
4	**Dingley v Bromley LBC**	[2000] CLY 4244	Bromley CC	PL	PI	Y	25	F	63	Failing to avoid tripping over pot hole despite knowing of its existence.	Failing to implement an adequate inspection system.
5	**M v Parsons**	2000 WL 33122496	High Ct	RA	PI	Y	20	F	14	Moving into path of traffic without looking or signalling.	Driving at excessive speed and too close to cyclist to overtake safely.

	Claim	Citation	Court	Claim type	Damage type	Guilty of CN	Discount	Gender	Age	Actual or alleged CN	Defendant's wrongful conduct
6	**M v Parsons**	2000 WL 33122496	High Ct	EL	PI	Y	20	F	14	Moving into path of traffic without looking or signalling.	Failing to ensure that claimant completed her newspaper round safely.
7	**Mullaney v CC of the West Midlands**	[2001] EWCA Civ 700	High Ct	EL	PI	N	N/A	M	29	Arresting suspect without backup from another police officer or ensuring that another officer was close by; persisting in efforts to arrest suspect after he had become violent.	Failing by police officer to assist claimant.
8	**Simpson v AI Dairies Farms Ltd**	2001 WL 14904	Mayor's and City of London CC	OL	PI	N	N/A	M	Adult	Failing to 'shuffle' through water, ie, to feel way through so as to avoid injury.	Failing to maintain drain.
9	**Futter v Bryceland**	2000 GWD 9-339	Court of Session (OH)	RA	PI	Y	60	M	15.25	Stepping into road without looking for oncoming traffic.	Driving at excessive speed; failing to keep a proper lookout for pedestrians.
10	**Methven v Comr of Police of the Metropolis**	2000 WL 1480108	Mayor's and City of London CC	RA	PI	N	N/A	M	Adult	Failing to see and avoid police van; driving at excessive speed on approach to the junction despite vehicle being so overloaded as to hamper braking.	Crossing the junction against a red light without keeping a proper lookout for other road users.

11	**Cook v Thorne**	[2001] EWCA Civ 81	High Ct	RA	PI	Y	30	M	Adult	Intoxicated; standing in road and vomiting.	Failing to slow down to an appropriate speed.
12	**Cook v Thorne**	[2001] EWCA Civ 81	High Ct	RA	PI	Y	30	M	Adult	Intoxicated; standing in road and vomiting.	Exiting vehicle whose headlights were blinding the first defendant; remaining stationary in road.
13	**McLeod v BRB**	2000 Rep LR 58	Court of Session (OH)	PL	PI	Y	20	M	12	Climbing onto pipe spanning railway line and walking along it.	Failing properly to fence section of embankment.
14	**Cottingham v Attey Bower & Jones**	[2000] PNLR 557	High Ct	PN	PEL	N	N/A	M	Adult	Proceeding with purchase of property despite recommendations for further investigations.	Failing to discover and advise claimant of pre-contractual misrepresentation.
15	**Cottingham v Attey Bower & Jones**	[2000] PNLR 557	High Ct	PN	PEL	N	N/A	F	Adult	Proceeding with purchase of property despite recommendations for further investigations.	Failing to discover and advise claimant of pre-contractual misrepresentation.
16	**Sousa v A&J Bull Ltd**	[2001] EWCA Civ 1039	High Ct	RA	PI	Y	30	M	20	Riding bicycle with passenger on front handlebar.	Failing to leave sufficient room to pass parked car.
17	**North v TNT Express (UK) Ltd**	[2001] EWCA Civ 853	High Ct	RA	PI	Y	75	M	Adult	Climbing up on to the front bumper of lorry when intoxicated.	Driving whilst claimant was on the front bumper of lorry.
18	**Bittles v Harland & Wolff Plc**	[2000] NIJB 209	High Ct (NI)	EL	PI	N	N/A	M	24	Unknown.	Exposing claimant to asbestos.

	Claim	Citation	Court	Claim type	Damage type	Guilty of CN	Discount	Gender	Age	Actual or alleged CN	Defendant's wrongful conduct
19	**Abouzaid v Mothercare (UK) Ltd**	2000 WL 1918530	Mayor's and City of London CC	O	PI	N	N/A	M	12	Unknown.	Unsafe design of sleeping bag intended for use with pram; failing to provide instructions; failing to appreciate risk that person using product improperly could suffer serious injury.
20	**Arnot v Sprake**	[2001] EWCA Civ 341	Wandsworth CC	RA	PI	N	N/A	M	U	Failing to appreciate that crop sprayer was towing a trailer until it was too late.	Failing to place red triangle in road to warn road users; failing to sound horn to ensure that traffic was alerted to and warned of defendant's presence.
21	**S (a child) v Keyse**	2000 WL 33201536	High Ct	RA	PI	Y	25	M	17.75	Stepping into road without looking for oncoming traffic.	Driving at excessive speed.
22	**Shinhan Bank Ltd v Sea Containers Ltd**	[2000] 2 Lloyd's Rep 406	High Ct	O	PEL	N	N/A	N/A	N/A	Advancing money before bills of exchange accepted.	Failing to ensure that 'clean receipts' recording receipt of containers were authentic.

23	**Beckley v Crowther**	2000 WL 1544758	High Ct	RA	PI	N	N/A	F	Adult	Effecting turn without considering oncoming traffic.	Driving at excessive speed and down central reservation.
24	**Thain v Aberdeenshire Council**	2000 GWD 25-951	Sheriff Ct (Grampian, Highland and Islands)	RA	PI	N	N/A	F	16	Driving on wrong side of road.	Driving on wrong side of road.
25	**Inglis (Alexander) & Son Ltd v Forth Ports Plc**	2000 GWD 27-1035	Court of Session (OH)	O	PD	N	N/A	N/A	N/A	Failing to instruct that all bins be turned regularly; failing to provide adequate specification for seed intended for long-term storage; failing to audit defender's facilities and procedures for storage.	Failing to inspect seed at regular and appropriate intervals and to report results.
26	**Watson v Skuse**	[2001] EWCA Civ 1158	Birmingham CC	RA	PI	Y	50	M	49	Crossing road without checking whether 'green man' signal was still showing and only checking red light directing traffic; crossing against red light; crossing very close to lorry.	Failing to keep a proper lookout for pedestrians.
27	**Ingram v Woodhouse**	[2001] EWCA Civ 1057	Exeter CC	RA	PI	N	N/A	F	Adult	Crossing road in a dangerous place where there was a restricted view of traffic coming from both directions.	Failing to perform an emergency stop.
28	**Sargent v Secretary of State for Scotland**	2001 SCLR 190	Court of Session (OH)	PL	PI	N	N/A	M	45	Driving over barrier at excessive speed; failing to keep the vehicle under control.	Failing to erect signs or temporary traffic lights so as to prevent an accident at hazardous location.

	Claim	Citation	Court	Claim type	Damage type	Guilty of CN	Discount	Gender	Age	Actual or alleged CN	Defendant's wrongful conduct
29	**Beech v Speare**	[2001] EWCA Civ 1164	Manchester CC	OL	PI	N	N/A	F	Adult	Failing to notice chain fence.	Erecting chain fence in dangerous position.
30	**Parker v PFC Flooring Supplies Ltd**	[2001] PIQR P7	High Ct	EL	PI	Y	50	M	28	Walking on roof of premises knowing it was a situation of obvious danger and without appropriate equipment/ clothing.	Failing to prevent employees from accessing roof.
31	**Secretary of State for the Environment, Transport and Regions v Unicorn Consultancy Services Ltd**	[2000] NPC 108	High Ct	PN	PEL	Y	50	N/A	N/A	Failing to look after own interests by punctually making an important payment; failing to take internal steps to remind of the need to make the payment.	Failing to remind claimant of need to make punctual payment in order to invoke break clause.
32	**Markowski v Elson**	[2001] CLY 4477	Weymouth CC	RA	PI	Y	33.3	F	Adult	Stepping into road without looking for oncoming traffic	Parking ambulance in a position whereby it caused a hazard.
33	**Ledger v Spurgeon**	[2001] EWCA Civ 1527	Kingston-Upon-Hull CC	RA	PI	Y	80	M	U	Driving without due care when driving directly towards low-hanging sun; failing to see the excavator and take appropriate action to avoid it despite the presence of warning signs.	Failing adequately to warn of the presence of excavator on road.

34	**Cross v UGC Ltd**	[2001] EWCA Civ 685	Milton Keynes CC	EL	PI	N	N/A	M	Adult	Resting spray gun on ladder.	Allowing an inherently unsafe system of work.
35	**DE (a child) v S Garages Ltd**	2000 WL 33281292	High Ct	O	PI	Y	33.3	M	14	Purchasing petrol knowing it was dangerous and inhaling fumes.	Selling petrol to claimant.
36	**B (a child) v Wynn**	[2001] EWCA Civ 710	Central London CC	RA	PI	Y	66.6	M	11.5	Stepping into road without looking for oncoming traffic.	Failing to keep a proper lookout for pedestrians.
37	**Taylor v Tyler**	2000 WL 33281237	High Ct	RA	PI	N	N/A	M	Adult	Driving at excessive speed; failing to observe the presence of the defendant's motor vehicle; overtaking a number of vehicles when unsafe to do so.	Effecting a right turn across path of oncoming traffic without making sure that there was no oncoming traffic that could be inconvenienced by manoeuvre.
38	**Cameron v Kvaerner Govan Ltd**	2001 Rep LR 52	Court of Session (OH)	EL	PI	Y	20	M	48	Failing to warn against loosening securing wire until box secured by crane.	Detaching cable from box before it was secured by crane.
39	**Regan v Chetwynd**	2000 WL 33122388	High Ct	RA	PI	N	N/A	M	21	Riding close to centre of road.	Failing to notice claimant's approaching motorcycle and turning into its path.
40	**W v Hardman**	[2001] CLY 4452	Leeds CC	RA	PI	Y	15	M	U	Failing to wear seat belt; travelling with intoxicated driver.	Driving while intoxicated.

	Claim	Citation	Court	Claim type	Damage type	Guilty of CN	Discount	Gender	Age	Actual or alleged CN	Defendant's wrongful conduct
41	**Gorringe v Calderdale MBC**	[2002] EWCA Civ 595; [2002] RTR 27	High Ct	PL	PI	N	N/A	F	35	Driving at excessive speed.	Failing to have adequate regard to conditions at crest/corner where accident occurred.
42	**Palfrey v Ark Offshore Ltd**	2001 WL 34034706	High Ct	EL	PI	N	N/A	M	40	Failing to have regard to obvious risk of malaria.	Failing effectively to advise employees of risk of tropical diseases whilst working abroad.
43	**Betts v Tokley**	[2002] EWCA Civ 52	Colchester CC	EL	PI	Y	60	F	Adult	Exiting the building through exit known to be unlit although aware of dangers doing so entailed.	Failing to illuminate premises.
44	**Currie v Clamp**	2002 SLT 196	Court of Session (OH)	RA	PI	Y	33.3	M	22	Travelling in a vehicle with intoxicated driver.	Driving while intoxicated.
45	**Mattar v Shenouda**	2001 WL 606384	High Ct	RA	PI	Y	15	M	51	Failing to wear seat belt.	Driving without due care and attention.
46	**George v Stagecoach South-East London**	2001 WL 513089	High Ct	RA	PI	Y	40	F	44	Walking into path of bus; failing to pay sufficient attention while crossing road.	Failing to keep a proper lookout for pedestrians; failing to accord claimant precedence.
47	**Perrin v Ministry of Defence**	[2001] All ER (D) 03 (May)	High Ct	EL	PI	Y	20	M	Adult	Failing to wear military helmet during training exercise.	Failing to ensure that helmets were worn during training exercise.

48	**Skinner v Aberdeen CC**	2001 Rep LR 118	Court of Session (OH)	EL	PI	N	N/A	M	63	Failing to use safer method of lifting and laying slabs.	Failing to train or instruct pursuer employee so as to reduce risk of injury to lowest possible level.
49	**White v Chapman**	2001 WL 825325	High Ct	RA	PI	Y	20	F	Adult	Crossing road at a point where there was no central refuge.	Failing to keep a proper lookout for pedestrians; failing to slow down or adjust position in road in order to avoid claimant.
50	**Sullivan v HWF Ltd**	[2001] CLY 3301	Bradford CC	EL	PI	Y	33.3	M	52	Failing to see bolt before kneeling down.	Failing to prevent tripping hazard in workplace.
51	**Toole v Bolton MBC**	[2002] EWCA Civ 588	Manchester CC	EL	PI	Y	75	M	Adult	Attempting to pick up syringe wearing only rubber glove.	Failing to provide adequate work equipment.
52	**Anderson v Newham College of Further Education**	[2002] EWCA Civ 505; [2003] ICR 212	Central London CC	EL	PI	Y	90	M	Adult	Failing to see legs of white board and avoid tripping over them.	Failing properly to store whiteboard.
53	**Powell v Hansen**	2001 WL 753470	High Ct	RA	PI	Y	20	M	52	Driving at excessive speed.	Undertaking a dangerous manoeuvre; failing to note oncoming traffic; failing to stop at stop line; driving on wrong side of road.

	Claim	Citation	Court	Claim type	Damage type	Guilty of CN	Discount	Gender	Age	Actual or alleged CN	Defendant's wrongful conduct
54	**Logical Computer Supplies Ltd v Euro Car Parks Ltd**	2001 WL 825094	High Ct	PN	PD	Y	50	N/A	N/A	Failing to put proper data back-up system in place; failing to check that back-up tapes were of correct type; failing to check that back-up system was working satisfactorily; failing to detect or understand error message produced by server.	Damaging hard-drive while undertaking repairs.
55	**Beck v United Closures & Plastics Plc**	2001 SLT 1299	Court of Session (OH)	EL	PI	N	N/A	M	Adult	Extending fingers and allowing them to become trapped.	Failing to provide suitable and safe work equipment.
56	**Young v Post Office**	[2002] EWCA Civ 661; [2002] IRLR 660	Barnsley CC	EL	PI	N	N/A	M	Adult	Burdening himself unnecessarily with work; failing to voice concerns about health to superiors.	Failing to provide sufficient support upon claimant's return to work following stress-related leave.
57	**Skerman v H Bollman Manufacturers Ltd**	[2002] EWCA Civ 919	Brighton CC	EL	PI	N	N/A	F	25	Unknown.	Failing properly to assess risk involved in task; failing to provide training and instruction.
58	**Chittock v Woodbridge School**	[2002] PIQR P13	High Ct	SI	PI	Y	50	M	17.5	Undertaking skiing manoeuvre which was too advanced; ignoring obvious associated risks.	Failing sufficiently to discipline claimant for skiing off piste.

59	**Oxley Plumbers Merchants v Davies**	[2002] EWCA Civ 540	Lincoln CC	OL	PI	N	N/A	M	Adult	Walking backwards towards trap door knowing it was in need of repair.	Failing to undertake remedial work to trap door.
60	**Holt v Holroyd Meek Ltd**	[2002] EWCA Civ 1004	Maidstone CC	EL	PI	N	N/A	M	Adult	Walking on surface made slippery by water and diesel.	Failing adequately to hose down surface.
61	**Irwin v Stevenson**	[2002] EWCA Civ 359	Basingstoke CC	RA	PI	Y	50	M	U	Attempting to overtake two slowing vehicles.	Failing to observe motorcycle.
62	**Barnett v Scottish Power**	[2002] EWCA Civ 104	Chester CC	EL	PI	N	N/A	F	44	Failing properly to assess suitability of chair.	Failing to provide necessary work equipment.
63	**Pidgeon v Doncaster HA**	[2002] Lloyd's Rep Med 130	Sheffield CC	PN	PI	Y	66.6	F	Adult	Repeatedly failing to undergo cervical smear tests.	Failing to interpret properly cervical smear test results.
64	**Poccia v Toussaint**	2001 WL 34008510	High Ct	RA	PI	N	N/A	M	Adult	Crossing a junction while parallel with defendant's car; overtaking on nearside.	Pulling to nearside of road to park and cutting across path of claimant's vehicle in doing so.
65	**Bailey v Command Security Services Ltd**	2001 WL 1535385	High Ct	EL	PI	Y	25	M	22	Failing to pay attention to surroundings and to notice unguarded edge.	Failing to ensure employees' safety.
66	**Bailey v Command Security Services Ltd**	2001 WL 1535385	High Ct	OL	PI	Y	25	M	22	Failing to pay attention to surroundings and to notice unguarded edge.	Failing to fence off dangerous areas.

	Claim	Citation	Court	Claim type	Damage type	Guilty of CN	Discount	Gender	Age	Actual or alleged CN	Defendant's wrongful conduct
67	**Rowntree v Comr of Police of the Metropolis**	[2001] Po LR 404	High Ct	EL	PI	N	N/A	F	34	Failing to complain about work pressure; failing to take a step back from a case on which she was working; failing to recognise own problems and seek advice.	Failing to supervise claimant properly and to give adequate support; failing to spot warning signs of mental stress; failing to recognise a second impending breakdown; failing to act and to protect the claimant from stressful involvement in child abuse trial.
68	**Purdue v Devon Fire and Rescue Service**	[2002] EWCA Civ 1538	Exeter CC	RA	PI	N	N/A	M	49	Failing to check for oncoming traffic whilst stationary at traffic lights.	Driving through a red light; failing to activate siren.
69	**Lunt v Khelifa**	2001 WL 1479700	High Ct	RA	PI	Y	33.3	M	Adult	Intoxicated; stepping into road without looking for oncoming traffic.	Failing to keep a proper lookout for pedestrians.
70	**Buyukardicli v Hammerson UK Properties Plc**	[2002] EWCA Civ 683	Central London CC	OL	PI	Y	75	F	Adult	Failing to pay attention while walking on unfinished and temporary surface.	Failing to take sufficient steps to reduce risk of injury to visitors walking across unfinished and temporary surface.

71	**Buyukardicli v Hammerson UK Properties Plc**	[2002] EWCA Civ 683	Central London CC	OL	PI	Y	75	F	Adult	Failing to pay attention while walking on unfinished and temporary surface.	Failing to take sufficient steps to reduce risk of injury to visitors walking across unfinished and temporary surface.
72	**Kirk v Fife Council**	2002 SCLR 407	Court of Session (OH)	OL	PI	N	N/A	M	27	Playing football on wet surface despite awareness that doing so presented increased risk of injury.	Allowing game to proceed knowing that part of the floor of the sports hall was wet.
73	**Donaldson v Brighton DC**	2001 WL 1743237	Lewes CC	OL	PI	Y	25	M	Adult	Failing to ask colleague to foot ladder.	Failing to implement required system to inspect ladders; failing to warn claimant of defective ladders.
74	**Donaldson v Brighton DC**	2001 WL 1743237	Lewes CC	EL	PI	Y	25	M	Adult	Failing to ask colleague to foot ladder.	Failing to provide claimant with a safe ladder; failing to train claimant adequately; failing to carry out risk assessment of task.
75	**Kane v New Forest DC (No 2)**	2001 WL 1903436	High Ct	PL	PI	Y	33.3	M	24	Stepping into road without looking for oncoming traffic.	Dangerous road design.
76	**Haughian v NI Railways Co Ltd**	[2001] NIQB 44	High Ct (NI)	OL	PI	N	N/A	M	15	Failing to realise danger of climbing over spiked metal fence.	Failing to eliminate or reduce risk of injury posed by spiked fence; failing to bend spikes.

	Claim	Citation	Court	Claim type	Damage type	Guilty of CN	Discount	Gender	Age	Actual or alleged CN	Defendant's wrongful conduct
77	**Miller v Perth and Kinross Council**	2002 Rep LR 22	Court of Session (OH)	EL	PI	N	N/A	F	Adult	Failing to keep a lookout and notice slope of path.	Failing to provide suitable and sufficient lighting.
78	**Kearn-Price v Kent CC**	[2002] EWCA Civ 1539	Tunbridge Wells CC	O	PI	N	N/A	F	14	Failing to stand in picnic area; standing too close to goalposts.	Failing to supervise pre-school activities of pupils.
79	**Butcher v Cornwall CC**	[2002] EWCA Civ 1640	Truro CC	EL	PI	Y	10	M	Adult	Failing to ensure that door was properly closed.	Failing to provide a safe means of securing open door.
80	**Kennedy v Harland & Wolff Plc**	[2002] NIQB 11; [2002] NI 169	High Ct (NI)	EL	PI	N	N/A	M	19	Unknown.	Exposing claimant to asbestos.
81	**Murray v Weldex International Offshore Ltd**	[2002] CSOH 52; 2002 SCLR 591	Court of Session (OH)	EL	PI	N	N/A	M	49	Signalling to crane operator to lift when it was unsafe to do so.	Proceeding to lift despite pursuer not standing clear of load.
82	**Wells v Trinder**	[2002] EWCA Civ 1030	Luton CC	RA	PI	N	N/A	F	Adult	Stepping into road without looking for oncoming traffic.	Driving at excessive speed; failing to keep a proper lookout for pedestrians.
83	**Arnesen v Heffey**	[2002] EWCA Civ 1058	Northampton CC	RA	PI	Y	25	M	U	Driving too close to vehicle in front; riding alongside another motorcyclist instead of riding one behind the other.	Failing to pull over to hard shoulder or pull closer to central reservation following a tyre blow-out.

84	**Beaton v Devon CC**	[2002] EWCA Civ 1675	Barnstaple CC	OL	PI	N	N/A	F	Adult	Putting foot in gully.	Failing to provide adequate lighting in tunnel.
85	**Smith v Hastie**	2002 SLT 1183	Court of Session (OH)	RA	PI	N	N/A	F	38	Driving at excessive speed; driving on wrong side of road.	Driving on the wrong side of road.
86	**Adlington v Comr of Police of the Metropolis**	[2002] EWCA Civ 1712	Central London CC	EL	PI	Y	33.3	M	Adult	Going down ramp and entering car park after seeing shutter open; failing to realise that shutter may start closing; going down ramp at excessive speed.	Failing to warn claimant and permitting him to travel into car park whilst shutter closing.
87	**Alpha Credit Bank v Stephenson Harwood**	[2002] EWHC 922 (Ch)	High Ct	PN	PEL	Y	60	N/A	N/A	Failing to make reasonably prudent enquiries into facts of transaction; negligent investigation of valuation; failing to instruct solicitor regarding occupiers whose status claimant wished to have investigated.	Failing to conduct proper investigations into occupiers of property.
88	**Marshall v Rennocks**	[2004] CLY 2702	Luton CC	RA	PI	N	N/A	U	U	Crossing centre line.	Parking vehicle in an unsafe and inappropriate manner.
89	**Renton v Riddell**	2002 Scot (D) 27/4	Court of Session (OH)	SI	N/A	N	N/A	M	36	Failing to take action to prevent collision; putting dominant right hand up to fend off defender's yacht.	Turning unexpectedly towards pursuer's yacht and striking it.
90	**Kiapasha v Laverton**	[2002] EWCA Civ 1656	Newcastle CC	OL	PI	N	N/A	F	30	Slipping on the wet tiled floor of the shop while intoxicated.	Failing to take steps to prevent accumulation of water on floor.

	Claim	Citation	Court	Claim type	Damage type	Guilty of CN	Discount	Gender	Age	Actual or alleged CN	Defendant's wrongful conduct
91	**Williams v Devon CC**	[2003] EWCA Civ 365; [2003] PIQR Q4	Plymouth CC	EL	PI	Y	33.3	F	Adult	Going through doorway carrying menu without first checking that path was clear.	Failing to keep floor free from obstructions.
92	**Annabil v George Payne & Co Ltd**	[2002] EWHC 1061 (QB)	High Ct	EL	PI	Y	25	M	Adult	Failing to notice roller door was closing and proceeding through door.	Failing to fit door with adequate safety mechanisms.
93	**Walker v Newham LBC**	[2002] CLY 3256	Central London CC	PL	PI	Y	33.3	M	U	Failing to take appropriate care to avoid danger of which claimant was well aware, in particular, failing to report gap to local authority.	Failing to maintain steps.
94	**Shaher v British Aerospace Flying College Ltd**	2002 Rep LR 96	Court of Session (OH)	O	PI	Y	50	M	19	Flying into clouds contrary to instructions.	Allowing solo flight to proceed.
95	**White v Harland & Wolff Plc**	[2002] NIQB 49	High Ct (NI)	EL	PI	N	N/A	M	24	Unknown.	Exposing claimant to asbestos.
96	**Patterson v Davis**	[2002] NIQB 36	High Ct (NI)	O	PI	N	N/A	M	48	Moving inside box while elevated on forklift.	Failing to secure potato box on tines of forklift.
97	**Patterson v Davis**	[2002] NIQB 36	High Ct (NI)	O	PI	N	N/A	M	48	Moving inside box while elevated on forklift.	Failing to secure potato box on tines of forklift.

98	**Credit Lyonnais SA v Russell Jones & Walker**	[2002] EWHC 1310 (Ch); [2003] PNLR 2	High Ct	PN	PEL	N	N/A	N/A	N/A	Failing to make a payment on time.	Failing to draw claimant's attention to need to make payment promptly.
99	**Pigford v City of Sunderland**	[2003] EWCA Civ 823	Newcastle upon Tyne CC	PL	PI	N	N/A	F	Adult	Unknown.	Failing to make surface safe despite repeated complaints about its dangerousness.
100	**Donoghue v Folkestone Properties Ltd**	[2003] EWCA Civ 231; [2003] QB 1008	High Ct	OL	PI	Y	75	M	31	Diving into unfamiliar water in harbour.	Failing to offer some protection against diving.
101	**Griffiths v Vauxhall Motors Ltd**	[2003] EWCA Civ 412	Tameside CC	EL	PI	Y	50	M	Adult	Failing to handle gun in required manner.	Failing to conduct risk assessment.
102	**Eagle v Chambers (No 1)**	[2003] EWCA Civ 1107; [2004] RTR 9	High Ct	RA	PI	Y	60	F	17	Stepping into road and walking in middle of it; ignoring warnings from passers by.	Intoxicated driver; driving at excessive speed; failing to stay in lane.
103	**Rogers v National Assembly for Wales**	[2004] EWCA Civ 250	High Ct	PL	PI	N	N/A	M	Adult	Driving at excessive speed; failing to keep a proper lookout for traffic coming in opposite direction.	Failing to maintain highway.
104	**Gartland v Hathaway Roofing Ltd**	[2003] EWCA Civ 957	Bishop Auckland CC	EL	PI	Y	25	M	27.5	Failing to clip safety harness to line.	Failing to operate safety system that had been established by second defendant.

	Claim	Citation	Court	Claim type	Damage type	Guilty of CN	Discount	Gender	Age	Actual or alleged CN	Defendant's wrongful conduct
105	**Gartland v Hathaway Roofing Ltd**	[2003] EWCA Civ 957	Bishop Auckland CC	EL	PI	Y	25	M	27.5	Failing to clip safety harness to line.	Failing to detect that its operating procedures were being breached.
106	**Noble v De Boer (No 2)**	2004 SLT 1085	Sheriff Ct (Grampian, Highland and Islands)	O	PI	Y	30	M	44	Knowing of stone's movement on deck and not disposing of it.	Failing to order that stone be disposed of overboard or at least to take reasonable steps to secure it in such a way that it could not move during fishing operations.
107	**Adjei v King**	[2003] EWCA Civ 414	High Ct	RA	PI	N	N/A	M	Adult	Stepping into road without looking for oncoming traffic.	Driving at excessive speed; failing to keep a proper lookout for pedestrians.
108	**Pratt v Smith**	2002 WL 31676426	High Ct	RA	PI	N	N/A	M	45	Driving car with defective brakes and bald/defective front tyre; driving at excessive speed; failing to notice defendant's indication of intention to turn right.	Cutting across claimant's path whilst driving.

109	**Alexander Forbes Europe Ltd v SBJ Ltd**	[2002] EWHC 3121 (Comm); [2003] PNLR 15	High Ct	PN	PEL	N	N/A	N/A	N/A	Failing to make claims under insurance policy.	Failing to notify underwriters properly as to possible 'any circumstances' claims.
110	**Cooper v Carillion Plc**	[2003] EWCA Civ 1811	Plymouth CC	EL	PI	Y	10	M	Adult	Failing to look underneath board before placing feet.	Failing to re-erect barriers around service hole.
111	**McCully v Farrans Ltd**	[2003] NIQB 6	High Ct (NI)	OL	PI	N	N/A	M	33	Failing to position lorry with near side to wall/boulders so as to avoid danger of slipping and falling between lorry and boulders.	Allowing boulders to be used as a means of access by many lorry drivers.
112	**Mackenzie v Perth & Kinross Council**	2003 Scot (D) 27/1	Court of Session (OH)	PL	PI	Y	33.3	M	Adult	Driving at excessive speed through roadworks.	Failing to erect a 'ramp ahead' warning sign at roadworks.
113	**Taylor v Liverpool CC**	[2004] CLY 2691	Liverpool CC	PL	PI	Y	U	F	U	Unknown.	Failing to maintain footway.
114	**Sahib Foods Ltd v Paskin KyriaKides Sands**	[2003] EWHC 142 (TCC); [2003] PNLR 30	High Ct	PN	PD	N	N/A	N/A	N/A	Cooking in room despite being advised that it was not appropriate for cooking.	Knowing that materials in room were not fireproof and failing to advise accordingly.
115	**Speshal Investments Ltd v Corby Kane Howard Partnership Ltd**	[2003] EWHC 390 (Ch)	High Ct	PN	PEL	Y	20	N/A	N/A	Failing to conclude that wide disparity between purchase price and valuation indicated unreliability of defendant's valuation; failing to pay adequate regard to another valuation; failing to undertake proper investigations.	Negligently valuing property.

	Claim	Citation	Court	Claim type	Damage type	Guilty of CN	Discount	Gender	Age	Actual or alleged CN	Defendant's wrongful conduct
116	**Constantine v Total Final Elf UK Ltd**	[2003] EWHC 428 (Ch)	High Ct	O	PD	N	N/A	M	Adult	Storing valuable antiques and furniture in garage close to oil storage tank and leaving them uncovered; requiring the defendant to deliver heating oil to storage tank in garage knowing that valuable antiques and furniture were in garage.	Spraying goods with oil whilst in storage.
117	**Moseley v Pell**	[2003] EWCA Civ 1533	Milton Keynes CC	RA	PI	N	N/A	M	39	Overtaking line of traffic in front of an entrance to event.	Effecting right turn without checking for oncoming traffic; failing to notice claimant's motorcycle.
118	**Delaney v McGregor Construction (Highlands) Ltd**	2003 Rep LR 56	Court of Session (OH)	EL	PI	Y	10	M	31	Standing at arms-length from heavy raised load; trying to dislodge load by pulling or tugging at it.	Failing to provide a safe way of unloading rods; failing to provide warnings or training in the lifting of rods; failing to provide sufficient supervision.
119	**Battley v Thomson Holidays Ltd**	[2004] CLY 1878	Central London CC	O	PI	Y	50	M	Adult	Error of judgment in thinking it possible to walk under large and obvious light.	Placing light fitting at an inappropriately low and unsafe level; failing to warn the claimant of the potential hazard.

120	**Marley v Cohen**	[2003] EWCA Civ 1536	Chester CC	O	PI	N	N/A	F	U	Stepping ashore whilst another boat was approaching.	Turning boat when it was unsafe to do so.
121	**Plumpton v Norfolk CC**	[2004] CLY 2750	Norwich CC	PL	PI	Y	50	F	U	Failing to apply brakes after seeing warning sign.	Failing to post adequate signs warning motorists of presence of loose chippings on highway.
122	**Green v Bannister**	[2003] EWCA Civ 1819	Barnsley CC	RA	PI	Y	60	M	U	Lying in road when intoxicated.	Failing to look over left shoulder or in nearside wing or rear-view mirror when reversing.
123	**Mathieson v Aberdeenshire Council**	2003 SLT (Sh Ct) 91	Sheriff Ct (Grampian, Highland and Islands)	PL	PI	N	N/A	M	U	Failing to avoid drop at recycling centre; unloading trailer in dangerous manner.	Failing to provide an effective barrier; failing to take the precautions deemed necessary by risk assessment.
124	**Coates v Jaguar Cars Ltd**	[2004] EWCA Civ 337	Birmingham CC	EL	PI	Y	25	M	58	Failing to look at steps whilst ascending them.	Failing to install a handrail on set of steps.
125	**Booth v White**	[2003] EWCA Civ 1708	Norwich CC	RA	PI	N	N/A	M	Adult	Failing to enquire of defendant whether he had drunk too much alcohol before accepting a lift home.	Driving while intoxicated.
126	**Costello v Birkby**	[2004] CLY 2744	Oldham CC	RA	PI	N	N/A	F	Adult	Edging taxi further out in the bus lane in order to reach a garage despite inability to see beyond about two car lengths down the bus lane.	Driving in bus lane when not entitled to do so; driving at excessive speed.

	Claim	Citation	Court	Claim type	Damage type	Guilty of CN	Discount	Gender	Age	Actual or alleged CN	Defendant's wrongful conduct
127	**Wright v Romford Blinds & Shutters Ltd**	[2003] EWHC 1165 (QB)	High Ct	EL	PI	N	N/A	M	55	Failing to advise of vertigo; standing on roof of the van when, by reason of such vertigo, it was unsafe to do so.	Failing to take reasonable care in the manner in which bundles of shuttering were passed to claimant.
128	**Barker v Corus UK Ltd**	[2006] UKHL 20; [2006] 2 AC 572	High Ct	EL	PI	Y	20	M	Adult	Self-exposure to asbestos while self-employed as a plasterer.	Exposing claimant to asbestos.
129	**Akasuc Enterprise Ltd v Farmar & Shirreff**	[2003] EWHC 1275 (Ch)	High Ct	PN	PEL	N	N/A	N/A	N/A	Failing to appreciate inadequate drafting.	Failing to insert mechanisms into conditional purchase agreement to protect overage fee.
130	**Lamoon v Fry**	[2004] EWCA Civ 591	Truro CC	RA	PI	Y	60	M	18	Cycling on wrong side of road.	Driving at excessive speed.
131	**Nixon v Thames Water Utilities Ltd**	[2006] CLY 2913	Romford CC	PL	PI	Y	50	F	U	Failing to notice and avoid trip hazard.	Failing to eliminate trip hazard.
132	**Lennon v Comr of Police of the Metropolis**	[2004] EWCA Civ 130	Central London CC	EL	PEL	N	N/A	M	28	Failing to read form and appreciate its effect.	Failing to advise claimant about preserving his housing allowance entitlement.

133	**Leitch v Reid**	[2003] NIQB 45	High Ct (NI)	O	PI	Y	50	M	Adult	Failing to examine ladder before using it.	Failing to examine the ladder for defects; failing to warn claimant not to use ladder; failing to remove ladder from premises.
134	**Duncan v Walshe**	2003 Scot (D) 15/7	Court of Session (OH)	RA	PI	N	N/A	M	23	Driving at excessive speed.	Straddling both carriageways while executing a right turn manoeuvre into a minor side road.
135	**Cemm v Bryant**	[2004] CLY 2701	Mansfield CC	RA	PI	N	N/A	F	29	Failing to see defendant's vehicle before it appeared on road; failing to stop motor vehicle before a collision occurred.	Losing control of vehicle and colliding with claimant's car.
136	**Great NE Rly Ltd v Railcare Ltd**	[2003] EWHC 1608 (Comm)	High Ct	PN	PD	N	N/A	N/A	N/A	Failing to detect crack in wheel that caused derailment.	Failing to deburr and chamfer edges of wheels.
137	**Gillespie v McFaddan McManus Construction Ltd**	[2003] EWHC 2067 (QB)	High Ct	EL	PI	N	N/A	M	30	Failing to ensure that skip was stabilised.	Using unsuitable skip and bogey in workplace.
138	**Owners of the Bow Spring v Owners of the Manzanillo II**	[2003] EWHC 1802 (Admlty); [2004] 1 Lloyd's Rep 647	High Ct	O	PD	Y	50	N/A	N/A	Grounding ship when other remedies were available.	Failing to alter course.

	Claim	Citation	Court	Claim type	Damage type	Guilty of CN	Discount	Gender	Age	Actual or alleged CN	Defendant's wrongful conduct
139	**Six Continents Retail Ltd v Carford Catering Ltd**	[2003] EWCA Civ 1790	High Ct	PN	PD	Y	100	N/A	N/A	Failing to respond to defendant's letter and to take steps to ascertain whether rotisserie was safe.	Failing safely to install rotisserie.
140	**Russell v Smith**	[2003] EWHC 2060 (QB)	High Ct	RA	PI	Y	50	M	10.25	Cycling across a road junction without regard to road markings.	Failing to bring car to halt soon enough to avoid the collision; failing to pay proper attention to the road.
141	**Slattery v Moore Stephens**	[2003] EWHC 1869 (Ch); [2004] PNLR 14	High Ct	PN	PEL	Y	50	M	Adult	Failing to discuss large tax refund with defendant accountants.	Failing to give appropriate advice.
142	**Blake v Galloway**	[2004] EWCA Civ 814; [2004] 3 All ER 315	Plymouth CC	O	PI	Y	50	M	15	Willingly engaging in game where bark chippings were thrown at participants.	Throwing bark chippings at claimant's face.
143	**Burridge v Airwork Ltd**	[2004] EWCA Civ 459	Manchester CC	RA	PI	N	N/A	M	47	Failing to take steps to guard against the possibility that driver, who had just pulled on to the hard shoulder, might open door and exit vehicle.	Opening driver's door without looking.

144	**Gilfillan v Barbour**	2003 SLT 1127	Court of Session (OH)	RA	PI	Y	50	M	61	Driving at excessive speed.	Entering junction despite having heard siren of police vehicle.
145	**Gilfillan v Barbour**	2003 SLT 1127	Court of Session (OH)	RA	PI	Y	50	M	39	Entering junction despite having heard police siren.	Failing to slow down at junction.
146	**Joseph v Braid**	2003 Rep LR 133	Court of Session (OH)	RA	PI	Y	66.6	M	U	Driving from minor road across path of car on major road without taking proper care; misjudging speed and distance of defender's car; using a mobile phone while driving and becoming distracted by it.	Failing to slow down at junction.
147	**Penny v McDermott Diving International Inc**	2004 SLT 253	Court of Session (OH)	EL	PI	N	N/A	M	34	Failing to inform supervisor that tag lines were too short; carrying on with operation perceived to be unsafe.	Failing to provide tag lines of sufficient length to secure pursuer's safety.
148	**Houghton v Stannard**	[2003] EWHC 2666 (QB)	High Ct	RA	PI	N	N/A	M	Adult	Driving on dual carriageway despite being aware of risk that car would break down; having broken down, or in the course of breaking down, failing to drive or park car; remaining inside car while it was stationary on road.	Driving at excessive speed; failing to see claimant's hazard warning lights and realising, much too late, that claimant's car was stationary.
149	**Edwards v Jerman**	[2004] CLY 2743	Liverpool CC	RA	PI	Y	25	M	Adult	Intoxicated; driving at excessive speed.	Driving on wrong side of road.

	Claim	Citation	Court	Claim type	Damage type	Guilty of CN	Discount	Gender	Age	Actual or alleged CN	Defendant's wrongful conduct
150	**Brownlow v Knight**	[2003] NIQB 71	High Ct (NI)	RA	PI	Y	40	F	59	Stepping into road without looking for oncoming traffic.	Failing to keep a proper lookout for pedestrians.
151	**Gilmour v East Renfrewshire Council (No 2)**	2004 Rep LR 40	Court of Session (OH)	EL	PI	N	N/A	F	57	Failing to keep a lookout for spillages on floor.	Failing to maintain ramp in a safe state; failing to keep surface of ramp free from any substance that might cause a person to slip and fall.
152	**Home Office v Lowles**	[2004] EWCA Civ 985	Leeds CC	EL	PI	Y	50	F	Adult	Failing to concentrate when walking over a step.	Failing adequately to maintain floor way.
153	**Delaney v Beechwood Nurseries Ltd**	[2004] CSOH 38	Court of Session (OH)	EL	PI	N	N/A	F	Adult	Failing to keep a proper lookout when descending staircase.	Failing adequately to illuminate staircase.
154	**Brown v Vosper Thornycroft (UK) Ltd**	[2004] EWHC 400 (QB)	High Ct	EL	PI	N	N/A	M	21	Placing hand in machine while in operation; failing to clean drill head.	Failing to provide adequate equipment.
155	**Hammond v Comr of Police of the Metropolis**	[2004] EWCA Civ 830; [2004] ICR 1467	Mayor's and City of London CC	EL	PI	Y	50	M	Adult	Unknown.	Failing to provide adequate work equipment.

156	**Hammond v Comr of Police of the Metropolis**	[2004] EWCA Civ 830; [2004] ICR 1467	Mayor's and City of London CC	EL	PI	Y	50	M	Adult	Unknown.	Failing to provide adequate work equipment.
157	**Parkinson v CC of Dyfed Powys**	[2004] EWCA Civ 802	Swansea CC	RA	PI	Y	35	M	U	Stepping into road without looking for incoming traffic.	Driving at 40 mph past parked taxi late at night in a built-up area in circumstances where defendant could and should have anticipated that there might be intoxicated pedestrians nearby.
158	**Hurst v Thomson Holidays Ltd**	[2004] CLY 1879	Cambridge CC	O	PI	Y	50	F	Adult	Failing to appreciate risk involved in jumping into swimming pool feet first.	Failing adequately to warn of risks of jumping into swimming pool feet first.
159	**Curran v Derbys and Lancs Gliding Club**	[2004] EWHC 687 (QB)	High Ct	SI	PI	Y	40	M	48	Executing a hazardous manoeuvre in glider.	Failing to take evasive action when deceased flew into her path.
160	**Curran v Derbys and Lancs Gliding Club**	[2004] EWHC 687 (QB)	High Ct	SI	PI	Y	40	M	48	Executing a hazardous manoeuvre in glider.	Failing to take evasive action when deceased flew into his path; wearing hood.
161	**Bici v Ministry of Defence**	[2004] EWHC 786 (QB)	High Ct	O	PI	N	N/A	M	22	Travelling in vehicle with person firing a gun in a potentially provocative manner.	Firing gun at vehicle when there was no justification for doing so.

	Claim	Citation	Court	Claim type	Damage type	Guilty of CN	Discount	Gender	Age	Actual or alleged CN	Defendant's wrongful conduct
162	**Bici v Ministry of Defence**	[2004] EWHC 786 (QB)	High Ct	O	PI	N	N/A	M	23	Travelling in vehicle with person firing a gun in a potentially provocative manner.	Firing gun at vehicle when there was no justification for doing so.
163	**Rose v SE London and Kent Bus Co Ltd**	[2004] EWHC 1106 (QB)	High Ct	RA	PI	Y	50	F	Adult	Crossing busy road in unsafe place when pedestrian crossing located approximately 30 metres away.	In a momentary lapse of concentration, failing to check for the claimant, whom he had been aware of previously.
164	**Eastgate v Oxfordshire CC**	[2005] CLY 1957	Reading CC	EL	PI	Y	30	M	Adult	Failing to inform occupational health physician of ongoing symptoms; sending caretaker home without seeking further help.	Failing to make reasonable assessment of task and to take appropriate steps to reduce risk of injury.
165	**Montlake v Lambert Smith Hampton Group Ltd**	[2004] EWHC 938 (Comm)	High Ct	PN	PEL	N	N/A	N/A	N/A	Failing to consider how club could keep ground or retain share in proceeds of any subsequent sale of ground; failing to obtain an open-market valuation of ground; failing to correct erroneous information about restrictive covenant.	Negligent valuation of club ground.

166	**Askey v Wood**	[2005] EWCA Civ 574	Leeds CC	RA	PI	Y	50	F	Adult	Driving on wrong side of road.	Driving at excessive speed around a blind bend.
167	**Lips v Older**	[2004] EWHC 1686 (QB); [2005] PIQR P14	High Ct	OL	PI	Y	66.6	M	42	Carrying heavy bag while intoxicated.	Failing to provide safe path at property.
168	**Fagan v Jeffers**	[2005] EWCA Civ 380	Central London CC	RA	PI	Y	50	M	U	Failing to exercise caution when travelling through 'keep clear' box.	Failing to keep a proper lookout when proceeding through stationary traffic.
169	**Firth v Hanley**	[2004] EWCA Civ 1714	Sheffield CC	RA	PI	N	N/A	F	Adult	Pulling up too fast in slippery conditions; being unaccompanied in car despite being provisional licence holder.	Driving carelessly.
170	**Swinton v Annabel's (Berkeley Square) Ltd**	[2005] CLY 2842	Lambeth CC	RA	PI	N	N/A	M	U	Failing to wear cycle helmet.	Failing to prevent dog from running into claimant bicyclist's path.
171	**Clare v Perry**	[2005] EWCA Civ 39	Exeter CC	OL	PI	Y	50	F	44	Jumping over six-foot high wall when too dark to see road below.	Failing to guard or fence off edge of wall.
172	**Warke v British Telecommuni-cations Plc**	[2004] NIQB 60	High Ct (NI)	EL	PI	Y	50	M	53	Failing properly to secure ladder.	Failing to provide sufficient health and safety information regarding use of ladders.

	Claim	Citation	Court	Claim type	Damage type	Guilty of CN	Discount	Gender	Age	Actual or alleged CN	Defendant's wrongful conduct
173	**Morgan v Twyford Tots Nursery Ltd**	[2006] CLY 2912	Telford CC	OL	PI	Y	25	F	Adult	Failing to heed warning cone having noticed the dampness of the floor.	Failing to prevent access to damp floor or to redirect visitors to an alternative door.
174	**Goodchild v Organon Laboratories Ltd**	[2004] EWHC 2341 (QB)	High Ct	EL	PI	Y	10	F	Adult	Lifting box without considering how heavy it was likely to be.	Failing to avoid the need for the claimant to undertake manual handling.
175	**Pesenti v London General Transport Services Ltd**	[2006] CLY 2903	Clerkenwell CC	RA	PI	N	N/A	F	U	Cycling erratically.	Passing too close to claimant.
176	**Pesenti v London General Transport Services Ltd**	[2006] CLY 2903	Clerkenwell CC	RA	PI	N	N/A	F	U	Cycling erratically.	Travelling too close behind claimant.
177	**Alli v Luton & Dunstable NHS Trust**	[2005] EWCA Civ 551	Central London CC	EL	PI	N	N/A	F	Adult	Failing to use light switches.	Failing to make sure there was sufficient light on the staircase.
178	**Carpenter v Lunnon**	[2004] EWHC 3079 (QB)	High Ct	RA	PI	Y	20	M	Adult	Walking on near side of carriageway with back to traffic and wearing dark clothing at night-time.	Failing to keep a proper lookout.

179	**Francis v Barclays Bank Plc**	[2004] EWHC 2787 (Ch); [2005] PNLR 18	High Ct	PN	PEL	N	N/A	F	Adult	Failing to obtain an independent report before sale of property.	Failing to enquire about status of planning permission.
180	**Dhillon v Aviation & Airport Services Ltd**	2004 WL 3520135	Central London CC	EL	PI	N	N/A	M	Adult	Unknown.	Failing to guard against risk that claimant employee would be injured by reversing van.
181	**Carter v Carter**	[2005] CSOH 2	Court of Session (OH)	RA	PI	N	N/A	M	58	Failing to instruct disabled wife properly in operation of vehicle.	Failing to operate hand controls and instead putting foot on accelerator.
182	**Neil v East Ayrshire Council**	[2005] CSOH 13; 2005 Rep LR 18	Court of Session (OH)	EL	PI	Y	50	M	54	Failing to take reasonable care of own safety by not trying to obtain a larger step ladder from supervisor before climbing into loft.	Failing to provide suitable work equipment.
183	**Murray v Royal County Down Golf Club**	[2005] NICA 52	High Ct (NI)	SI	PI	N	N/A	M	68	Unknown.	Cordoning off pathway and redirecting golfers to an alternative route in slippery area.
184	**Baird v Thurrock BC**	[2005] EWCA Civ 1499	Southend CC	EL	PI	Y	25	M	U	Standing too close to hoist.	Failing to maintain dustcart.
185	**Young v Kent CC**	[2005] EWHC 1342 (QB)	High Ct	OL	PI	Y	50	M	12.5	Climbing onto roof.	Failing to prevent climbing onto roof.

	Claim	Citation	Court	Claim type	Damage type	Guilty of CN	Discount	Gender	Age	Actual or alleged CN	Defendant's wrongful conduct
186	**Stephen v Peters**	[2005] CSOH 38; 2005 SCLR 513	Court of Session (OH)	EL	PI	Y	90	M	Adult	Driving at excessive speed.	Failing to ensure that tachograph and speed limiter were properly maintained.
187	**Davis v Stena Line Ltd**	[2005] EWHC 420 (QB); [2005] 2 Lloyd's Rep 13	High Ct	O	PI	N	N/A	M	35	Deliberately going over side of ship.	Failing properly to train captain or crew.
188	**Kerr v East Ayrshire Council**	2005 SLT (Sh Ct) 67	Sheriff Ct (North Strathclyde)	OL	PI	N	N/A	F	Adult	Pushing hand against glass panel thereby causing it to break.	Failing to install safety glass in door.
189	**Honnor v Lewis**	[2005] EWHC 747 (QB)	High Ct	RA	PI	Y	20	M	11	Failing to pay due attention when crossing a road.	Failing to observe pedestrian, sound horn, or slow down.
190	**Keown v Coventry Healthcare NHS Trust**	[2006] EWCA Civ 39; [2006] 1 WLR 953	Nuneaton CC	OL	PI	Y	66.6	M	11.75	Climbing fire escape knowing it was dangerous.	Failing to prevent individuals from climbing up fire escape.

191	**Drinnan v Bone Group Ltd**	2005 SLT (Sh Ct) 119	Sheriff Ct (South Strathclyde, Dumfries and Galloway)	EL	PI	Y	25	M	40	Neglecting risks involved in bringing great force to bear on crowbar.	Failing to provide a suitable crowbar for operation of repairing bearing; failing to ensure that pursuer employee was given adequate information and instructions.
192	**Burgess v Plymouth CC**	[2005] EWCA Civ 1659; [2006] ICR 579	Plymouth CC	EL	PI	Y	50	F	Adult	Failing to keep a proper lookout for obstructions on floor.	Failing to comply with system of placing lunch-boxes in storage at end of day.
193	**Large v Mamani**	[2005] EWHC 1271 (QB)	High Ct	RA	PI	Y	20	M	Adult	Failing to slow motorcycle having seen defendant's van moving across road.	Driving into claimant's path; failing to keep a proper lookout for pedestrians.
194	**Whitehead v Thomson Holidays Ltd**	2005 WL 3749695	Sheffield CC	O	PI	N	N/A	F	64	Failing to hold onto rail firmly enough.	Failing to mop water on stairs; failing to place warning signs.
195	**Smith v S Notaro Ltd**	[2006] EWCA Civ 775	Taunton CC	OL	PI	Y	60	M	Adult	Striding up plank walkway without considering suitable alternative access.	Failing to make walkway safe; failing to provide suitable access.
196	**Beattie v McConnell**	[2005] NIQB 47	High Ct (NI)	O	PI	Y	20	F	38	Calling on kennel outside normal opening hours thus being aware of possibility that dogs might be free and staff would be less alert to risks to visitors; standing close to the gate after seeing five dogs loose in yard and one standing up against gate.	Failing to foresee that dog could put its head through bars of gate and to take suitable precautions.

	Claim	Citation	Court	Claim type	Damage type	Guilty of CN	Discount	Gender	Age	Actual or alleged CN	Defendant's wrongful conduct
197	**CTO Gesellschaft v Dziennik**	[2006] EWCA Civ 1456	High Ct	EL	PI	Y	60	M	52	Removing entire basin when only part of it needed removing; failing to follow instructions.	Failing to confirm that entire basin did not need to be removed.
198	**Tompkins v Royal Mail Group Plc**	[2005] EWHC 1902 (QB); [2006] RTR 5	High Ct	RA	PI	Y	65	M	Adult	Failing to brake, slow down, or take evasive action.	Parking trailer in manner that could cause accident.
199	**Wells v Mutchmeats Ltd**	[2006] EWCA Civ 963	Oxford CC	OL	PI	Y	40	M	Adult	Stepping into foot bath known to be unstable.	Placing foot bath in doorway so as to create an obstruction which might cause a person to slip, trip or fall.
200	**Wells v Mutchmeats Ltd**	[2006] EWCA Civ 963	Oxford CC	EL	PI	Y	40	M	Adult	Stepping into foot bath known to be unstable.	Placing foot bath in doorway so as to create an obstruction which might cause a person to slip, trip or fall.
201	**Rodger v BHS Ltd**	[2006] CLY 1968	Medway CC	OL	PI	Y	60	M	Adult	Failing properly to check door before kneeling to look at it.	Failing to address defective 'door closer' and inadequate inspection system.

202	**Hodson Development Ltd v CTA Civils**	[2006] EWHC 1913 (TCC)	High Ct	PN	PEL	N	N/A	N/A	N/A	Failing to check architect's drawing.	Failing to notify of change in plot of land.
203	**Shine v Tower Hamlets LBC**	[2006] EWCA Civ 852	Romford CC	PL	PI	N	N/A	M	9	Seeking to leap-frog knowing it was dangerous.	Failing to make bollard stable and secure when it was foreseeable children would leap-frog it.
204	**O'Gara v Paul John Construction (Leicester) Ltd**	[2005] EWHC 2829 (QB)	High Ct	EL	PI	N	N/A	M	63	Selecting the wrong place to turn near the edge of the forecourt and in the mouth of the ramp; failing to keep a proper lookout; driving his dumper over the edge of the forecourt and off the tarmac into an observable hole or depression beside the ramp.	Failing to make site safe for dumper driving.
205	**Davis v Schrogin**	[2006] EWCA Civ 974	Leeds CC	RA	PI	N	N/A	M	Adult	Failing to avoid collision despite having had time to see defendant's manoeuvre.	Executing U-turn without looking.
206	**Craigie v Lanarkshire Health Board**	[2005] CSOH 118	Court of Session (OH)	EL	PI	Y	20	F	61	Realizing that pavement was very slippery but nevertheless attempting to walk across it.	Failing to devise a safe system of access to workplaces by employees.
207	**Feakins v Burstow**	[2005] EWHC 1931 (QB); [2006] PNLR 6	High Ct	PN	PEL	N	N/A	M	Adult	Failing to keep adequate records; filling in forms incorrectly and telling defendant that they had been completed correctly; failing to provide sufficient instructions as to basis on which defence could be pleaded; failing to contest figures.	Failing to manage litigation properly.

	Claim	Citation	Court	Claim type	Damage type	Guilty of CN	Discount	Gender	Age	Actual or alleged CN	Defendant's wrongful conduct
208	**Welsh v Messenger**	[2006] CLY 2875	Newcastle upon Tyne CC	RA	PI	N	N/A	F	68	Failing to wear seat belt.	Failing to keep coach on road.
209	**Morrison v Gardiner**	[2005] CSOH 156	Court of Session (OH)	RA	PI	Y	25	M	44	Failing to activate siren; proceeding too close to traffic at an excessive speed.	Failing to check for oncoming traffic on right or use mirror before starting manoeuvre.
210	**Badger v Ministry of Defence**	[2005] EWHC 2941 (QB); [2006] 3 All ER 173	High Ct	EL	PI	Y	20	M	Adult	Continuing to smoke when claimant knew or ought to have known that it was dangerous to health.	Exposing claimant to asbestos.
211	**McGowan v W&JR Watson Ltd**	[2006] CSIH 62; 2007 SC 272	Court of Session (OH)	EL	PI	N	N/A	M	40	Failing to clamp saw; being inadvertent in using saw.	Failing to take measures to prevent access to dangerous parts of machinery.
212	**Potter v Sinclair**	2006 SLT (Sh Ct) 102	Sheriff Ct (North Strathclyde)	EL	PI	N	N/A	M	57	Standing too close to vehicle when it was being positioned.	Failing to ensure that employees involved in loading process were clear of vehicle.
213	**Plymouth & South West Co-operative Society v Architecture Structure & Management Ltd**	[2006] EWHC 5 (TCC); (2006) 108 Con LR 77	High Ct	PN	PEL	N	N/A	N/A	N/A	Increasing project costs by delaying access, increasing phasing of works, ordering of variations, and providing information late.	Failing to warn of cost implications of two-stage tenure process.

214	**Donkin v Reid**	[2006] NIQB 2	High Ct (NI)	O	PI	Y	50	F	30	Attempting to attack defendant.	Headbutting claimant.
215	**Black v CB Richard Ellis Management Services Ltd**	2006 Rep LR 36	Sheriff Ct (Tayside, Central and Fife)	OL	PI	N	N/A	F	Adult	Failing to notice the water on tiles.	Failing properly to repair leaking roof.
216	**Millar v Rooney**	[2006] NIQB 7	High Ct (NI)	OL	PI	Y	30	M	48	Failing to secure planks or to ensure that they fully covered open box upon which claimant was standing.	Failing to make sure that contractor was competent.
217	**Millar v Rooney**	[2006] NIQB 7	High Ct (NI)	OL	PI	Y	30	M	48	Failing to secure planks or to ensure that they fully covered open box upon which claimant was standing.	Failing to make sure that contractor was competent.
218	**McKenzie v Bonar Yarns & Fabrics Ltd**	[2006] CSOH 23	Court of Session (OH)	EL	PI	Y	25	M	57	Leaving spool in precarious position without knowing whether any strands of yarn were still holding and, if so, how many.	Failing to instruct operators to report cobwebbed spools and have the maintenance department deal with the problem; failing to provide appropriate platform.
219	**McFarlane v Corus Construction & Industrial**	[2006] CSOH 38; 2006 SLT 375	Court of Session (OH)	EL	PI	Y	20	M	43	Failing to put down edger.	Failing to provide safe plant and equipment.
220	**BP Plc v AON Ltd (No 2)**	[2006] EWHC 424 (Comm); [2006] 1 CLC 881	High Ct	PN	PEL	N	N/A	N/A	N/A	Failing to confirm with defendant that it had received email instructions and that it had acted on them.	Failing to make effective declarations to underwriters.

	Claim	Citation	Court	Claim type	Damage type	Guilty of CN	Discount	Gender	Age	Actual or alleged CN	Defendant's wrongful conduct
221	**McEwan v Lothian Buses Plc**	[2006] CSOH 56; 2006 SCLR 592	Court of Session (OH)	EL	PI	Y	75	M	Adult	Spilling coolant; failing to take steps to neutralise or clear coolant; walking or running on spillage when no pressing need to do so.	Failing to provide an effective method of preventing coolant from contaminating floor.
222	**Jukes v Etti**	[2006] EWHC 2493 (QB); [2007] RTR 2	High Ct	RA	PI	Y	40	M	37	Seeking to cross road when there was oncoming traffic.	Failing to keep a proper lookout for pedestrians.
223	**Ashbridge v Christian Salvesen Plc**	[2006] CSOH 79; 2006 SLT 697	Court of Session (OH)	EL	PI	Y	50	M	Adult	Failing properly to check level of water in tank before cracking open sludge door.	Inadequate system for checking whether tanks were empty.
224	**McCue v North Lanarkshire Council**	[2006] CSOH 80; 2006 SLT 693	Court of Session (OH)	PL	PI	N	N/A	M	70	Losing footing due to intoxication.	Failing properly to maintain footpath.
225	**Maughan v Boylan**	[2006] NIQB 38	High Ct (NI)	RA	PI	Y	80	M	77	Stepping into road without looking for oncoming traffic.	Failing to keep a proper lookout; failing to react sufficiently quickly to emergency.
226	**Graham v Richard Lawson Autologistics Ltd**	[2006] CSOH 89	Court of Session (OH)	EL	PI	N	N/A	M	Adult	Failing to protect against risk posed by tubing on pathway.	Leaving a piece of tubing on pathway.

227	**Ehrari v Curry**	[2006] EWHC 1319 (QB)	High Ct	RA	PI	Y	70	F	13.75	Stepping into road from behind parked car and walking without looking.	Failing to see claimant despite knowing that it was necessary to pay attention (having had to stop previously so as to allow children to cross road).
228	**Pankhurst v White**	[2006] EWHC 2093 (Admin)	High Ct	RA	PI	N	N/A	M	48	Driving at excessive speed before sharp corner.	Driving at excessive speed.
229	**Weir v Robertson Group (Construction) Ltd**	[2006] CSOH 107; 2006 Rep LR 114	Court of Session (OH)	EL	PI	N	N/A	M	36	Putting himself in proximity to hole so that he could slip, trip or fall.	Failing to protect against risk posed by hole in roof; failing to place safety net beneath gap; failing to inform pursuer that safety net had been removed.
230	**Nicolson v Willis**	[2006] EWHC 2402 (Admin)	High Ct	RA	PI	Y	33.3	M	36	Driving at excessive speed; failing to take action despite seeing multi-purpose vehicle starting to emerge.	Turning corner when unsafe to do so.
231	**Riddell v Leisure Link Electronic Entertainment Ltd**	[2008] CSIH 16	Sheriff Ct (Aberdeen)	EL	PI	N	N/A	F	42	Unknown.	Unknown.
232	**Clark v CC of Essex**	[2006] EWHC 2290 (QB)	High Ct	EL	PI	N	N/A	M	Adult	Failing to use opportunities made available to police officers to manage stress.	Failing to prevent bullying at work.

	Claim	Citation	Court	Claim type	Damage type	Guilty of CN	Discount	Gender	Age	Actual or alleged CN	Defendant's wrongful conduct
233	**Crowther v Kirklees MDC**	[2007] CLY 2958	Huddersfield CC	PL	PI	N	N/A	F	Adult	Stepping from vehicle without looking down.	Failing to maintain highway.
234	**Al Gouri v Achkar**	[2007] CLY 3079	High Ct	RA	PI	Y	25	M	17	Failing to wear seat belt.	Driving without due care and attention.
235	**B (a child) v JJB Sports Plc**	[2007] CLY 4195	Wigan CC	OL	PI	N	N/A	M	10	Running.	Cleaning floor of football school when large number of children present.
236	**Given v James Watt College**	[2006] CSOH 189; 2007 SLT 39	Court of Session (OH)	EL	PI	N	N/A	F	58	Overreacting to fright given by malfunctioning machine.	Failing properly to maintain drinks dispensing machine.
237	**Evans v Kosmar Villa Holidays Plc**	[2007] EWCA Civ 1003; [2008] 1 All ER 530	High Ct	O	PI	Y	50	M	18	Diving into shallow end of swimming pool.	Failing to put no diving sign in appropriate position.
238	**Dabinett v Somerset CC**	Taunton CC, 15 Dec 2006	Taunton CC	PL	PI	N	N/A	M	Adult	Unknown.	Failing effectively to clear gravel and loose chippings from road that was resurfaced seven months before accident.

239	**Urquhart v Fife Primary Care NHS Trust**	[2007] CSOH 2; 2007 SCLR 317	Court of Session (OH)	EL	PI	N	N/A	F	52	Employing cross-arm lift to move patient as opposed to swivel transfer.	Failing sufficiently to reduce the risks of manual handling.
240	**Day v Suffolk CC**	[2007] EWCA Civ 1436	Cambridge CC	PL	PI	Y	40	M	Adult	Driving at excessive speed in the circumstances.	Failing to keep road in proper repair.
241	**Bulk Atalanta (Owners) v Ship Forest Pioneer (Owners)**	[2007] EWHC 84 (Admlty)	High Ct	O	PD	Y	15	N/A	N/A	Failing to keep proper lookout for other vessels.	Carelessness in altering course and speed.
242	**Ellis v William Cook Leeds Ltd**	[2007] EWCA Civ 1232	Leeds CC	EL	PI	Y	25	M	38	Standing in a unsafe position while attempting to 'unstick' crane; failing to notify supervisor of malfunction and attempting to remedy it himself.	Failing to replace malformed crane hook.
243	**Donaldson v Hays Distribution Services Ltd**	[2007] CSOH 31	Court of Session (OH)	RA	PI	Y	25	F	50	Walking between rear of trailer and loading bay wall.	Failing to keep a proper lookout for pedestrians and, in particular, failing to look underneath length of trailer before entering cab; failing to use lookout when reversing lorry.
244	**Brown v Glasgow CC**	[2007] CSOH 33	Court of Session (OH)	EL	PI	N	N/A	M	Adult	Lifting a load that was too heavy; throwing load over shoulder; carelessness in placing feet.	Failing to reduce risk posed by hole; engaging pursuer in manual handling operation.

	Claim	Citation	Court	Claim type	Damage type	Guilty of CN	Discount	Gender	Age	Actual or alleged CN	Defendant's wrongful conduct
245	**Brown v Glasgow CC**	[2007] CSOH 33	Court of Session (OH)	OL	PI	N	N/A	M	Adult	Lifting a load that was too heavy; throwing load over shoulder; carelessness in placing feet.	Failing to reduce risk posed by hole; engaging pursuer in manual handling operation.
246	**McNab v Bluebird Buses Ltd**	[2007] CSOH 36; 2007 Rep LR 36	Court of Session (OH)	RA	PI	Y	50	M	37	Failing to walk facing oncoming traffic.	Failing to keep a proper lookout for pedestrians.
247	**Gawler v Raettig**	[2007] EWHC 373 (QB)	High Ct	RA	PI	Y	25	M	24	Failing to wear seat belt.	Losing control of car during cornering.
248	**N (a child) v Newham LBC**	[2007] CLY 2931	Central London CC	O	PI	Y	60	M	7	Punching a pane of glass.	Failing to supervise children on school premises.
249	**Arbory Group Ltd v West Craven Insurance Services**	[2007] Lloyd's Rep IR 491	High Ct	PN	PEL	N	N/A	N/A	N/A	Failing to read and follow explanatory notes.	Failing properly to advise, resulting in claimant being significantly underinsured for business interruption.
250	**MacKenzie v Co-Operative Group (CWS) Ltd**	2007 Scot (D) 14/6	Sheriff Ct (Grampian, Highland and Islands)	EL	PI	Y	40	F	46	Being oblivious to possibility of presence of ice.	Failing to keep area outside front door of shop free of ice.

251	**Taylor v Rashid**	[2008] CLY 2661	Bow CC	RA	PI	N	N/A	U	U	Failing to wear seat belt.	Driving car into passenger side rear door of vehicle.
252	**Keating v Wirral MBC**	[2008] CLY 2647	Liverpool CC	EL	PI	Y	25	F	Adult	Failing to call on staff on hand for help with challenging child known to be prone to violence.	Failing to carry out risk assessment with regard to safety and welfare of staff; failing to ensure appropriate staffing levels and proper handover.
253	**Wilson v BAE Systems Plc**	[2007] CSOH 79	Court of Session (OH)	EL	PI	Y	20	M	Adult	Unknown.	Permitting manhole cover to protrude onto path.
254	**Morton v Glasgow CC**	2007 SLT (Sh Ct) 81	Sheriff Ct (Glasgow and Strathkelvin)	OL	PI	Y	25	M	14	Climbing up scaffolding poles.	Failing to protect children from entering area of scaffolding.
255	**Hanks v Ministry of Defence**	[2007] EWHC 966 (QB)	High Ct	EL	PI	Y	15	M	27	Reading map instead of looking straight ahead.	Carrying out manoeuvre without warning.
256	**Carleton v Strutt & Parker**	[2007] EWHC 999 (QB); [2007] PNLR 29	High Ct	PN	PEL	N	N/A	M	Adult	Failing to forfeit leases.	Failing to take rent into account when negotiating lease.
257	**Ahanonu v SE London and Kent Bus Co Ltd**	[2008] EWCA Civ 274	Central London Civic Justice Centre	RA	PI	Y	50	F	18	Taking extremely dangerous path when crossing road.	Failing to check rear-view mirror.
258	**Wakeling v McDonagh**	[2007] EWHC 1201 (QB)	High Ct	RA	PI	N	N/A	M	17	Entering road on bicycle without looking.	Driving under influence of drugs; driving at excessive speed.

	Claim	Citation	Court	Claim type	Damage type	Guilty of CN	Discount	Gender	Age	Actual or alleged CN	Defendant's wrongful conduct
259	**Garth v Grant**	[2007] All ER (D) 459 (May)	High Ct	RA	PI	Y	15	F	41	Failing to wear seat belt.	Driving on wrong side of road.
260	**SH (a child) v Farrell**	[2007] NIQB 42	High Ct (NI)	RA	PI	Y	15	F	11	Stepping into road without looking for oncoming traffic.	Failing to slow down at junction; driving at excessive speed; failing to keep a proper lookout for pedestrians.
261	**Robertson v Glasgow CC**	[2007] CSOH 89	Court of Session (OH)	EL	PI	Y	50	M	57	Failing to notice boards on tipper that were being supported by board pursuer moved; failing to raise tipper to its full height or return the tipper to horizontal position and remove remaining boards from side of lorry.	Failing to instruct employee in use of the tipper for loading and unloading loads such as boards.
262	**Jones v BBC**	QBD, 22 Jun 2007	High Ct	EL	PI	N	N/A	M	Adult	Walking beneath object being lowered.	Failing to discuss identified hazard.
263	**Jones v BBC**	QBD, 22 Jun 2007	High Ct	EL	PI	N	N/A	M	Adult	Walking beneath object being lowered.	Deliberately passing beneath mast; leading claimant on same route and into same hazardous area.

264	**Jones v BBC**	QBD, 22 Jun 2007	High Ct	OL	PI	N	N/A	M	Adult	Walking beneath object being lowered.	Failing to prevent BBC crew from passing under mast during its lowering.
265	**Thorpe v Aberdeen CC**	2007 Rep LR 105	Sheriff Ct (Grampian, Highland and Islands)	PL	PI	Y	25	M	U	Failing to keep a proper look out; failing to pay attention to placement of feet.	Failing properly to maintain footpath.
266	**Newline Corporate Name Ltd v Morgan Cole**	[2007] EWHC 1628 (Comm); [2008] PNLR 2	High Ct	PN	PEL	N	N/A	N/A	N/A	Insufficiency of staff to review policy in detail.	Negligence in advising regarding insurance policy.
267	**Poppleton v Trustees of the Portsmouth Youth Activities Committee**	[2008] EWCA Civ 646; [2009] PIQR P1	Winchester CC	OL	PI	Y	75	M	25	Attempting to jump from one section of climbing wall to another.	Failing to warn that the thick safety matting did not make climbing wall safe.
268	**Lawson v The Broomfield Holiday Park**	2007 Scot (D) 9/7	Sheriff Ct (Grampian, Highland and Islands)	OL	PI	Y	20	F	68	Failing to pay attention to footing; failing to look out for speed hump.	Failing to illuminate speed hump or otherwise warn of its presence.
269	**Piccolo v Larkstock Ltd**	2007 WL 2024863	High Ct	OL	PI	N	N/A	M	45.5	Failing to notice petal on floor.	Failing to implement an effective means of clearing petals from floor.
270	**Dawes v Aldis**	[2007] EWHC 1831 (QB)	High Ct	RA	PI	N	N/A	M	40	Intoxicated; running across road.	Driving at excessive speed; driving on wrong side of road.

	Claim	Citation	Court	Claim type	Damage type	Guilty of CN	Discount	Gender	Age	Actual or alleged CN	Defendant's wrongful conduct
271	**McCrory v Hutchison's Coaches (Overtown) Ltd**	2007 SLT (Sh Ct) 187	Sheriff Ct (South Strathclyde, Dumfries and Galloway)	RA	PI	N	N/A	F	47	Standing and walking on moving bus; failing to hold onto handrail.	Braking suddenly.
272	**McCrory v Hutchison's Coaches (Overtown) Ltd**	2007 SLT (Sh Ct) 187	Sheriff Ct (South Strathclyde, Dumfries and Galloway)	RA	PI	N	N/A	F	47	Failing to hold onto handrail.	Stopping suddenly, without indication, to perform right-hand manoeuvre.
273	**Wilson v Glasgow CC**	[2007] CSOH 143	Court of Session (OH)	OL	PI	Y	25	F	57	Failing to exercise sufficient care in navigating staircase.	Failing properly to maintain staircase.
274	**Sahakian v McDonnell**	[2007] EWHC 3242 (QB); [2008] RTR 19	High Ct	RA	PI	Y	50	F	Adult	Walking into road without looking from behind parked car.	Driving at excessive speed; failing to see claimant in time to effect any proper braking.
275	**St George v Home Office**	[2007] EWHC 2774 (QB)	High Ct	O	PI	Y	15	M	29	Becoming addicted to alcohol and drugs.	Allocating claimant drug addict to top bunk in prison despite knowing that he had previously had withdrawal seizures.

276	**Gleeson v Court**	[2007] EWHC 2397 (QB); [2008] RTR 10	High Ct	RA	PI	Y	30	M	20	Travelling with intoxicated driver; travelling in car boot.	Driving while intoxicated.
277	**Hughes v Guise Motors Ltd**	[2007] EWHC 2529 (QB)	High Ct	RA	PI	N	N/A	M	U	Failing to steer or coast car onto the hard shoulder; remaining in car.	Failing to slow down sufficiently to create space between himself and the preceding vehicle.
278	**Lindesay v Lamb**	[2007] EWHC 2948 (QB)	High Ct	RA	PI	Y	20	M	38	Moving into closing gap between lorry and taxi and failing to brake in time to avoid colliding with either vehicle.	Failing to brake in time so as to avoid collision.
279	**Lees v North Lanarkshire Council**	[2008] CSOH 8	Court of Session (OH)	PL	PI	Y	40	M	U	Failing to walk around roughened area of footpath.	Failing to maintain footpath.
280	**Bollito v Arriva London**	[2008] EWHC 48 (QB)	High Ct	RA	PI	N	N/A	M	Adult	Deliberately blocking bus doors and jumping from doors.	Closing bus doors knowing claimant was between them; driving off and accelerating with claimant trapped between partially closed doors.
281	**Standard Life Assurance Ltd v Oak Dedicated Ltd**	[2008] EWHC 222 (Comm); [2008] 2 All ER (Comm) 916	High Ct	PN	PEL	N	N/A	N/A	N/A	Failing to obtain insurance cover meeting client's requirements.	Failing to appreciate risks in wording of insurance policy.

	Claim	Citation	Court	Claim type	Damage type	Guilty of CN	Discount	Gender	Age	Actual or alleged CN	Defendant's wrongful conduct
282	**Easdon v A Clarke & Co (Smethwick) Ltd**	[2008] CSOH 29	Court of Session (OH)	RA	PI	N	N/A	M	32	Driving at excessive speed so that unable to stop within range of vision.	Driving on the wrong side of road.
283	**Moreh v O'Neill**	[2008] NIQB 28	High Ct (NI)	RA	PI	Y	50	M	78	Failing to notice defendant's vehicle on road.	Failing to keep proper lookout for other vehicles; failing to brake; failing to give warning.
284	**Ruddy v Monte Marco**	[2008] CSOH 40	Court of Session (OH)	EL	PI	N	N/A	M	51	Failing to apply brakes of three out of four wheels of scaffold.	Failing to install sufficient guards on scaffolding.
285	**Berry v Hayden**	[2008] NIQB 134	High Ct	RA	PI	Y	66.6	F	47	Standing in the path of vehicle; shouting at driver of vehicle; failing to move out of the vehicle's way despite hearing its engine revving and seeing it move.	Failing to stop vehicle in time to prevent it from striking claimant.
286	**Greenwood v Cummings**	QBD, 9 Apr 2008	High Ct	RA	PI	Y	33.3	F	U	Failing to stop and check whether road was clear before crossing at a designated pedestrian crossing.	Failing to slow down when visibility affected by sun.
287	**Parmer v Big Security Co Ltd**	[2008] EWHC 1414 (QB)	High Ct	O	PI	Y	30	M	Adult	Engaging in act of violence against bouncer.	Pushing claimant into barrier.

288	**Heaton v Herzog**	[2008] EWCA Civ 1636; [2009] RTR 30	Cambridge CC	RA	PI	N	N/A	F	Adult	Failing to keep observation to right in order to have the opportunity to see motorcycle, brake and avoid colliding with it.	Driving at excessive speed.
289	**Lees v Northants Heartlands NHS PCT**	[2008] EWHC 2484 (QB)	High Ct	EL	PI	N	N/A	F	48	Failing to alert superiors to perceived inadequacies of chair.	Failing to provide adequate equipment.
290	**McGhee v Diageo Plc**	[2008] CSOH 74	Court of Session (OH)	EL	PI	N	N/A	M	20	Standing on screw feeder despite having been told that it was about to start.	Unknown.
291	**Shortell v BICAL Construction Ltd**	2008 WL 2148256	High Ct	EL	PI	Y	15	M	Adult	Smoking.	Exposing claimant to asbestos.
292	**Minh Lac v Clayton**	[2009] EWCA Civ 106	High Ct	RA	PI	N	N/A	M	Adult	Failing to move away from car after collision.	Driving without due care and striking vehicle from behind.
293	**Minh Lac v Clayton**	[2009] EWCA Civ 106	High Ct	RA	PI	N	N/A	M	Adult	Failing to move away from car after collision.	Driving without due care and striking vehicle from behind.
294	**Minh Lac v Clayton**	[2009] EWCA Civ 106	High Ct	RA	PI	N	N/A	M	Adult	Failing to move away from car after collision.	Driving without due care and striking vehicle from behind.
295	**Halkett v South Ayrshire Council**	2008 GWD 21-350	Sheriff Ct (South Strathclyde, Dumfries and Galloway)	EL	PI	N	N/A	M	36	Failing to follow the instructions of the clerk of works; failing to resign from employment.	Failing to conduct sufficient risk assessment for handling kerbstones; failing to provide suitable training; failing sufficiently to reduce risk of injury when lifting kerbstones.

	Claim	Citation	Court	Claim type	Damage type	Guilty of CN	Discount	Gender	Age	Actual or alleged CN	Defendant's wrongful conduct
296	**Clayton v Lambert**	[2009] EWCA Civ 237; [2010] RTR 3	Leeds CC	RA	PI	Y	75	M	Adult	Driving at excessive speed.	Continuing turn after seeing claimant approaching.
297	**Don v Eastern Holdings Ltd**	Edinburgh Sheriff Ct, 18 Jun 2008	Sheriff Ct (Edinburgh)	RA	PI	Y	25	M	19	Failing to pause or stop to allow defender's car either fully to enter nearside northbound lane or to continue forward and resume occupancy only of offside northbound lane.	Encroaching further into nearside northbound lane when pursuer was passing.
298	**National Grid Gas Plc v Stanley Stores (Strathclyde) Ltd**	[2008] CSOH 94	Court of Session (OH)	O	PD	N	N/A	N/A	N/A	Providing inadequate map regarding pipes.	Damaging pipes.
299	**Gower-Smith v Hampshire CC**	S'hampton CC, 27 Jun 2008	S'hampton CC	EL	PI	Y	25	M	68.5	Climbing to top platform of ladder.	Failing sufficiently to train an employee on an identified risk.
300	**Flavio v Jeffrey**	[2008] EWHC 2331 (QB)	High Ct	RA	PI	Y	66.6	M	Adult	Failing to look when turning onto main road.	Failing to look before turning.
301	**Armsden v Kent Police**	[2009] EWCA Civ 631; [2009] RTR 31	Canterbury CC	RA	PI	N	N/A	F	29	Failing to look properly before moving off from junction.	Failing to activate siren.

302	**Ministry of Defence v Radclyffe**	[2009] EWCA Civ 635	High Ct	EL	PI	Y	40	M	24	Diving into water from bridge.	Army officer giving permission to jump into water.
303	**Sowmez v Kebaberry Wholesale Ltd**	[2008] EWHC 3366 (QB)	High Ct	EL	PI	Y	20	M	U	Cleaning machine whilst in operation; failing to follow instructions.	Failing to prevent overriding of locking mechanism.
304	**Duffy v Enterprise Engineering Services Ltd**	[2008] CSOH 141	Court of Session (OH)	EL	PI	Y	25	M	Adult	Failing to use safer method to cross pipe.	Failing to make and keep safe an access route.
305	**Williams v Jervis**	[2008] EWHC 2346 (QB)	High Ct	RA	PI	N	N/A	F	Adult	Driving with defective brake lights and while using mobile telephone.	Failing to stop vehicle in time to prevent it striking claimant's car from behind.
306	**Ormsby v CC of Strathclyde**	[2008] CSOH 143; 2008 SCLR 783	Court of Session (OH)	EL	PI	N	N/A	F	30	Failing to wear stab-proof vest; failing to follow instructions.	Continuing to deploy officer even once risk of serious injury had become apparent.
307	**Chrysalis Scotland Ltd v Clydesdale Bank Insurance Brokers Ltd**	[2008] CSOH 144	Court of Session (OH)	PN	PEL	N	N/A	N/A	N/A	Failing to read certain documents.	Failing to bring to pursuers' attention risk that a market value adjustment might be applied upon withdrawing funds from bond after five years.
308	**Kern v Bridgend CBC**	Bridgend CC, 17 Oct 2008	Bridgend CC	EL	PI	Y	15	F	Adult	Mishandling container and probably withdrawing it too quickly causing hot liquid to spill from it.	Failing to assess and adjust suitability of protective jacket to ensure it fitted a school kitchen assistant correctly.

	Claim	Citation	Court	Claim type	Damage type	Guilty of CN	Discount	Gender	Age	Actual or alleged CN	Defendant's wrongful conduct
309	**Collins-Williamson v Silverlink Train Services Ltd**	[2008] EWHC 2945 (QB)	High Ct	O	PI	Y	50	M	27	Walking alongside train while unsteady on feet due to intoxication; walking close to the edge of platform.	Failing to have a window capable of being opened in guard's vestibule.
310	**Craggy v CC of Cleveland Police**	[2009] EWCA Civ 1128; [2009] Po LR 349	Middlesbrough CC	RA	PI	Y	66.6	M	Adult	Turning when unsafe to do so.	Failing to drive so that vehicle could be stopped if another emergency vehicle emerged.
311	**Buchan v Whiting**	[2008] EWHC 2951 (QB)	High Ct	RA	PI	Y	50	M	20	Driving at excessive speed.	Failing to look before turning.
312	**Anderson v Lyotier**	[2008] EWHC 2790 (QB)	High Ct	SI	PI	Y	33.3	M	41	Failing to inform instructor that ski route was too difficult.	Inviting claimant to ski in place where there was risk of hitting tree.
313	**Palmer v Kitley**	[2008] EWHC 2819 (QB)	High Ct	RA	PI	Y	15	F	16.75	Failing to wear seat belt.	Cornering at excessive speed.
314	**Connor v Jackson**	[2008] NIQB 102	High Ct (NI)	RA	PI	N	N/A	M	18	Failing to notice defendant's vehicle sooner.	Attempting to cross road when it was risky to do so; failing to wait for clear view.

315	**Crew v Ash**	[2008] EWHC 3068 (QB)	High Ct	RA	PI	N	N/A	F	18	Intoxicated; stepping into road without looking for oncoming traffic; crossing road when view obscured by car; failing to appreciate speed at which the defendant was travelling; failing to use crossing.	Driving without due care and striking the claimant as a result.
316	**Devine v McAteer**	[2008] NICh 18	High Ct (NI)	PN	PEL	N	N/A	M	U	Unknown.	Failing to ensure that monies were employed consistently with statutory requirements and that they were invested lawfully.
317	**Callier v Deacon**	[2009] EWHC 245 (QB)	High Ct	RA	PI	Y	55	M	17	Wearing dark, non-reflective clothing; cycling without lights; being stationary in a restricted area of the road; failing to pay any proper attention to oncoming traffic.	Overtaking vehicle in front when unsafe to do so.
318	**Smith v Finch**	[2009] EWHC 53 (QB)	High Ct	RA	PI	N	N/A	M	51	Failing to wear cycle helmet.	Driving at excessive speed; driving too close to claimant cyclist while attempting to overtake him.
319	**Spencer v Wincanton Holdings Ltd**	[2009] EWCA Civ 1404; [2010] PIQR P8	Sheffield CC	EL	PI	Y	33.3	M	Adult	Failing to use crutches or prosthesis for support while filling car with petrol.	Colliding with stationary tractor that claimant was driving.

	Claim	Citation	Court	Claim type	Damage type	Guilty of CN	Discount	Gender	Age	Actual or alleged CN	Defendant's wrongful conduct
320	**McLellan v Dundee CC**	[2009] CSOH 9; 2009 Rep LR 61	Court of Session (OH)	EL	PI	Y	20	M	38	Holding crowbar so that hand was in close proximity to cutting blades.	Failing to provide adequate health and safety information.
321	**Nationwide Building Society v Dunlop Haywards (DHL) Ltd**	[2009] EWHC 254 (Comm); [2009] 2 All ER (Comm) 715	High Ct	O	PEL	Y	50	N/A	N/A	Failing to appreciate fraudulent transaction.	Fraudulent overvaluing of property.
322	**Stanton v Collinson**	[2009] EWHC 342 (QB)	High Ct	RA	PI	N	N/A	M	16	Failing to wear seat belt.	Driving at excessive speed.
323	**Teviotdale v Norwich Union Insurance Ltd**	2009 SCLR 660	Sheriff Ct (Dumfries)	RA	PI	N	N/A	F	U	Driving without due care.	Failing to keep a proper lookout for other vehicles, in particular, failing to see pursuer's vehicle when entering car park.
324	**Smeaton v Duncan**	2009 GWD 13-210	Sheriff Ct (Grampian, Highland and Islands)	RA	PI	N	N/A	M	15	Driving at excessive speed.	Failing to keep a lookout for oncoming traffic.

325	**Causby v Seagoe Technologies Ltd**	[2009] NIQB 24	High Ct (NI)	EL	PI	Y	33.3	M	Adult	Attempting to release cage for the second time without any thought or planning.	Failing to make a sufficient assessment of manual handling operation.
326	**Forbes v Ferguson**	2009 GWD 21-353	Sheriff Ct (Tayside, Central and Fife)	RA	PI	Y	50	M	Adult	Putting hand on stationary van to steady himself and falling into road.	Failing to keep a proper lookout for pedestrians before reversing.
327	**Drew v Whitbread Plc**	[2010] EWCA Civ 53; [2010] 1 WLR 1725	Exeter CC	EL	PI	Y	25	M	Adult	Unknown.	Unknown.
328	**Russell v West Sussex CC**	[2009] EWHC 1063 (QB)	High Ct	PL	PI	Y	50	F	48	Driving at excessive speed.	Failing properly to maintain highway.
329	**Woods v Police Service for NI**	[2009] NIQB 35	High Ct (NI)	EL	PI	Y	50	M	48	Failing to 'dry fire' weapon prior to dismantling it; failing to point weapon in a safe direction; depressing the trigger and activating slide locks at the same time; failing to prepare a risk assessment for the activity of weapon function testing and dismantling.	Absence of a second 'inspector' or 'range officer' to check weapon before it was dismantled; failing to conduct risk assessment in respect of weapons test firing range.
330	**Chubb Fire Ltd v Vicar of Spalding**	[2010] EWCA Civ 981; [2010] 2 CLC 277	Nottingham CC	O	PD	N	N/A	N/A	N/A	Failing to place 'theft stoppers' on fire extinguishers.	Failing to warn of consequences of releasing dry powder from extinguisher.

	Claim	Citation	Court	Claim type	Damage type	Guilty of CN	Discount	Gender	Age	Actual or alleged CN	Defendant's wrongful conduct
331	**Taylor v Wincanton Group Ltd**	[2009] EWCA Civ 1581	Doncaster CC	EL	PI	Y	50	M	36	Carrying box and thereby obscuring view of step.	Failing to prevent use of an unsuitable route.
332	**Osei-Antwi v SE London & Kent Bus Co Ltd**	[2010] EWCA Civ 132	High Ct	RA	PI	Y	33.3	F	17	Standing very close to edge of road; failing to keep a good lookout for bus.	Permitting rear end of bus to mount pavement when turning.
333	**Campbell v Elliot Group Ltd**	[2009] CSOH 63	Court of Session (OH)	EL	PI	Y	20	M	56	Knowing dangerous conditions in yard and nevertheless taking route through it.	Leaving yard in a dangerous condition; failing to take reasonable care to provide safe access.
334	**Dines v Clifton**	[2009] EWHC 1254 (QB)	High Ct	RA	PI	N	N/A	M	40	Negligent parking; failing to place cones in road; standing in road while using mobile phone.	Crashing into back of lorry and hitting claimant in the process.
335	**Tibbatts v British Airways Plc**	[2009] EWHC 815 (QB)	High Ct	EL	PI	Y	33.3	M	58	Lifting bag knowing that two people were needed to do so.	Failing to comply with Manual Handling Regulations 1992.
336	**Stanley v Close**	[2009] EWHC 2849 (QB)	High Ct	SI	PI	N	N/A	M	U	Stalling at top of jump.	Failing to employ experienced or trained staff.

337	**Owners of 'Western Neptune' v Owners of 'Philadelphia Express'**	[2009] EWHC 1274 (Admlty); [2010] 2 All ER (Comm) 154	High Ct	O	PD	Y	33.3	N/A	N/A	Failing to inform approaching vessels of presence of flashing lights on tail buoys; failing to confirm need to avoid entering the 'safety zone'; failing to communicate when altering course to port; failing thereafter to alert vessel that she was in danger; failing to dive streamers.	Entering exclusion zone; improper alteration of course; failing to see or to appreciate significance of blue strobe lights on stern buoys.
338	**Anderson v Scottish Ministers**	[2009] CSOH 92; 2009 Rep LR 122	Court of Session (OH)	OL	PI	N	N/A	M	40	Leaving the path and cycling into drain and gully.	Failing to conduct a proper risk assessment; leaving gully and drain too close to cycle path.
339	**Berry v Laytons**	[2009] EWHC 1591 (QB)	High Ct	PN	PEL	N	N/A	M	Adult	Misreading letter from solicitors.	Giving inadequate advice.
340	**Bell v Havering LBC**	[2010] EWCA Civ 689	Central London CC	PL	PI	Y	33.3	F	44	Failing to pay sufficient attention to placement of feet.	Failing properly to maintain highway.
341	**Martin v Triggs Turner Bartons**	[2009] EWHC 1920 (Ch); [2010] PNLR 3	High Ct	PN	PEL	N	N/A	F	Adult	Failing to follow up enquiry regarding pension.	Inadequate drafting.
342	**Smith v Hammond**	[2010] EWCA Civ 725; [2010] RTR 30	High Ct	RA	PI	Y	60	M	13	Cycling into road without looking.	Failing to sound horn.

	Claim	Citation	Court	Claim type	Damage type	Guilty of CN	Discount	Gender	Age	Actual or alleged CN	Defendant's wrongful conduct
343	**Bhatt v Fontain Motors Ltd**	[2010] EWCA Civ 863; [2010] PIQR P17	Central London CC	EL	PI	Y	33.3	M	49.5	Failing properly to foot ladder.	Failing to store goods other than in loft; failing to install fixed ladder.
344	**Toropdar v D (a minor)**	[2009] EWHC 2997 (TCC)	High Ct	RA	PI	Y	33.3	M	10	Stepping into road without looking for oncoming traffic.	Driving at excessive speed; failing to undertake precautionary braking.
345	**Parkinson v NI Fire and Rescue Service**	[2009] NIQB 87	High Ct (NI)	O	PI	Y	25	M	40	Proceeding with some speed in circumstances of poor underfoot conditions and manifestly inadequate illumination.	Failing to warn about the prevailing conditions and topography.
346	**Ievers v Prebble**	[2010] EWCA Civ 1615	Leicester CC	RA	PI	Y	70	F	Adult	Cutting across the path of another driver.	Being insufficiently alert to difficulties of claimant, who had been forced into wrong lane; failing to avoid collision by accelerating rather than slowing down and stopping.

347	**Harvey v Plymouth CC**	[2010] EWCA Civ 860; [2010] PIQR P18	High Ct	OL	PI	Y	75	M	21	Running in dark while intoxicated.	Failing securely to fence edge of land; allowing fence to constitute tripping hazard.
348	**Horsley v Cascade Insulation Services Ltd**	[2009] EWHC 2945 (QB)	High Ct	EL	PI	Y	20	M	Adult	Smoking.	Exposing claimant to asbestos.
349	**Horsley v Cascade Insulation Services Ltd**	[2009] EWHC 2945 (QB)	High Ct	EL	PI	Y	20	M	Adult	Smoking.	Exposing claimant to asbestos.
350	**Dunlop Haywards Ltd v Barbon Insurance Group Ltd**	[2009] EWHC 2900 (Comm); [2010] Lloyd's Rep IR 149	High Ct	PN	PEL	N	N/A	N/A	N/A	Failing to review terms of insurance cover.	Failing to obtain required insurance cover.
351	**Dunlop Haywards Ltd v Barbon Insurance Group Ltd**	[2009] EWHC 2900 (Comm); [2010] Lloyd's Rep IR 149	High Ct	PN	PEL	Y	80	N/A	N/A	Failing to identify change in cover.	Failing to query change in insurance.
352	**Sklair v Haycock**	[2009] EWHC 3328 (QB)	High Ct	RA	PI	Y	10	M	46	Crossing road when unsafe to do so.	Unknown.

	Claim	Citation	Court	Claim type	Damage type	Guilty of CN	Discount	Gender	Age	Actual or alleged CN	Defendant's wrongful conduct
353	**Howe v Houlton**	[2009] EWHC 3344 (QB)	High Ct	RA	PI	N	N/A	M	27.5	Parking within controlled area of pedestrian crossing in breach of Highway Code.	Hitting claimant's car door when driving past.
354	**Scout Association v Barnes**	[2010] EWCA Civ 1476	Birmingham CC	O	PI	N	N/A	M	13	Failing to avoid collision with bench.	Turning lights off, which introduced an unacceptable degree of risk to game.
355	**Limbrick v Ron Green & Son**	[2010] CLY 2413	Cardiff CC	EL	PI	Y	20	M	Adult	Failing to appreciate risk that lead flashing might suddenly come away.	Failing to carry out a risk assessment.
356	**Moore v Hotelplan Ltd**	[2010] EWHC 276 (QB)	High Ct	SI	PI	Y	30	F	37	Riding too close to vehicle in front and applying the throttle instead of the brake.	Defendant tour operator said to be liable for failure of ski instructor to provide the claimant with proper training on the use of ski mobiles.
357	**Waters v Hayley**	[2010] EWHC 920 (QB)	High Ct	OL	PI	N	N/A	M	39	Opening lift door when claimant would have known that the lift was not in fact there.	Allowing lift doors to open when unsafe.
358	**Tom Hoskins Plc v EMR Law**	[2010] EWHC 479 (Ch)	High Ct	PN	PEL	N	N/A	N/A	N/A	Delaying obtaining landlord's consent.	Delaying completing transaction.

359	**Valentine v Ministry of Defence**	[2010] CSOH 40; 2010 SLT 473	Court of Session (OH)	EL	PI	Y	20	M	22	Letting guard down despite being aware of risk of falling into trench.	Failing to carry out a sufficient risk assessment; failing to devise and institute a safe system of taking soil samples.
360	**Edwards v Martin**	[2010] EWHC 570 (QB)	High Ct	RA	PI	Y	15	M	34	Failing to wear seat belt.	Unknown.
361	**Dalling v RJ Heale & Co Ltd**	[2011] EWCA Civ 365	Swansea CC	EL	PI	Y	33.3	M	25	Falling over due to intoxication.	Failing to implement safe work system.
362	**Stoddart v Perucca**	[2011] EWCA Civ 290	Newcastle CC	RA	PI	Y	50	F	14	Failing to look before crossing road on horse.	Failing to slow down to allow for the possibility of a second horse.
363	**Ceva Logistics Ltd v Lynch**	[2011] EWCA Civ 188; [2011] ICR 746	High Ct	EL	PI	Y	25	M	47	Accessing area on foot without blocking off both ends.	Failing to provide a proper briefing; failing to employ a safe system of work in situations where vehicles were in close proximity to other workers.
364	**Ceva Logistics Ltd v Lynch**	[2011] EWCA Civ 188; [2011] ICR 746	High Ct	EL	PI	Y	25	M	47	Accessing area on foot without blocking off both ends.	Failing to provide a proper briefing; failing to employ a safe system of work in situations where vehicles were in close proximity to other workers.

	Claim	Citation	Court	Claim type	Damage type	Guilty of CN	Discount	Gender	Age	Actual or alleged CN	Defendant's wrongful conduct
365	**Tolley v Carr**	[2010] EWHC 2191 (QB); [2011] RTR 7	High Ct	RA	PI	N	N/A	M	Adult	Moving car that had crashed on the road.	Losing control of vehicle when driving at 65–70mph in adverse weather conditions and stopping car with driver's door facing oncoming traffic in outside lane.
366	**Tolley v Carr**	[2010] EWHC 2191 (QB); [2011] RTR 7	High Ct	RA	PI	N	N/A	M	Adult	Moving car that had crashed on the road.	Driving without due care in adverse weather conditions and colliding with first defendant's stopped vehicle.
367	**Tolley v Carr**	[2010] EWHC 2191 (QB); [2011] RTR 7	High Ct	RA	PI	N	N/A	M	Adult	Moving car that had crashed on the road.	Driving without due care in adverse weather conditions and colliding with first defendant's stopped vehicle.
368	**Caerphilly CBC v Button**	[2010] EWCA Civ 1311; [2011] ICR D3	Cardiff CC	EL	PI	Y	20	F	Adult	Failing to pay sufficient attention to placement of feet.	Failing to provide safe access route from car park.

369	**Swain v Geoffrey Osborne Ltd**	[2010] EWHC 1108 (QB)	High Ct	PL	PI	Y	25	M	39	Walking too quickly on muddy surface.	Failing to ensure that second defendant put in place and implemented a satisfactory system in post-remediation period.
370	**Swain v Geoffrey Osborne Ltd**	[2010] EWHC 1108 (QB)	High Ct	PL	PI	Y	25	M	39	Walking too quickly on muddy surface.	Failing to ensure mud removed.
371	**Willard v Boswell**	[2010] EWHC 2037 (QB)	High Ct	RA	PI	N	N/A	M	Adult	Driving on wrong side of road.	Swerving onto wrong side of road.
372	**Kotula v EDF Energy Networks (EPN) Plc**	[2010] EWHC 1968 (QB)	High Ct	PL	PI	N	N/A	M	24	Riding bicycle through roadworks.	Failing to erect and maintain a pedestrian access point during works.
373	**Belka v Prosperini**	[2011] EWCA Civ 623	Newcastle Upon Tyne CC	RA	PI	Y	66.6	M	Adult	Running across road in front of defendant's vehicle.	Failing to slow down upon noticing pedestrians.
374	**Doran v Shanks Waste Management**	[2010] CSOH 91	Court of Session (OH)	EL	PI	Y	20	M	61	Climbing onto lorry; failing to wait until skip was on ground; skipping forward to create some room despite knowing that ram on the lorry moved; failing to take sufficient care in placing feet.	Failing to instruct pursuer not to climb onto lorry.
375	**Hyndman v Brown**	[2010] NIQB 94	High Ct (NI)	EL	PI	Y	20	M	20	Attempting to dislodge a blockage from the harvester while the power was turned on.	Failing to take proper steps to ensure that claimant was in a safe position before turning on power to machinery.

	Claim	Citation	Court	Claim type	Damage type	Guilty of CN	Discount	Gender	Age	Actual or alleged CN	Defendant's wrongful conduct
376	**Toner v George Morrison Builders**	[2010] CSOH 125; 2011 Rep LR 18	Court of Session (OH)	EL	PI	Y	50	M	Adult	Using ladder despite obvious danger in doing so.	Failing to take sufficient steps to prevent use of ladder.
377	**Clark v Bourne Leisure Ltd**	[2011] EWCA Civ 753	Norwich CC	OL	PI	Y	33.3	F	55	Driving wheelchair down steps.	Failing to ensure that premises were reasonably safe for wheelchair users.
378	**Scullion v Bank of Scotland Plc**	[2010] EWHC 2253 (Ch); [2011] PNLR 5	High Ct	PN	PEL	N	N/A	M	Adult	Signing application form without reading and checking it.	Negligently overstating both capital value and expected rental income of flat.
379	**Boardman v Ministry of Defence**	QBD, 12 Nov 2010	High Ct	RA	PI	N	N/A	M	6	Stepping into road from behind lorry.	Driving at excessive speed; failing to wait for lorry to pass before continuing.
380	**Burton v Evitt**	[2011] EWCA Civ 1378	Preston CC	RA	PI	Y	66.6	M	Adult	Overtaking line of traffic; driving at excessive speed.	Failing to inch out of traffic queue so as to see traffic behind.
381	**MacDonald v Wood Group Engineering (North Sea) Ltd**	[2010] CSOH 165	Court of Session (OH)	EL	PI	Y	50	M	48	Placing fingers in a place of danger.	Failing to carry out a sufficient risk assessment

382	**Hill v Master Concrete Ltd**	[2010] EWHC 3613 (QB)	High Ct	RA	PI	Y	50	F	Adult	Failing to look before crossing road.	Failing to look before turning.
383	**Smith v CC of Notts**	[2012] EWCA Civ 161; [2012] RTR 23	Nottingham CC	RA	PI	Y	75	F	16	Crossing road when unsafe to do so.	Failing to slow down when travelling through red light on emergency call.
384	**Hadlow v Peterborough CC**	[2011] EWCA Civ 1329	Lincoln CC	EL	PI	N	N/A	F	63	Tripping over chair.	Failing to provide claimant with another staff member.
385	**Sedge v Prime**	[2011] EWHC 820 (QB)	High Ct	RA	PI	Y	25	M	21	Intoxicated; stepping into road without looking for oncoming traffic.	Failing to drive at safe speed; failing to keep a proper lookout for pedestrians; failing to sound horn.
386	**Lightfoot v Go-Ahead Group Plc**	[2011] EWHC 89 (QB); [2011] RTR 27	High Ct	RA	PI	Y	40	M	52	Stepping into road when intoxicated to flag down an oncoming bus.	Reading timetable while driving.
387	**Ground Gilbey Ltd v Jardine Lloyd Thompson UK Ltd**	[2011] EWHC 124 (Comm); [2012] Lloyd's Rep IR 12	High Ct	PN	PEL	N	N/A	N/A	N/A	Failing to enforce prohibition against portable heaters.	Failing to take reasonable care in advising on terms of insurance cover.
388	**McLachlan v Early Learning Centre Ltd**	[2011] CSOH 25; 2011 SCLR 629	Court of Session (OH)	EL	PI	Y	25	F	37	Putting one foot on shelf and then attempting to return that part of her weight to ladder prior to descending.	Placing box high above ground.

	Claim	Citation	Court	Claim type	Damage type	Guilty of CN	Discount	Gender	Age	Actual or alleged CN	Defendant's wrongful conduct
389	**Douglas v O'Neill**	[2011] EWHC 601 (QB)	High Ct	RA	PI	Y	12.5	M	34.5	Stepping into road without looking for oncoming traffic.	Driving while intoxicated.
390	**Maynard v Wigan MBC**	[2011] EWCA Civ 1694	Wigan CC	OL	PI	Y	50	F	Adult	Failing to notice hole.	Negligently failing to fill in hole on verge.
391	**Phethean-Hubble v Coles**	[2011] EWHC 363 (QB)	High Ct	RA	PI	Y	33.3	M	16	Entering road from pavement on bicycle without looking for oncoming traffic.	Driving at excessive speed.
392	**Peverill v Hillingdon LBC**	Central London CC, 9 Mar 2011	Central London CC	PL	PI	N	N/A	F	U	Failing to identify hazard in course of crossing access point.	Failing to detect a dangerous defect on a cross-over at entrance to school.
393	**P (decd) v Sedar**	[2011] EWHC 1266 (QB)	High Ct	PN	PI	N	N/A	F	Adult	Failing to follow up appointment.	Failing to contact claimant regarding breast lump.
394	**O'Neill v University of the West of Scotland**	[2011] CSOH 52; 2011 Rep LR 58	Court of Session (OH)	EL	PI	N	N/A	F	Adult	Failing to take reasonable care in placement of feet; failing to take account of surroundings.	Failing to highlight hazard created by a step placed in a corridor circulation area.
395	**Thomas v Warwickshire CC**	[2011] EWHC 772 (QB)	High Ct	PL	PI	Y	60	M	Adult	Riding too close to cyclist in front.	Failing to maintain highway.

396	**Kelly v Nugent**	[2011] NIQB 79	High Ct (NI)	RA	PI	Y	15	M	9.75	Taking tricycle onto road.	Failing to keep a proper lookout for pedestrians; driving at excessive speed.
397	**Rehill v Rider Holdings Ltd**	[2012] EWCA Civ 628; [2013] RTR 5	Bradford CC	RA	PI	Y	33.3	M	45.5	Crossing road when traffic signal was red and in sight of bus.	Failing to notice pedestrian and brake sufficiently quickly.
398	**Bellingham v Todd**	[2011] CSOH 74; 2011 SLT 1124	Court of Session (OH)	RA	PI	Y	80	M	40	Riding too close to vehicle in front.	Braking hard without considering other road users.
399	**Stangroom v Brown**	[2012] EWCA Civ 424	Norwich CC	RA	PI	Y	75	M	Adult	Driving at excessive speed.	Failing to take sufficient safety precautions when pulling out from a lay-by.
400	**Cheung v Zhu**	[2011] EWHC 2913 (QB)	High Ct	EL	PI	Y	15	F	53	Failing to take proper care on wet floor known to be slippery.	Failing to keep floor free from slippery substance.
401	**Anderson v Warburtons Ltd**	[2011] CSOH 77	Court of Session (OH)	RA	PI	Y	66.6	F	Adult	Failing to notice two signs indicating presence of lay-by (or lay-by itself) which would have afforded a safe stopping place; stopping car on road after end of the lay-by; failing to remove car from danger.	Failing to slow down sufficiently.
402	**Tafa v Matsim Properties Ltd**	[2011] EWHC 1302 (QB)	High Ct	EL	PI	Y	10	M	42	Failing to take care when working at height and in the vicinity of fragile materials.	Failing to ensure work at height was properly planned and supervised.

	Claim	Citation	Court	Claim type	Damage type	Guilty of CN	Discount	Gender	Age	Actual or alleged CN	Defendant's wrongful conduct
403	**Tafa v Matsim Properties Ltd**	[2011] EWHC 1302 (QB)	High Ct	EL	PI	Y	10	M	42	Failing to take care when working at height and in the vicinity of fragile materials.	Failing to ensure work at height was properly planned and supervised.
404	**Costa v Imperial London Hotels Ltd**	[2012] EWCA Civ 672	Mayor's and City of London CC	EL	PI	Y	35	F	41	Undertaking unsafe lifting.	Failing to provide refresher training.
405	**Whiteford v Kubas UAB**	[2012] EWCA Civ 1017	Cambridge CC	RA	PI	Y	50	M	Adult	Driving too close to centre line on motorcycle.	Failing to drive closer to edge of road given size of vehicle and narrowness of road.
406	**Woodham v JM Turner**	[2011] EWHC 1588 (QB); [2012] RTR 7	High Ct	RA	PI	Y	30	M	16	Overtaking stationary traffic on offside when approaching junction; travelling at excessive speed.	Performing manoeuvre with obstructed view.
407	**Brown v Brent**	Croydon CC, 21 Jun 2011	Croydon CC	RA	PI	Y	33.3	M	Adult	Failing to heed warning signs and race marshal indicating that race was in progress; driving at excessive speed.	Driving at excessive speed; crossing onto wrong side of road by a considerable margin; and riding into claimant's path.
408	**Coldridge v Bury MBC**	Manchester CC, 24 Jun 2011	Manchester CC	EL	PI	Y	20	F	Adult	Failing to use oven gloves provided; being selective in reading or taking note of instructions on packet.	Failing to carry out risk assessment in relation to ready-meal containers.

409	**Harrison v Jagged Globe (Alpine) Ltd**	[2012] EWCA Civ 835	Central London CC	SI	PI	Y	40	F	30	Undertaking two-staged fall.	Initiating climbing stunts.
410	**Reynolds v Strutt & Parker LLP**	[2011] EWHC 2263 (QB)	High Ct	SI	PI	Y	66.6	M	46	Failing to wear a cycle helmet.	Failing to carry out a sufficient and suitable risk assessment.
411	**Trebor Bassett Holdings Ltd v ADT Fire & Security Plc**	[2011] EWHC 1936 (TCC); [2011] BLR 661	High Ct	PN	PD	Y	75	N/A	N/A	Failing to segregate production area from rest of building; failing to install sprinklers; taking inappropriate action upon discovery of fire.	Failing to take reasonable care in connection with design and installation.
412	**Trebor Bassett Holdings Ltd v ADT Fire & Security Plc**	[2011] EWHC 1936 (TCC); [2011] BLR 661	High Ct	PN	PD	Y	75	N/A	N/A	Failing to segregate the production area from the rest of the building, failing to install sprinklers, and failing to ensure that staff members were fully trained in the manual activation of the system.	Design and installation faults.
413	**Smith v Wilgar**	[2011] NIQB 67	High Ct (NI)	EL	PI	Y	33.3	M	27	Climbing 20-foot ladder; failing to inform employer about previous falls from ladders or scaffolding.	Failing to provide a mobile scaffold tower that would have afforded sufficient protection against a fall from a ladder due to a hypoglycaemic attack.

	Claim	Citation	Court	Claim type	Damage type	Guilty of CN	Discount	Gender	Age	Actual or alleged CN	Defendant's wrongful conduct
414	**Ellis v Lokat**	QBD, 6 Oct 2011	High Ct	RA	PI	Y	20	M	U	Driving at excessive speed.	Turning too slowly at junction; failing to look for oncoming traffic and to see claimant.
415	**McKeever v Ministry of Defence**	[2011] NIQB 87	High Ct (NI)	O	PI	N	N/A	M	21	Driving a getaway car; getting on knees at front of car and presenting head and shoulders above bonnet and adopting a firing stance.	Shooting unarmed person without justification.
416	**Johnson v Castle Combe Circuit Ltd**	QBD, 7 Oct 2011	High Ct	EL	PI	N	N/A	M	59	Sitting in a dangerous position whilst on a moving vehicle.	Failing to provide proper equipment.
417	**Devereux v Hayward**	[2011] EWHC 2780 (QB)	High Ct	RA	PI	N	N/A	F	37	Failing to move horse to verge.	Driving at excessive speed.
418	**Phee v Gordon**	[2011] CSOH 181; 2011 Rep LR	Court of Session (OH)	SI	PI	N	N/A	M	40	Failing to duck when hearing shout of 'fore'.	Underestimating degree of risk of golf shot.
419	**Phee v Gordon**	[2011] CSOH 181; 2011 Rep LR	Court of Session (OH)	OL	PI	N	N/A	M	40	Failing to duck when hearing shout of 'fore'.	Failing to conduct a risk assessment of golf course; failing to take precautions to reduce risk of accident; failing to place warning signs.

420	**McDermott v Pettit**	[2011] EWHC 3074 (QB)	High Ct	RA	PI	Y	10	M	18	Failing to use pedestrian crossing.	Driving at excessive speed; driving while intoxicated.
421	**Malasi v Ahmed**	[2011] EWHC 4083 (QB)	High Ct	RA	PI	Y	80	M	19	Failing to stop at red light.	Driving at excessive speed.
422	**Palfrey v WM Morrisons Supermarkets Plc**	[2012] EWCA Civ 1917	Plymouth CC	OL	PI	Y	50	F	79	Tripping over container having already seen it.	Using low lying container to stack shelves in circumstances where customers' attention would be on products.
423	**Ringe v Eden Springs (UK) Ltd**	[2012] EWHC 14 (QB)	High Ct	RA	PI	Y	80	M	U	Driving at excessive speed; overtaking lorry when unsafe to do so.	Undertaking manoeuvre without clear sight.
424	**Rehman v Brady**	[2012] EWHC 78 (QB)	High Ct	RA	PI	N	N/A	F	7.25	Running into road from behind a parked vehicle.	Driving at excessive speed in built-up area where presence of children was likely.
425	**Paramasivan v Wicks**	[2013] EWCA Civ 262	High Ct	RA	PI	Y	50	M	13	Stepping into road without looking for oncoming traffic.	Failing to look out for pedestrians.
426	**Tavares v Hudson-Rotin**	[2012] EWHC 3171 (QB)	High Ct	RA	PI	Y	15	M	37	Failing to follow advice contained in Green Cross Code when attempting to cross road.	Driving at excessive speed.
427	**Pinchbeck v Craggy Island Ltd**	[2012] EWHC 2745 (QB)	High Ct	SI	PI	Y	33.3	F	41	Jumping from climbing wall rather than climbing down.	Failing to give clear instructions.

	Claim	Citation	Court	Claim type	Damage type	Guilty of CN	Discount	Gender	Age	Actual or alleged CN	Defendant's wrongful conduct
428	**AC v Devon CC**	[2012] EWHC 796 (QB); [2012] RTR 32	High Ct	PL	PI	N	N/A	M	Adult	Failing to notice pot hole while overtaking a slower-moving vehicle.	Failing to maintain highway.
429	**Tacagni v Cornwall CC**	[2013] EWCA Civ 702	Truro CC	OL	PI	Y	66.6	F	Adult	Walking on raised path in dark while intoxicated and without a torch.	Failing to erect a fence to prevent risk of falling over edge.
430	**Argos Ltd v Leather Trade House Ltd**	[2012] EWHC 1348 (QB)	High Ct	PN	PEL	N	N/A	N/A	N/A	Failing to take measures to clarify safety of chemical.	Failing to inform of potential harm caused by chemical when requested.
431	**Starks v CC of Herts**	[2013] EWCA Civ 782; [2014] RTR 4	Cambridge CC	RA	PI	Y	55	M	Adult	Entering roundabout late and not slowing down.	Failing to observe roundabout; driving straight over roundabout.
432	**Jackson v Murray**	[2012] CSOH 100; 2012 SCLR 605	Court of Session (OH)	RA	PI	Y	90	F	13	Crossing road when unsafe to do so.	Failing to keep a proper lookout for pedestrians; failing to reduce speed when approaching minibus.
433	**Meaney v Link Rider Coaches Ltd**	B'mouth CC, 21 Jun 2012	B'mouth CC	RA	PI	Y	25	M	U	Failing to abort attempt to leave road.	Failing to leave sufficient stopping distance.

434	**Hannon v Hillingdon Homes Ltd**	[2012] EWHC 1437 (QB); [2012] PTSR D37	High Ct	OL	PI	N	N/A	M	46	Rushing down stairs.	Failing to maintain premises.
435	**Hook v Eatons Solicitors**	Leeds CC, 17 Jul 2012	Leeds CC	EL	PI	N	N/A	F	Adult	Momentary misjudgement of a few inches that led to loss of footing.	Failing to carry out a risk assessment regarding suitability of route.
436	**Ireland v David Lloyd Leisure Ltd**	[2013] EWCA Civ 665	Bristol CC	OL	PI	Y	25	F	U	Resting hand on gym equipment while in use.	Failing to take sufficient steps to warn of dangers associated with equipment.
437	**Condie v Blight**	Newcastle upon Tyne CC, 25 Jul 2012	Newcastle upon Tyne CC	RA	PI	N	N/A	M	U	Failing to look in defendant's direction.	Failing to move so as to be able to see cars coming from claimant's direction.
438	**Smith v Fowler**	2012 GWD 26-552	Sheriff Ct (Grampian, Highland and Islands)	RA	PI	N	N/A	M	56	Failing to exercise special care in proceeding forward despite having seen van stop and having view obstructed.	Turning into path of oncoming traffic without checking if road was clear.
439	**Beasley v Alexander**	[2012] EWHC 2197 (QB)	High Ct	RA	PI	N	N/A	M	25	Driving at excessive speed.	Performing turn without looking.
440	**Probert v Moore**	[2012] EWHC 2324 (QB)	High Ct	RA	PI	N	N/A	F	13.5	Walking along country road on winter's night; failing to wear high-visibility clothing; wearing headphones.	Driving at excessive speed; failing to appreciate other road users.

	Claim	Citation	Court	Claim type	Damage type	Guilty of CN	Discount	Gender	Age	Actual or alleged CN	Defendant's wrongful conduct
441	**Alleyne v Comr of Police of the Metropolis**	[2012] EWHC 3955 (QB)	High Ct	O	PI	N	N/A	M	57.5	Failing to comply with police instructions.	Failing to exercise reasonable care when handcuffing claimant.
442	**McCarrick v Park Resorts Ltd**	QBD, 26 Oct 2012	High Ct	OL	PI	Y	33.3	M	19.5	Failing to take sufficient steps to ascertain depth of water before diving into it.	Failing to erect adequate signage regarding diving.
443	**McGlinchey v McCaughan**	[2012] NIQB 111	High Ct (NI)	O	PI	N	N/A	F	19	Swapping seats throughout journey.	Driving boat recklessly.
444	**Proctor v City Facilities Management Ltd**	[2012] NIQB 99	High Ct (NI)	EL	PI	Y	33.3	M	56	Using ladder knowing of the risk that it could fall.	Requiring claimant to carry out a painting job while standing on a ladder in a stairwell.
445	**Smith v James Strang Ltd**	[2012] CSOH 173; 2013 Rep LR 19	Court of Session (OH)	EL	PI	Y	50	M	26	Failing to read instruction manual.	Failing to design a safe system of work.
446	**West Sussex CC v Pierce**	[2013] EWCA Civ 1230	Brighton CC	OL	PI	N	N/A	M	9.5	Accidentally punching a metal water fountain.	Failing to safeguard children from risk of harm posed by fountain.
447	**Japp v Virgin Holidays Ltd**	[2013] EWCA Civ 1371; [2014] PIQR P8	Brighton CC	O	PI	Y	20	F	Adult	Unknown.	Inadequate safety standards at hotel.

448	**Hill v Norside Ltd**	[2012] CSOH 187; 2013 Rep LR 22	Court of Session (OH)	EL	PI	Y	20	M	Adult	Failing to tie ladder to scaffold before descent.	Failing to provide a proper plan or safe system for use of portable ladder.
449	**Biddick (decd) v Morcom**	[2014] EWCA Civ 182	High Ct	OL	PI	Y	66.6	M	Adult	Overreaching himself to get to a screw knowing it was unsafe to do so.	Failing to hold pole having assumed a responsibility by saying that he would.
450	**Webb Resolutions Ltd v E.Surv Ltd**	[2012] EWHC 3653 (TCC); [2013] PNLR 15	High Ct	PN	PEL	Y	50	N/A	N/A	Lending on a loan-to-value ratio that was dangerously high; lending on a self-certified basis where application had not been made on that basis; failing to obtain confirmation of amount of earnings from accountant; failing to take into account very substantial credit card defaults.	Negligent valuation.
451	**Blemain Finance Ltd v E.Surv Ltd**	[2012] EWHC 3654 (TCC)	High Ct	PN	PEL	N	N/A	N/A	N/A	Failing to act as a reasonably competent second charge lender.	Negligent valuation.
452	**Brown v First Glasgow Ltd**	[2012] CSOH 192	Court of Session (OH)	RA	PI	Y	80	M	Adult	Opening door while close to the centre of road without checking if it was safe to do so.	Driving unnecessarily close to van; intruding onto southbound carriageway without being alert to possibility of activity at rear of van.

	Claim	Citation	Court	Claim type	Damage type	Guilty of CN	Discount	Gender	Age	Actual or alleged CN	Defendant's wrongful conduct
453	**French v Strathclyde Fire Board**	[2013] CSOH 3; 2013 SLT 247	Court of Session (OH)	EL	PI	N	N/A	M	31	Failing to appreciate that complying with request was dangerous and that the gable could collapse.	Failing to conduct a suitable risk assessment; instructing the pursuer fireman to enter the building rather than attempting to eliminate the fire from a side window.
454	**French v Strathclyde Fire Board**	[2013] CSOH 3; 2013 SLT 247	Court of Session (OH)	EL	PI	N	N/A	M	24	Failing to appreciate that complying with request was dangerous and that the gable could collapse.	Failing to conduct a suitable risk assessment; instructing the pursuer fireman to enter the building rather than attempting to eliminate the fire from a side window.
455	**Steele v WH Malcolm Ltd**	2013 GWD 25-511	Sheriff Ct (North Strathclyde)	EL	PI	Y	30	M	39	Failing to wear a seat belt while driving a forklift; misjudging a turn.	Failing to organise workplace such that vehicles could circulate safely.

456	**Cowan v Hopetoun House Preservation Trust**	[2013] CSOH 9; 2013 Rep LR 62	Court of Session (OH)	OL	PI	Y	75	M	61	Failing to follow instructions at beginning of walk; leaving path in darkness; failing to keep a proper look out.	Failing to provide clear directions to all participants in walk; failing to take reasonable care to get visitors safely off premises in darkness.
457	**McGee v RJK Building Services Ltd**	[2013] CSOH 10; 2013 SLT 428	Court of Session (OH)	O	PI	N	N/A	M	71	Consuming alcohol in evening preceding fall.	Failing properly to fit handrail.
458	**Ayres v Odedra**	[2013] EWHC 40 (QB)	High Ct	RA	PI	Y	20	M	24	Walking while intoxicated and with trousers around ankles resulting in inability to move at normal speed.	Driving in pedestrian only area; misjudging amount of time it would take claimant to get to position clear of car.
459	**Cruikshanks v Amlin UK Ltd**	[2013] CSOH 12	Court of Session (OH)	RA	PI	N	N/A	M	U	Failing to pay proper attention to what was happening in right-hand lane and thus failing to see tractor unit or defender signalling.	Failing to keep a proper lookout for other cars; moving from right-hand lane into left-hand lane of roundabout when unsafe to do so.
460	**Wheeler v CC of Glos**	[2013] EWCA Civ 1791	High Ct	RA	PI	Y	50	M	Adult	Driving at excessive speed.	Failing to stop or check for oncoming traffic before turning right.

	Claim	Citation	Court	Claim type	Damage type	Guilty of CN	Discount	Gender	Age	Actual or alleged CN	Defendant's wrongful conduct
461	**Germaine v Epsom and St Helier University Hospitals NHS Trust**	[2013] EWHC 761 (QB)	High Ct	EL	PI	N	N/A	F	54	Failing to implement manual handling training.	Failing to provide safe means of lifting furniture.
462	**Wilson v Haden**	[2013] EWHC 229 (QB)	High Ct	OL	PI	N	N/A	M	46	Failing to wrap legs around pole.	Failing to demonstrate adequately how to use fireman's pole.
463	**Wallace v Stewart Homes (Scotland) Ltd**	[2013] CSOH 30; 2014 SCLR 1	Court of Session (OH)	EL	PI	Y	33.3	M	Adult	Going onto roof despite absence of scaffold protection.	Failing to provide a safe work environment; failing to instruct pursuer not to work on roof following removal of scaffolding.
464	**Sharp v Top Flight Scaffolding Ltd**	[2013] EWHC 479 (QB)	High Ct	EL	PI	Y	60	M	40	Building scaffolding without internal ladders and descending in unsafe manner.	Failing properly to train employees.
465	**Rockliffe v Liverpool CC**	Liverpool CC, 18 Mar 2013	Liverpool CC	PL	PI	N	N/A	F	U	Unknown.	Failing to clear a footpath of ice.
466	**Taylor v Bank of Ireland (UK) Plc**	[2013] NIQB 50	High Ct (NI)	PN	PEL	N	N/A	N/A	N/A	Failing to carry out checks in relation to buyer.	Assuring claimant that buyer's funds had cleared.

467	**Gray v Gibson**	[2014] EWCA Civ 355	Stoke-on-Trent CC	RA	PI	Y	40	F	Adult	Driving at excessive speed.	Driving over central line.
468	**Quinn v Keenan**	[2013] NIQB 55	High Ct (NI)	EL	PI	Y	50	M	Adult	Lifting a heavy piece of work equipment without assistance.	Failing to maintain and rigorously enforce a safe system of working.
469	**Corbett v Cumbria Kart Racing Club**	[2013] EWHC 1362 (QB)	High Ct	OL	PI	Y	10	M	46.5	Failing to tighten seat belt sufficiently before race.	Failing to take sufficient steps to prevent vehicles coming off the track; positioning ambulance behind tyres on corner.
470	**Corbett v Cumbria Kart Racing Club**	[2013] EWHC 1362 (QB)	High Ct	SI	PI	Y	10	M	46.5	Failing to tighten seatbelt sufficiently before race.	Failing to take sufficient steps to prevent vehicles coming off track; positioning ambulance behind tyres on corner.
471	**Heary v Phinn**	2013 SLT (Sh Ct) 145	Sheriff Ct (Tayside, Central and Fife)	OL	PI	Y	50	M	Adult	Underestimating risk of injury in climbing over obstacle.	Failing to take reasonable care to ensure that when yard was vacated no visitors thereto were left locked in.
472	**Hickman v London Central Bus Co Ltd**	[2013] EWHC 1703 (QB)	High Ct	RA	PI	Y	40	M	Adult	Crossing road in potentially hazardous area; failing to wait until buses had moved before crossing road.	Failing to keep a proper lookout for pedestrians; moving off when pedestrian already crossing road.

	Claim	Citation	Court	Claim type	Damage type	Guilty of CN	Discount	Gender	Age	Actual or alleged CN	Defendant's wrongful conduct
473	**Mills v JP Barnes & Sons Ltd**	2013 WL 8182338	Leeds CC	EL	PI	N	N/A	M	Adult	Failing to wear a mask; failing to ensure when using electric tile cutter that water tray was filled so as to absorb some of dust generated.	Exposing the claimant to silica dust.
474	**Manorgate Ltd v First Scottish Property Services Ltd**	[2013] CSOH 108; [2014] PNLR 1	Court of Session (OH)	PN	PEL	N	N/A	N/A	N/A	Failing to query or double-check accuracy of information in Property Enquiry Certificate.	Failing to produce an accurate Property Enquiry Certificate.
475	**Ali v Caton**	[2013] EWHC 1730 (QB)	High Ct	RA	PI	Y	20	M	17	Unknown.	Unknown.
476	**Dickson v Kinsman**	[2013] CSOH 111	Court of Session (OH)	RA	PI	N	N/A	M	35	Driving at excessive speed; misjudging direction.	Failing to look out for cyclists such as pursuer; braking too late; conveying impression that vehicle might not stop at junction.
477	**Wembridge Claimants v Winter**	[2013] EWHC 2331 (QB)	High Ct	EL	PI	N	N/A	M	63	Failing to leave site of fire when advised to do so.	Storing fireworks in an unsafe manner.

478	**Kennedy v Cordia (Services) LLP**	[2013] CSOH 130; 2013 Rep LR 126	Court of Session (OH)	EL	PI	N	N/A	F	41	Failing to keep a proper look out and watch where feet placed; failing to wear suitable footwear; failing to report weather and underfoot conditions to management.	Failing to conduct suitable and sufficient risk assessments; failing to consider using protective personal equipment for footwear.
479	**Bennett v Southwell**	[2013] EWHC 2382 (QB)	High Ct	RA	PI	Y	50	F	Adult	Steering into defendant's path while braking and turning a corner.	Driving too far over line while cornering.
480	**Aurora Leasing Ltd v Colliers International Belfast Ltd**	[2013] NIQB 116	High Ct (NI)	PN	PEL	Y	20	N/A	N/A	Advancing loan without adequate inquiry as to circumstances of borrower and guarantors and property that was to provide security.	Negligent valuation.
481	**McKeown v Inverclyde Council**	[2013] CSOH 141; 2013 SLT 937	Court of Session (OH)	EL	PI	N	N/A	M	58	Slipping on steps which pursuer had salted earlier that day.	Failing to maintain pathways on school premises during wintery conditions.
482	**Khan v Harrow LBC**	[2013] EWHC 2687 (TCC)	High Ct	O	PD	Y	15	F	Adult	Failing to act on warnings and recommendations.	Permitting roots to damage property.
483	**Khan v Harrow LBC**	[2013] EWHC 2687 (TCC)	High Ct	O	PD	Y	15	M	Adult	Failing to act on warnings and recommendations.	Permitting roots to damage property.

	Claim	Citation	Court	Claim type	Damage type	Guilty of CN	Discount	Gender	Age	Actual or alleged CN	Defendant's wrongful conduct
484	**United Central Bakeries Ltd v Spooner Industries Ltd**	[2013] CSOH 150	Court of Session (OH)	O	PD	Y	20	N/A	N/A	Failing to consider data sheet carefully.	Failing to emphasise advice about temperatures and flammability in data sheet; failing to emphasise that product should not cause belting to exceed 90°C; failing to advise investigation regarding effect of burning naan bread on belting.
485	**United Central Bakeries Ltd v Spooner Industries Ltd**	[2013] CSOH 150	Court of Session (OH)	O	PD	Y	20	N/A	N/A	Failing to consider data sheet carefully.	Failing to emphasise advice about temperatures and flammability in data sheet; failing to advise investigation regarding effect of burning naan bread on belting.
486	**Forsta AP-Fonden v Bank of New York Mellon SA/NV**	[2013] EWHC 3127 (Comm)	High Ct	PN	PEL	N	N/A	N/A	N/A	Failing to monitor portfolio; omitting entries from list of prohibited investments; failing to appreciate potential impact of 'credit crunch' on portfolio.	Failing to give appropriate advice in light of financial crisis.

487	**Doyle v Advocate General for Scotland**	[2013] CSOH 164	Court of Session (OH)	EL	PI	Y	25	M	56	Failing to report problem to employers.	Exposing pursuer to excessive noise.
488	**Farmer v FTV Proclad (UK) Ltd**	[2013] CSOH 165	Court of Session (OH)	EL	PI	Y	33.3	M	61	Failing to use an alternative route.	Permitting employees to use a dangerous shortcut.
489	**Nadarajah v Sotnick**	[2013] EWHC 3389 (QB)	High Ct	RA	PI	N	N/A	F	Adult	Driving at excessive speed.	Performing U-turn when unsafe to do so.
490	**Everett v London Fire and Emergency Planning Authority**	[2013] All ER (D) 289 (Nov)	High Ct	EL	PI	N	N/A	F	39	Failing to take reasonable care in climbing ladder.	Removing foot from stabilizing bar on ladder.
491	**McCracken v Smith**	[2013] EWHC 3620 (QB)	High Ct	RA	PI	Y	45	M	16	Travelling as pillion passenger on trail bike with dangerous driver; failing to wear helmet.	Failing to keep a proper lookout for other vehicles at junction.
492	**Butcher v Southend-on-Sea BC**	[2014] EWCA Civ 1556	Southend CC	OL	PI	Y	50	F	Adult	Failing to pay attention regarding edge of path.	Failing to rectify hazard when it was foreseeable that visitors might inadvertently step off path and lose their balance.
493	**Law Society of NI v Bank of Ireland**	[2013] NIQB 130	High Ct (NI)	PN	PEL	N	N/A	N/A	N/A	Failing properly to investigate and to challenge cheques prepared by solicitor and regarding other activities.	Violating s 79(2) of the Bills of Exchange Act 1882.

	Claim	Citation	Court	Claim type	Damage type	Guilty of CN	Discount	Gender	Age	Actual or alleged CN	Defendant's wrongful conduct
494	**Jones v Lawton**	[2013] EWHC 4108 (QB)	High Ct	RA	PI	Y	33.3	M	U	Driving at excessive speed; failing to see gap in traffic and defendant emerging from side road.	Being unaware of possibility that motorcycle was proceeding outside of slow-moving lanes of traffic; failing to look to right when turning.
495	**Train v Secretary of State for Defence**	[2014] EWHC 1928 (QB); [2014] RTR 28	High Ct	RA	PI	Y	80	M	Adult	Driving at excessive speed.	Turning when unsafe to do so.
496	**Sabir v Osei-Kwabena**	[2015] EWCA Civ 1213; [2016] RTR 9	High Ct	RA	PI	Y	25	F	30	Misjudging car's position and/or time available to cross road.	Failing to keep a proper lookout for pedestrians.
497	**Hazlett v Robinson**	[2014] NIQB 17	High Ct (NI)	RA	PI	Y	20	M	29	Failing to wear seat belt.	Driving without due care.
498	**McAllister v Campbell**	[2014] NIQB 24	High Ct (NI)	RA	PI	Y	25	M	21	Not looking where cycling; looking down at heart rate monitor.	Stopping vehicle when claimant cyclist was approaching from behind.

499	**Wellesley Partnership LLP v Withers LLP**	[2014] EWHC 556 (Ch); [2014] PNLR 22	High Ct	PN	PEL	N	N/A	N/A	N/A	Failing to read the agreement in its entirety.	Unknown.
500	**Curtis v Hertfordshire Council**	[2014] EWHC 1672 (QB)	High Ct	PL	PI	N	N/A	M	52	Failing to take action to avoid crack in road.	Failing to maintain highway.
501	**MacLeod v Comr of Police of the Metropolis**	[2014] EWHC 977 (QB)	High Ct	RA	PI	N	N/A	M	59	Intoxicated; proceeding in front of defendant's car without looking.	Driving at excessive speed in poor visibility; failing to keep a proper lookout for cyclists.
502	**Cowan v Lewis**	[2014] NIQB 47	High Ct (NI)	EL	PI	N	N/A	M	52	Working in a prohibited area.	Failing to take sufficient measures to prevent a fall from height; failing adequately to cover holes in storm tank.
503	**Rainford v Lawrenson**	[2014] EWHC 1188 (QB)	High Ct	RA	PI	Y	50	F	14.75	Stepping into road without looking for oncoming traffic.	Failing to anticipate risk of children stepping into road; failing to re-position vehicle closer to centre of road, reduce speed or cover foot brake; failing to use horn so as to alert claimant.

	Claim	Citation	Court	Claim type	Damage type	Guilty of CN	Discount	Gender	Age	Actual or alleged CN	Defendant's wrongful conduct
504	**West Sussex CC v Fuller**	[2015] EWCA Civ 189	Brighton CC	EL	PI	N	N/A	F	40	Misjudging footing when ascending a staircase.	Failing to carry out a risk assessment before asking a receptionist to deliver post in office.
505	**Smith v Bluebird Buses Ltd**	[2014] CSOH 75; 2014 Rep LR 91	Court of Session (OH)	RA	PI	Y	85	M	Adult	Intoxicated; stepping into road without looking for oncoming traffic.	Failing to keep a proper lookout for pedestrians; failing to stop bus so as to avoid collision.
506	**Groves v Studley**	[2014] EWHC 1522 (QB)	High Ct	RA	PI	Y	40	M	34	Jumping onto car bonnet.	Manoeuvring car in such a manner so as deliberately to dislodge claimant.
507	**Terminal Contenitori Porto di Genova SpA v China Shipping Container Lines Ltd**	[2014] EWHC 1629 (Comm)	High Ct	O	PD	N	N/A	N/A	N/A	Failing to move crane away from ship in light of the prevailing winds.	Failing properly to moor ship.
508	**Group Seven Ltd v Allied Investment Corp Ltd**	[2014] EWHC 2046 (Ch)	High Ct	O	PEL	N	N/A	N/A	N/A	Failing to take sufficient steps to investigate transaction.	Obtaining loan through misrepresentation.

509	**Playboy Club London Ltd v Banca Nazionale del Lavoro SpA**	[2014] EWHC 2613 (QB)	High Ct	PN	PEL	Y	15	N/A	N/A	Failing to check creditworthiness of party; failing to notice that cheques were obvious forgeries.	Failing to provide an accurate reference as to creditworthiness.
510	**Hay v Advanced Stairlifts (Scotland) Ltd**	[2014] CSOH 118; 2014 Rep LR 102	Court of Session (OH)	EL	PI	N	N/A	F	40	Failing to be careful regarding sitting when in control of equipment.	Allowing employees to use equipment giving rise to a risk of injury which was reasonably foreseeable.
511	**McLaughlin v Morrison**	[2014] CSOH 123; 2014 SLT 862	Court of Session (OH)	RA	PI	N	N/A	M	30	Provoking assault.	Assaulting pursuer who was run down by defender's car.
512	**Pearson v Anwar**	[2015] EWCA Civ 1011	Manchester CC	RA	PI	Y	25	M	23	Failing to wear seat belt.	Driving at excessive speed.
513	**Blackmore v Dept for Communities and Local Government**	2014 WL 5411779	Exeter CC	EL	PI	Y	30	M	Adult	Smoking.	Exposing claimant to asbestos.
514	**Ali v Siddique**	[2015] EWCA Civ 1258	Bradford CC	O	PEL	Y	50	M	Adult	Allowing transaction to proceed despite knowing that it was an unconventional method of transfer involving a higher risk of loss; handing over signed blank cheques knowing that doing so would put own funds at risk.	Transferring claimant's money to fraudster.

	Claim	Citation	Court	Claim type	Damage type	Guilty of CN	Discount	Gender	Age	Actual or alleged CN	Defendant's wrongful conduct
515	**Wilson v North Star Shipping (Aberdeen) Ltd**	[2014] CSOH 156	Court of Session (OH)	EL	PI	Y	40	M	45	Assuming an unsafe position on vessel.	Using a method of transferring sampling kits that created an avoidable risk.
516	**Wilson v North Star Shipping (Aberdeen) Ltd**	[2014] CSOH 156	Court of Session (OH)	O	PI	Y	40	M	45	Assuming an unsafe position on vessel.	Using a method of transferring sampling kits that created an avoidable risk.
517	**Russell v NFU Mutual Insurance Society Ltd**	[2014] CSOH 157	Court of Session (OH)	RA	PI	N	N/A	M	23	Driving at excessive speed.	Driving onto main road once pursuer had come round corner and should have been visible to defender; failing to take due care in the driving of vehicle.
518	**Ferguson v Ferguson**	[2015] CSIH 63; 2015 SLT 561	Court of Session (OH)	O	PI	Y	85	F	54	Grabbing the dog's cheeks and putting face close to its.	Violating section 1 Animals (Scotland) Act 1987.
519	**Wormald v Ahmed**	[2014] EWHC 4498 (QB)	High Ct	RA	PI	Y	40	M	20	Crossing road when unsafe to do so.	Failing to check mirror and blind spot and to monitor whole of road ahead; not looking ahead and thus failing to see claimant.

520	**Smith v Muir Construction Ltd**	[2014] CSOH 171; 2015 Rep LR 8	Court of Session (OH)	EL	PI	N	N/A	M	Adult	Failing to foot or otherwise secure ladder.	Failing to prevent ladder from being used; failing to issue warnings in respect of ladder's use.
521	**Brown v Dept for Regional Development**	[2014] NIQB 126	High Ct (NI)	PL	PI	Y	25	M	35	Failing to see the missing flagstone.	Failing properly to maintain the footpath.
522	**Edwards v Sutton LBC**	[2014] EWHC 4378 (QB)	High Ct	OL	PI	Y	40	M	Adult	Failing to let go of bicycle when falling on a bridge; failing to exercise necessary vigilance when crossing an old bridge.	Failing to undertake a risk assessment.
523	**Belkovic v DSG International Plc**	[2014] NIQB 139	High Ct (NI)	EL	PI	N	N/A	M	Adult	Failing to use system of work provided by employer.	Failing to take sufficient steps to ensure that migrant worker understood tasks and risks.
524	**McCaughey v Mullan**	[2014] NIQB 132	High Ct (NI)	RA	PI	Y	60	F	20	Being intoxicated in the middle of road.	Driving at excessive speed.
525	**English Heritage v Taylor**	[2016] EWCA Civ 448; [2016] PIQR P14	Newport (Isle of Wight) CC	OL	PI	Y	50	M	60	Standing on steep bank.	Failing to provide sign warning visitors of sheer drop.
526	**Suiter v Eves**	[2015] NIQB 31	High Ct (NI)	RA	PI	N	N/A	M	54	Driving at excessive speed.	Driving on the wrong side of road.
527	**Milroy v British Telecommunications Plc**	[2015] EWHC 532 (QB)	High Ct	EL	PI	Y	33.3	M	49	Moving bucket close to power line; allowing site engineer into bucket.	Failing to provide adequate training.

	Claim	Citation	Court	Claim type	Damage type	Guilty of CN	Discount	Gender	Age	Actual or alleged CN	Defendant's wrongful conduct
528	**Wilkinson v Hjaltland Housing Association Ltd**	2015 Rep LR 62	Sheriff Ct (Grampian, Highland and Islands)	OL	PI	N	N/A	F	31	Taking a shortcut rather than sticking to designated pathways.	Failing to take any safety precautions in respect of a hole in occupier's premises.
529	**Taberna Europe CDO II Plc v Selskabet (in bankruptcy)**	[2015] EWHC 871 (Comm)	High Ct	O	PEL	N	N/A	N/A	N/A	Failing to carry out due diligence competently.	Making untrue representations in public documents on which claimant relied when deciding to purchase subordinated notes issued by defendant.
530	**Rochester Cathedral v Debell**	[2016] EWCA Civ 1094	Brighton CC	PL	PI	Y	20	M	72	Failing to take sufficient care to see where he was walking.	Failing properly to maintain the concrete.
531	**Spencer v Hillingdon Hospital NHS Trust**	[2015] EWHC 1058 (QB)	High Ct	PN	PI	N	N/A	M	49	Failing to report symptoms.	Failing to inform claimant about risks of general anaesthetic.
532	**Hicks v Young**	[2015] EWHC 1144 (QB)	High Ct	RA	PI	Y	50	M	23	Misjudging speed at which taxi was travelling; jumping from taxi while it was moving.	Accelerating while claimant passenger was standing up in rear of vehicle.

533	**Wagner v Grant**	[2015] CSOH 51	Court of Session (OH)	RA	PI	Y	40	M	18	Not being aware of hazard warning lights and working lights; failing to slow motorcycle down; failing to keep lookout ahead.	Blocking the other lane by the trailer in darkness; failing to give some form of advance warning to westbound traffic, either by way of a warning sign or someone appointed to provide a form of advance warning.
534	**Whyte v Bluebird Buses Ltd**	[2015] CSOH 56; 2015 SLT 338	Court of Session (OH)	RA	PI	N	N/A	M	11	Striking bus while on pavement.	Driving too close to pavement.
535	**Warren v Inventive Leisure Ltd**	[2015] CLY 1939	Birmingham CC	O	PI	Y	20	F	22	Unknown.	Failing to keep toilet floor clear of water.
536	**Smithson v Calderdale MBC**	2015 WL 5949384	Manchester CC	PL	PI	N	N/A	F	42	Driving at excessive speed; failing to be cautious when there was black ice on the road.	Failing to keep the road clear of ice.
537	**Buswell v Symes**	[2015] EWHC 1379 (QB)	High Ct	RA	PI	Y	66.6	M	40	Driving at excessive speed.	Blocking road beyond hill with tractor.
538	**Rollinson v Dudley MBC**	[2015] EWHC 3330 (QB); [2016] RTR 19	Birmingham CC	PL	PI	N	N/A	M	52	Walking on moss even though there were clear strips on both sides of path.	Failing to keep path clear of moss.

	Claim	Citation	Court	Claim type	Damage type	Guilty of CN	Discount	Gender	Age	Actual or alleged CN	Defendant's wrongful conduct
539	**Jones v Scottish Opera**	[2015] CSOH 64; 2015 SLT 401	Court of Session (OH)	EL	PI	N	N/A	M	Adult	Making an awkward manoeuvre to get down from a height of a metre or more without any assistance.	Failing to provide a ramp.
540	**HP v Terex Equipment Ltd**	[2015] CSOH 76; 2015 Rep LR 106	Court of Session (OH)	EL	PI	N	N/A	M	Adult	Not being careful in placement of feet; failing to notice water on floor.	Unknown.
541	**Sinclair v Joyner**	[2015] EWHC 1800 (QB); [2015] RTR 29	High Ct	RA	PI	Y	25	F	58	Cycling in the middle of road.	Failing to stop and allow cyclist to pass safely.
542	**Orientfield Holdings Ltd v Bird & Bird LLP**	[2015] EWHC 1963 (Ch); [2015] PNLR 33	High Ct	PN	PEL	N	N/A	N/A	N/A	Failing to obtain a valuation of development on property.	Failing to reveal information adversely affecting property to be purchased.
543	**Pollock v Cahill**	[2015] EWHC 2260 (QB)	High Ct	OL	PI	N	N/A	M	34	Failing to use bed as a guide to door.	Leaving a window open.
544	**Pollock v Cahill**	[2015] EWHC 2260 (QB)	High Ct	OL	PI	N	N/A	M	34	Failing to use bed as a guide to door.	Leaving a window open.

545	**Southern v Adventure Forest Ltd**	[2016] EWCA Civ 1178	Oldham CC	OL	PI	Y	50	F	U	Holding on to metal work of swing despite having been instructed not to do so.	Providing inadequate warning signs.
546	**Lloyds Bank Plc v McBains Cooper Consulting Ltd**	[2015] EWHC 2372 (TCC)	High Ct	PN	PEL	Y	33,3	N/A	N/A	Failing to take sufficient steps to investigate transaction.	Failing to alert bank to reality of overall financial position.
547	**Low v Duncan**	[2015] CSOH 133	Court of Session (OH)	RA	PI	Y	10	M	U	Behaving in an aggressive manner; being in middle of road.	Swerving car towards pursuer; driving at excessive speed.
548	**AB v Main**	[2015] EWHC 3183 (QB)	High Ct	RA	PI	Y	20	M	9	Stepping into road without looking for oncoming traffic.	Failing to keep young child playing at side of road under proper observation; failing to ensure that child was aware of car's presence before proceeding; failing to take foot off accelerator, cover brakes or sound horn.
549	**McLellan v Mitie Group Plc**	[2015] CSOH 151; 2015 SLT 861	Court of Session (OH)	EL	PI	Y	20	F	Adult	Failing to secure the bucket sufficiently so that boiling water fell and splashed legs.	Failing to provide a safe system for obtaining hot water.
550	**McGeer v Macintosh**	2015 WL 6966174	High Ct	RA	PI	Y	30	F	47	Violating rule 73 of the Highway Code requiring cyclists to pay particular attention when long vehicles make left turns at junctions.	Failing to check nearside rear-view mirrors.

	Claim	Citation	Court	Claim type	Damage type	Guilty of CN	Discount	Gender	Age	Actual or alleged CN	Defendant's wrongful conduct
551	**McCreery v Letson**	[2015] CSOH 153	Court of Session (OH)	RA	PI	Y	50	F	61	Stepping into road without looking for oncoming traffic.	Driving at excessive speed.
552	**Mansion Estates Ltd v Hayre & Co**	[2016] EWHC 96 (Ch)	High Ct	PN	PEL	N	N/A	N/A	N/A	Providing solicitor with wrong plan to attach to form.	Handling a conveyancing transaction negligently.
553	**Mosson v Spousal (London) Ltd**	[2016] EWHC 53 (QB); [2016] 4 WLR 28	High Ct	EL	PI	N	N/A	M	15.5	Exposure to asbestos while self-employed.	Exposing claimant to asbestos.
554	**Sandison v Coope**	2016 Rep LR 70	Sheriff Ct (Tayside, Central and Fife)	RA	PI	Y	30	F	42	Failing to avoid animals on quiet country road.	Allowing dog to cross public road at blind corner without checking for hazards.
555	**MacDonald v Myerscough College**	2016 WL 01377226	High Ct	O	PI	Y	65	M	34	Releasing the safety device.	Failing to monitor trainee.
556	**Glass v Donnelly**	[2016] NIQB 36	High Ct (NI)	RA	PI	Y	66.6	F	31	Stepping into road without looking for oncoming traffic.	Driving at excessive speed; failing to keep a proper lookout for pedestrians.

557	**Robinson v Scottish Borders Council**	[2016] CSOH 47; 2016 SLT 435	Court of Session (OH)	PL	PI	N	N/A	M	50	Driving at excessive speed; cycling without due care.	Failing to keep the road safe for the people using it (metal strips on the road posed a hazard to two wheeled vehicles).
558	**Commodities Research Unit International (Holdings) Ltd v King and Wood Mallesons LLP**	[2016] EWHC 727 (QB); [2016] PNLR 29	High Ct	PN	PEL	N	N/A	N/A	N/A	Failing to send conditions of service to solicitors.	Failing to identify CEO's conditions of service; failing to request conditions of service.
559	**Sparrow v Andre**	[2016] EWHC 739 (QB)	High Ct	RA	PI	Y	60	M	49	Trying to restrain car from rolling down slope; failing to put car into 'park' mode, to apply foot brake or switch off ignition.	Failing to keep a proper lookout for other cars in car park and reversing into claimant's car.
560	**AB v Pro-Nation Ltd**	[2016] EWHC 1022 (QB)	High Ct	OL	PI	N	N/A	M	53	Failing to take reasonable care whilst descending staircase when intoxicated.	Failing to install adequate handrails to staircase.
561	**Lawrence v NCL (Bahamas) Ltd**	QBD, 6 May 2016	High Ct	O	PI	Y	25	M	76	Proceeding too closely behind those ahead of claimant thus tripping over sill.	Failing to inspect tender to ensure that there were no obvious hazards; failing to take appropriate steps once hazards were identified.
562	**Scott v EAR Sheppard Consulting Civil and Structural Engineers Ltd**	[2016] EWHC 1949 (TCC)	High Ct	PN	PEL	N	N/A	M	Adult	Failing to inform defendant of plans to carry out works to property; failing to seek advice from structural engineer prior to committing to purchase of property.	Failing properly to inspect property and report structural condition prior to its purchase by claimant.

	Claim	Citation	Court	Claim type	Damage type	Guilty of CN	Discount	Gender	Age	Actual or alleged CN	Defendant's wrongful conduct
563	**Scott v EAR Sheppard Consulting Civil and Structural Engineers Ltd**	[2016] EWHC 1949 (TCC)	High Ct	PN	PEL	N	N/A	M	Adult	Failing to inform defendant of plans to carry out works to property; failing to seek advice from structural engineer prior to committing to purchase of property.	Failing properly to inspect property and report structural condition prior to its purchase by claimant.
564	**Scott v EAR Sheppard Consulting Civil and Structural Engineers Ltd**	[2016] EWHC 1949 (TCC)	High Ct	PN	PEL	N	N/A	F	Adult	Failing to inform defendant of plans to carry out works to property; failing to seek advice from structural engineer prior to committing to purchase of property.	Failing properly to inspect property and report structural condition prior to its purchase by claimant.
565	**Cassidy v British Telecommuni-cations Plc**	2016 WL 08116614	Manchester CC	EL	PI	N	N/A	M	45	Failing to report defective equipment; failing to wear protective equipment.	Failing to provide suitable and safe work equipment.
566	**Barclays Bank Plc v Christie Owen & Davies Ltd**	[2016] EWHC 2351 (Ch); [2017] PNLR 8	High Ct	PN	PEL	Y	40	N/A	N/A	Failing to carry out financial analysis before making lending decision.	Providing claimant with two negligent valuation reports.
567	**Adams v Gibson**	QBD, 26 Oct 2016	High Ct	RA	PI	Y	33.3	M	U	Stepping into road without looking for oncoming traffic; failing to use crossing.	Failing to keep an eye on claimant pedestrian or to slow down in case claimant continued into road.

568	**Ahmed v MacLean**	[2016] EWHC 2798 (QB)	High Ct	O	PI	Y	20	M	43	Overestimating ability to ride down slope at a greater speed than his first ride.	Failing sufficiently to instruct claimant to enable claimant safely to ride down slope.
569	**Adams v Atlas International Property Services Ltd**	[2016] EWHC 3120 (QB)	High Ct	PN	PEL	N	N/A	N/A	N/A	Paying purchase price in full without receiving proof of seller's ability to pass legal title and without requesting legal advice from any source; failing to sue defendant in time.	Failing to warn claimants that there was no bank guarantee in place as required by law; failing to warn claimants that there was no proof that seller was able to pass an unencumbered title; failing to advise claimants not to pay anything in these circumstances; failing to take reasonable steps to ensure that the seller provided required guarantee before the purchase monies were paid.
570	**Anderson v Imrie**	[2016] CSOH 171; 2017 Rep LR 21	Court of Session (OH)	OL	PI	Y	25	M	8	Failing to comply with instructions not to leave courtyard and, in particular, not to go into race.	Failing to prevent pursuer from going into race; failing properly to supervise pursuer.

	Claim	Citation	Court	Claim type	Damage type	Guilty of CN	Discount	Gender	Age	Actual or alleged CN	Defendant's wrongful conduct
571	**Harlequin Property (SVG) Ltd v Wilkins Kennedy**	[2016] EWHC 3188 (TCC); [2017] 4 WLR 30	High Ct	PN	PEL	Y	50	N/A	N/A	Understanding need for payments to reflect what had actually been done but nevertheless not carrying out proper checks.	Negligently advising claimant not to enter into contract.
572	**SSE Generation Ltd v Hochtief Solutions AG**	[2016] CSOH 177	Court of Session (OH)	O	PD	N	N/A	N/A	N/A	Failing to discover collapse earlier; failing to appreciate significance of odd readings.	Failing to exercise reasonable skill and care in the construction of scheme so as to prevent collapse; failing to return to repair tunnel.

APPENDIX 2

APPELLATE CLAIMS

	Claim	Citation	Claim Type	Damage Type	CN at FI	Discount at FI	Gender	Age	Actual or alleged CN	Defendant's wrongful conduct	CN post-appeal	Discount post-appeal	Discount Difference
1	**UCB Corporate Services Ltd v Clyde & Co**	[2000] 2 All ER (Comm) 257	PN	PEL	N	N/A	N/A	N/A	Failing to pursue guarantors; releasing a second charge against director's home.	Failing to complete guarantee documents properly.	N	N/A	N/A
2	**Great Scottish & Western Rly Co Ltd v BRB**	2000 WL 389473	O	PD	N	N/A	N/A	N/A	Failing to follow train shunter's instructions as to need for scotches.	Failing to secure a train carriage that had been left on an incline.	N	N/A	N/A
3	**Selat Arjuna (Owners) v Contship Success (Owners)**	[2000] 1 All ER (Comm) 905	O	PD	N	N/A	N/A	N/A	Failing to ascertain earlier that another ship had altered course; failing to take remedial action by going hard to port.	Failing to keep a proper lookout; wrongly altering course.	N	N/A	N/A

	Claim	Citation	Claim Type	Damage Type	CN at FI	Discount at FI	Gender	Age	Actual or alleged CN	Defendant's wrongful conduct	CN post-appeal	Discount post-appeal	Discount Difference
4	**Slack v Glenie**	2000 WL 544172	OL	PI	Y	50	M	24	Riding with a side-car passenger with whom he had never ridden before, whose racing experience related to a different track, and with whom he had no established means of communication.	Unsafe track.	Y	50	N/A
5	**Slack v Glenie**	2000 WL 544172	OL	PI	Y	50	M	24	Riding with a side-car passenger with whom he had never ridden before, whose racing experience related to a different track and with whom he had no established means of communication.	Unsafe track.	Y	50	N/A
6	**Jebson v Ministry of Defence**	[2000] 1 WLR 2055	RA	PI	Y	75	M	21	Climbing onto roof of moving lorry when intoxicated.	Failing to supervise adequately; failing to provide suitable vehicle for the journey.	Y	75	N/A
7	**Ward v CC of the RUC**	[2000] NI 543	O	PI	N/A	N/A	F	U	Provoking officer by making minor physical contact with him.	Pushing claimant over wall.	Y	33.3	N/A

8	**Methven v Comr of Police of the Metropolis**	2000 WL 1480108	RA	PI	N	N/A	M	Adult	Failing to see and avoid police van; speeding on approach to the junction despite vehicle being so overloaded as to hamper braking.	Crossing junction against red light without keeping a proper lookout for other road users.	N	N/A	N/A
9	**Robinson v Midland Bank Plc**	2000 WL 1675148	EL	PI	Y	U	F	33	Failing to notice obstacles on the floor while carrying the trays.	Failing to warn of obstruction on the floor.	N	N/A	N/A
10	**Coe v The Waddesdon Estate**	2000 WL 1720288	EL	PI	Y	33.3	M	52	Failing to drive tractor properly; failing to follow employer's instructions.	Requiring the claimant employee to operate a tractor the seat of which was defective.	Y	33.3	N/A
11	**Richards v Quinton**	2000 WL 1675223	RA	PI	Y	50	M	U	Driving at excessive speed; failing to cycle on a safer part of the cycle track.	Failing to keep a proper lookout for other road users.	Y	75	25
12	**C (a child) v Imperial Design Ltd**	[2001] Env LR 33	OL	PI	Y	70	M	13	Lighting a can of flammable liquid despite knowing the dangers associated with doing so and being warned by friends of the consequences.	Leaving flammable liquid in an unsafe area in breach of section 73(6) of the Environmental Protection Act 1990.	Y	50	-20

	Claim	Citation	Claim Type	Damage Type	CN at FI	Discount at FI	Gender	Age	Actual or alleged CN	Defendant's wrongful conduct	CN post-appeal	Discount post-appeal	Discount Difference
13	**Tasci v Pekalp of London Ltd**	[2001] ICR 633	EL	PI	N/A	N/A	M	Adult	Placing hand too close to circular wood-cutter.	Failing to provide sufficient training.	Y	60	N/A
14	**King v RCO Support Services Ltd**	[2001] ICR 608	EL	PI	Y	100	M	57	Failing to concentrate on where to place feet while gritting.	Failing to take steps to avoid risk of slipping on ice.	Y	50	-50
15	**Simpson v AI Dairies Farms Ltd**	[2001] NPC 14	OL	PI	N	N/A	M	Adult	Failing to 'shuffle' through water, ie, to feel way through so as to avoid injury.	Failing to maintain drain.	N	N/A	N/A
16	**Cook v Thorne**	[2001] EWCA Civ 81	RA	PI	Y	30	M	Adult	Intoxicated; standing in road and vomiting.	Failing to slow down to an appropriate speed.	Y	30	N/A
17	**Cook v Thorne**	[2001] EWCA Civ 81	RA	PI	Y	30	M	Adult	Intoxicated; standing in road and vomiting.	Leaving vehicle whose headlights were blinding the first defendant stationary on road.	Y	30	N/A
18	**Sykes v Harry**	[2001] EWCA Civ 169; [2001] QB 1014	OL	PI	Y	80	M	Adult	Failing to inform defendant landlord of defect in gas fire.	Failing to service gas fire regularly or make appropriate inquiries into its state.	Y	80	N/A

19	**Billington v Maguire**	[2001] EWCA Civ 273	RA	PI	Y	100	F	Adult	Failing to look ahead and see vehicle until it was too late to take evasive action.	Parking van in cycle lane of busy dual carriageway thereby creating foreseeable source of danger.	Y	70	-30
20	**P (a child) v National Floor Coverings Ltd**	[2001] EWCA Civ 288	RA	PI	Y	66.6	M	16	Stepping into road without looking and from behind a bus.	Failing to brake.	Y	66.6	N/A
21	**Cross v UGC Ltd**	[2001] EWCA Civ 685	EL	PI	N	N/A	M	Adult	Resting spray gun on ladder.	Allowing an inherently unsafe system of work.	N	N/A	N/A
22	**Hatton v Cooper**	[2001] EWCA Civ 623; [2001] RTR 36	RA	PI	N	N/A	M	Adult	Driving on wrong side of road; failing to keep a proper lookout for other road users.	Driving on wrong side of road; failing to keep a proper lookout for other road users.	Y	50	N/A
23	**Mullaney v CC of the West Midlands**	[2001] EWCA Civ 700	EL	PI	N	N/A	M	29	Arresting suspect without backup from another police officer or ensuring that another officer was close by; persisting in efforts to arrest suspect after he had become violent.	Police officer failing to assist claimant.	N	N/A	N/A
24	**Ingram v Woodhouse**	[2001] EWCA Civ 1057	RA	PI	N	N/A	F	Adult	Crossing the road in a dangerous place where there was a restricted view of traffic coming from both directions.	Failing to perform emergency stop.	Y	30	N/A

	Claim	Citation	Claim Type	Damage Type	CN at FI	Discount at FI	Gender	Age	Actual or alleged CN	Defendant's wrongful conduct	CN post-appeal	Discount post-appeal	Discount Difference
25	**Pride Valley Foods Ltd v Hall and Partners Ltd (No 1)**	[2001] EWCA Civ 1001	PN	PD	Y	50	N/A	N/A	Failing to clean oven and/or modify pipe.	Failing to advise of highly combustible panels.	Y	50	N/A
26	**Watson v Skuse**	[2001] EWCA Civ 1158	RA	PI	Y	50	M	49	Crossing road without checking whether 'green man' signal was still showing and only checking red light directing traffic; crossing against red light; crossing very close to lorry.	Failing to keep a proper lookout for pedestrians.	Y	80	30
27	**Parker v PFC Flooring Supplies Ltd**	[2001] EWCA Civ 1533	EL	PI	Y	50	M	28	Walking on roof of premises knowing it was a situation of obvious danger and without appropriate equipment/clothing.	Failing to prevent employees from accessing roof.	Y	50	N/A
28	**Betts v Tokley**	[2002] EWCA Civ 52	EL	PI	Y	60	F	Adult	Exiting the building through exit known to be unlit although aware of dangers that doing so entailed.	Failing to illuminate premises.	Y	60	N/A
29	**Barnett v Scottish Power**	[2002] EWCA Civ 104	EL	PI	N	N/A	F	44	Failing properly to assess suitability of chair.	Failing to provide necessary work equipment.	N	N/A	N/A

30	**Anderson v Newham College for Further Education**	[2002] EWCA Civ 505; [2003] ICR 212	EL	PI	Y	90	M	Adult	Failing to see legs of whiteboard and avoid tripping over them.	Failing properly to store whiteboard.	Y	50	-40
31	**Toole v Bolton MBC**	[2002] EWCA Civ 588	EL	PI	Y	75	M	Adult	Attempting to pick up syringe wearing only rubber glove.	Failing to provide adequate work equipment.	N	N/A	N/A
32	**Oxley Plumbers Merchants v Davies**	[2002] EWCA Civ 540	OL	PI	N	N/A	M	Adult	Walking backwards towards trap door knowing it was in need of repair.	Failing to undertake remedial work to trap door.	N	N/A	N/A
33	**Young v Post Office**	[2002] EWCA Civ 661; [2002] IRLR 660	EL	PI	N	N/A	M	Adult	Burdening himself unnecessarily with work; failing to voice concerns about health to superiors.	Failing to provide sufficient support upon claimant's return to work following stress-related leave.	N	N/A	N/A
34	**Buyukardicli v Hammerson UK Properties Plc**	[2002] EWCA Civ 683	OL	PI	Y	75	F	Adult	Failing to pay attention while walking on unfinished and temporary surface.	Failing to take sufficient steps to reduce risk of injury to visitors walking across unfinished and temporary surface.	Y	75	N/A
35	**Buyukardicli v Hammerson UK Properties Plc**	[2002] EWCA Civ 683	OL	PI	Y	75	F	Adult	Failing to pay attention while walking on unfinished and temporary surface.	Failing to take sufficient steps to reduce risk of injury to visitors walking across unfinished and temporary surface.	Y	75	N/A

	Claim	Citation	Claim Type	Damage Type	CN at FI	Discount at FI	Gender	Age	Actual or alleged CN	Defendant's wrongful conduct	CN post-appeal	Discount post-appeal	Discount Difference
36	**Lunt v Khelifa**	[2002] EWCA Civ 801	RA	PI	Y	33.3	M	Adult	Stepping into the road without looking for oncoming traffic.	Failing to keep a proper lookout for pedestrians.	Y	33.3	N/A
37	**Eden v West & Co**	[2002] EWCA Civ 991; [2003] PIQR Q2	OL	PI	N	N/A	M	Adult	Removing window frames though aware that window might not have lintels.	Failing to warn that some windows might not have lintels.	N	N/A	N/A
38	**Holt v Holroyd Meek Ltd**	[2002] EWCA Civ 1004	EL	PI	N	N/A	M	Adult	Walking on surface made slippery by water and diesel.	Failing adequately to hose down surface.	N	N/A	N/A
39	**Wells v Trinder**	[2002] EWCA Civ 1030	RA	PI	N	N/A	F	Adult	Stepping into the road without looking for oncoming traffic.	Driving at excessive speed; failing to keep a proper lookout for pedestrians.	Y	25	N/A
40	**Purdue v Devon Fire and Rescue Service**	[2002] EWCA Civ 1538	RA	PI	N	N/A	M	48.5	Failing to check for oncoming traffic whilst stationary at traffic lights.	Driving through a red light; failing to activate siren.	Y	20	N/A
41	**Butcher v Cornwall CC**	[2002] EWCA Civ 1640	EL	PI	Y	10	M	Adult	Failing to ensure that door was properly closed.	Failing to provide safe means of securing open door.	Y	33.3	23.3

42	**Goddard v Greenwood**	[2002] EWCA Civ 1590; [2003] RTR 10	RA	PI	Y	80	F	U	Crossing road when traffic signal was green.	Failing to slow down or stop knowing that pedestrians might still be on crossing.	Y	80	N/A
43	**Goddard v Greenwood**	[2002] EWCA Civ 1590; [2003] RTR 10	RA	PI	Y	80	F	U	Crossing road when traffic signal was green.	Failing to slow down or stop knowing that pedestrians might still be on crossing.	Y	80	N/A
44	**Grealis v Opuni**	[2003] EWCA Civ 177; [2004] RTR 7	RA	PI	N/A	N/A	M	18	Cutting a corner; crossing path of oncoming traffic; failing to keep a proper lookout for other road users.	Driving at excessive speed.	Y	80	N/A
45	**Grace v Tanner**	[2003] EWCA Civ 354	RA	PI	N	N/A	F	Adult	Driving at excessive speed; failing to keep a proper lookout for other vehicles before exiting roundabout.	Failing to keep a proper lookout for other road users.	Y	50	N/A
46	**Griffiths v Vauxhall Motors Ltd**	[2003] EWCA Civ 412	EL	PI	Y	50	M	Adult	Failing to handle gun in required manner.	Failing to conduct a risk assessment.	Y	50	N/A
47	**Williams v Devon CC**	[2003] EWCA Civ 365; [2003] PIQR Q4	EL	PI	Y	33.3	F	Adult	Going through doorway carrying menu without first checking that path was clear.	Failing to keep floor free from obstructions.	N	N/A	N/A
48	**Adjei v King**	[2003] EWCA Civ 414	RA	PI	N	N/A	M	Adult	Stepping into the road without looking for oncoming traffic.	Driving at excessive speed; failing to keep a proper lookout for pedestrians.	Y	40	N/A

	Claim	Citation	Claim Type	Damage Type	CN at FI	Discount at FI	Gender	Age	Actual or alleged CN	Defendant's wrongful conduct	CN post-appeal	Discount post-appeal	Discount Difference
49	**Eagle v Chambers (No 1)**	[2003] EWCA Civ 1107; [2004] RTR 9	RA	PI	Y	60	F	17	Stepping into road and walking in middle of it; ignoring warnings from passers-by.	Intoxicated driver; speeding; failing to stay in lane.	Y	40	-20
50	**Marley v Cohen**	[2003] EWCA Civ 1536	O	PI	N	N/A	F	U	Stepping ashore whilst another boat was approaching.	Turning boat when it was unsafe to do so.	N	N/A	N/A
51	**Moseley v Pell**	[2003] EWCA Civ 1533	RA	PI	N	N/A	M	39	Overtaking line of traffic in front of an entrance to event.	Effecting right turn without checking for oncoming traffic; failing to notice claimant's motorcycle.	Y	50	N/A
52	**Six Continents Retail Ltd v Carford Catering Ltd**	[2003] EWCA Civ 1790	PN	PD	Y	100	N/A	N/A	Failing to respond to defendant's letter and to take steps to ascertain whether rotisserie was safe.	Failing safely to install rotisserie.	N	N/A	N/A
53	**Booth v White**	[2003] EWCA Civ 1708	RA	PI	N	N/A	M	Adult	Failing to enquire of defendant whether he had drunk too much alcohol before accepting a lift home.	Driving while intoxicated.	N	N/A	N/A

54	**Cooper v Carillion Plc**	[2003] EWCA Civ 1811	EL	PI	Y	10	M	Adult	Failing to look underneath board before placing feet.	Failing to re-erect barriers around service hole.	N	N/A	N/A
55	**Green v Bannister**	[2003] EWCA Civ 1819	RA	PI	Y	60	M	U	Lying in road when intoxicated.	Failing to look over left shoulder or in nearside wing or rear-view mirror when reversing.	Y	60	N/A
56	**Sahib Foods Ltd v Paskin KyriaKides Sands**	[2003] EWCA Civ 1832; [2004] PNLR 22	PN	PD	N	N/A	N/A	N/A	Cooking in room despite being advised that it was not appropriate for cooking.	Knowing that materials in room were not fireproof and failing to advise accordingly.	Y	66.6	N/A
57	**Sherlock v Chester CC**	[2004] EWCA Civ 201	EL	PI	N/A	N/A	M	27	Using bench saw without proper structural support.	Failing to conduct a risk assessment.	Y	60	N/A
58	**Noble v De Boer (No 2)**	2004 SC 548	O	PI	Y	30	M	44	Knowing of stone's movement on deck and not disposing of it.	Failing to order that stone be disposed of overboard or at least to take reasonable steps to secure it in such a way that it could not move during fishing operations.	N	N/A	N/A
59	**Burridge v Airwork Ltd**	[2004] EWCA Civ 459	RA	PI	N	N/A	M	47	Failing to take steps to guard against the possibility that driver, who had just pulled on to the hard shoulder, might open door and exit vehicle.	Opening driver's door without looking.	N	N/A	N/A

	Claim	Citation	Claim Type	Damage Type	CN at FI	Discount at FI	Gender	Age	Actual or alleged CN	Defendant's wrongful conduct	CN post-appeal	Discount post-appeal	Discount Difference
60	**Lamoon v Fry**	[2004] EWCA Civ 591	RA	PI	Y	60	M	18	Cycling on wrong side of road.	Driving at excessive speed.	Y	60	N/A
61	**Nixon v Thames Water Utilities Ltd**	[2006] CLY 2913	PL	PI	Y	50	F	U	Failing to notice and avoid trip hazard.	Failing to eliminate trip hazard.	N	N/A	N/A
62	**Smyth v Smyth**	[2004] NICA 16	OL	PI	N/A	N/A	M	12	Unknown.	Parking tractor, link box, and pallets too close to basketball net despite knowing that children were playing nearby.	Y	40	N/A
63	**Bow Spring (Owners) v Manzanillo II (Owners)**	[2004] EWCA Civ 1007; [2004] 4 All ER 899	O	PD	Y	50	N/A	N/A	Grounding ship when other remedies were available.	Failing to alter course.	Y	50	N/A
64	**Home Office v Lowles**	[2004] EWCA Civ 985	EL	PI	Y	50	F	Adult	Failing to concentrate when walking over a step.	Failing adequately to maintain floorway.	Y	50	N/A
65	**Ball v Street**	[2005] EWCA Civ 76; [2005] PIQR P22	EL	PI	N/A	N/A	M	Adult	Failing to wear eye goggles; failing to notice loose spring.	Failing to maintain machinery.	Y	25	N/A

66	**McFarlane v Scottish Borders Council**	[2005] CSIH 23; 2005 SLT 359	EL	PI	Y	75	M	U	Failing to exercise reasonable care in controlling a machine.	Failing to provide a safe place of work; failing to provide equipment suitable for use at that place.	Y	50	-25
67	**Fagan v Jeffers**	[2005] EWCA Civ 380	RA	PI	Y	50	M	U	Failing to exercise caution when travelling through 'keep clear' box.	Failing to keep a proper lookout when proceeding through stationary traffic.	Y	50	N/A
68	**Askey v Wood**	[2005] EWCA Civ 574	RA	PI	Y	50	F	Adult	Driving on wrong side of road.	Driving at excessive speed around a blind bend.	Y	50	N/A
69	**Duncan v Walshe**	[2005] CSIH 49	RA	PI	N	N/A	M	23	Driving at excessive speed.	Straddling both carriageways while executing a right-turn manoeuvre into a minor side road.	N	N/A	N/A
70	**Burgess v Plymouth CC**	[2005] EWCA Civ 1659; [2006] ICR 579	EL	PI	Y	50	F	Adult	Failing to keep a proper lookout for obstructions on floor.	Failing to comply with system of placing lunch-boxes in storage at end of day.	Y	50	N/A
71	**Wells v Mutchmeats Ltd**	[2006] EWCA Civ 963	OL	PI	Y	40	M	Adult	Stepping into foot bath known to be unstable.	Placing foot bath in doorway so as to create an obstruction which might cause a person to slip, trip, or fall.	Y	40	N/A

	Claim	Citation	Claim Type	Damage Type	CN at FI	Discount at FI	Gender	Age	Actual or alleged CN	Defendant's wrongful conduct	CN post-appeal	Discount post-appeal	Discount Difference
72	**Wells v Mutchmeats Ltd**	[2006] EWCA Civ 963	EL	PI	Y	40	M	Adult	Stepping into foot bath known to be unstable.	Placing foot bath in doorway so as to create an obstruction which might cause a person to slip, trip or fall.	Y	40	N/A
73	**Davis v Schrogin**	[2006] EWCA Civ 974	RA	PI	N	N/A	M	Adult	Failing to avoid collision despite seeing defendant's manoeuvre.	Executing U-turn without looking.	N	N/A	N/A
74	**CTO Gesellschaft Co v Dziennik**	[2006] EWCA Civ 1456	EL	PI	Y	60	M	52	Removing entire basin when only part of it needed removing; failing to follow instructions.	Failing to confirm that entire basin did not need to be removed.	N	N/A	N/A
75	**Robb v Salamis (M&I) Ltd**	[2006] UKHL 56; [2007] 2 All ER 97	EL	PI	Y	100	M	34	Failing to check ladders despite awareness that they were removable and were frequently removed and replaced.	Failing to clamp ladders or otherwise fix to sides of bunks.	Y	50	-50
76	**McGowan v W&JR Watson Ltd**	[2006] CSIH 62; 2007 SC 272	EL	PI	N	N/A	M	U	Failing to clamp saw; being inattentive in using saw.	Failing to take measures to prevent access to dangerous parts of machinery.	N	N/A	N/A
77	**Eyres v Atkinsons Kitchens & Bedrooms Ltd**	[2007] EWCA Civ 365	EL	PI	Y	25	M	20	Failing to wear a seat belt; failing to take action when realizing a real risk of falling asleep at wheel.	Allowing claimant employee to drive after being awake for 19 hours.	Y	33.3	8.3

78	**Ellis v Bristol CC**	[2007] EWCA Civ 685; [2007] ICR 1614	EL	PI	N/A	N/A	F	Adult	Failing to keep a proper lookout despite being aware of risk of slip hazard.	Failing to take sufficient steps to prevent floor from becoming slippery.	Y	33.3	N/A
79	**Ellis v William Cook Leeds Ltd**	[2007] EWCA Civ 1232	EL	PI	Y	25	M	38	Standing in unsafe position while attempting to 'unstick' crane; failing to notify supervisor of malfunction and attempting to remedy it himself.	Failing to replace malformed crane hook.	Y	50	25
80	**Dorning v Rigby (decd)**	[2007] EWCA Civ 1315	RA	PI	N/A	N/A	M	Adult	Travelling too close to motorcycle in front.	Driving at excessive speed.	Y	20	N/A
81	**Neeson v Acheson**	[2008] NIQB 12	O	PI	N/A	N/A	F	U	Putting face too close to dog.	Breaching article 29 of the Dogs (Northern Ireland) Order 1983.	Y	33.3	N/A
82	**St George v Home Office**	[2008] EWCA Civ 1068; [2008] 4 All ER 1039	O	PI	Y	15	M	29	Becoming addicted to alcohol and drugs.	Allocating claimant drug addict to a top bunk in prison despite knowing that he had previously had withdrawal seizures.	N	N/A	N/A
83	**Heaton v Herzog**	[2008] EWCA Civ 1636; [2009] RTR 30	RA	PI	N	N/A	F	Adult	Failing to keep observation to right in order to have the opportunity to see motorcycle, brake, and avoid colliding with it.	Driving at excessive speed.	Y	25	N/A

	Claim	Citation	Claim Type	Damage Type	CN at FI	Discount at FI	Gender	Age	Actual or alleged CN	Defendant's wrongful conduct	CN post-appeal	Discount post-appeal	Discount Difference
84	**Egan v Central Manchester NHS Trust**	[2008] EWCA Civ 1424; [2009] ICR 585	EL	PI	N/A	N/A	F	Adult	Carelessly undertaking patient lifting.	Failing to implement a risk assessment for patient lifting.	Y	50	N/A
85	**Minh Lac v Clayton**	[2009] EWCA Civ 106	RA	PI	N	N/A	M	Adult	Failing to move away from car after collision.	Driving without due care and striking vehicle from behind.	N	N/A	N/A
86	**Minh Lac v Clayton**	[2009] EWCA Civ 106	RA	PI	N	N/A	M	Adult	Failing to move away from car after collision.	Driving without due care and striking vehicle from behind.	N	N/A	N/A
87	**Minh Lac v Clayton**	[2009] EWCA Civ 106	RA	PI	N	N/A	M	Adult	Failing to move away from car after collision.	Driving without due care and striking vehicle from behind.	N	N/A	N/A
88	**Armsden v Kent Police**	[2009] EWCA Civ 631; [2009] RTR 31	RA	PI	N	N/A	F	29	Failing to look properly before moving off from junction.	Failing to activate siren.	Y	60	N/A
89	**Ministry of Defence v Radclyffe**	[2009] EWCA Civ 635	EL	PI	Y	40	M	24	Diving into water from bridge.	Army officer giving permission to jump into water.	Y	40	N/A

90	**Collins-Williamson v Silverlink Train Services Ltd**	[2009] EWCA Civ 850	O	PI	Y	50	M	27	Walking alongside train while unsteady on feet due to intoxication; walking close to the edge of platform.	Failing to have a window capable of being opened in guard's vestibule.	Y	50	N/A
91	**Henry v CC of Thames Valley**	[2010] EWCA Civ 5; [2010] RTR 14	RA	PI	N/A	N/A	M	Adult	Failing to surrender to police when initially prompted.	Pulling car too close to claimant in an effort to prevent him from escaping.	Y	60	N/A
92	**Osei-Antwi v SE London & Kent Bus Co**	[2010] EWCA Civ 132	RA	PI	Y	33.3	F	17	Standing very close to edge of road; failing to keep a good lookout for bus.	Permitting rear end of bus to mount pavement when turning.	N	N/A	N/A
93	**West Sussex CC v Russell**	[2010] EWCA Civ 71; [2010] RTR 19	PL	PI	Y	50	F	48	Driving at excessive speed on slippery road.	Failing to maintain highway properly.	Y	50	N/A
94	**Stanton v Collinson**	[2010] EWCA Civ 81; [2010] RTR 26	RA	PI	N	N/A	M	16	Failing to wear seat belt.	Speeding.	N	N/A	N/A
95	**Bell v Havering LBC**	[2010] EWCA Civ 689	PL	PI	Y	33.3	F	44	Failing to pay sufficient attention in placing feet.	Failing to maintain highway adequately.	Y	33.3	N/A
96	**Johnstone v AMEC Construction Ltd**	[2010] CSIH 57; 2011 SCLR 178	EL	PI	Y	60	M	U	Failing to keep a proper lookout in stepping over rubber boot; failing to appreciate where placing feet.	Failing properly to maintain barrier fence.	Y	40	-20

	Claim	Citation	Claim Type	Damage Type	CN at FI	Discount at FI	Gender	Age	Actual or alleged CN	Defendant's wrongful conduct	CN post-appeal	Discount post-appeal	Discount Difference
97	**Yetkin v Mahmood**	[2010] EWCA Civ 776; [2011] QB 827	PL	PI	Y	75	F	47.5	Crossing road without waiting for lights to change.	Planting shrubs in a place that obscured view of road.	Y	75	N/A
98	**Chubb Fire Ltd v Vicar of Spalding**	[2010] EWCA Civ 981; [2010] 2 CLC 277	O	PD	N	N/A	N/A	N/A	Failing to place 'theft stoppers' on fire extinguishers.	Failing to warn of the consequences of releasing dry powder from extinguisher.	N	N/A	N/A
99	**Swilas v Clyde Pumps Ltd**	2012 SLT (Sh Ct) 146	EL	PI	Y	75	M	U	Failing to avoid or mitigate injury by ceasing forward movement.	Failing to provide safe and suitable work equipment.	Y	75	N/A
100	**Wardle v Scottish Borders Council**	2011 SLT (Sh Ct) 199	OL	PI	N/A	N/A	F	9	Climbing into rafters despite having been warned of risks of doing so.	Failing to take sufficient measures to prevent climbing into rafters.	Y	50	N/A
101	**Stoddart v Perucca**	[2011] EWCA Civ 290	RA	PI	Y	50	F	14	Failing to look before crossing road on horse.	Failing to slow down to allow for the possibility of a second horse.	Y	50	N/A
102	**Dalling v RJ Heale & Co Ltd**	[2011] EWCA Civ 365	EL	PI	Y	33.3	M	25	Falling over due to intoxication.	Failing to implement safe work system.	Y	33.3	N/A

103	**Belka v Prosperini**	[2011] EWCA Civ 623	RA	PI	Y	66.6	M	Adult	Running across road in front of defendant's vehicle.	Failing to slow down upon noticing pedestrians.	Y	66.6	N/A
104	**Wallace v Glasgow CC**	[2011] CSIH 57; 2011 Rep LR 96	EL	PI	Y	50	F	60	Standing on toilet bowl in order to reach window.	Failing to provide a window pole in toilet area.	Y	50	N/A
105	**Burton v Evitt**	[2011] EWCA Civ 1378	RA	PI	Y	66.6	M	Adult	Overtaking line of traffic; driving at excessive speed.	Failing to inch out of traffic queue so as to see traffic behind.	Y	80	13.4
106	**Ali v D'Brass**	[2011] EWCA Civ 1594	RA	PI	N/A	N/A	M	Adult	Braking sharply without explanation.	Driving too close to vehicle in front.	Y	40	N/A
107	**Woodham v JM Turner**	[2012] EWCA Civ 375	RA	PI	Y	30	M	16	Overtaking stationary traffic on offside when approaching junction; travelling at excessive speed.	Performing manoeuvre with obstructed view.	Y	50	20
108	**Smith v CC of Notts**	[2012] EWCA Civ 161; [2012] RTR 23	RA	PI	Y	75	F	16	Crossing road when unsafe to do so.	Failing to slow down when travelling through red light on emergency call.	Y	33.3	-41.7
109	**Phethean-Hubble v Coles**	[2012] EWCA Civ 349; [2012] RTR 31	RA	PI	Y	33.3	M	16	Entering road from pavement on bicycle without looking for oncoming traffic.	Driving at excessive speed.	Y	50	16.7

	Claim	Citation	Claim Type	Damage Type	CN at FI	Discount at FI	Gender	Age	Actual or alleged CN	Defendant's wrongful conduct	CN post-appeal	Discount post-appeal	Discount Difference
110	**Rehill v Rider Holdings Ltd**	[2012] EWCA Civ 628; [2013] RTR 5	RA	PI	Y	33.3	M	45.5	Crossing road when traffic signal was red and in sight of bus.	Failing to notice pedestrian and brake sufficiently quickly.	Y	50	16.7
111	**Palfrey v WM Morrisons Supermarkets Plc**	[2012] EWCA Civ 1917	OL	PI	Y	50	F	79	Tripping over container having already seen it.	Using low-lying container to stack shelves in circumstances where customers' attention would be on products.	Y	20	-30
112	**Paramasivan v Wicks**	[2013] EWCA Civ 262	RA	PI	Y	50	M	13	Stepping into road without looking for oncoming traffic.	Failing to look out for pedestrians.	Y	75	25
113	**Phee v Gordon**	[2013] CSIH 18; 2013 SLT 439	O	PI	N	N/A	M	40	Failing to duck when hearing shout of 'fore'.	Underestimating degree of risk of golf shot.	N	N/A	N/A
114	**AC v Devon CC**	[2013] EWCA Civ 418; [2014] RTR 1	PL	PI	N	N/A	M	Adult	Failing to notice pot hole while overtaking the claimant's slower-moving vehicle.	Failing to maintain highway.	Y	50	N/A

115	**Hill v Norside Ltd**	[2013] CSIH 44	EL	PI	Y	20	M	Adult	Failing to tie ladder to scaffold before descent.	Failing to provide a proper plan or safe system for use of portable ladder.	Y	20	N/A
116	**Ireland v David Lloyd Leisure Ltd**	[2013] EWCA Civ 665	OL	PI	Y	25	F	U	Resting hand on gym equipment while in use.	Failing to take sufficient steps to warn of dangers associated with gym equipment.	Y	25	N/A
117	**Birch v Ministry of Defence**	[2013] EWCA Civ 676; [2014] PIQR P1	EL	PI	Y	50	M	18	Driving vehicle while neither qualified nor trained.	Allowing claimant to drive vehicle despite knowing that claimant was neither qualified nor trained.	N	N/A	N/A
118	**Kennedy v Chivas Brothers Ltd**	[2013] CSIH 57; 2013 SLT 981	EL	PI	Y	U	F	U	Placing hands on extremities of trolley despite having been told not to do so.	Using unsuitable work equipment.	N	N/A	N/A
119	**Starks v CC of Herts**	[2013] EWCA Civ 782; [2014] RTR 4	RA	PI	Y	55	M	Adult	Entering roundabout late and not slowing down.	Failing to observe roundabout; driving straight over roundabout.	Y	35	-20
120	**Wheeler v CC of Glos**	[2013] EWCA Civ 1791	RA	PI	Y	50	M	Adult	Driving at excessive speed.	Failing to stop or check for oncoming traffic before turning right.	Y	50	N/A

	Claim	Citation	Claim Type	Damage Type	CN at FI	Discount at FI	Gender	Age	Actual or alleged CN	Defendant's wrongful conduct	CN post-appeal	Discount post-appeal	Discount Difference
121	**Biddick (decd) v Morcom**	[2014] EWCA Civ 182	OL	PI	Y	66.6	M	Adult	Overreaching himself to get to a screw knowing it was unsafe to do so.	Failing to hold pole having assumed a responsibility by saying that he would.	Y	66.6	N/A
122	**Gray v Gibson**	[2014] EWCA Civ 355	RA	PI	Y	40	F	Adult	Driving at excessive speed.	Driving over central line.	N	N/A	N/A
123	**Gray v Botwright**	[2014] EWCA Civ 1201	RA	PI	N/A	N/A	M	Adult	Failing to look for oncoming traffic when turning at traffic lights.	Travelling through red light.	Y	50	N/A
124	**Jackson v Murray**	[2015] UKSC 5; [2015] 2 All ER 805	RA	PI	Y	90	F	13	Crossing road when unsafe to do so.	Failing to keep a proper lookout for pedestrians; failing to reduce speed when approaching minibus.	Y	50	-40
125	**McCracken v Smith**	[2015] EWCA Civ 380; [2015] PIQR P19	RA	PI	Y	45	M	16	Travelling as pillion passenger on trail bike with dangerous driver; failing to wear helmet.	Failing to keep a proper lookout for other vehicles at junction.	Y	65	20

126	**Ferguson v Ferguson**	[2015] CSIH 63; 2015 SLT 561	O	PI	Y	85	F	54	Grabbing dog's cheeks and putting face close to its face.	Breaching section 1 of the Animals (Scotland) Act 1987.	Y	85	N/A
127	**Sabir v Osei-Kwabena**	[2015] EWCA Civ 1213; [2016] RTR 9	RA	PI	Y	25	F	30	Misjudging car's position and/or time available to cross road.	Failing to keep a proper lookout for pedestrians.	Y	25	N/A
128	**English Heritage v Taylor**	[2016] EWCA Civ 448; [2016] PIQR P14	OL	PI	Y	50	M	60	Standing on steep bank.	Failing to provide sign warning visitors of sheer drop.	Y	50	N/A
129	**Wagner v Grant**	[2016] CSIH 34; 2016 SLT 699	RA	PI	Y	40	M	18	Failing to keep a proper lookout.	Blocking lane with trailer in darkness; failing to give advance warning to westbound traffic.	Y	60	20

APPENDIX 3

ROAD ACCIDENT CLAIMS AT FIRST INSTANCE

	Claim	Citation	CN	Discount	Gender	Age	Claimant Type	Recurrent type of CN	Actual or alleged CN	Defendant's wrongful Conduct
1	**McDonald v Chambers**	2000 SLT 454	Y	33.3	F	25	Pedestrian	Pedestrian entering carriageway	Stepping into road before confirming that the traffic had stopped.	Failing to brake, swerve or sound horn upon seeing pursuer.
2	**Ameen v Hunter**	2000 SLT 954	Y	50	F	27	Driver	N/A	Failing to stop car to check what was wrong with it; failing to move car off the carriageway; failing to activate hazard lights once car had come to rest.	Failing to move to inside lane to avoid collision.
3	**Pritchard v Ralph**	2000 WL 1791426	Y	50	M	Adult	Pedestrian	Pedestrian entering carriageway	Stepping into road without looking for oncoming traffic.	Failing to keep a proper lookout for pedestrians.
4	**M v Parsons**	2000 WL 33122496	Y	20	F	14	Bicyclist	N/A	Moving into path of traffic without looking or signalling.	Driving at excessive speed and too close to cyclist to overtake safely.
5	**Futter v Bryceland**	2000 GWD 9-339	Y	60	M	15.25	Pedestrian	Pedestrian entering carriageway	Stepping into road without looking for oncoming traffic.	Driving at excessive speed; failing to keep a proper lookout for pedestrians.

	Claim	Citation	CN	Discount	Gender	Age	Claimant Type	Recurrent type of CN	Actual or alleged CN	Defendant's wrongful Conduct
6	**Methven v Comr of Police of the Metropolis**	2000 WL 1480108	N	N/A	M	Adult	Driver	N/A	Failing to see and avoid police van; driving at excessive speed on approach to the junction despite vehicle being so overloaded as to hamper braking.	Crossing the junction against a red light without keeping a proper lookout for other road users.
7	**Cook v Thorne**	[2001] EWCA Civ 81	Y	30	M	Adult	Pedestrian	Pedestrian entering carriageway	Intoxicated; standing in road and vomiting.	Failing to slow down to an appropriate speed.
8	**Cook v Thorne**	[2001] EWCA Civ 81	Y	30	M	Adult	Passenger in D's vehicle	N/A	Intoxicated; standing in road and vomiting.	Exiting vehicle whose headlights were blinding the first defendant; remaining stationary in road.
9	**Sousa v A&J Bull Ltd**	[2001] EWCA Civ 1039	Y	30	M	20	Bicyclist	N/A	Riding bicycle with passenger on front handlebar.	Failing to leave sufficient room to pass parked car.
10	**North v TNT Express (UK) Ltd**	[2001] EWCA Civ 853	Y	75	M	Adult	Pedestrian	N/A	Climbing up on to the front bumper of lorry when intoxicated.	Driving whilst claimant was on the front bumper of lorry.

11	**Arnot v Sprake**	[2001] EWCA Civ 341	N	N/A	M	U	M'cyclist	N/A	Failing to appreciate that crop sprayer was towing a trailer until it was too late.	Failing to place red triangle in road to warn road users; failing to sound horn to ensure that traffic was alerted to and warned of defendant's presence.
12	**S (a child) v Keyse**	2000 WL 33201536	Y	25	M	17.75	Pedestrian	Pedestrian entering carriageway	Stepping into road without looking for oncoming traffic.	Driving at excessive speed.
13	**Beckley v Crowther**	2000 WL 1544758	N	N/A	F	Adult	Driver	N/A	Effecting turn without considering oncoming traffic.	Driving at excessive speed and down central reservation.
14	**Thain v Aberdeenshire Council**	2000 GWD 25-951	N	N/A	F	16	M'cyclist	N/A	Driving on wrong side of road.	Driving on wrong side of road.
15	**Watson v Skuse**	[2001] EWCA Civ 1158	Y	50	M	49	Pedestrian	Pedestrian entering carriageway	Crossing road without checking whether 'green man' signal was still showing and only checking red light directing traffic; crossing against red light; crossing very close to lorry.	Failing to keep a proper lookout for pedestrians.
16	**Ingram v Woodhouse**	[2001] EWCA Civ 1057	N	N/A	F	Adult	Pedestrian	N/A	Crossing road in a dangerous place where there was a restricted view of traffic coming from both directions.	Failing to perform an emergency stop.
17	**Markowski v Elson**	[2001] CLY 4477	Y	33.3	F	Adult	Pedestrian	Pedestrian entering carriageway	Stepping into road without looking for oncoming traffic.	Parking ambulance in a position whereby it caused a hazard.

	Claim	Citation	CN	Discount	Gender	Age	Claimant Type	Recurrent type of CN	Actual or alleged CN	Defendant's wrongful Conduct
18	**Ledger v Spurgeon**	[2001] EWCA Civ 1527	Y	80	M	U	M'cyclist	N/A	Driving without due care when driving directly towards low-hanging sun; failing to see the excavator and take appropriate action to avoid it despite the presence of warning signs.	Failing adequately to warn of the presence of excavator on road.
19	**B (a child) v Wynn**	[2001] EWCA Civ 710	Y	66.6	M	11.5	Pedestrian	Pedestrian entering carriageway	Stepping into road without looking for oncoming traffic.	Failing to keep a proper lookout for pedestrians.
20	**Taylor v Tyler**	2000 WL 33281237	N	N/A	M	Adult	M'cyclist	N/A	Driving at excessive speed; failing to observe the presence of the defendant's motor vehicle; overtaking a number of vehicles when unsafe to do so.	Effecting a right turn across path of oncoming traffic without making sure that there was no oncoming traffic that could be inconvenienced by manoeuvre.
21	**Regan v Chetwynd**	2000 WL 33122388	N	N/A	M	21	M'cyclist	N/A	Riding close to centre of road.	Failing to notice claimant's approaching motorcycle and turning into its path.

22	**W v Hardman**	[2001] CLY 4452	Y	15	M	U	Passenger in D's vehicle	No seat belt or helmet	Failing to wear seat belt; travelling with intoxicated driver.	Driving while intoxicated.
23	**Currie v Clamp**	2002 SLT 196	Y	33.3	M	22	Passenger in D's vehicle	N/A	Travelling in a vehicle with intoxicated driver.	Driving while intoxicated.
24	**Mattar v Shenouda**	2001 WL 606384	Y	15	M	51	Passenger in D's vehicle	No seat belt or helmet	Failing to wear seat belt.	Driving without due care and attention.
25	**George v Stagecoach SE London**	2001 WL 513089	Y	40	F	44	Pedestrian	Pedestrian entering carriageway	Walking into path of bus; failing to pay sufficient attention while crossing road.	Failing to keep a proper lookout for pedestrians; failing to accord claimant precedence.
26	**White v Chapman**	2001 WL 825325	Y	20	F	Adult	Pedestrian	Pedestrian entering carriageway	Crossing road at a point where there was no central refuge.	Failing to keep a proper lookout for pedestrians; failing to slow down or adjust position in road in order to avoid claimant.
27	**Powell v Hansen**	2001 WL 753470	Y	20	M	52	M'cyclist	Speeding	Driving at excessive speed.	Undertaking a dangerous manoeuvre; failing to note oncoming traffic; failing to stop at stop line; driving on wrong side of road.
28	**Irwin v Stevenson**	[2002] EWCA Civ 359	Y	50	M	U	M'cyclist	N/A	Attempting to overtake two slowing vehicles.	Failing to observe motorcycle.
29	**Poccia v Toussaint**	2001 WL 34008510	N	N/A	M	Adult	M'cyclist	N/A	Crossing a junction while parallel with defendant's car; overtaking on nearside.	Pulling to nearside of road to park and cutting across path of claimant's vehicle in doing so.

	Claim	Citation	CN	Discount	Gender	Age	Claimant Type	Recurrent type of CN	Actual or alleged CN	Defendant's wrongful Conduct
30	**Purdue v Devon Fire and Rescue Service**	[2002] EWCA Civ 1538	N	N/A	M	49	Driver	N/A	Failing to check for oncoming traffic whilst stationary at traffic lights.	Driving through a red light; failing to activate siren.
31	**Lunt v Khelifa**	2001 WL 1479700	Y	33.3	M	Adult	Pedestrian	Pedestrian entering carriageway	Intoxicated; stepping into road without looking for oncoming traffic.	Failing to keep a proper lookout for pedestrians.
32	**Wells v Trinder**	[2002] EWCA Civ 1030	N	N/A	F	Adult	Pedestrian	N/A	Stepping into road without looking for oncoming traffic.	Driving at excessive speed; failing to keep a proper lookout for pedestrians.
33	**Arnesen v Heffey**	[2002] EWCA Civ 1058	Y	25	M	U	M'cyclist	N/A	Driving too close to vehicle in front; riding alongside another M'cyclist instead of riding one behind the other.	Failing to pull over to hard shoulder or pull closer to central reservation following a tyre blow-out.
34	**Smith v Hastie**	2002 SLT 1183	N	N/A	F	38	Driver	N/A	Driving at excessive speed; driving on wrong side of road.	Driving on the wrong side of road.
35	**Marshall v Rennocks**	[2004] CLY 2702	N	N/A	U	U	Driver	N/A	Crossing centre line.	Parking vehicle in an unsafe and inappropriate manner.

36	**Eagle v Chambers (No 1)**	[2003] EWCA Civ 1107; [2004] RTR 9	Y	60	F	17	Pedestrian	Pedestrian entering carriageway	Stepping into road and walking in middle of it; ignoring warnings from passers by.	Intoxicated driver; driving at excessive speed; failing to stay in lane.
37	**Adjei v King**	[2003] EWCA Civ 414	N	N/A	M	Adult	Pedestrian	N/A	Stepping into road without looking for oncoming traffic.	Driving at excessive speed; failing to keep a proper lookout for pedestrians.
38	**Pratt v Smith**	2002 WL 31676426	N	N/A	M	45	M'cyclist	N/A	Driving car with defective brakes and bald/defective front tyre; driving at excessive speed; failing to notice defendant's indication of intention to turn right.	Cutting across claimant's path whilst driving.
39	**Moseley v Pell**	[2003] EWCA Civ 1533	N	N/A	M	39	M'cyclist	N/A	Overtaking line of traffic in front of an entrance to event.	Effecting right turn without checking for oncoming traffic; failing to notice claimant's motorcycle.
40	**Green v Bannister**	[2003] EWCA Civ 1819	Y	60	M	U	Pedestrian	Pedestrian entering carriageway	Lying in road when intoxicated.	Failing to look over left shoulder or in nearside wing or rear-view mirror when reversing.
41	**Booth v White**	[2003] EWCA Civ 1708	N	N/A	M	Adult	Passenger in D's vehicle	N/A	Failing to enquire of defendant whether he had drunk too much alcohol before accepting a lift home.	Driving while intoxicated.

	Claim	Citation	CN	Discount	Gender	Age	Claimant Type	Recurrent type of CN	Actual or alleged CN	Defendant's wrongful Conduct
42	**Costello v Birkby**	[2004] CLY 2744	N	N/A	F	Adult	Driver	N/A	Edging taxi further out in the bus lane in order to reach a garage despite inability to see beyond about two car lengths down the bus lane.	Driving in bus lane when not entitled to do so; driving at excessive speed.
43	**Lamoon v Fry**	[2004] EWCA Civ 591	Y	60	M	18	Bicyclist	N/A	Cycling on wrong side of road.	Driving at excessive speed.
44	**Duncan v Walshe**	2003 Scot (D) 15/7	N	N/A	M	23	M'cyclist	N/A	Driving at excessive speed.	Straddling both carriageways while executing a right turn manoeuvre into a minor side road.
45	**Cemm v Bryant**	[2004] CLY 2701	N	N/A	F	29	Driver	N/A	Failing to see defendant's vehicle before it appeared on road; failing to stop motor vehicle before a collision occurred.	Losing control of vehicle and colliding with claimant's car.
46	**Russell v Smith**	[2003] EWHC 2060 (QB)	Y	50	M	10.25	Bicyclist	N/A	Cycling across a road junction without regard to road markings.	Failing to bring car to halt soon enough to avoid the collision; failing to pay proper attention to the road.

47	**Burridge v Airwork Ltd**	[2004] EWCA Civ 459	N	N/A	M	47	Bicyclist	N/A	Failing to take steps to guard against the possibility that driver, who had just pulled on to the hard shoulder, might open door and exit vehicle.	Opening driver's door without looking.
48	**Gilfillan v Barbour**	2003 SLT 1127	Y	50	M	61	Driver	Speeding	Driving at excessive speed.	Entering junction despite having heard siren of police vehicle.
49	**Gilfillan v Barbour**	2003 SLT 1127	Y	50	M	39	Driver	N/A	Entering junction despite having heard police siren.	Failing to slow down at junction.
50	**Joseph v Braid**	2003 Rep LR 133	Y	66.6	M	U	Driver	N/A	Driving from minor road across path of car on major road without taking proper care; misjudging speed and distance of defender's car; using a mobile phone while driving and becoming distracted by it.	Failing to slow down at junction.
51	**Houghton v Stannard**	[2003] EWHC 2666 (QB)	N	N/A	M	Adult	Driver	N/A	Driving on dual carriageway despite being aware of risk that car would break down; having broken down, or in the course of breaking down, failing to drive or park car; remaining inside car while it was stationary on road.	Driving at excessive speed; failing to see claimant's hazard warning lights and realizing, much too late, that claimant's car was stationary.

	Claim	Citation	CN	Discount	Gender	Age	Claimant Type	Recurrent type of CN	Actual or alleged CN	Defendant's wrongful Conduct
52	**Edwards v Jerman**	[2004] CLY 2743	Y	25	M	Adult	Driver	Speeding	Intoxicated; driving at excessive speed.	Driving on wrong side of road.
53	**Brownlow v Knight**	[2003] NIQB 71	Y	40	F	59	Pedestrian	Pedestrian entering carriageway	Stepping into road without looking for oncoming traffic.	Failing to keep a proper lookout for pedestrians.
54	**Parkinson v CC of Dyfed Powys**	[2004] EWCA Civ 802	Y	35	M	U	Pedestrian	Pedestrian entering carriageway	Intoxicated; stepping into road when claimant could and should have been aware of presence of defendant's car.	Driving at 40 mph past parked taxi late at night in a built-up area in circumstances where defendant could and should have anticipated that there might be intoxicated pedestrians nearby.
55	**Rose v SE London and Kent Bus Co Ltd**	[2004] EWHC 1106 (QB)	Y	50	F	Adult	Pedestrian	Pedestrian entering carriageway	Crossing busy road in unsafe place when pedestrian crossing located approximately 30 metres away.	In a momentary lapse of concentration, failing to check for the claimant, whom he had been aware of previously.
56	**Askey v Wood**	[2005] EWCA Civ 574	Y	50	F	Adult	Driver	N/A	Driving on wrong side of road.	Driving at excessive speed around a blind bend.

57	**Fagan v Jeffers**	[2005] EWCA Civ 380	Y	50	M	U	M'cyclist	N/A	Failing to exercise caution when travelling through 'keep clear' box.	Failing to keep a proper lookout when proceeding through stationary traffic.
58	**Firth v Hanley**	[2004] EWCA Civ 1714	N	N/A	F	Adult	Driver	N/A	Pulling up too fast in slippery conditions; being unaccompanied in car despite being provisional licence holder.	Driving carelessly.
59	**Swinton v Annabel's (Berkeley Square) Ltd**	[2005] CLY 2842	N	N/A	M	U	Bicyclist	N/A	Failing to wear cycle helmet.	Failing to prevent dog from running into claimant bicyclist's path.
60	**Pesenti v London General Transport Services Ltd**	[2006] CLY 2903	N	N/A	F	U	Bicyclist	N/A	Cycling erratically.	Passing too close to claimant.
61	**Pesenti v London General Transport Services Ltd**	[2006] CLY 2903	N	N/A	F	U	Bicyclist	N/A	Cycling erratically.	Travelling too close behind claimant.
62	**Carpenter v Lunnon**	[2004] EWHC 3079 (QB)	Y	20	M	Adult	Pedestrian	Pedestrian entering carriageway	Walking on near side of carriageway with back to traffic and wearing dark clothing at night-time.	Failing to keep a proper lookout.

	Claim	Citation	CN	Discount	Gender	Age	Claimant Type	Recurrent type of CN	Actual or alleged CN	Defendant's wrongful Conduct
63	**Carter v Carter**	[2005] CSOH 2	N	N/A	M	58	Passenger in D's vehicle	N/A	Failing to instruct disabled wife properly in operation of vehicle.	Failing to operate hand controls and instead putting foot on accelerator.
64	**Honnor v Lewis**	[2005] EWHC 747 (QB)	Y	20	M	11	Pedestrian	Pedestrian entering carriageway	Failing to pay due attention when crossing a road.	Failing to observe pedestrian, sound horn, or slow down.
65	**Large v Mamani**	[2005] EWHC 1271 (QB)	Y	20	M	Adult	M'cyclist	Speeding	Failing to slow motorcycle having seen defendant's van moving across road.	Driving into claimant's path; failing to keep a proper lookout for pedestrians.
66	**Tompkins v Royal Mail Group Plc**	[2005] EWHC 1902 (QB); [2006] RTR 5	Y	65	M	Adult	Driver	Speeding	Failing to brake, slow down, or take evasive action.	Parking trailer in manner that could cause accident.
67	**Davis v Schrogin**	[2006] EWCA Civ 974	N	N/A	M	Adult	M'cyclist	N/A	Failing to avoid collision despite having had time to see defendant's manoeuvre.	Executing U-turn without looking.
68	**Welsh v Messenger**	[2006] CLY 2875	N	N/A	F	68	Passenger in D's vehicle	N/A	Failing to wear seat belt.	Failing to keep coach on road.
69	**Morrison v Gardiner**	[2005] CSOH 156	Y	25	M	44	M'cyclist	Speeding	Failing to activate siren; proceeding too close to traffic at an excessive speed.	Failing to check for oncoming traffic on right or use mirror before starting manoeuvre.

70	**Jukes v Etti**	[2006] EWHC 2493 (QB); [2007] RTR 2	Y	40	M	37	Pedestrian	Pedestrian entering carriageway	Seeking to cross road when there was oncoming traffic.	Failing to keep a proper lookout for pedestrians.
71	**Maughan v Boylan**	[2006] NIQB 38	Y	80	M	77	Pedestrian	Pedestrian entering carriageway	Stepping into road without looking for oncoming traffic.	Failing to keep a proper lookout; failing to react sufficiently quickly to emergency.
72	**Ehrari v Curry**	[2006] EWHC 1319 (QB)	Y	70	F	13.75	Pedestrian	Pedestrian entering carriageway	Stepping into road from behind parked car and walking without looking.	Failing to see claimant despite knowing that it was necessary to pay attention (having had to stop previously so as to allow children to cross road).
73	**Pankhurst v White**	[2006] EWHC 2093 (Admin)	N	N/A	M	48	Bicyclist	N/A	Driving at excessive speed before sharp corner.	Driving at excessive speed.
74	**Nicolson v Willis**	[2006] EWHC 2402 (Admin)	Y	33.3	M	36	M'cyclist	Speeding	Driving at excessive speed; failing to take action despite seeing multi-purpose vehicle starting to emerge.	Turning corner when unsafe to do so.
75	**Al Gouri v Achkar**	[2007] CLY 3079	Y	25	M	17	U	No seat belt or helmet	Failing to wear seat belt.	Driving without due care and attention.
76	**Donaldson v Hays Distribution Services Ltd**	[2007] CSOH 31	Y	25	F	50	Pedestrian	N/A	Walking between rear of trailer and loading bay wall.	Failing to keep a proper lookout for pedestrians and, in particular, failing to look underneath length of trailer before entering cab; failing to use lookout when reversing lorry.

	Claim	Citation	CN	Discount	Gender	Age	Claimant Type	Recurrent type of CN	Actual or alleged CN	Defendant's wrongful Conduct
77	**McNab v Bluebird Buses Ltd**	[2007] CSOH 36; 2007 Rep LR 36	Y	50	M	37	Pedestrian	Pedestrian entering carriageway	Failing to walk facing oncoming traffic.	Failing to keep a proper lookout for pedestrians.
78	**Gawler v Raettig**	[2007] EWHC 373 (QB)	Y	25	M	24	Passenger in D's vehicle	No seat belt or helmet	Failing to wear seat belt.	Losing control of car during cornering.
79	**Taylor v Rashid**	[2008] CLY 2661	N	N/A	U	U	Passenger in other vehicle	N/A	Failing to wear seat belt.	Driving car into passenger side rear door of vehicle.
80	**Ahanonu v SE London and Kent Bus Co Ltd**	[2008] EWCA Civ 274	Y	50	F	18	Pedestrian	Pedestrian entering carriageway	Taking extremely dangerous path when crossing road.	Failing to check rear-view mirror.
81	**Wakeling v McDonagh**	[2007] EWHC 1201 (QB)	N	N/A	M	17	Bicyclist	N/A	Entering road on bicycle without looking.	Driving under influence of drugs; driving at excessive speed.
82	**Garth v Grant**	[2007] All ER (D) 459 (May)	Y	15	F	41	Passenger in other vehicle	No seat belt or helmet	Failing to wear seat belt.	Driving on wrong side of road.
83	**SH (a child) v Farrell**	[2007] NIQB 42	Y	15	F	11	Pedestrian	Pedestrian entering carriageway	Stepping into road without looking for oncoming traffic.	Failing to slow down at junction; driving at excessive speed; failing to keep a proper lookout for pedestrians.

84	**Dawes v Aldis**	[2007] EWHC 1831 (QB)	N	N/A	M	40	Pedestrian	N/A	Intoxicated; running across road.	Driving at excessive speed; driving on wrong side of road.
85	**McCrory v Hutchison's Coaches (Overtown) Ltd**	2007 SLT (Sh Ct) 187	N	N/A	F	47	Passenger in D's vehicle	N/A	Standing and walking on moving bus; failing to hold onto handrail.	Braking suddenly.
86	**McCrory v Hutchison's Coaches (Overtown) Ltd**	2007 SLT (Sh Ct) 187	N	N/A	F	47	Passenger in other vehicle	N/A	Failing to hold onto handrail.	Stopping suddenly, without indication, to perform right-hand manoeuvre.
87	**Sahakian v McDonnell**	[2007] EWHC 3242 (QB); [2008] RTR 19	Y	50	F	Adult	Pedestrian	Pedestrian entering carriageway	Walking into road without looking from behind parked car.	Driving at excessive speed; failing to see claimant in time to effect any proper braking.
88	**Gleeson v Court**	[2007] EWHC 2397 (QB); [2008] RTR 10	Y	30	M	20	Passenger in D's vehicle	N/A	Travelling with intoxicated driver; travelling in car boot.	Driving while intoxicated.
89	**Hughes v Guise Motors Ltd**	[2007] EWHC 2529 (QB)	N	N/A	M	U	Driver	N/A	Failing to steer or coast car onto the hard shoulder; remaining in car.	Failing to slow down sufficiently to create space between himself and the preceding vehicle.

	Claim	Citation	CN	Discount	Gender	Age	Claimant Type	Recurrent type of CN	Actual or alleged CN	Defendant's wrongful Conduct
90	**Lindesay v Lamb**	[2007] EWHC 2948 (QB)	Y	20	M	38	M'cyclist	N/A	Moving into closing gap between lorry and taxi and failing to brake in time to avoid colliding with either vehicle.	Failing to brake in time so as to avoid collision.
91	**Bollito v Arriva London**	[2008] EWHC 48 (QB)	N	N/A	M	Adult	Passenger in D's vehicle	N/A	Deliberately blocking bus doors and jumping from doors.	Closing bus doors knowing claimant was between them; driving off and accelerating with claimant trapped between partially closed doors.
92	**Easdon v A Clarke & Co (Smethwick) Ltd**	[2008] CSOH 29	N	N/A	M	32	M'cyclist	N/A	Driving at excessive speed so that unable to stop within range of vision.	Driving on the wrong side of road.
93	**Moreh v O'Neill**	[2008] NIQB 28	Y	50	M	78	Bicyclist	N/A	Failing to notice defendant's vehicle on road.	Failing to keep proper lookout for other vehicles; failing to brake; failing to give warning.

94	**Berry v Hayden**	[2008] NIQB 134	Y	66.6	F	47	Driver	Pedestrian entering carriageway	Standing in the path of vehicle; shouting at driver of vehicle; failing to move out of the vehicle's way despite hearing its engine revving and seeing it move.	Failing to stop vehicle in time to prevent it from striking claimant.
95	**Greenwood v Cummings**	QBD, 9 Apr 2008	Y	33.3	F	U	Pedestrian	Pedestrian entering carriageway	Failing to stop and check whether road was clear before crossing at a designated pedestrian crossing.	Failing to slow down when visibility affected by sun.
96	**Heaton v Herzog**	[2008] EWCA Civ 1636; [2009] RTR 30	N	N/A	F	Adult	Driver	N/A	Failing to keep observation to right in order to have the opportunity to see motorcycle, brake and avoid colliding with it.	Driving at excessive speed.
97	**Minh Lac v Clayton**	[2009] EWCA Civ 106	N	N/A	M	Adult	Driver	N/A	Failing to move away from car after collision.	Driving without due care and striking vehicle from behind.
98	**Minh Lac v Clayton**	[2009] EWCA Civ	N	N/A	M	Adult	Passenger in other vehicle	N/A	Failing to move away from car after collision.	Driving without due care and striking vehicle from behind.
99	**Minh Lac v Clayton**	[2009] EWCA Civ 106	N	N/A	M	Adult	Passenger in other vehicle	N/A	Failing to move away from car after collision.	Driving without due care and striking vehicle from behind.
100	**Clayton v Lambert**	[2009] EWCA Civ 237; [2010] RTR 3	Y	75	M	Adult	M'cyclist	Speeding	Driving at excessive speed.	Continuing turn after seeing claimant approaching.

	Claim	Citation	CN	Discount	Gender	Age	Claimant Type	Recurrent type of CN	Actual or alleged CN	Defendant's wrongful Conduct
101	**Don v Eastern Holdings Ltd**	Edinburgh Sheriff Court, 18 Jun 2008	Y	25	M	19	Driver	N/A	Failing to pause or stop to allow defender's car either fully to enter nearside northbound lane or to continue forward and resume occupancy only of offside northbound lane.	Encroaching further into nearside northbound lane when pursuer was passing.
102	**Flavio v Jeffrey**	[2008] EWHC 2331 (QB)	Y	66.6	M	Adult	Bicyclist	N/A	Failing to look when turning onto main road.	Failing to look before turning.
103	**Armsden v Kent Police**	[2009] EWCA Civ 631; [2009] RTR 31	N	N/A	F	29	Driver	N/A	Failing to look properly before moving off from junction.	Failing to activate siren.
104	**Williams v Jervis**	[2008] EWHC 2346 (QB)	N	N/A	F	Adult	Driver	N/A	Driving with defective brake lights and while using mobile telephone.	Failing to stop vehicle in time to prevent it striking claimant's car from behind.
105	**Craggy v CC of Cleveland Police**	[2009] EWCA Civ 1128	Y	66.6	M	Adult	Driver	N/A	Turning when unsafe to do so.	Failing to drive so that vehicle could be stopped if another emergency vehicle emerged.

106	**Buchan v Whiting**	[2008] EWHC 2951 (QB)	Y	50	M	20	M'cyclist	Speeding	Driving at excessive speed.	Failing to look before turning.
107	**Palmer v Kitley**	[2008] EWHC 2819 (QB)	Y	15	F	16.75	Passenger in D's vehicle	No seat belt or helmet	Failing to wear seat belt.	Cornering at excessive speed.
108	**Connor v Jackson**	[2008] NIQB 102	N	N/A	M	18	M'cyclist	N/A	Failing to notice defendant's vehicle sooner.	Attempting to cross road when it was risky to do so; failing to wait for clear view.
109	**Crew v Ash**	[2008] EWHC 3068 (QB)	N	N/A	F	18	Pedestrian	N/A	Intoxicated; stepping into road without looking for oncoming traffic; crossing road when view obscured by car; failing to appreciate speed at which the defendant was travelling; failing to use crossing.	Driving without due care and striking the claimant as a result.
110	**Callier v Deacon**	[2009] EWHC 245 (QB)	Y	55	M	17	Bicyclist	Pedestrian entering carriageway	Wearing dark, non-reflective clothing; cycling without lights; being stationary in a restricted area of the road; failing to pay any proper attention to oncoming traffic.	Overtaking vehicle in front when unsafe to do so.

	Claim	Citation	CN	Discount	Gender	Age	Claimant Type	Recurrent type of CN	Actual or alleged CN	Defendant's wrongful Conduct
111	**Smith v Finch**	[2009] EWHC 53 (QB)	N	N/A	M	51	Bicyclist	N/A	Failing to wear cycle helmet.	Driving at excessive speed; driving too close to claimant cyclist while attempting to overtake him.
112	**Stanton v Collinson**	[2009] EWHC 342 (QB)	N	N/A	M	16	Passenger in D's vehicle	N/A	Failing to wear seat belt.	Driving at excessive speed.
113	**Teviotdale v Norwich Union Insurance Ltd**	2009 SCLR 660	N	N/A	F	U	Driver	N/A	Driving without due care.	Failing to keep a proper lookout for other vehicles, in particular, failing to see pursuer's vehicle when entering car park.
114	**Smeaton v Duncan**	2009 GWD 13-210	N	N/A	M	15	M'cyclist	N/A	Driving at excessive speed.	Failing to keep a lookout for oncoming traffic.
115	**Forbes v Ferguson**	2009 GWD 21-353	Y	50	M	Adult	Pedestrian	N/A	Putting hand on stationary van to steady himself and falling into road.	Failing to keep a proper lookout for pedestrians before reversing.
116	**Osei-Antwi v SE London & Kent Bus Co Ltd**	[2010] EWCA Civ 132	Y	33.3	F	17	Pedestrian	N/A	Standing very close to edge of road; failing to keep a good lookout for bus.	Permitting rear end of bus to mount pavement when turning.

117	**Dines v Clifton**	[2009] EWHC 1254 (QB)	N	N/A	M	40	Pedestrian	N/A	Negligent parking; failing to place cones in road; standing in road while using mobile phone.	Crashing into back of lorry and hitting claimant in the process.
118	**Smith v Hammond**	[2010] EWCA Civ 725; [2010] RTR 30	Y	60	M	13	Bicyclist	N/A	Cycling into road without looking.	Failing to sound horn.
119	**Toropdar v D (a minor)**	[2009] EWHC 2997 (TCC)	Y	33.3	M	10	Pedestrian	Pedestrian entering carriageway	Stepping into road without looking for oncoming traffic.	Driving at excessive speed; failing to undertake precautionary braking.
120	**Ievers v Prebble**	[2010] EWCA Civ 1615	Y	70	F	Adult	Driver	N/A	Cutting across the path of driver.	Being insufficiently alert to difficulties of claimant, who had been forced into wrong lane; failing to avoid collision by accelerating rather than slowing down and stopping.
121	**Sklair v Haycock**	[2009] EWHC 3328 (QB)	Y	10	M	46	Pedestrian	Pedestrian entering carriageway	Crossing road when unsafe to do so.	Unknown.
122	**Howe v Houlton**	[2009] EWHC 3344 (QB)	N	N/A	M	27.5	Pedestrian	N/A	Parking within controlled area of pedestrian crossing in breach of Highway Code.	Hitting claimant's car door when driving past.
123	**Edwards v Martin**	[2010] EWHC 570 (QB)	Y	15	M	34	U	No seat belt or helmet	Failing to wear seat belt.	Unknown.

	Claim	Citation	CN	Discount	Gender	Age	Claimant Type	Recurrent type of CN	Actual or alleged CN	Defendant's wrongful Conduct
124	**Stoddart v Perucca**	[2011] EWCA Civ 290	Y	50	F	14	N/A	N/A	Failing to look before crossing road on horse.	Failing to slow down to allow for the possibility of a second horse.
125	**Tolley v Carr**	[2010] EWHC 2191 (QB); [2011] RTR 7	N	N/A	M	Adult	Driver	N/A	Moving car that had crashed on the road.	Losing control of vehicle when driving at 65–70mph in adverse weather conditions and stopping car with driver's door facing oncoming traffic in outside lane.
126	**Tolley v Carr**	[2010] EWHC 2191 (QB); [2011] RTR 7	N	N/A	M	Adult	Driver	N/A	Moving car that had crashed on the road.	Driving without due care in adverse weather conditions and colliding with first defendant's stopped vehicle.
127	**Tolley v Carr**	[2010] EWHC 2191 (QB); [2011] RTR 7	N	N/A	M	Adult	Driver	N/A	Moving car that had crashed on the road.	Driving without due care in adverse weather conditions and colliding with first defendant's stopped vehicle.
128	**Willard v Boswell**	[2010] EWHC 2037 (QB)	N	N/A	M	Adult	Driver	N/A	Driving on wrong side of road.	Swerving onto wrong side of road.

129	**Belka v Prosperini**	[2011] EWCA Civ 623	Y	66.6	M	Adult	Pedestrian	Pedestrian entering carriageway	Running across road in front of defendant's vehicle.	Failing to slow down upon noticing pedestrians.
130	**Boardman v Ministry of Defence**	QBD, 12 Nov 2010	N	N/A	M	6	Pedestrian	N/A	Stepping into road from behind lorry.	Driving at excessive speed; failing to wait for lorry to pass before continuing.
131	**Burton v Evitt**	[2011] EWCA Civ 1378	Y	66.6	M	Adult	M'cyclist	Speeding	Overtaking line of traffic; driving at excessive speed.	Failing to inch out of traffic queue so as to see traffic behind.
132	**Hill v Master Concrete Ltd**	[2010] EWHC 3613 (QB)	Y	50	F	Adult	Pedestrian	Pedestrian entering carriageway	Failing to look before crossing road.	Failing to look before turning.
133	**Smith v CC of Notts**	[2012] EWCA Civ 161; [2012] RTR 23	Y	75	F	16	Pedestrian	Pedestrian entering carriageway	Crossing road when unsafe to do so.	Failing to slow down when travelling through red light on emergency call.
134	**Sedge v Prime**	[2011] EWHC 820 (QB)	Y	25	M	21	Pedestrian	Pedestrian entering carriageway	Intoxicated; stepping into road without looking for oncoming traffic.	Failing to drive at safe speed; failing to keep a proper lookout for pedestrians; failing to sound horn.
135	**Lightfoot v Go-Ahead Group Plc**	[2011] EWHC 89 (QB); [2011] RTR 27	Y	40	M	52	Pedestrian	Pedestrian entering carriageway	Stepping into road when intoxicated to flag down an oncoming bus.	Reading timetable while driving.
136	**Douglas v O'Neill**	[2011] EWHC 601 (QB)	Y	12.5	M	34.5	Pedestrian	Pedestrian entering carriageway	Stepping into road without looking for oncoming traffic.	Driving while intoxicated.

	Claim	Citation	CN	Discount	Gender	Age	Claimant Type	Recurrent type of CN	Actual or alleged CN	Defendant's wrongful Conduct
137	**Phethean-Hubble v Coles**	[2011] EWHC 363 (QB)	Y	33.3	M	16	Bicyclist	N/A	Entering road from pavement on bicycle without looking for oncoming traffic.	Driving at excessive speed.
138	**Kelly v Nugent**	[2011] NIQB 79	Y	15	M	9.75	Bicyclist	N/A	Taking tricycle onto road.	Failing to keep a proper lookout for pedestrians; driving at excessive speed.
139	**Rehill v Rider Holdings Ltd**	[2012] EWCA Civ 628; [2013] RTR 5	Y	33.3	M	45.5	Pedestrian	Pedestrian entering carriageway	Crossing road when traffic signal was red and in sight of bus.	Failing to notice pedestrian and brake sufficiently quickly.
140	**Bellingham v Todd**	[2011] CSOH 74; 2011 SLT 1124	Y	80	M	40	M'cyclist	N/A	Riding too close to vehicle in front.	Braking hard without considering other road users.
141	**Stangroom v Brown**	[2012] EWCA Civ 424	Y	75	M	Adult	M'cyclist	Speeding	Driving at excessive speed.	Failing to take sufficient safety precautions when pulling out from a lay-by.

142	**Anderson v Warburtons Ltd**	[2011] CSOH 77	Y	66.6	F	Adult	Driver	N/A	Failing to notice two signs indicating presence of lay-by (or lay-by itself) which would have afforded a safe stopping place; stopping car on road after end of the lay-by; failing to remove car from danger.	Failing to slow down sufficiently.
143	**Whiteford v Kubas UAB**	[2012] EWCA Civ 1017	Y	50	M	Adult	M'cyclist	N/A	Driving too close to centre line on motorcycle.	Failing to drive closer to edge of road given size of vehicle and narrowness of road.
144	**Woodham v JM Turner**	[2011] EWHC 1588 (QB); [2012] RTR 7	Y	30	M	16	M'cyclist	Speeding	Overtaking stationary traffic on offside when approaching junction; travelling at excessive speed.	Performing manoeuvre with obstructed view.
145	**Brown v Brent**	Croydon CC, 21 Jun 2011	Y	33.3	M	Adult	Bicyclist	Speeding	Failing to heed warning signs and race marshal indicating that race was in progress; driving at excessive speed.	Driving at excessive speed; crossing onto wrong side of road by a considerable margin; and riding into claimant's path.
146	**Ellis v Lokat**	QBD, 6 Oct 2011	Y	20	M	U	M'cyclist	Speeding	Driving at excessive speed.	Turning too slowly at junction; failing to look for oncoming traffic and to see claimant.

	Claim	Citation	CN	Discount	Gender	Age	Claimant Type	Recurrent type of CN	Actual or alleged CN	Defendant's wrongful Conduct
147	**Devereux v Hayward**	[2011] EWHC 2780 (QB)	N	N/A	F	37	N/A	N/A	Failing to move horse to verge.	Driving at excessive speed.
148	**McDermott v Pettit**	[2011] EWHC 3074 (QB)	Y	10	M	18	Pedestrian	Pedestrian entering carriageway	Failing to use pedestrian crossing.	Driving at excessive speed; driving while intoxicated.
149	**Malasi v Ahmed**	[2011] EWHC 4083 (QB)	Y	80	M	19	Bicyclist	N/A	Failing to stop at red light.	Driving at excessive speed.
150	**Ringe v Eden Springs (UK) Ltd**	[2012] EWHC 14 (QB)	Y	80	M	U	M'cyclist	Speeding	Driving at excessive speed; overtaking lorry when unsafe to do so.	Undertaking manoeuvre without clear sight.
151	**Rehman v Brady**	[2012] EWHC 78 (QB)	N	N/A	F	7.25	Pedestrian	N/A	Running into road from behind a parked vehicle.	Driving at excessive speed in built-up area where presence of children was likely.
152	**Paramasivan v Wicks**	[2013] EWCA Civ 262	Y	50	M	13	Pedestrian	Pedestrian entering carriageway	Stepping into road without looking for oncoming traffic.	Failing to look out for pedestrians.
153	**Tavares v Hudson-Rotin**	[2012] EWHC 3171 (QB)	Y	15	M	37	Pedestrian	Pedestrian entering carriageway	Failing to follow advice contained in Green Cross Code when attempting to cross road.	Driving at excessive speed.

154	**Starks v CC of Herts**	[2013] EWCA Civ 782; [2014] RTR 4	Y	55	M	Adult	Driver	Speeding	Entering roundabout late and not slowing down.	Failing to observe roundabout; driving straight over roundabout.
155	**Jackson v Murray**	[2012] CSOH 100; 2012 SCLR 605	Y	90	F	13	Pedestrian	Pedestrian entering carriageway	Crossing road when unsafe to do so.	Failing to keep a proper lookout for pedestrians; failing to reduce speed when approaching minibus.
156	**Meaney v Link Rider Coaches Ltd**	B'mouth CC, 21 Jun 2012	Y	25	M	U	Driver	N/A	Failing to abort attempt to leave road.	Failing to leave sufficient stopping distance.
157	**Condie v Blight**	Newcastle upon Tyne CC, 25 Jul 2012	N	N/A	M	U	Driver	N/A	Failing to look in defendant's direction.	Failing to move so as to be able to see cars coming from claimant's direction.
158	**Smith v Fowler**	2012 GWD 26-552	N	N/A	M	56	Driver	N/A	Failing to exercise special care in proceeding forward despite having seen van stop and having view obstructed.	Turning into path of oncoming traffic without checking if road was clear.
159	**Beasley v Alexander**	[2012] EWHC 2197 (QB)	N	N/A	M	25	M'cyclist	N/A	Driving at excessive speed.	Performing turn without looking.
160	**Probert v Moore**	[2012] EWHC 2324 (QB)	N	N/A	F	13.5	Pedestrian	N/A	Walking along country road on winter's night; failing to wear high-visibility clothing; wearing headphones.	Driving at excessive speed; failing to appreciate other road users.

	Claim	Citation	CN	Discount	Gender	Age	Claimant Type	Recurrent type of CN	Actual or alleged CN	Defendant's wrongful Conduct
161	**Brown v First Glasgow Ltd**	[2012] CSOH 192	Y	80	M	Adult	Pedestrian	N/A	Opening door while close to the centre of road without checking if it was safe to do so.	Driving unnecessarily close to van; intruding onto southbound carriageway without being alert to possibility of activity at rear of van.
162	**Ayres v Odedra**	[2013] EWHC 40 (QB)	Y	20	M	24	Pedestrian	Pedestrian entering carriageway	Walking while intoxicated and with trousers around ankles resulting in inability to move at normal speed.	Driving in pedestrian only area; misjudging amount of time it would take claimant to get to position clear of car.
163	**Cruikshanks v Amlin UK Ltd**	[2013] CSOH 12	N	N/A	M	U	Driver	N/A	Failing to pay proper attention to what was happening in right-hand lane and thus failing to see tractor unit or defender signalling.	Failing to keep a proper lookout for other cars; moving from right-hand lane into left-hand lane of roundabout when unsafe to do so.
164	**Wheeler v CC of Glos**	[2013] EWCA Civ 1791	Y	50	M	Adult	Driver	Speeding	Driving at excessive speed.	Failing to stop or check for oncoming traffic before turning right.
165	**Gray v Gibson**	[2014] EWCA Civ 355	Y	40	F	Adult	Driver	Speeding	Driving at excessive speed.	Driving over central line.

166	**Hickman v London Central Bus Co Ltd**	[2013] EWHC 1703 (QB)	Y	40	M	Adult	Pedestrian	Pedestrian entering carriageway	Crossing road in potentially hazardous area; failing to wait until buses had moved before crossing road.	Failing to keep a proper lookout for pedestrians; moving off when pedestrian already crossing road.
167	**Ali v Caton**	[2013] EWHC 1730 (QB)	Y	20	M	17	Pedestrian	N/A	Unknown.	Unknown.
168	**Dickson v Kinsman**	[2013] CSOH 111	N	N/A	M	35	Bicyclist	N/A	Driving at excessive speed; misjudging direction.	Failing to look out for cyclists such as pursuer; braking too late; conveying impression that vehicle might not stop at junction.
169	**Bennett v Southwell**	[2013] EWHC 2382 (QB)	Y	50	F	Adult	Driver	N/A	Steering into defendant's path while braking and turning a corner.	Driving too far over line while cornering.
170	**Nadarajah v Sotnick**	[2013] EWHC 3389 (QB)	N	N/A	F	Adult	M'cyclist	N/A	Driving at excessive speed.	Performing U-turn when unsafe to do so.
171	**McCracken v Smith**	[2013] EWHC 3620 (QB)	Y	45	M	16	M'cyclist	No seat belt or helmet	Travelling as pillion passenger on trail bike with dangerous driver; failing to wear helmet.	Failing to keep a proper lookout for other vehicles at junction.
172	**Jones v Lawton**	[2013] EWHC 4108 (QB)	Y	33.3	M	U	M'cyclist	Speeding	Driving at excessive speed; failing to see gap in traffic; and defendant emerging from side road.	Being unaware of possibility that motorcycle was proceeding outside slow-moving lanes of traffic; failing to look to right when turning.

	Claim	Citation	CN	Discount	Gender	Age	Claimant Type	Recurrent type of CN	Actual or alleged CN	Defendant's wrongful Conduct
173	**Train v Secretary of State for Defence**	[2014] EWHC 1928 (QB); [2014] RTR 28	Y	80	M	Adult	M'cyclist	Speeding	Driving at excessive speed.	Turning when unsafe to do so.
174	**Sabir v Osei-Kwabena**	[2015] EWCA Civ 1213; [2016] RTR 9	Y	25	F	30	Pedestrian	Pedestrian entering carriageway	Misjudging car's position and/or time available to cross road.	Failing to keep a proper lookout for pedestrians.
175	**Hazlett v Robinson**	[2014] NIQB 17	Y	20	M	29	Passenger in D's vehicle	No seat belt or helmet	Failing to wear seat belt.	Driving without due care.
176	**McAllister v Campbell**	[2014] NIQB 24	Y	25	M	21	Bicyclist	N/A	Not looking where cycling; looking down at heart-rate monitor.	Stopping vehicle when claimant cyclist was approaching from behind.
177	**MacLeod v Comr of Police of the Metropolis**	[2014] EWHC 977 (QB)	N	N/A	M	59	Bicyclist	N/A	Intoxicated; proceeding in front of defendant's car without looking.	Driving at excessive speed in poor visibility; failing to keep a proper lookout for cyclists.
178	**Rainford v Lawrenson**	[2014] EWHC 1188 (QB)	Y	50	F	14.75	Pedestrian	Pedestrian entering carriageway	Stepping into road without looking for oncoming traffic.	Failing to anticipate risk of children stepping into road; failing to re-position vehicle closer to centre of road, reduce speed, or cover foot brake; failing to use horn so as to alert claimant.

179	**Smith v Bluebird Buses Ltd**	[2014] CSOH 75; 2014 Rep LR 91	Y	85	M	Adult	Pedestrian	Pedestrian entering carriageway	Intoxicated; stepping into road without looking for oncoming traffic.	Failing to keep a proper lookout for pedestrians; failing to stop bus so as to avoid collision.
180	**Groves v Studley**	[2014] EWHC 1522 (QB)	Y	40	M	34	Pedestrian	N/A	Jumping onto car bonnet.	Manoeuvring car in such a manner so as deliberately to dislodge claimant.
181	**McLaughlin v Morrison**	[2014] CSOH 123; 2014 SLT 862	N	N/A	M	30	Pedestrian	N/A	Provoking assault.	Assaulting pursuer who was run down by defender's car.
182	**Pearson v Anwar**	[2015] EWCA Civ 1011	Y	25	M	23	Passenger in D's vehicle	No seat belt or helmet	Failing to wear seat belt.	Driving at excessive speed.
183	**Russell v National Farmers' Union Mutual Insurance Society Ltd**	[2014] CSOH 157	N	N/A	M	23	M'cyclist	N/A	Driving at excessive speed.	Driving onto main road once pursuer had come round corner and should have been visible to defendant; failing to take due care in the driving of vehicle.
184	**Wormald v Ahmed**	[2014] EWHC 4498 (QB)	Y	40	M	20	Pedestrian	Pedestrian entering carriageway	Crossing road when unsafe to do so.	Failing to check mirror and blind spot and to monitor whole of road ahead; not looking ahead and thus failing to see claimant.
185	**McCaughey v Mullan**	[2014] NIQB 132	Y	60	F	20	Pedestrian	Pedestrian entering carriageway	Being intoxicated in the middle of road.	Driving at excessive speed.

	Claim	Citation	CN	Discount	Gender	Age	Claimant Type	Recurrent type of CN	Actual or alleged CN	Defendant's wrongful Conduct
186	**Suiter v Eves**	[2015] NIQB 31	N	N/A	M	54	M'cyclist	N/A	Driving at excessive speed.	Driving on the wrong side of road.
187	**Hicks v Young**	[2015] EWHC 1144 (QB)	Y	50	M	23	Passenger in D's vehicle	N/A	Misjudging speed at which taxi was travelling; jumping from taxi while it was moving.	Accelerating while claimant passenger was standing up in rear of vehicle.
188	**Wagner v Grant**	[2015] CSOH 51	Y	40	M	18	M'cyclist	Speeding	Not being aware of hazard warning lights and working lights; failing to slow motorcycle down; failing to keep lookout ahead.	Blocking the other lane by the trailer in darkness; failing to give some form of advance warning to westbound traffic, either by way of a warning sign or someone appointed to provide a form of advance warning.
189	**Whyte v Bluebird Buses Ltd**	[2015] CSOH 56; 2015 SLT 338	N	N/A	M	11	Pedestrian	N/A	Striking bus while on pavement.	Driving too close to pavement.
190	**Buswell v Symes**	[2015] EWHC 1379 (QB)	Y	66.6	M	40	M'cyclist	Speeding	Driving at excessive speed.	Blocking road beyond hill with tractor.

191	**Sinclair v Joyner**	[2015] EWHC 1800 (QB); [2015] RTR 29	Y	25	F	58	Bicyclist	N/A	Cycling in the middle of road.	Failing to stop and allow cyclist to pass safely.
192	**Low v Duncan**	[2015] CSOH 133	Y	10	M	U	Pedestrian	Pedestrian entering carriageway	Behaving in an aggressive manner; being in middle of road.	Placing himself in a position of danger for pedestrians by swerving car towards pursuer; driving at excessive speed.
193	**AB v Main**	[2015] EWHC 3183 (QB)	Y	20	M	9	Pedestrian	Pedestrian entering carriageway	Stepping into road without looking for oncoming traffic.	Failing to keep young child playing at side of road under proper observation; failing to ensure that child was aware of car's presence before proceeding; failing to take foot off accelerator, cover brakes, or sound horn.
194	**McGeer v Macintosh**	2015 WL 6966174	Y	30	F	47	Bicyclist	N/A	Violating rule 73 of the Highway Code requiring cyclists to pay particular attention when long vehicles make left turns at junctions.	Failing to check nearside rear-view mirrors.
195	**McCreery v Letson**	[2015] CSOH 153	Y	50	F	61	Pedestrian	Pedestrian entering carriageway	Stepping into road without looking for oncoming traffic.	Driving at excessive speed.

	Claim	Citation	CN	Discount	Gender	Age	Claimant Type	Recurrent type of CN	Actual or alleged CN	Defendant's wrongful Conduct
196	**Sandison v Coope**	2016 Rep LR 70	Y	30	F	42	Bicyclist	N/A	Failing to avoid animals on quiet country road.	Allowing dog to cross public road at blind corner without checking for hazards.
197	**Glass v Donnelly**	[2016] NIQB 36	Y	66.6	F	31	Pedestrian	Pedestrian entering carriageway	Stepping into road without looking for oncoming traffic.	Driving at excessive speed; failing to keep a proper lookout for pedestrians.
198	**Sparrow v Andre**	[2016] EWHC 739 (QB)	Y	60	M	49	Driver	N/A	Trying to restrain car from rolling down slope; failing to put the car into 'park' mode, to apply foot brake, or switch off ignition.	Failing to keep a proper lookout for other cars in car park and reversing into claimant's car.
199	**Adams v Gibson**	QBD, 26 Oct 2016	Y	33.3	M	U	Pedestrian	Pedestrian entering carriageway	Stepping into road without looking for oncoming traffic; failing to use crossing.	Failing to keep an eye on claimant pedestrian or to slow down in case claimant continued into road.

APPENDIX 4

PROFESSIONAL NEGLIGENCE CLAIMS AT FIRST INSTANCE

	Claim	Citation	Professional Type	Damage Type	Contributory Negligence	Discount (%)
1	**Cottingham v Attey Bower & Jones**	[2000] PNLR 557	Legal practitioner	Pure economic loss	No	N/A
2	**Cottingham v Attey Bower & Jones**	[2000] PNLR 557	Legal practitioner	Pure economic loss	No	N/A
3	**Secretary of State for the Environment, Transport and Regions v Unicorn Consultancy Services Ltd**	[2000] NPC 108	Legal practitioner	Pure economic loss	Yes	50
4	**Logical Computer Supplies Ltd v Euro Car Parks Ltd**	2001 WL 825094	Other	Property damage	Yes	50
5	**Pidgeon v Doncaster HA**	[2002] Lloyd's Rep Med 130	Medical practitioner	Personal injury	Yes	66.6
6	**Alpha Credit Bank v Stephenson Harwood**	[2002] EWHC 922 (Ch)	Legal practitioner	Pure economic loss	Yes	60
7	**Credit Lyonnais SA v Russell Jones & Walker**	[2002] EWHC 1310 (Ch); [2003] PNLR 2	Legal practitioner	Pure economic loss	No	N/A
8	**Alexander Forbes Europe Ltd v SBJ Ltd**	[2002] EWHC 3121 (Comm); [2003] PNLR 15	Insurance broker	Pure economic loss	No	N/A
9	**Sahib Foods Ltd v Paskin KyriaKides Sands**	[2003] EWHC 142 (TCC); [2003] PNLR 30	Architect	Property damage	No	N/A
10	**Speshal Investments Ltd v Corby Kane Howard Partnership Ltd**	[2003] EWHC 390 (Ch)	Valuer	Pure economic loss	Yes	20

	Claim	Citation	Professional Type	Damage Type	Contributory Negligence	Discount (%)
11	**Akasuc Enterprise Ltd v Farmar & Shirreff**	[2003] EWHC 1275 (Ch)	Legal practitioner	Pure economic loss	No	N/A
12	**Great NE Rly Ltd v Railcare Ltd**	[2003] EWHC 1608 (Comm)	Other	Property damage	No	N/A
13	**Six Continents Retail Ltd v Carford Catering Ltd**	[2003] EWCA Civ 1790	Project manager	Property damage	Yes	100
14	**Slattery v Moore Stephens**	[2003] EWHC 1869 (Ch); [2004] PNLR 14	Accountant	Pure economic loss	Yes	50
15	**Montlake v Lambert Smith Hampton Group Ltd**	[2004] EWHC 938 (Comm)	Surveyor and valuer	Pure economic loss	No	N/A
16	**Francis v Barclays Bank Plc**	[2004] EWHC 2787 (Ch); [2005] PNLR 18	Surveyor	Pure economic loss	No	N/A
17	**Hodson Development Ltd v CTA Civils**	[2006] EWHC 1913 (TCC)	Architect	Pure economic loss	No	N/A
18	**Feakins v Burstow**	[2005] EWHC 1936 (QB); [2006] PNLR 6	Legal practitioner	Pure economic loss	No	N/A
19	**Plymouth & South West Co-operative Society v Architecture Structure & Management Ltd**	[2006] EWHC 5 (TCC)	Architect	Pure economic loss	No	N/A
20	**BP Plc v AON Ltd (No 2)**	[2006] EWHC 424 (Comm); [2006] 1 CLC 881	Insurance broker	Pure economic loss	No	N/A
21	**Arbory Group Ltd v West Craven Insurance Services**	[2007] Lloyd's Rep IR 491	Insurance broker	Pure economic loss	No	N/A
22	**Carleton v Strutt & Parker**	[2007] EWHC 999 (QB); [2007] PNLR 29	Surveyor	Pure economic loss	No	N/A

23	**Newline Corporate Name Ltd v Morgan Cole**	[2007] EWHC 1628 (Comm); [2008] PNLR 2	Legal practitioner	Pure economic loss	No	N/A
24	**Standard Life Assurance Ltd v Oak Dedicated Ltd**	[2008] EWHC 222 (Comm); [2008] 2 All ER (Comm) 916	Insurance broker	Pure economic loss	No	N/A
25	**Chrysalis Scotland Ltd v Clydesdale Bank Insurance Brokers Ltd**	[2008] CSOH 144	Other	Pure economic loss	No	N/A
26	**Devine v McAteer**	[2008] NICh 18	Accountant	Pure economic loss	No	N/A
27	**Berry v Laytons**	[2009] EWHC 1591 (QB)	Legal practitioner	Pure economic loss	No	N/A
28	**Martin v Triggs Turner Bartons**	[2009] EWHC 1920 (Ch); [2010] PNLR 3	Legal practitioner	Pure economic loss	No	N/A
29	**Dunlop Haywards Ltd v Barbon Insurance Group Ltd**	[2009] EWHC 2900 (Comm); [2010] Lloyd's Rep IR 149	Insurance broker	Pure economic loss	No	N/A
30	**Dunlop Haywards Ltd v Barbon Insurance Group Ltd**	[2009] EWHC 2900 (Comm); [2010] Lloyd's Rep IR 149	Insurance broker	Pure economic loss	Yes	80
31	**Tom Hoskins Plc v EMR Law**	[2010] EWHC 479 (Ch)	Legal practitioner	Pure economic loss	No	N/A
32	**Scullion v Bank of Scotland Plc**	[2010] EWHC 2253 (Ch); [2011] PNLR 5	Valuer	Pure economic loss	No	N/A
33	**Ground Gilbey Ltd v Jardine Lloyd Thompson UK Ltd**	[2011] EWHC 124 (Comm); [2012] Lloyd's Rep IR 12	Insurance broker	Pure economic loss	No	N/A
34	**P (decd) v Sedar**	[2011] EWHC 1266 (QB)	Medical practitioner	Personal injury	No	N/A
35	**Trebor Bassett Holdings Ltd v ADT Fire & Security Plc**	[2011] EWHC 1936 (TCC)	Other	Property damage	Yes	75

	Claim	Citation	Professional Type	Damage Type	Contributory Negligence	Discount (%)
36	**Trebor Bassett Holdings Ltd v ADT Fire & Security Plc**	[2011] EWHC 1936 (TCC)	Other	Property damage	Yes	75
37	**Argos Ltd v Leather Trade House Ltd**	[2012] EWHC 1348 (QB)	Other	Pure economic loss	No	N/A
38	**Webb Resolutions Ltd v E.Surv Ltd**	[2012] EWHC 3653 (TCC); [2013] PNLR 15	Surveyor	Pure economic loss	Yes	50
39	**Blemain Finance Ltd v E.Surv Ltd**	[2012] EWHC 3654 (TCC)	Valuer	Pure economic loss	No	N/A
40	**Taylor v Bank of Ireland (UK) Plc**	[2013] NIQB 50	Banker	Pure economic loss	No	N/A
41	**Manorgate Ltd v First Scottish Property Services Ltd**	[2013] CSOH 108; [2014] PNLR 1	Other	Pure economic loss	No	N/A
42	**Aurora Leasing Ltd v Colliers International Belfast Ltd**	[2013] NIQB 116	Surveyor and valuer	Pure economic loss	Yes	20
43	**Forsta AP-Fonden v Bank of New York Mellon SA/NV**	[2013] EWHC 3127 (Comm)	Banker	Pure economic loss	No	N/A
44	**Law Society of Northern Ireland v Bank of Ireland**	[2013] NIQB 130	Banker	Pure economic loss	No	N/A
45	**Wellesley Partnership LLP v Withers LLP**	[2014] EWHC 556 (Ch); [2014] PNLR 22	Legal practitioner	Pure economic loss	No	N/A
46	**Playboy Club London Ltd v Banca Nazionale del Lavoro SpA**	[2014] EWHC 2613 (QB)	Banker	Pure economic loss	Yes	15

47	**Spencer v Hillingdon Hospital NHS Trust**	[2015] EWHC 1058 (QB)	Medical practitioner	Personal injury	No	N/A
48	**Orientfield Holdings Ltd v Bird & Bird LLP**	[2015] EWHC 1963 (Ch); [2015] PNLR 33	Legal practitioner	Pure economic loss	No	N/A
49	**Lloyds Bank Plc v McBains Cooper Consulting Ltd**	[2015] EWHC 2372 (TCC)	Project manager	Pure economic loss	Yes	33.3
50	**Mansion Estates Ltd v Hayre & Co**	[2016] EWHC 96 (Ch)	Legal practitioner	Pure economic loss	No	N/A
51	**Commodities Research Unit International (Holdings) Ltd v King and Wood Mallesons LLP**	[2016] EWHC 727 (QB); [2016] PNLR 29	Legal practitioner	Pure economic loss	No	N/A
52	**Scott v EAR Sheppard Consulting Civil and Structural Engineers Ltd**	[2016] EWHC 1949 (TCC)	Engineer	Pure economic loss	No	N/A
53	**Scott v EAR Sheppard Consulting Civil and Structural Engineers Ltd**	[2016] EWHC 1949 (TCC)	Engineer	Pure economic loss	No	N/A
54	**Scott v EAR Sheppard Consulting Civil and Structural Engineers Ltd**	[2016] EWHC 1949 (TCC)	Engineer	Pure economic loss	No	N/A
55	**Barclays Bank Plc v Christie Owen & Davies Ltd**	[2016] EWHC 2351 (Ch); [2017] PNLR 8	Valuer	Pure economic loss	Yes	40
56	**Adams v Atlas International Property Services Ltd**	[2016] EWHC 3120 (QB)	Legal practitioner	Pure economic loss	No	N/A
57	**Harlequin Property (SVG) Ltd v Wilkins Kennedy**	[2016] EWHC 3188 (TCC); [2017] 4 WLR 30	Accountant	Pure economic loss	Yes	50

INDEX

Index